Women of the Wall

Women of the Wall

Navigating Religion in Sacred Sites

YUVAL JOBANI
NAHSHON PEREZ

OXFORD
UNIVERSITY PRESS

OXFORD
UNIVERSITY PRESS

Oxford University Press is a department of the University of Oxford. It furthers
the University's objective of excellence in research, scholarship, and education
by publishing worldwide. Oxford is a registered trade mark of Oxford University
Press in the UK and certain other countries.

Published in the United States of America by Oxford University Press
198 Madison Avenue, New York, NY 10016, United States of America.

Library of Congress Cataloging-in-Publication Data
Names: Jobani, Yuval, author. | Perez, Nahshon, 1973– author.
Title: Women of the Wall : navigating religion in sacred sites /
Jobani Yuval & Perez Nahshon.
Description: New York : Oxford University Press, [2017] |
Includes bibliographical references and index.
Identifiers: LCCN 2016047079 (print) | LCCN 2016048399 (ebook) |
ISBN 9780190280444 (cloth) | ISBN 9780190280451 (updf) |
ISBN 9780190280468 (oso)
Subjects: LCSH: Western Wall (Jerusalem) | Women of the Wall (Organization : Israel) |
Jewish women—Religious life—Israel. |
Women in Judaism—Israel. | Feminism—Religious aspects—Judaism.
Classification: LCC DS109.32.W47 J63 2017 (print) |
LCC DS109.32.W47 (ebook) | DDC 296.4/82082—dc23
LC record available at https://lccn.loc.gov/2016047079

To Keren,
without whom this book would have been completed much earlier
but would not have been necessary.
Y.J.

To Alma,
with love.
N.P.

Contents

Acknowledgments   xi

*Introduction—Drama in Jerusalem: Who Are the Women of the
Wall and Why Does Their Struggle Matter?*   xv

    I.I. Overview of Women of the Wall: Navigating Religion
    in Sacred Sites   xix

1. Laying the Groundworks: Concepts, Definitions,
and Methodology   1

    1.1. The Western Wall as a "Thick Site": Categorizing the Wall   1

    1.2. Defining Religion, State, and the Public Sphere: Locating
    Thick Sites Conceptually   7

    1.3. Methodology   14

2. Women of the Wall in Focus: Examining the
Various Aspects of the WoW Struggle   19

    2.1. Liberating the Wall: The Religious-Feminist Challenge
    of the WoW   19

        2.1.1. Women-Only Prayer Group (*Tfila*)   20

        2.1.2. Women's Torah Reading (Torah)   26

        2.1.3. Women Wrapped in the Tallit   29

    2.2. Religion and State in Israel: An Overview   35

    2.3. Legal Analysis: An Exploration of Three Major Supreme
    Court Decisions (1994–2003)   39

        2.3.1. The First Ruling of the Supreme Court   40

        2.3.2. The Second Ruling of the Supreme Court   42

        2.3.3. The Third Ruling of the Supreme Court   43

2.4. Recent Developments   44

2.5. Conclusion   52

Introduction to chapters 3 to 5   53

3. The Dominant Culture View and the Women of the Wall: Competing
Significances, Elusive Tradition, and Inegalitarianism   56

    3.1. Challenging "Shared Understandings": On the Competing
    Significances of the Western Wall   60

        3.1.1. The Archaeological Significance of the Western Wall   61

        3.1.2. The Orthodox Significance   63

        3.1.3. Non-Orthodox Significance   66

        3.1.4. National Significance   68

    3.2. The Elusive Traditions of the Wall: A Subversive Historical Survey of
    Prayer Practices at the Western Wall   75

    3.3. The DCV and Egalitarianism: The Democratic Challenge   80

        3.3.1. The DCV as an Instrumental Good   81

        3.3.2. DCV as an Expression of the Wish of the Majority   85

            3.3.2.1. Violation of Rights   88

            3.3.2.2. Procedural Aspects: Duress, Monopoly, and
                Sour Grapes   88

            3.3.2.3. Irreversibility   91

            3.3.2.4. Concluding Remarks on the DCV   94

    3.4. DCV and the Management of Contested Sacred Sites   96

    3.5. Conclusion   100

4. Evenhandedness, Thick Sites, and the Women of the Wall: Permissible
but Inapplicable?   102

    4.1. End-Result-Oriented Evenhandedness   105

        4.1.1. The Result-Oriented Evenhanded Model:
        Justifications and Policy Implications   107

        4.1.2. The End-Results Evenhanded Model: Critiques   111

    4.2. The Procedural Evenhanded Model   115

        4.2.1. Justifications for the Procedural Evenhanded Model   120

        4.2.2. Critiques of the Procedural Evenhanded Model   125

            4.2.2.1. The Individual and Her/His Religion:
                An *Imbalanced* Connection   126

4.2.2.2. The Institutional Aspects of Procedural
Evenhandedness 128

4.2.2.3. Is there a Real Need for Evenhandedness in
Democratic Societies? 133

4.3. Evenhandedness and Thick Sites 135

4.4. Conclusion 142

5. Privatization, Thick Sites, and the Women of the Wall: A
Suggested Solution 143

5.1. Privatizing Religion: Defining and Illustrating the Model 143

5.2. Two Potential Misrepresentations of the Privatization Model 148

5.3. Four Justifications of the Privatization Model of
Religion-State Relations 150

5.4. Privatizing "Thick Sites": Keeping the State at a
Proper Distance 158

5.4.1. Privatizing Thick Sites 159

5.4.2. Three Potential Objections to the Application of the
Privatization Model to Thick Sites 164

5.4.2.1. Fear of Violence or the Backlash Problem 164

5.4.2.2. Baseline Problems 167

5.4.2.3. Problems of Religious Incompatibility 169

5.5. Conclusion 175

Concluding Remarks 177

Appendix: Thick Sites, "Gag Solutions," and the Ayodhya Dispute 183

A.1. A Brief Methodological Explanation 184

A.2. The Ayodhya Dispute: The Details of the Case 186

A.2.1. The Hindu Narrative 186

A.2.2. The Muslim Narrative 187

A.2.3. The Historical and Legal Dispute 187

A.3. Gag Solutions and the Ayodhya Dispute: Returning to
the Models 192

A.3.1. Ayodhya: Restricting Access and Worship,
"Gag Solutions," and Thick Sites 193

A.3.2. "Gagging" Solutions: Evaluating the Instrument
vis-à-vis the Models of DCV, Evenhandedness,
and Privatization   195

A.3.3. The Particulars of Ayodhya: Gagging
or Evenhandedness?   195

A.4. Concluding Remarks   198

References 201

Index 233

Acknowledgments

THE QUEST FOR a comprehensive theoretical compass with which to navigate religion in a wide variety of differing public spaces worldwide has recently gained greater urgency and wider scholarly attention. This is a problem that has preoccupied us for several years now. We began our joint inquiry into the issue, in general, and the complexities it evokes in the Israeli context, in particular, with a paper, published in the *Journal of Political Ideologies*, on the Israeli ultra-Orthodox Jews' request to win an exemption from mandatory military conscription. While working on this article, we became fascinated with the challenges the Women of the Wall pose to the ultra-Orthodox hold on Judaism's holiest prayer site, the Western Wall, and the difficulties encountered by democratic states asked to respond to requests from minorities—in this case, religious women—that conflict with (what is often) a state-endorsed mainstream interpretation of a given tradition. Our first foray into the case of the Women of the Wall, an article published in the *Oxford Journal of Law and Religion* in 2014 made it clear to us that this complex and sensitive case touches on a wide variety of fundamental, often nuanced issues and problems, such as the need to conceptualize "contested sacred sites" and the normative status of "tradition." These reflections ultimately led us to the present book-length study.

It is said that writing a book is a long and lonely process. Long it has been, but we have had the good fortune of not finding it lonely. Principal thanks are owed to the supportive community of friends and colleagues without whose encouragement and assistance this book could not have been written and whose advice and insightful comments were invaluable to the research project. We wish to thank the following people (in alphabetical order): Adam Afterman, Allan Arkush, Dan Avnon, Avner Ben Amos, David Biale, Joseph Carens, Nitzan Caspi-Shilony, Emanuela Ceva, Asher Cohen, Andrew I. Cohen, Andrew J. Cohen, Julie Cooper, Avigail Eisenberg, Orly Erez-Likhovski, Rainer Forst, Jonathan Fox, Tammy Gottlieb, Aviad Hacohen, Ayelet Harel-Shalev, Moshe Hellinger, Noam Hofstadter, Yotam Hotam, Deeana Klepper, Cecile Labourde, Hagar

Lahav, Pnina Lahav, Hannah Lerner, Assaf Likhovski, Wendy Lochner, Patrick Loobuyck, Menachem Lorberbaum, Ron Margolin, Yehudah Mirsky, Darrel Moellendorf, Víctor M. Muniz-Fraticelli, David Myers, Amikam Nachmani, Glen Newey, Vered Noam, Alan Patten, Derek Penslar, Oren Perez, Roland Pierik, Meital Pinto, Frances Raday, Shalom Ratzaby, Itzhak Reiter, Elisheva Rosman-Stollman, Aviad Rubin, Andy Sabl, Maxime St-Hilaire, Gidi Sapir, Jeff Spinner-Halev, Geetanjali A. Srikantan, Bernard Susser, Simon Thompson, Michael Walzer, Daniel Weinstock, Melissa Williams, and Ami Wolansky. Jonathan Rynhold and Richard A. Shweder devoted a great deal of time to discussing the thesis developed in this book. Their comments and criticisms were invaluable. At Oxford University Press, we especially would like to thank Cynthia Read for her sage advice at various stages of this project. Jeremy Fogel and David Larson carefully read the manuscript and very much contributed to its final shape. Our research assistants, Hanit Ben-Glass (Tel Aviv University), Ruth Klein (Bar-Ilan University), and Yarin Raban (Tel Aviv University), provided highly valuable and professional support.

We would like to thank the organizers and participants of the conferences and workshops at which we presented various parts of this research project. The stimulating conversations we engaged in and the feedback we received in these venues were challenging and helped to greatly improve this monograph: Pavia Permanent Political Theory Seminar at the University of Pavia (2013); the 16th World Congress of Jewish Studies, in Jerusalem (2013); the 5th German-Israeli Frontiers of Humanities Symposium, organized by the Israel Academy of Sciences and Humanities and the Alexander Von Humboldt Foundation in Kibbutz Tzuba (2013); the British-Jewish Educational Charity Limmud, in Modi'in (2014); the ASPP (Association for Social and Political Philosophy) conference at the University of Amsterdam (2015); the 31st Association for Israel Studies Annual Conference at Concordia University Montreal (2015); the ASPP conference at the London School of Economics and Political Science (2016); the European Consortium for Political Research General Conference, in Prague (2016); the Colloquium of Political Theory at the Goethe-Universitat Frankfurt (2015); and the School for Interdisciplinary Area Studies at Oxford University (2016).

While writing we were fortunate to receive the generous support of various institutions and foundations, for which we are grateful (in alphabetical order): Alexander von Humboldt Foundation; EU Marie Curie Re-Integration Grants (2012–2016, no. 321680 and no. 276694); Israel Science Foundation Grant (ISF, 760/15); Publication Grant, School of Education, Tel Aviv University (2016); Schnizter Fund, the Dean of Social Sciences, Bar-Ilan University, 2014, 2016; 2016–2017 Fellowship from the Katz Center for Advanced Judaic Studies at University of Pennsylvania; grant from the Unit of Sociology of Education and the Community at Tel Aviv University (2014, 2015); and Publication Grant, Faculty of Humanities, Tel Aviv University (2015, 2016).

It is customary to end acknowledgments by thanking one's family, and for good reason. Sharing one's life with someone who is writing a book, especially an academic one, is sometimes harder than actually writing it.

Yuval Jobani: I am grateful to my parents, Moshe and Miriam, and my brother Itamar for their unconditional support and love throughout the years. To their loving encouragement I owe more than I can say. Thanks also to my beloved Keren and our wonderful children, Yonatan, Tom, and Uriah for reminding me repeatedly that writing academic books and articles is not the most important thing in life.

Nahshon Perez: I dedicate this book to Alma Gadot-Perez, who has been the best companion I could ask for, in so many ways (intellectual and others), in the near impossible mission of raising two kids, writing this book, and handling thousands of other obligations; I am grateful to my parents, Nurit and Ran, and my brothers, Oren and Gilad, for always providing me with the rich intellectual environment where precise critical thinking thrives; and to Eyal and Alon, my two marvelous, beloved sons, may they grow in a society in which the government is kept at the *right*, rather far, distance from the religious belief and practice (or lack thereof) of each autonomous individual.

Introduction—Drama in Jerusalem: Who Are the Women of the Wall and Why Does Their Struggle Matter?

SASHA LUTT, a twelve-year-old girl from Be`er Sheva in the south of Israel, made history in October 2014 when she became the first female person to read from a Torah scroll at the Western Wall in Jerusalem. It was a culmination of a quarter-century-long struggle in which the Women of the Wall (WoW), a multi-denominational Jewish feminist group, sought legal permission to perform at the women's section practices reserved solely for men under the current arrangements at the Western Wall—namely, to pray collectively and read aloud from a Torah scroll while wearing fringed prayer shawls.

With police assistance, the rabbinical authorities at the Western Wall bar the members of the WoW from bringing a Torah scroll into the women's section of the Western Wall or from using one of the over one hundred scrolls available in the men's section. This policy continues well into 2016, in defiance of a 2013 decision by the Jerusalem District court that effectively canceled the prevailing ban on the WoW's manner of prayer at the Western Wall. However, early on Friday morning, on October 24, 2014, the WoW's monthly prayer service on the first day of the Jewish month—a habitual custom since 1988—took an unusual turn. The WoW were prevented, as expected, from entering the Western Wall plaza with a normal-sized Torah scroll by security guards and the police. Subsequently, the members of the WoW demanded to meet with ultra-Orthodox rabbi Shmuel Rabinowitz, the Rabbi of the Western Wall and the chairman of the Western Wall Heritage Foundation, in order to ask for his permission to read from one of the Torah scrolls available in the men's section (a request he was expected to reject). As he was not present at that time, they seemingly accepted the ban and entered the Women's section without the Torah scroll that they had brought. However, one of the members of the WoW smuggled a tiny Torah scroll, measuring just twenty-eight centimeters, into the women's section. During their service, surrounded and sheltered by members of the WoW, Sasha read the tiny script of the smuggled scroll with a piece of magnifying plastic as part of her bat mitzvah (the Jewish coming-of-age ceremony) and became the first female person to read from a Torah scroll at the Western Wall.

In an ironic twist of history, the tiny Torah scroll the WoW brought especially from the United Kingdom to enable the celebration of Sasha's bat mitzvah, was a two-hundred-year-old scroll used, on various occasions, by Jews who were banned from publicly practicing their religion in the diaspora. Sasha's mother, Irina Lutt, had moved to Israel with the then infant Sasha from Russia, where, for decades, Jews were forbidden to practice their religion. Sasha has acknowledged her excitement, but the magnitude of her act, and the fact that she's a true celebrity, does not seem to have registered with her. When told by a reporter, "You made the *New York Times*!" she looked quizzically at her mother. She had never heard of that newspaper (Kashner, 2014).

Of course, Sasha is not everyone's hero. The Rabbi of the Western Wall, Shmuel Rabinowitz, responded by accusing the WoW of deception, and other ultra-Orthodox figures have unleashed a fierce and violent backlash. The response to the WoW's bat mitzvah's poster campaign on Jerusalem buses, in which Sasha's photo was featured with those of three other girls, provides one example. The posters read in Hebrew: "Mom, I want a bat mitzvah at the Kotel [Western Wall], too." In a violent response, half of the fifty posters were slashed and defaced and, according to the police, the tires of several buses bearing the posters were slashed in ultra-Orthodox neighborhoods of Jerusalem.[1]

A *New York Times* reader encountering the story of Sasha's bat mitzvah might be understandably confused: why are Jews smuggling a Torah scroll to the Western Wall in Jerusalem? Isn't Israel the place where Jews are supposed to be able to practice their religion safely and freely? The answer to these questions is complex and multifaceted, especially because the specific location of the dispute—the Western Wall is one of the holiest places for Judaism—and the more general difficulty posed by religious conflicts over sacred sites. The WoW's struggle is a fascinating, unusual story in which a multi-denominational group of Jewish women brought about important, unprecedented changes in the prayer arrangements, legal reality, and spatial environment of one of the most complex and controversial sacred sites in the world. Amazingly, no full-length scholarly book has been published on their story. The goal of *Women of the Wall: Navigating Religion in Sacred Sites* is to fill this gap.

---

1. Ferber (2014); Kershner (2014); Kashner (2014).

THE CASE OF the Women of the Wall combines several issues that make it unusual and, thus, a fascinating and challenging case study for religion and state relations: *first*, it exemplifies a dramatic scenario in which religious and political establishments are faced with strong, explicit demands for gender egalitarianism; *second*, as a portion of the WoW are Jewish-American and their goal is to expand religious freedoms at the Wall, they gained the support of many liberal American Jews (especially from Reform and Conservative Jewish communities). This significant support adds a further transnational complexity to this religious conflict;[2] *third*, while the core group of the WoW is Orthodox, its multi-denominational membership defies easy classification and undercuts simplistic solutions; *fourth*, the specific location—the Western Wall—is a highly significant and irreplaceable site for both observant Jews and Israel's civil religion. This raises both the tensions and the stakes of the already difficult case; any attempt to change a given (or invented) tradition at the Wall will face charges of offending another group's religious feelings,[3] as well as accusations of provoking and disturbing public order.

The WoW case hence elucidates several crucial dilemmas addressed in the current literature on religion and state by raising them all at once: How should governments manage religious plurality within their borders?[4] Is it permissible for a democratic government to endorse one particular denomination and, if so, to what extent?[5] How should the government respond to the requests of minorities—in this case, religious women—that conflict with the mainstream interpretation of a given tradition (in many cases endorsed by the state)?[6] How should the government manage disputed sacred sites located in the public sphere?[7]

---

2. As Michael Oren, the former Israeli ambassador to the United States wrote:

> Women of the Wall nevertheless tweaked one of the most sensitive U.S.-Israeli nerves. Many of the group's members, and the bulk of its foreign supporters, were American. And, once again, what Israelis viewed through the lens of law and public order . . . Americans saw from the perspectives of freedom of speech and religion as well as women's rights. (Oren 2015, 264)

3. On this category, see Feinberg (1985); Dworkin (2006); Pinto (2010).

4. The literature on this question is vast. See, for example, Audi (2011).

5. See, for comparative data, Robinstein and Yakobson (2008); Fox (2013). For a defense of state support of one church, see Weiler (2010). The classic critical discussion of the family of arguments suggested by Weiler is Hart (1963).

6. See, for example, Spinner, Halev, & Eisenberg (2005).

7. See Hassner (2009); Berkovits (2000); Friedland & Hecht (1996).

The WoW case, like the challenges it poses to theories of religion-state relations, does not float in thin air. Not only are the participants and relevant decision-makers in this case influenced by other struggles and evolving norms in religion and state relations, the struggle itself is part of a new wave of problems concerning religion-state relations in general, and conflicts over sacred sites in particular.

The relations between religion and the state, as well as the issue of religious tolerance, have been treated, for some time, as almost exhausted topics of research. Many view religion-state separation as simply the best model for guiding religion-state relations—one that will ultimately culminate with the termination of violent struggles between different religions.[8] Recently, however, more attention is being given to different models for the relations between religion and state. This attention stems from several different sources. First, many European states and courts (including the prestigious European Court of Human Rights) challenge the separation model and argue that models such as an established or endorsed church are also legitimate. As such claims arose in perfectly democratic states and courts in Europe, this has created renewed attention towards religion-state relations.[9] Second, several scholars—such as Joseph Weiler, a leading jurist and the president of the European University Institute in Florence, and David Miller of Oxford University—recently provided theoretical arguments for adopting non-separation models.[10] Hence, alternative models (such as the established or endorsed church) exist not only as political and legal realities and as case studies, but also receive support from major intellectual figures. Lastly, several US Supreme Court decisions, as well as recent historical studies of religion-state relations in the United States, have offered important critiques of the separation model and argued that such a strict model was not actually in place throughout most of United States' existence; these criticisms also maintain that it *should not* be the dominant model for religion-state relations. A case in point would be traditions such as prayers opening legislative sessions in various US towns, a practice seemingly in violation of the strict separation model. Such developments strongly point to renewed interest in religion-state relations, which notable theorists had previously deemed almost a closed matter.[11] Our goal is to illuminate and

---

8. See Nussbaum (2008); Rawls (1993); Epstein (1995).

9. See, for example, the Lautsi vs. Italy case (ECHR 30814/06, 2011) that legitimated the mandatory placement of crucifixes in all public schools in Italy. This policy received support from many European states. See Temperman (2012); Pin (2014); Perez (2015).

10. Weiler (2011); Miller (2016).

11. See, for example, the recent US Supreme Court decision in Town of Greece v. Galloway, 572 U.S. 2014; Hamburger (2004).

contribute to such recent developments in the theorizing regarding religion-state relations while focusing on the specific and challenging religious struggle of the WoW. Now, this struggle has attracted the attention of several important scholars who have attempted to situate the WoW in various specific social, legal, political, and gender-related contexts.[12] These investigations are all highly valuable and our research draws from their significant insights. However, our research locates the WoW's struggle within the renewed interest in the separation model, in order to clarify, and contribute to, an adequate modeling of the relations between religion and state, with a special reference to the somewhat neglected category of sacred sites.

I.1. Overview of Women of the Wall: Navigating Religion in Sacred Sites

The following overview aims at illustrating the structure of the book, providing a succinct description of the content of the chapters, and assisting the reader in navigating her/his way to the issues in which s/he is most interested. We are well aware that readers have limited time and diverse interests. We have tried to respect both by writing in a succinct style and by focusing in each one of the chapters on one specific topic or category, while avoiding the temptations of discussing "neighboring" subjects. Our wish, of course, is that the reader will be interested enough to read the whole monograph. However, we are well aware that this might not be the case for some readers, and therefore we made the following "road map," so a reader interested in a particular topic or issue would easily find her/his way in the monograph.

Chapter 1 introduces several major concepts central to our study and explains our methodological framework. It opens with a categorization of the Western Wall as what we propose to label a "thick site." Echoing Geertz's "thick description" approach, this new concept denotes a site typically but not necessarily religious, which is loaded with different and incompatible meanings attributed to it by different agents. From these agents' perspective, such meanings are highly significant, and consequently, these sites are irreplaceable. This conceptualization

---

12. See Charme (2005); Lahav (2015); Raday (2007); Shakdiel (2002); Reiter (2016). The only book available on the subject is by Phyllis Chesler and Rivka Haut (Eds.), *Women of the Wall: Claiming Sacred Ground at Judaism's Holy Site* (2002). This collection of essays and reminiscences, edited by two of the WoW's American members, offers an accessible assemblage of passionate primary accounts and traces the genesis and first years of the WoW struggle. However, it is not an academic book and does not contain a systematic, scholarly study of the WoW. Additionally, since it was published more than a decade ago, it does not cover the crucial legal and political developments in this complex affair since 2002.

elucidates the most important characteristics of sacred sites, enabling us to clas-sify the WoW struggle within a larger context of similar struggles regarding such thick sites, and helps us indicate possible solutions. We then move to define basic, and often contested, concepts that are necessary for illustrating the contours of our discussion: "state," "religion" and "public sphere." The chapter concludes with a discussion that explains, in detail, the contextual research methodology chosen for this study.

Chapter 2 explores the WoW's struggle from various perspectives in order to provide a clear picture of this complex conflict. It opens with an in-depth Halakhic analysis of the religious-feminist challenge that the WoW pose to the patriarchy of mainstream Jewish Orthodoxy. Then, we situate the WoW's strug-gle in the framework of Israel's complex religion-state arrangement and critically examine the various rulings that the Israeli Supreme Court has issued on the mat-ter (delivered in 1994, 2000, and 2003). Finally, we conclude with a survey of the recent dramatic developments of 2013–2016: the reversal of the legal ban on the WoW manner of prayer, the "third plaza" plan, and the split within the WoW over the proper response to the "third plaza" plan.

Chapters 3, 4, and 5 examine three prevalent alternative models of religion-state relations: the "dominant culture view" (DCV), evenhandedness, and pri-vatization, respectively—with a special reference to thick sites in general and the WoW struggle in particular. Moving between the thick-site category, the WoW case details and the analyses of these models, will enrich our efforts to develop these theories, while also providing a fuller comparative and theoretical context to the WoW case-study. This will allow us to point to what are, arguably, adequate solutions to this and similar complex conflicts.

The first theory examined (chapter 3), the *dominant culture view* (DCV) argues that, in any given country, majorities can legitimately advance their reli-gious traditions and shared cultural understandings through the acts of the government, so long as such shared understandings and traditions are effec-tively demonstrated and present, and their advancement by the state does not violate the rights of minority groups. The DCV, thus, identifies the state with one denomination. Many European countries (England, Greece, Denmark, Italy) have adopted the DCV by, for example, arranging an established or endorsed church. Chapter 3 critically considers the DCV approach as a whole, and its applicability to thick sites in general and to the WoW case in particular. Our examination will focus on three assumptions of the DCV approach: the existence of shared-understandings, a robust tradition rooted in the past and in respect for democratic standards. The "shared-understandings" assumption will be chal-lenged through an examination of the different, often incompatible meanings attributed to the Western Wall. The "tradition" assumption is challenged via the presentation of a subversive historical survey, of over a hundred years, of prayer practices and women's attendance at the Wall; this survey will show that it is impossible to identify a single, coherent tradition at the Wall. Finally, the "democratic" assumption is challenged by noting that, as no Western democracy is religiously homogenous, the DCV approach might create unjustified inequality between citizens belonging to different denominations. The nontrivial exploration of this "unjustified inequality" will be detailed in the chapter itself.

In the second model (chapter 4), *evenhandedness*, the state remains unaffiliated with any given denomination. It does, however, adopt a hands-on approach in which governmental resources are allocated to different religious denominations and groups. Importantly, preference is not given to any one religious group, and the allocation of resources is impartial (Germany, for example, employs a version of the evenhanded approach). Chapter 4 carefully examines the evenhanded approach in general, and its applicability to thick sites and the Western Wall in particular. This hands-on approach aims to treat all citizens of the state with equal concern and respect, an equality maintained through an impartial, egalitarian governmental involvement in religion-state relations. However, there are two principled drawbacks to the even-handed approach, noteworthy even at this preliminary stage: *first*, an evenhanded approach to religious claims tends to lead to the adoption of end-result solutions that potentially violate religious freedoms. As applied to the WoW case, this would mean granting particular prayer customs a preferential, and perhaps exclusive, status that could make their adoption a condition of access to the Wall; *second*, the burden that this approach places on the government—to continually assess and respond to the demands of different groups—requires unjustifiable optimism with regard to the abilities of any governmental apparatus. These points require much elaboration that will be done in the chapter itself.

Privatization, the third model (chapter 5), keeps the state unaffiliated with any given denomination via a strict "hands off" approach towards religions. It attempts, primarily, to reduce governmental entanglement with religion both by strictly limiting the role that religion can play in political institutions and by respecting the autonomy of religions. The privatization model of religion-state relations aims to neither assist nor hinder any religious establishment, belief or practice, leaving religious decisions, as much as possible, to be made by each individual citizen (France's model of secularism and the American principle of separation between religion and state share some important features of privatization, although neither is identical to it).

Chapter 5 carefully examines the privatization approach in general, and its applicability to thick sites and the Western Wall in particular. The main argument to be advanced in it is that the most adequate governmental response for the Women of the Wall case, as well as for similar religious conflicts over sacred sites, is a specific version of the privatization approach that we label *context-sensitive privatization*. The privatization approach is a promising framework for managing the WoW struggle and similar struggles over thick sites as, among other considerations, it neither encourages hostile factionalism nor burdens the government with complex decisions stemming from entanglement with diverse religious beliefs; the privatization approach views all worshipers as equally entitled to respect and concern; and it protects religions from the heavy hand of the state (especially in such contested sites). Therefore, in the vein of the privatization approach, we tentatively posit that the Israeli government should retreat from its dominant presence at and exclusive management of the Western Wall and limit itself to providing law and order.

However, given that the Wall is indeed a highly contested thick site, the government should demonstrate sensitivity while applying the privatization policy. A context sensitive approach is appropriate, we argue, as applying rigid privatization to thick sites could mean that members of many denominations would be unable to maintain core practices of their religion, as members of these groups often have preferences concerning the public aspect of such sites. However, context sensitivity is qualified, so that the suggested approach will not violate core liberties of the members of other religious groups. To mention one example in which such sensitivity would be appropriate, even under a privatized scenario, it may be necessary to allow a temporary gender-divider at the Western Wall so as to avoid (among other considerations) the alienation of Orthodox members of the WoW themselves (who require a divider in order to pray). Here, in order not to violate the core principles of the privatization approach, specific details must be added: the praying party itself (and not the state) would have to place such a divider (during prayers only), nor would the government enforce its presence. The government, therefore, tolerates some adjustments to the privatization approach but does not initiate or support them.

In order to avoid selection bias, and to add what we consider a necessary comparative perspective to our exploration of disputes over contested sacred sites or "thick sites," we examine, in the appendix, an additional case-study where a government had to manage a highly disputed sacred site: the Ram Janmabhoomi / Babri masjid conflict in Uttar Pradesh, India, that became a focal point of encounters between Hindus and Muslims. The examination of a non-Jewish, non-Israeli case, adds much data and helpful insights to the ways such conflicts are managed and might be resolved.

We conclude the *Women of the Wall: Navigating Religion in Sacred Sites* by underscoring the impressive achievements of the Women of the Wall struggle; of which arguably the most distinctive achievement is leading the Israeli government and courts, to make substantial changes in the prayer arrangements and physical reality at the Western Wall, one of the most sacred sites for Jews worldwide, while being posed against a dominant patriarchal order. It should be noted that when the WoW began their struggle (1988), the idea of establishing the egalitarian third plaza at the Western Wall seemed as implausible as an outlandish science-fiction premise. However, the current fierce debate and split within the WoW—regarding the "third plaza" proposal—demonstrates, it will be argued in this monograph, the need to abandon this plan in favor of the context-sensitive privatization model.

Women of the Wall

I

Laying the Groundworks

CONCEPTS, DEFINITIONS, AND METHODOLOGY

IN THIS CHAPTER, we introduce the main concepts, definitions, and the research methodology employed throughout this monograph. We begin in the first section (1.1) by introducing the new concept of a "thick site," which we define as "a site typically but not necessarily religious, which is loaded with different and incompatible meanings that are attributed to it by different agents. From these agents' view, such meanings are highly significant, and, consequently, these sites are irreplaceable." This novel concept aims to elucidate the characteristics of a pattern to which an entire class of disputed sacred sites, the Western Wall included, belong. Approaching sacred sites through the lens of "thick sites" can provide us not only with a better understanding of the struggles over these sites but also a better evaluation of policy options aimed at managing these conflicted sites. Since the conflicts over sacred sites unfold in the intersection of religion, state, and the public sphere, the second section (1.2) takes up the challenging endeavor of defining these three basic yet contested concepts. In the third section (1.3), we provide a detailed analysis of the contextual methodology we have adopted in this monograph in order to clarify how we conducted and structured our research. By presenting our methodology, we also hope to facilitate the evaluation of both our results and the applicability of our conclusions to other cases. As such, this methodological discussion is not tailored to, or limited by, the contours of the Women of the Wall (WoW) case study.

1.1. The Western Wall as a "Thick Site": Categorizing the Wall

Any attempt to adequately understand and, further, to suggest solutions to the WoW struggle requires a nuanced understanding of the various groups involved and a careful tracing of the political and legal developments of the case;

additionally, and this is crucial, it also requires an in-depth inquiry into the various meanings and characteristics of the site at which the conflict takes place—that is, the Western Wall. Along with its unique and particular significance,[1] the Western Wall shares important attributes with other disputed sacred sites. It is necessary, therefore, to analyze it as belonging to a larger class of similar sites. The concept of a "thick site" that is suggested in this section aims to advance comparative understanding by placing the Western Wall in a broad context that will assist us in better conceptualizing the conflictual nature of many sacred sites.[2] The section opens with a detailed discussion of the characteristics of "thick sites" and considers the complex relation between Geertzian "thick description" and "thick sites"; it closes with a demonstration of the relevance of this new concept to the WoW struggle.

By thick site we denote a site, typically but not necessarily religious, which is loaded with different and incompatible meanings that are attributed to it by different agents. From these agents' view, such meanings are highly significant and, consequently, these sites are irreplaceable.

A few comments on this parsimonious definition are in order. The definition of a "thick site" suggests four major features of such sites: (1) being loaded with different meanings, (2) incompatibility of those meanings, (3) significance of those meanings, and (4) irreplaceability. We shall briefly comment on all four.

The first feature of the concept "thick site"—being loaded with different meanings—echoes Geertz's influential cross-disciplinary thick-description approach, adding several important and distinct attributes.[3] According to Geertz (2014), to thickly describe social action is to conduct an in-depth inquiry into the

---

1. Many excellent analyses of the religious, historical, and national significances of the Western Wall are available, including Ben-Dov, Naor, and Aner (1983); and Barkay and Schiller (2007).

2. There are somewhat legalistic definitions of holy places or sacred sites. However, without offering a critique of such definitions, we note that they serve to describe and identify, whereas our goal in the conceptualization of thick sites is also to further our understanding of the noted conflictual nature of such sites. Two mainly legal definitions found in the literature are as follows (we indicate the main parts of these definitions): (1) "Holy places or sacred places are geographically determined localities to which one or more religious communities attribute extraordinary religious significance or consider as subjects of divine consecration" (Rumpf, 1995). And (2) Benzo, after examining various existing definitions, offers the four following features as characteristics of a sacred place: a link to manifestation of the sacred; an important role played in the history of a religion as a permanent landmark; the fact that it is the object of veneration and interest not only for local communities but also for believers from different parts of the world and even for members of different religions; the fact that a general consensus within the religious community (or communities) exists, or throughout history and tradition, has developed to consider it as such (2014: p. 21).

3. Geertz (1973, pp. 3–32). The term "thick description," as Geertz himself notes, originates with the works of the philosopher Gilbert Ryle, specifically the lectures "Thinking and Reflecting" and "The Thinking of Thoughts: What Is 'le Penseur' Doing?" both published in

circumstances, meanings, intentions, motivations, and so on, of a particular act (or, in cases of sets of interconnected acts, "events"). A thin description, in contrast, offers only a dry description of facts, independent of any cultural context. As a "context-less description," a thin description should be dismissed, according to Geertz, since acts and events cannot maintain their full meaning without the complex webs of significance and interaction in which they are located.[4]

Following Geertz, we shall argue that in order to reach an adequate understanding of a given sacred site, a thick description of its meanings is required. A thin description—picking up what seem to be naked or dry facts without situating them in the relevant cultural webs of significance—might lead to mistakes and misunderstandings of a site's meaning.[5]

While Geertz focused on actions or clusters of actions that constitute events and their proper understanding, we focus on sites and the proper understanding of their meanings. A "site," the Oxford English Dictionary tells us, is "the ground or area upon which a building, town, etc., has been built, or which is set apart for some purpose."[6] This definition suggests geographical points; specific terrains, such as rocks or sand; and constructs, such as streets and avenues. But this is only a thin description. The sites that interest us here are located within complex webs of significances, and without an adequate understanding of those webs of cultural meanings, such locations cannot be understood. A further adaption of Geertz's approach to sacred sites is that different agents often attribute different meanings to them. This description arises from observing the struggles over these sites and naturally arises from being loyal to an adequate, sensitive-to-details description to such sites a la Geertz.

We turn now to the second feature of thick sites: that the various meanings attributed to them are not only different; they are also incompatible with each other. Disputes over access, legitimate and permissible conduct, and the management of thick sites reflect these vehemently different understandings of them. This incompatibility is increased by the deep concern that individuals—already

---

Ryle's *Collected Essays, 1929–1968*, the second volume of his Collected Papers (1971). Geertz's term "thick description" and the methodology embedded in it became milestones in the social sciences and beyond. See, for example, Walzer (1994); Scarboro, Campbell, and Stave (1994); Denzin (1989), esp. chap. 6; and Ponterotto (2006).

4. Geertz (1973, pp. 5–10). These webs of significance, according to Geertz (1973) constitute culture itself. In his words, "[C]ulture is not a power, something to which social events, behaviours, institutions, or processes can be causally attributed; it is a context, something within which they can be intelligibly—that is, thickly described" (p. 14; italics added).

5. See also Skinner (1969).

6. "Site," (n.d.), *Oxford English Dictionary Online*, retrieved from http://www.oed.com/ (accessed June 15, 2014).

holding different beliefs regarding the "correct" meaning of such sites—have regarding the behavior of other persons in such sites, even if such behavior does not impinge in any simple and direct physical manner on one's ability to practice one's own rituals (religious, national, or any other). This attribute of regard for the actions of other persons explains much of the intractability of the disputes regarding the management of thick sites.

Note that deciding which meaning constitutes a proper understanding of a given thick site cannot be settled by favoring thin descriptions over thick descriptions or by declaring just one given description to be the thick description; these competing meanings are typically all thick descriptions. Though it is always possible to point to a shallow common denominator and to thinly describe the sites as "mere" religious, national, or historical sites, such a step would amount to a flat description that is inadequate to such sites and conflicts. Only by taking into account all the various thick descriptions of these sites can the depth and significance of the disputes over them be fully understood. The third feature of thick sites is that the meanings attributed to them by the relevant agents are highly significant; that is, the sites are central to the agents' beliefs and identities. This might apply to many different religious beliefs, national narratives, and so on. Note that the significance attributed to a thick site depends neither on the agents being physically present at the site nor on the specific activities they conduct there. Even people who do not reside near a specific thick site, or actually visit it, often care deeply about its management.

Finally, the fourth feature of such sites concerns their irreplaceability owing to their significance to believers' beliefs and identities. By definition, thick sites are those to which significant meanings—religious, national, and so on—are attributed; they are never merely a platform on which significant activities are performed (such as religious rituals or ceremonies of a state's civil religion). As such, the beliefs and identities of those who share similar beliefs, typically members of a given community or denomination, might be undermined by any request to move those significant activities to different locations.

Taken together, the different, highly significant, and incompatible meanings attributed to these irreplaceable sites explain the recurrent disputes over access to, ownership of, permissible conduct in, and management and even the desecration (which sometimes even degenerates into destruction) of thick sites around the globe.[7] Moreover, the analysis just outlined clarifies why conflicts over thick

---

7. There is no official index of worldwide conflicts over sacred sites, though some catalogs exist for various countries. In The Battle for Holy Places, Berkovits lists—in Israel and the Palestinian Territories alone—some 450 sacred sites under conflict. In India, to mention but one additional example, Eaton points to eighty incidents of temple desecrations in the premodern era. See Eaton (2000); Berkovits (2000); and Hassner (2009, p. 184, n. 1).

sites can rarely be reduced to and consequently resolved via technical or logistical measures.[8]

Approaching the Western Wall as a thick site enables us to advance our understanding of the conflict over its management by placing it in a broad comparative context. In addition to the Western Wall, we point to Ayodhya's Ramjanmabhoomi / Babri Masjid in Uttar Pradesh as an example of a thick site that has become the focal point of violent encounters between Hindus and Muslims.[9] These deep collisions have led to severe disagreements regarding the proper way to manage both sites, as well as to attempts to recruit the state to maintain control over them.[10]

It is important to note that many different locations require a thick description in order to fully understand the activities taking place within them but also that not all such locations qualify as thick sites. Consider, for example, a trivial location such as a post office. People visit the post office to do various things: send a letter, pick up a package, buy stamps, and so on. To properly understand such familiar activities requires a thick description. Think, for example, of two persons mailing letters: one sends a complaint to an airline about its luggage policy; the second mails a job application for a tenure-track position, which, because many previous applications have been denied, she has decided will be the last attempt before she abandons her life-long dream of being a university professor. Indeed, a thin description would miss the complex and very different meanings of the seemingly identical and trivial acts of sending a letter.

There are, however, two main differences between a postal office and what we label a thick site. The first important difference relates to the irreplaceability feature: a post office can be replaced by other postal offices or by similar services, such as Federal Express. This is not the case with thick sites like the Western Wall. In the post-office example, the thickness refers to the acts of the relevant agents and the networks of meanings and emotions that surround those acts; the thickness

---

8. Thick sites are by definition sites of contestation and disagreement. However, not all contested sacred sites are thick sites. Contestation has to be enduring and substantial in order for a given sacred site to become a thick site.

9. For detailed surveys of the Ayodhya case and comparative studies of the religious conflicts in Ayodhya and Jerusalem, see Rajamony (2007); Noorani (2003, 2003b, 2014); Friedland and Hecht (1998); and Bakker (1991). See also the appendix for a detailed discussion.

10. Note that we don't ask at this stage what the normative strengths of the various constituent attributes of thick sites are or what governmental policies in response to those attributes should be. We merely aim to identify and conceptualize what we believe to be an important, largely overlooked phenomenon belonging to the religious-political landscape (see chapters 3–5 for further discussion of this point). For general literature on the justification and scope of religious freedom, see Barry (2001, chap. 2); Dorfman (2008); Sapir and Statman (2014); McConnell (1990).

does not refer to the locations in which the acts take place (a specific branch of the post office). This point applies to both examples—both the ordinary letter (complaining about baggage policy), and the more emotionally charged letter (the job-seeking one)—because to gain a proper understanding of each case, a thick description is required; but the site itself, a post office, is not thick.

The second difference is that in a thick site the relevant agents care deeply not only about the meanings they attribute to the site and their own activities there, but also about the presence and activities (broadly understood to include dress codes, for example) of other persons at the site. Furthermore, these agents would view some of these activities and attributed meanings as an interruption of their own (typically religious) activities and even, in some cases, a desecration of a holy site. In many cases, they even argue that the "interruption" prevents them from carrying out their own religious activities and maintaining their own identities. This other-regarding characteristic is not typical of the ways people conceive of, and conduct themselves at, places that are not characteristically thick sites.[11] Persons do not usually care what other persons do, for example, at the post office.

It is important to note that the Western Wall fits into the thick-site category perfectly because it exhibits all four features of those sites: different and incompatible meanings are attributed to it by various agents for whom it is highly important and, as such, irreplaceable. The disagreement between the ultra-Orthodox and the members of the WoW demonstrates this point, as it stems from the following: *first*, for both parties, the Wall is highly important and as such irreplaceable; *second*, the different meanings that each group attributes to the Wall have their roots in deep, incommensurable religious understandings from which their different religious practices arise.

The members of the WoW, as well as their opponents, are well aware (even though they do not use this particular vocabulary) of the fact that it is the thickness of the Wall that so complicates the debate over prayer arrangements at this

---

11. We focus exclusively on conflicts over thick sites situated in the public sphere. Obviously, there are other kinds of conflicts pertaining to sacred sites, but we intentionally omit the following two categories of disputes from our considerations: first, cases in which one side in the dispute attributes "irreplaceability" to the site, while the other side attributes only an instrumental or "thin" meaning to the site, which makes it replaceable; second, cases in which the thick site is privately owned. The omission of such cases, not merely a technical concession for "limitations of space," intrinsically follows from the contours of this research project. The focus of our monograph is thick sites that, in the definition that we use, denote contested sacred sites to which all the concerned parties attribute the feature of irreplaceability. Since our interest is in the public sphere, even related conflicts at privately owned sites reside outside of the contours of the current study. For a survey of some legal cases and relevant literature related to these excluded categories, see *Lyng v. Northwest Indian Cemetery Protective Association* (485 U.S. 439, 1988); *Tsilhqot'in Nation v. British Columbia*, (2014) 2 SCR 257; Ross (2006); Villaroman (2015); Carpenter (2005); Wygoda (2010); Garrick (1998); Collins (2003).

location. Rivka Haut (2003), one of the founders of the WoW, has noted that the location has intensified their conflict, "Unlike Tefilah ('prayer') groups which meet behind closed doors . . . WoW is the only 'Women Tefilah Group' to have come under direct physical attack" (p. 280). Menachem Elon (2005), who occupied the seat in the Israeli Supreme Court traditionally designated for a scholar in Jewish Law, in his long and encyclopedic ruling rejecting the WoW petition (see section 2.3 in chapter 2), also noted the relevance of the location: "[T]he praying site at the Western Wall, is not the right location for a war of opinions and acts in this topic [Women Tefilah (prayer) Group]" (p. 156). Elon admits that, in principle, there is a need to acknowledge the growing Halakhic legitimacy of Women Tefilah Groups, yet he fiercely opposes the WoW because the location of their struggle is one of the most holy locations in Judaism. In other words, it is the thickness of the Wall that particularly pushes him to an adversarial view vis-à-vis the WoW.

1.2. Defining Religion, State, and the Public Sphere: Locating Thick Sites Conceptually

Conflicts over sacred sites are conducted in the intersection between religion, the state, and the public sphere; it is in between these conceptual "locations" that thick sites are situated. Thus, if we wish to properly understand thick sites, as well as to suggest adequate policies for managing them, a clear understanding of these difficult and contested concepts is required. We therefore turn to the challenging endeavor of defining these basic yet contested concepts: religion, state, and public sphere.

A preliminary note is required: we are well aware of the familiar trap of favoring definitions that support one's normative presuppositions. However, without clear definitions, there is an even graver danger that readers will, legitimately, attribute different meanings to contested concepts than those meant by the authors. Furthermore, misunderstandings and inconsistencies can develop for the authors themselves, as Hobbes' (1651/1968) puts it in his *Leviathan*:

> [A] man that seeketh precise truth had need to remember what every name he uses stands for, and to place it accordingly; or else he will find himself entangled in words, as a bird in lime twigs; the more he struggles, the more belimed. (p. 105: I:5)

We turn therefore to the Sisyphean task of defining the three basic concepts without which no proper understanding of the WoW struggle will be possible: religion, state, and public sphere.

Although rival definitions of "religion," the first concept to be explored here, have proliferated, they can conveniently be grouped into two approaches: functional and substantive (Berger, 1974). Succinctly put, the functional approach defines religion in terms of the social and psychological functions it fulfills; the substantive approach defines religion in terms of its believed content. A prevalent example of a functional definition of religion is suggested by Geertz (1966), for whom religion is

> a system of symbols which acts to establish powerful, pervasive, and long-lasting moods and motivations in men by formulating conceptions of a general order of existence and clothing these conceptions with such an aura of factuality that the moods and motivations seem uniquely realistic. (p. 4)[12]

Geertz's definition includes key functional characteristics, such as the existence of symbols and the motivating of individuals to certain actions, but not concrete content, such as a specific deity or god. The definition can fit, therefore, not only established historical religions, but also nationalism and other ideological movements. Geertz's functional definition, and the functional approach as a whole, can be contrasted with Rudolph Otto's (1917/1958) substantive approach that identifies the religious realm with the realm of the "numinous," a term Otto uses to denote a nonrational and nonsensory experience or feeling that is both terrifying and fascinating at the same time. This is a typical substantive approach; its focal point is the substance of religion as it is perceived from the perspective of the faithful. By identifying the religious realm with the realm of the numinous, Otto aimed to grasp religion from within instead of from the outside (as suggested by the functional approach).[13]

While both types of definitions have distinct advantages, we will favor functional definitions over substantive definitions of religion; that is, we will define religion in terms of social and psychological functions rather than in terms of its believed content (Berger, 1974, pp. 125–133). We do so for three main reasons. *First*, functional definitions are better suited for tracing the effects of religion in the public sphere and for determining how to best assess claims grounded in

---

12. Bellah's (1964) definition of religion is another example of a functionalist approach: "a set of symbolic forms and acts which relate to ultimate condition of his existence" (p. 358).

13. In this context, Ninian Smart claims that the phenomenological study of religion (which attempts, through a suspension of the researcher's own personal position, to grasp religion as it is grasped by the believers themselves) must be based on what he calls "informed empathy" toward religion, an empathy anchored in the symbols, narratives, rituals, and works of art of the religious world. See, for example, Smart (1996, p. xxiii).

differing religious identities and doctrines; our interests here, simply, are not in the inner lives of religious persons. *Second*, functional definitions of religion, by their nature, are broad (or soft) and include established historical religions as well as various kinds of ideological systems that are prevalent in thick sites like the Western Wall—such as nationalism, cultural ethoses, and traditions. *Lastly*, and following the previous point, the definitions of religion in social, political, and legal contexts determine eligibility for the allocation of resources, such as legal standing, material goods, and so on. Therefore, adopting a strict substantive definition of religion not only begs the analytical question, it can also create privileges based on the particular values and expectations favored by a contested definition. Given that our context is exactly the struggles over such definitions and their effects on the allocation of resources, a strict substantial definition is inadequate, as it would predetermine the outcome of our examination.

Moving on, we must search for a useful definition of the state. Although history displays a great variety of forms of states, "the first impulse of the philosopher," as Walzer (1983) observed in another context, "is to resist the display of history, the world of appearances, and to search for some underlying unity" (p. 4). The most famous definition to which most scholars return is Weber's. In the first chapter of Economy and Society, Weber asserts that "a compulsory political organization with continuous operations (politischer Anstaltsbetrieb) will be called a 'state' insofar as its administrative staff successfully upholds the claim to the monopoly of the legitimate use of physical force in the enforcement of its order" (p. 54; see also Weber, 1946, p. 78). This definition connects some of the essential characteristics of a state: physical force, administration, legitimation, and territory.[14] Weber emphasized that a major characteristic of any state is control over legitimate physical force combined with a given territory, population, and the existence of differentiated organizations[15] (such as bureaucratic organizations and the apparatus of the modern state, the development of which are hallmarks of Weber scholarship).[16]

In the context of our study, two important points about this definition must be made. First, the major focus of states in Weber's approach is connected to

---

14. Weber (1978, p. 54) adds "territory" to his definition of a state.

15. C. Tilly (1985) offers a definition that is indebted to Weber yet more developed, as: "relatively centralized, differentiated organizations the officials of which more or less successfully claim control over the chief concentrated means of violence within a population inhabiting a large, contiguous territory" (p. 170), thus demonstrating the continued relevance of Weber's definition.

16. On Weber's well-known theory of bureaucracy, see, for example, Mommsen (1989, pp. 109–120).

their ability to control and use force through their technical-bureaucratic appa-ratuses, rather than, for example, the advancement of a given set of ideals or val-ues (Dunleavy, 1993, p. 612; Swedberg, 2005, p. 265).[17] However, moving to the second point, physical force is a necessary but insufficient feature.[18] The use of physical force by the state must rest on some form of legitimation, Weber asserts, otherwise the state would be highly unstable. The citizenry must not only fear retaliation if laws are violated but also believe that, to a certain degree, following the state's laws is justified behavior. Various theorists have offered different views regarding the source, nature, essence, and best techniques of acquiring such legit-imation, from Plato's well-known "noble lies" (1968, pp. 93–95: 414c–414d) and Rousseau's "civil religion" (1997, pp. 142–151) to Habermas' "constitutional patri-otism" (1995). Noting that states' need to gain legitimacy is important in order to avoid the temptation to view the state solely through its monopoly on physical force, bureaucracy, and institutions. If they wish to maintain legitimation and stability, states must concern themselves with the creation, preservation, and cultivation of such legitimacy, typically via public education, symbols, national anthems, memorials, national commemoration days, and the like. A state is never, to put this point in a different way, solely mere institutions and a coercive appara-tus; it has to suggest some kind of self-justification in order to achieve legitimacy and long-term stability.

In terms of our overall aim in this study—learning how to navigate religion in thick sites located in the public sphere—these two aspects of the Weberian definition of a state that we have adopted necessitate a succinct analysis.

Like the functional definition of religion, this definition of a state's first group of attributes—control over means of violence and institutional frameworks—does not assume a given normative content of the state. As such, these attributes are compatible with many different states and regimes and, in our context, pro-vide a framework that does not beg the question of what the preferred model of religion-state relations is (see chapters 3–5). The second group of attributes—regarding the search for legitimacy—are also compatible with many differ-ent states and regimes and do not assume, in an a priori way, a given particular

---

17. Some critics have argued that behind Weber's allegedly "value-free" theoretical discourse on politics in general and the modern state in particular, one can find Weber's own value-laden standpoint, which tends to be adversarial or even conflictual (Lassman, 2000, p. 87). We are well aware of the general framework in which Weber located his definition, but we argue that it is possible to adopt a variation of his valuable definition without committing to his entire system of thought.

18. As Seneca puts it, "No one who has ruled by violence has ever ruled for long" (violenta imperia nemo continuit diu). See Trojan Women in Seneca (1986, p. 260).

religion-state institutional arrangement; this group is, nonetheless, more complex. As various philosophers, such as Hobbes in his Leviathan (1651) and Spinoza in his Theological-Political Treatise (1670),[19] have argued the set of ideals advanced by the state to insure its legitimacy is an ongoing source of conflict between the state and religion.[20] As religions contain their own sets of ideals and produce guidelines for conduct in various spheres, the possibility of competing authorities can arise. This study explores three models (in chapters 3–5 correspondingly) that attempt to illustrate the proper relations between religion and state. Note that in the context of conflicts over sacred or "thick" sites, the contest is not only between a given religion and the state, but between many religions and the state. This point proves significant in determining the adequate arrangement between the noted religions and the state. We shall return to this point in the noted chapters.

We can now turn to the third and final organizing concept of this section, the "public sphere." As with the concepts "religion" and "state," the public sphere is highly contested and loaded with different meanings and expectations. A good starting point for our discussion is the prevailing definition, by Habermas (1993), of the public sphere as

> the sphere of private people coming together as a public; they soon claimed the public sphere regulated from above against the public authorities themselves, to engage them in a debate over the general rules governing relations in the basically privatized but publicly relevant sphere of commodity exchange and social labor. The medium of this political confrontation was peculiar and without historical precedent: people's public use of their reason. (p. 27)

---

19. According to Hobbes (1588–1679) and Spinoza (1632–1677), who were among the first philosophers to analyze the theological-political problem in the modern era, the clash between religion and the state is the result of a firm mutual demand for supremacy. Religion proclaims its supremacy in the absolute nature of the source of its authority: God; and it is therefore not prepared to bow down to the authority of the state. Political authority, by contrast, perceives its supremacy to be a factual-conceptual matter; in the same way that an item cannot be considered a chair if it was not intended to be used for sitting, no social institution can be considered a political authority if it does not demand for itself, and prove capable of realizing, supremacy (this perspective is also shared, mutatis mutandis, by Weber's definition of the state). Spinoza devoted his entire Theological-Political Treatise to the clash between religion and the state, and Hobbes deals with the issue at length in part 3, "Of a Christian Commonwealth," and part 4, "Of the Kingdom of Darkness," of Leviathan (1968, pp. 409–626). See also Lorberbaum (2007); Jobani (2008, 2016).

20. Contemporary scholars also note this tension. See Liebman and Don Yehiya (1983); Gill (2008).

Habermas' famous definition includes the crucial distinction between the public sphere and the state and the important insight that the public sphere is where the free, potentially critical, process of public thinking and arguing on public affairs is conducted. However, Habermas' definition has two main shortcomings. *First*, it burdens the public sphere with heavy expectations of what should happen in it: that is, debate and the public use of reason to craft a shared critique of the government. This seems idealistic in that it does not sufficiently recognize that public debates tend to be adversarial, conflictual, and, many times, simply messy. *Second*, it does not, as Nancy Frazer (1990) pointed out, take into account heterogeneous distinctions among the public, especially marginalized groups, such as (in certain contexts) women; therefore, it does not consider the variety of groups and interests that are not explicitly represented in the public sphere.

Rather than provide a full alternative to this definition, we adopt a minimal approach to delimiting the public sphere. Incorporating crucial elements of Habermas' and Frazer's discussions, we aim to move beyond both in two specific ways. *First*, we emphasize that the public sphere is an "in-between" sphere. That is, it is a sphere that is outside the sphere of the state, on the one hand, and beyond the private sphere on the other. A park in the middle of a given town, used for making speeches for or against a given policy, nicely illustrates this "in-between" nature of the public sphere: it is not in the private sphere (i.e., Jane Doe's house), nor is it "the state." The speaker in this example is not employed by or sent by the state, the content of his or her speech is not dictated by the state, and the speech is not delivered from within a state institution such as a parliament or a court house. The boundaries of the public sphere are admittedly ambiguous, and it is far from trivial to formulate them against both the state[21] and the private sphere.[22] However, as in other cases, problems of demarcation should not hasten our jettisoning of the notion or lead us to conclude that the concept is fictitious and devoid of any content.

Second, beyond defining the public sphere as an in-between space, we do not specify any set of characteristics that the activities taking place in it must exhibit,

---

21. Certain rules and legal norms apply to all spaces; while some are trivial (such as "no littering" rules), some—such as public education, civil religion, etc.—are controversial. In such cases, the demarcation between the public sphere and the state would be difficult to define and is often contested (Stepan, 1978, p. xii).

22. Feminist scholars, for example, have pointed to the artificiality, tendentious character, and interest-oriented nature of demarcations between the public and the private spheres. Such demarcations may hide other motivations, such as economic or religious goals. To point to well-known examples: paid maternity leave and subsidized childcare facilities in workplaces can be, and at times are, defined as "belonging" to not only the private sphere but also to the state and the public sphere (Gavison, 1992).

nor do we burden it with expectations. While Habermas' description of the people's public use of reason is inspiring, we must wonder whether he does not set the bar a tad too high. What happens in the public sphere, in our approach, is a factual, not a definitional or philosophical, issue. Such a minimal, thin, or "naked" definition of a public sphere has a major advantage in that it is not biased toward a previously defined set of assumptions or rules rooted in a given political or moral theory (Schumpeter, 1943/2003).[23] Note that we do not object to deliberations or to the setting of circumstances that would promote better decision-making processes of various kinds in the public sphere; we simply do not view these as necessary features of the public sphere.

As the decision to examine thick sites within the conceptual space of the "public sphere" is not trivial, a brief explanation is required. *First*, thick sites such as the Western Wall and many others are located in the public sphere, and they are not directly part of the state apparatus; this preliminary condition is therefore satisfied in the cases that interest us here.[24] *Second*, in the vein of Habermas' approach, given the significance of these sites, decisions regarding their management have central consequences for the identity of the state, its values, its relations with the various religions inside its boundaries, and the standing of its heterogeneous body of citizens. While the phrase "public use of reason" may seem inadequate or exaggerated given the messy nature of this decision-making process, there certainly exists a critical, multilayered, and important thinking process regarding central aspects of state's policies with regard to the management of sacred sites. Struggles over thick sites certainly belong to the "public sphere." *Finally*, the way in which such struggles are conducted—via adversarial means—exemplifies the problems noted with Habermas' view of the public sphere: its lack of realism and the danger of its imposing certain values on this sphere and thus predetermining the results of such struggles.[25]

Therefore, our "thin" view of the public sphere has both the advantage of functioning as an adequate conceptual platform for analyzing the struggles over

---

23. Many worry that without institutionalized deliberation, decision-making will be flawed or otherwise problematic; others worry that minorities will be left unrepresented or marginalized (Richardson, 2002). We take these worries seriously but consider such dangers to be as or even more pertinent when directed at established deliberative models (that may reflect existing power structures) than when directed at a "minimally" defined public sphere. Moreover, as we shall argue in chapter 5, such a minimal approach is especially suitable when assessing the proper relations between religion and the state.

24. See chapter 5, the "baseline issue" (section 5.4.2.2), for an extended discussion of this point.

25. Miller's (2016) view of the Swiss referendum regarding the building of minarets is a good example of how a conception of the state as pronouncing (Christian) values can predetermine and legitimate a certain outcome in a struggle over the public sphere.

thick sites—that is, for acknowledging the importance and centrality of such sites to religion-state relations and states' identities as a whole—and the advantage of not imposing on such struggles a predetermined solution.

To conclude the discussion of these three key definitions, we present the following basic empirical assertion that constitutes the background for our research. We assume that in our examined case (and many others), the state, religions, and the public sphere all function under conditions of plurality—that is, under conditions in which shared understandings do not exist—and that there are significant, deep disagreements among different groups within the societies that we analyze regarding questions of belief, religion, and values that translate into practical questions regarding the proper management of (among other things) thick sites. Therefore, a major challenge to models attempting to illustrate adequate or proper state and religion relations is to demonstrate their ability to cope satisfactorily with this plurality. Note that this "plurality condition" is not a normative assumption; it is a factual assertion for all modern democracies and all but a negligible minority of states as a whole. This plurality condition is reflected in the scenario at the Western Wall, as exemplified by the WoW struggle, involving the WoW, the reform and conservative movements, Israel's civil religion, and ultra-Orthodox factions.[26]

1.3. Methodology

Here we discuss the methodology we adopted for this book in order to facilitate better understanding of how we conducted and structured our research. By presenting our methodology, we also aim to enable a more complete evaluation of the validity of our results and of whether our conclusions can be applied to other cases. As such, the following methodological discussion is not tailored to, or limited by, the contours of our selected case study. We adopted a contextual methodology in our research that, briefly stated, entails carefully attending to the specific details of a given case and moving between the details of the case and the relevant theories in order to sharpen our understanding of both. Joseph Carens (2004), one of the leading scholars of this approach, described the nature of the method:

> In a contextual approach to theory, one moves back and forth between practice and theory, connecting theoretical claims . . . and . . . moral categories to actual cases and practices where we have some intuitive views

---

26. See Jobani and Perez (2014). For an empirical study regarding the veracity of this point in the Israeli context, see Susser and Cohen (2000); Peres and Yaar (1998). Generally, see Rawls (1993); Sen (2009, pp. 11–12).

about the rightness or wrongness, goodness or badness of what is going on. The idea is to engage in an ongoing dialectic that involves mutual challenging of theory by practice and of practice by theory. (p. 123)

In applying this method to our current case study, we aim to reach, *first*, an adequate understanding of both the WoW case study via an in-depth examination of its various aspects and the wider class of struggles over sacred sites to which this case belongs and, *second*, a conclusion regarding the most adequate governmental response for religious conflicts over sacred sites. We will attempt this through the noted back and forth between several major religion-state theories (privatization, evenhandedness, and the "dominant culture view"; see chapters 3–5) and the WoW case study. We shall therefore organize our inquiry in the following way:

First, we aim to provide a rigorous study of a single case in order to further our understanding of a larger class of similar cases.[27] In order to do so, we will provide, in the next chapter, a survey of the historical, legal, and social aspects of the WoW struggle. This survey will include a detailed analysis of the rulings that the Israeli Supreme Court has issued on the matter; the reports of numerous governmental committees; newspaper articles; a survey of developments that took place at the Western Wall during the entire conflict (emphasizing recent events); and other sources that will help characterize the full extent of the struggle.

Here it should be noted that because the WoW case study is not only a legal and social struggle but also a religious one, delving into the religious dimension of the struggle is necessary in order to provide a comprehensive, thicker understanding of the case. This kind of in-depth inquiry enables a fuller understanding of the intractable nature of the conflict and why it is not merely "technical" or simply "about the details" of "prayer arrangements." Furthermore, by gaining a thicker understanding of the case, we will be better positioned to point to both shortcomings and potential improvements of various models for managing sacred sites such as the Western Wall (see the discussion of "contextual privatization" in chapter 5).

A case in point is that of Judge Elon, of the Israeli Supreme Court, in his highly influential and encyclopedic ruling according to which the WoW manner of prayer was not to be permitted at the Western Wall (HCJ 257/89 and 2410/90). By examining (in chapter 2) the inner-religious perspective via a detailed analysis of the relevant literature by key Halakhic figures—such as David ben Josef ben David Abudarham (Seville, Spain, fourteenth century) and Rabbi Samson Raphael Hirsch (Germany, 1808–1888)—we critically examine Judge

---

27. Note that our research uses case-study-based methodology derived from both political science and political theory. See Rogowski (1995, pp. 467–470); Gerring (2004); Gomm Hammersley, and Foster (2009); Thompson (1984, pp. 193–197); Galston (2010, pp. 385–411).

Elon's claim that the WoW's manner of prayer challenges the dominant Jewish custom of prayer. This critical examination, crucial in the context of our discussion of the "dominant culture view" model for religion and state relations (which will be elaborated in chapter 3), would not have been possible without the noted thick description of the case.

This is the place to note that the literature on religious toleration (broadly understood to include the variety of institutions and laws aiming to regulate religious institutions and behaviors) has surprisingly produced very little research regarding sacred sites; we aim to enrich this literature through our intensive study of the WoW case.[28]

Second, to avoid selection bias, we shall succinctly present another case in which a given government had to decide how to manage conflicting claims at a highly disputed sacred site. We chose to focus, in the appendix, on the Ram Janmabhoomi / Babri masjid (RJBM, hereafter) conflict in Uttar Pradesh, which became a focal point of encounters between Hindus and Muslims.[29] The choice of the RJBM case follows a growing body of literature that compares India and Israel and emphasizes certain similarities between the two countries.[30] Additionally, the two sites are both "thick sites," and examining the ways in which governments manage them provides needed perspective and data that are necessary for any attempt to recommend a policy aimed at the further management of such sites. There are also important differences between the two cases, for example, the Indian case involves an interreligious conflict (Hindus and Muslims), while the WoW case is an intra-Jewish-religious conflict, so that we avoid replicating the "same" case. Additionally, the gendered aspect, central to the WoW case, is not obviously present at the RJBM.[31]

Third, since this book has a prescriptive[32] aspect to it, our methodology relies on literature in religious toleration (broadly conceived) that suggests various models, theories, or "designs" for political institutions and public policy that

---

28. There is literature regarding the management and handling of sacred sites in legal and comparative politics scholarship (Winslow, 1996; Collins, 2003; Hassner, 2009; Sapir & Statman, 2014), but it proves challenging to locate a source that directly and fully deals with sacred sites in the literature on religious toleration. For example, one of the most comprehensive studies of toleration, Rainer Forst's Toleration in Conflict (2013), contains no such discussion.

29. See Noorani (2003, 2003b, 2014); Rajamony (2007); and the appendix in this volume.

30. See Harel-Shalev (2010); Friedland and Hecht (1998); Perez (2002).

31. Selecting cases in a comparative small-N research is a complex endeavor, but we cannot enter into a fuller discussion here. See the appendix and Collier and Mahoney (1996, pp. 56–91).

32. To use a Weberian term, we are asking a "value judgment" question, not an empirical question—that is, "what should be done," not "what is the situation"—in the context of religion-state relations and liberal toleration. On the distinction between empirical and prescriptive (or "normative"), see Weber (2011, pp. 1–49).

manage, regulate, and engage with religions.[33] In this respect, the adoption of the contextual methodology (following J. Carens's, A. Sen's, and J. Levy's analyses of this methodology)[34] enables us to tease out the implications of major religion-state theories (privatization, evenhandedness, and the "dominant culture view"; see chapters 3–5) and illuminate their strengths and shortcomings in order to further develop them.

Note that the adoption of the contextual methodology for our prescriptive exploration has two central goals: the first is to consider the suitability of each model to a given case or class of cases; the second is to improve the models or theories themselves. The first goal of a contextual methodology is to reflect on how a given model would function if it were to be applied to a given case or class of cases; this enables us to reach a conclusion about its adequacy to that particular case or set of cases. If, for example, the model works well under conditions of social homogeneity, but the given case involves different factions with no shared understandings and considerable social heterogeneity, an application of the model to the case is likely inadequate and already suspect. Furthermore, given some reasonable assumptions and comparative data, we can predict what would happen if a given model were to be applied to a case or class of cases and count the expected consequences as a consideration for or against the adoption of this given model. If, for example, a state chooses to support one denomination among many, which would likely bring about resentment on the part of believers from other denominations, this should count against adopting such a policy for reasons both of equal treatment and of long-term stability.

The second, equally important, goal of a contextual methodology is to improve existing models or theories, that is, to use the examination of a given case as a "theory improving mechanism." This use of contextual inquiry enables us, in the adroit words of Levy (2007),

> to identify circumstances, conditions, and situations in which an already-developed theory's application takes on importantly new, unusual, or surprising turns. Here theory precedes the context; but, unlike when cases are merely illustrative, it does not emerge unchanged from its encounter with the context. (p. 180)

For example, in light of the Western Wall case study, we shall argue that a strict version of the privatization approach, a major theory in religion and state

---

33. See chapters 3–5 for an elaborate discussion of this point. Some notable examples include Barry (2001); Carens (2000); Miller (2016).

34. Carens (2004); Sen (2009, pp. 7–8); J. Levy (2007, pp. 173–197).

relations, is inappropriate for many thick sites. If it were applied as is, the privatization approach would fail to allow some of the core practices of religious groups
typical to such locations, revealing a blind spot in the theory itself. This extends
beyond merely illustrating or applying the privatization theory and, if correct,
constitutes a theory improving step (see chapter 5).[35]

A final note on our research design concerns the choice of Israel as the main
focus for research on religious-based conflict regarding sacred sites. Our research
does not depend on evaluating Israel as belonging (or not belonging) to the liberal Western camp; it is specifically the "in-between" or an "in-transition" characteristic of Israel that helps to elucidate several crucial dilemmas of religion and
state relations. The WoW struggle would not have been possible in a completely
illiberal political system (the WoW would simply be outlawed and repressed in
such a scenario), nor would it have been a problem in a completely liberal political system (the WoW would have been embraced as contributing to an already
existing plurality). The WoW thus provide an illuminating opportunity for a contextual examination and analysis—as if in a laboratory—of the ways in which a
divided society (India fits here as well) struggles to navigate religion in sacred
sites located in the public sphere vis-à-vis the demands of different religious
groups and of gender egalitarianism.

---

35. Further discussion of the intricacies of the contextual methodology, as well as its advantages
and disadvantages, can be found at Carens (2013, pp. 297–313); Anderson (2010, pp. 5–7).

2

Women of the Wall in Focus

EXAMINING THE VARIOUS ASPECTS OF
THE WOW STRUGGLE

THIS CHAPTER PRESENTS the details of the WoW struggle over prayer arrangements at the Western Wall in their full complexity. Our exploration of the case is contextual in the sense described in the previous chapter; that is, significant attention is given to the details of the case, details that a theoretical perspective, examining conflicts over sacred sites with only cursory attention to actual case studies, might overlook. We have adopted this approach with the goal of using this case to further our understanding of theories of religion-state relations, especially as applied to thick or sacred sites. As part of this contextual exploration, special attention must be given to the Halakhic aspects of the debate, both as part of a proper description of the involved parties' concerns, and because the Halakhic aspects formed a crucial part of the legal deliberations over the case in the Israeli Supreme Court.

The chapter is divided into four sections: section 2.1 analyzes the Halakhic debate over the WoW manner of prayer; section 2.2 provides an overview of religion and state relations in Israel in order to adequately understand the legal and social-political arenas in which the WoW struggle takes place; section 2.3 examines the three Supreme Court decisions that have been made regarding the WoW case; finally, section 2.4 reports on the most recent developments in the WoW case, including their dramatic gains via the Jerusalem District Court's 2013 decision, which provided the legal backing for many of their requests.

2.1. Liberating the Wall: The Religious-Feminist Challenge of the WoW

This section explores the Halakhic aspects of the WoW's manner of prayer in order to explore, and bring into clear focus, the religious-feminist challenge that they pose to the patriarchy of mainstream Jewish Orthodoxy. We examine the three main aspects of the WoW's manner of prayer, which they have labeled the three *T*s: (1) praying aloud in a women-only group (*Tfila*), (2) public reading from a handwritten copy of the five books of Moses (Torah), and (3) wearing the ceremonial prayer shawl (tallit).

In the framework of the patriarchal Orthodox approach to public worship, women are excluded from each of these noted aspects of Jewish prayer rituals. As will be demonstrated below, the exclusion of women from these aspects of prayer has significance not only in the religious sphere but also in the social and political spheres, because it excludes women from symbols of knowledge, power, and leadership in their communities.[1]

Three important preliminary comments are in order before we proceed. *First*, a rather lengthy volume would be required to discuss all of the Halakhic perspectives related to issues of women-only prayer groups in general, and the WoW's manner of prayer in particular.[2] We shall, therefore, limit our survey to the details that are absolutely necessary to provide an accessible point of entry into this intricate subject matter. *Second*, it must be noted that Orthodox authorities have not strictly forbidden women from performing the three different aspects of the WoW's manner of prayer, at least not unanimously; the practices are, nevertheless, considered offensive and unacceptable by the mainstream patriarchal Jewish Orthodoxy.[3] *Third*, it is crucial to note that, while the WoW are a multi-denominational group, they made a conscious decision to avoid alienating their Orthodox members by conducting their prayers according to an Orthodox Halakhic approach, albeit in a specific and controversial interpretation.[4]

2.1.1. Women-Only Prayer Group (*Tfila*)

Let us begin with the first *T* of the three aspects of the WoW manner of prayer: praying aloud in a women-only prayer group (*Tfila*). The Orthodoxy's objection to women's active participation in public prayer at Orthodox synagogues in general

---

1. See Ross (2004); Raday (2007); Hartman-Halbertal (2002).

2. There are several excellent analyses of Halakhic perspectives on women-only prayer groups, which have emerged with increasing frequency since the 1970s. These groups largely, but not exclusively, originate from the United States. See Cohen (1999); Haut (1992); Haut (2003); Weiss (2001); Friedland Ben Arza (2003); Twersky (1998); Adler (2001); Frimer (1998); Ross (2004). On non-Jewish women-only prayer groups, see, for example, Day (2010).

3. See Elon (2005, pp. 119–193); Weiss (2001, pp. 43–56); and Raday (2007, p. 257, nn. 3, 4).

4. Unsurprisingly, many Orthodox Jews do not classify the Orthodox core of the WoW as legitimately Orthodox. We are well aware that such claims of "belonging" not only reveal inner-religious assumptions regarding the place and status of women within Orthodoxy, but also have very real social and political implications given the dominance of Orthodoxy in Israel

and to women's prayer groups in particular stems from the fact that according to the Halakha, prayers are held at fixed times and that women are exempt from performing active religious duties at fixed times (*mitzvot asse she-ha-zman gramman*).[5] Moreover, and this is crucial, the Halakha maintains that women are not only exempt from public prayer but are also legally (i.e., from a Halakhic perspective) excluded from joining the religious quorum (minyan), the basic public prayer unit consisting of at least ten Israelite men. Women are simply not counted in the minyan. The Halakhic basis for this conclusion is that those who are not obligated in a matter cannot discharge others from their obligations (Mishnah Rosh Hashanah 3:8; see also Haut, 2003, p. 267; and Meiselman, 1978, p. 136). In what follows, we investigate some of the reasons given for exempting women from performing active religious duties at fixed times, especially as this exemption is transformed into both a de facto general ban on women's active participation in public prayer at Orthodox synagogues and a particular proscription against women's prayer groups, such as the WoW.

Both ancient and modern scholars hold conflicting opinions regarding the rationale behind this exemption of women from performing active religious duties at fixed times (Ross, 2004, pp. 35–37). We shall focus on the opinions of three notable scholars: Rabbi Samson Raphael Hirsch, Rabbi Judah b. Bezalel Loew [Maharal], and David ben Josef ben David Abudarham. Though their opinions obviously do not exhaust the full range of approaches explored within the Halakhic literature, they are influential and used with enough frequency to serve as the primary focus of our analysis.[6] Furthermore, given the dominance of Orthodoxy in Israel, the discussion has important consequences for the status of women in the Israeli public sphere as a whole.

Rabbi Samson Raphael Hirsch (1808–1888), a leader of nineteenth-century German Orthodoxy, argues that the exemption of women from performing religious active duties at fixed times is anchored in the socioeconomic fabric of the community. Briefly stated, Hirsch (1962) argues that the passivity of women in the socioeconomic sphere is the reason for their exemption from performing

---

(Shakdiel, 2002; Lahav, 2015). However, our goal here is not to judge such claims of "belonging," but simply to note them in order to advance a thick understanding of the WoW case study.

5. There are many exceptions to this principle. For example, women are obligated to eat matzah on Passover and to pray after meals (*birkat hamazon*) even though these commandments must be performed at fixed times. Nevertheless, the exceptions do not undermine the principle itself. See Alexander (2013); Meiselman (1978, pp. 43–57); Sassoon (2011, pp. 44–59); Hauptman (1993); Puterkovsky (2014, pp. 114–118); Ross (2004, pp. 15–16).

6. For a more comprehensive survey of approaches to gender hierarchy in the Jewish tradition from biblical times to the present, see Walzer (2003, pp. 150–230). See also, among many excellent studies, Meiselman (1978); Ross (2004); Sassoon (2011).

active religious duties at fixed times. Unlike men, he argues, women do not fully participate in public socioeconomic activities and, therefore, face fewer "temptations which occur in the course of business and professional life" (pp. 711–712)[7] that necessitate the strict and orderly structure of religious duties conducted at fixed times.

Other scholars turn to metaphysical, even mystical avenues in their attempts to justify this exemption. Rabbi Judah b. Bezalel Loew [Maharal] (Prague, *c.* 1525–1609)—Talmudist, Kabbalist, and a major transitional figure between medieval and modern Jewish thought—held that women have, by what he describes as their *passive nature*, greater potential for spiritual growth and thus do not need to perform active duties at fixed times to achieve spiritual perfection.[8] According to the Maharal of Prague, women's natural passivity makes them metaphysically closer to the world to come (*Olam Haba*), which he characterized as a pure and blissful state of total rest and tranquility (Loew, 1972, p. 28). Considering the context of the WoW, it is noteworthy that the Maharal inverts the common patriarchal argument that women are less holy than men because they have been given fewer commandments (Walzer, 2003, p. 154). According to the Maharal, the exemption of women does not suggest their inferiority but, rather, reflects their superiority over men.

Both Hirsch and the Maharal of Prague point to what they characterize as the "passivity" of women as the basis for their exemption from active religious duties at fixed times, even though they locate this passivity in different spheres: Hirsch grounds the passivity of women in the public socioeconomic sphere, the Maharal anchors the "passivity" of women in the metaphysical order of nature. These arguments, however, cannot be accepted at face value. Using either the special role of women in society (as suggested by Hirsch) or their metaphysical nature (as suggested by the Maharal of Prague) in order to justify exempting them from highly valued religious rituals is suspicious; in many cases, such explanations are merely an excuse to exclude women from valuable public activities and positions in economic, political, and legal life (Eisenstadt, 2007, pp. 406–407). In US Supreme Court Justice Brennan's adroit words, sex discrimination has often been "rationalized by an attitude of 'romantic paternalism,' which in practical effect, put women, not on a pedestal, but in a cage" (*Frontiero v. Richardson*, 411 U.S. 677 (1973)).

---

7. From Hirsch's (1962) commentary on Leviticus 23:43 (p. 712). On Hirsch's position, see Baader (2012, pp. 56–58); Weiss-Goldman (1999, pp. 108–109); Elon (2005, p. 128, n. 36).

8. See Loew (1972, p. 28). The Maharal anchors the passivity of women in the Talmudic interpretation of the term *Nashim Sha'ananot* (lit. carefree Women; Isaiah 32:9). See BT Barcot 17:1. See also Meiselman (1978, pp. 43–44).

David ben Josef ben David Abudarham (Seville, Spain, fourteenth century), a liturgical commentator, offered one of the most blatantly patriarchal justifications for the exemption of women from religious active duties at fixed times. In his tract *The Book of Abudarham*, which provides detailed explanations of various prayers and liturgical customs, he argues that the reason for the exemption of women from religious active duties at fixed times is that a woman is subject to her husband to tender to his needs. And had she been obliged to do religious active duties at fixed times, it might happen that while in the process of carrying out one of the commandments (*mitzvah*) [religious active duties at fixed times] the husband might order her to do his *mitzvah*. And if she carries out the Creator's *mitzvah* and neglects his *mitzvah*, woe is she on account of her husband. And if she carries out her husband's *mitzvah* and neglects the Creator's *mitzvah*, woe is she on account of her Creator. Hence, the Creator exempted her from his commandments so that she should be at peace with her husband.[9]

In this account, firmly rooted in a patriarchal attitude, the woman is portrayed as submissive and obedient—almost a slave—to two masters: God and her husband. In order to avoid potential conflict, God *withdraws* by exempting women from religious active duties at fixed times so that they remain available to follow the orders of their husbands (which Abudarham noticeably labels as a *mitzva*—a religious duty).

According to Abudarham, by exempting the married woman from performing time-bound commandments for him, God "gives up his honor . . . in order to make peace between husband and wife."[10] Of course, the term "peace in the family," according to a patriarchal view, means nothing more than maintaining the husband's control of his wife.[11] Indeed, according to Abudarham, the exemption of women from active religious duties at fixed times is nothing more than

---

9. The Book of Abudraham (*Seder tefilot shel chol*, chapter 3, *brachat hamizvot*), see Abudarham (1927, pp. 107–108). We are using Sassoon's (2011, pp. 45–46) translation of this passage with minor modifications.

10. Aburdarham, quoted in Sassoon (2011, pp. 45–46). In his long and encyclopedic ruling rejecting the WoW petition (see section 2.3), Judge Elon presents Abudarham in a perplexing way. According to Elon, Abudarham did not intend to maintain the submission of women to men, but rather to "ease women's [familial] duties" and household tasks (Elon, 2005, p. 125; see also the judgment by Elon in HCJ 257/89 and 2410/90, at p. 304). As we aim to demonstrate, this is a distortion of Abudarham's position.

11. As Walzer (2006) points out, this view, which is

common among many nations and cultures, or at least among their male members, is that the subordination of women is justified by the work they have to do in the home—and will do, if the biblical story is right, only if their husbands 'rule over [them]' [Gen. 3:16]. (p. 154)

an expression of their enslavement to their husbands.[12] Tellingly, he later notes in his tract that "all the commandments which are obligatory for women are also obligatory for slaves" (Abudarham, 1927, p. 111).[13]

In conclusion, the different rationales for exempting women from religious active duties at fixed times (including active participation in public prayers) transcend the narrow Halakhic sphere as they are anchored in wide-ranging attitudes toward women's social, spiritual, and familial status. Moreover, this exclusion from the religious realm is not only derived from wider inequities, it also reinforces and amplifies the wider exclusion of women from active and equal participation in other realms: marriage and family (Abudarham), society and economy (Hirsch), spirituality and personal development (the Maharal of Prague). It is therefore not surprising that, in the framework of patriarchal orthodoxy, the exemption of women from active participation in public prayer (i.e., *minyan*, the basic public prayer units consisting of at least ten Israelite men) effectively prohibits the active participation of women in public prayer generally, and particularly prevents women's prayer groups that aim to constitute a minyan.

The WoW are united by their desire to challenge this prevalent exclusion of women from public prayers and, through this venue, the general framework of mainstream patriarchal orthodoxy. Since the membership of the WoW comes from different Jewish denominations (Orthodox, Conservative, Reform, etc.),

---

12. It should be noted that, according to mainstream Halakhic perceptions, Abudarham's views are certainly not without limits. As Raday (2007) notes,

> It does not relate to women's childbearing role or even to child rearing but concentrates solely on the competing duties which a woman has to her husband and to God . . . there are sources which deny that a wife has to be submissive and obedient to her husband and, in particular, it is clearly provided that it is forbidden for a husband to coerce his wife to have intercourse with him. (p. 261, n. 12)

For a detailed discussion, see Elon (2005, pp. 213–228).

13. In the same vein, Jacob ben Abba Mari Anatoli (southern France–Italy, thirteenth century) asserts, in his influential collection of philosophical sermons *Malmad he-Talmidim*:

> It is because woman was created to be a fitting helper to man, and necessity dictated that he rule over her, that the stature of her form was diminished [by God] relative to that of man in the majority of cases. He put into her nature that she serve her husband out of love and fear to preserve peace in the home. So much so, that the Torah, all of whose paths are peaceful, has—as ascertained by tradition—relieved woman of the yoke of commandments determined by time. For if she were obligated she would be preoccupied by their timely performance and would not have the free time to serve her husband and do the housework, and that would lead them to strife. Moreover, her obligations are diminished in accordance with her diminished intellect. (Anatoli, 1866, p. 152, quoted and translated in Walzer, 2003, pp. 176–177)

they have different preferences regarding the concrete expression of this common objection to patriarchal exclusion. Some believe that women should pray exactly like men do, even if this necessitates the partial or complete abandonment of orthodox Halakhic prayer. Others believe that, though women's prayer is legitimate and necessary, it must be conducted in an alternative, reduced format that takes into account various Halakhic restrictions. Rivka Haut, one of the founding Orthodox members of the WoW, insists that women praying publically do not, by themselves, constitute a minyan. Practically speaking, this means omitting the few passages of the prayer whose recitation demands a minyan, that is, those known in the Halakha as *devarim shebekdusha* (sanctifications).[14] This restricts the liturgy to prayer that is recited by an individual, male or female, who prays alone. Women praying in this fashion are, therefore, a collection of individuals praying together, without forming a congregation (*tzibur*) in the technical Halakhic sense. The adherence to the Halakha, Haut emphasizes, compels women to relinquish complete equality, even as it enables them to perform a legitimate prayer that is "equally important and desirable before God as the prayers of men" (Haut, 2003, p. 269). By adhering to the Halakha in their prayer manner, the WoW prove to be both deeply traditional and challenging to tradition by pressing it to its limits. On the one hand, they form a women-only prayer group, while, on the other hand, they pray as though they are merely aggregated individuals rather than a formal Halakhic group (*tzibur*). As Tova Hartman-Halbertal puts it in another context, instead of being passive collaborators in a patriarchal system, they prefer to be active agents in the transformation of tradition itself (Hartman-Halbertal, 2002, p. 16).

Now, as the WoW are a diverse group, some members wish to pray exactly as men pray, whereas others prefer to maintain some version of the restrictions that orthodox Halakha places on women's prayer. This variation within the WoW's vision was visible primarily in legal terms, as seen in the first two petitions the organization submitted to the Israeli Supreme Court. The women from Jerusalem who submitted the first petition, in 1989 (257/89), demanded the right of women to pray exactly the way men do (as a minyan, etc.) at the Western Wall. In 1990, an additional petition (2410/90) was submitted by women from the United States who made a separate demand for allowing women only prayer groups to pray at the Wall while adhering to Orthodox Halakhic restrictions (see sect. 2.3).

In practice, however, members of both groups, those seeking equal prayer and those with more Orthodox tendencies, all pray together at the Wall. Thus the

---

14. These include Kaddish, Kedusha, Barekhu, etc. See Weiss (2001, pp. 37–39); Ross (2004, pp. 176–177).

manner of prayer that is employed is, in many ways, determined by whoever happens to serve as prayer leader (*Hazzanit*).[15] The prayer leaders include or exclude passages from the group's prayers according to their own religious sensitivities, and the other members of the WoW demonstrate flexibility and understanding toward the plurality of prayer manners within the group.

It is important to note that, as Justice Elon made clear in his ruling, even if the WoW accept all the Orthodox Halakhic prohibitions, the Orthodox opposition to their request to be allowed to pray in their manner stands. This opposition has been asserted by Orthodox leaders such as the Chief Rabbis of Israel. Indeed, even if a formally Halakhic perspective accepts the manner of prayer of the WoW, such prayers will still be perceived by their opponents as an obvious change to the custom of the place at the Western Wall. As Elon (2005) writes, "In the prayer plaza at the Western Wall . . . [t]he custom of women prayer has never been carried out"; and, citing various sources in the Jewish tradition, he further claims that "in order to avoid controversy one should stick to the existing customs" (p. 153).

This argument—that to protect the Orthodox custom, the WoW should not be allowed to pray in their manner—has also been used in opposing the WoW reading of the Torah, which we will now turn to explore.

2.1.2. Women's Torah Reading (Torah)

The second element of the WoW manner of prayer—public reading from the Torah—should be approached through a consideration of the broader context of the Orthodox approach to Torah reading.[16] Public readings from the Torah, which were initiated by Ezra the Scribe (fifth century B.C.E.), are part of the morning or afternoon prayer services on certain days of the week or holidays, including Rosh Hodesh (the day of the new moon), which is when the WoW habitually conduct their prayers at the Western Wall.

---

15. This feature of the WoW manner of prayer can be seen in various video clips of their prayers that can be found on their official website: http://womenofthewall.org.il/; it has also been verified in conversation with members of the group.

16. In the past few years, women's Torah reading has attracted much attention and has been examined in thorough detail by numerous scholars and rabbis in Modern Orthodox circles; some of them fiercely oppose it (e.g., Professor Shochetman and Rabbi Riskin) while others enthusiastically support it (Rabbi Shapiro and Rabbi and Professor Sperber, among others). See Shochetman (2005); Riskin (2008); Shapiro (2001); Sperber (2002). It should be noted that Professor Shochetman, who opposes women's Torah reading, was selected in what might be considered a controversial move to serve as the Halakhic expert for the respondent (the State) in the Supreme Court proceedings concerning the WoW petitions. On women's Torah reading, see also Rothstein (2005); Brown (2008).

The most common and prevalent reason given for the prohibition against women reading the Torah as part of the service in Orthodox congregations is to be found in the baraita,[17] a collection of traditions and teachings from the Tannaitic period (*c.* 200 C.E.). According to the baraita (in Megillah 23a), women are not called up to read from the Torah during public prayer because doing so would be an affront to the "congregation honor" (*kevod ha-tsibur*). The *baraita* does not explain why a woman publically reading the Torah is improper and what, precisely, is meant by the highly contested concept "congregation honor." According to a common Orthodox understanding, the term signifies the "fitting atmosphere," which requires the separation of the sexes, for communal worship.[18] This understanding of the term "congregation honor" is couched in an essentialist (and therefore highly problematic) view of gender. At this point, however, we only wish to clarify the sources of the orthodox opposition to the WoW manner of prayer. The "congregation honor" argument justifies the prohibition on Women's Torah reading by pointing to essential attributes of the two genders, and therefore the argument should withstand shifting cultural sensibilities and historical realities; it presumes to be absolute, durable, and timeless.[19]

Though the notion has persisted in the orthodox world for many generations,[20] "congregation honor" cannot justify the prohibition against Women's

---

17. Literally meaning "external" to signify that these traditions and teachings were not included in the Mishnah, the early third-century codification of Jewish oral laws.

18. Shochetman, for example, claims that the prohibition against women reading the Torah dates back to the original arrangement of worship space in the Temple. Just as the women's and the men's enclosure in the Temple were separate in order to prevent inappropriate behavior and sinful thoughts, so too does the synagogue, which is considered a "tiny Temple," require that the separation of the sexes be kept stringently in order to ensure appropriate conditions for worship. According to this view, women reading the Torah out loud as part of a prayer service would be an obvious transgression of this proper atmosphere (Shochetman, 2005, pp. 275–279).

19. Irshai (2013) describes this view (which she opposes) as follows:

The connection between modesty and "congregation honor" (*kevod ha-tzibur*) leads to the understanding that we are dealing with an objective concept that is not subject to change, just as human nature isn't, and that the prohibition is therefore an absolute one that is independent of the *tzibur* [congregation] itself and cannot be waived. (p. 336)

On the various understandings of the term "congregation honor," see also Rosenak (2008); Issacs (2006); Porat-Rouash (2008).

20. A few scholars have claimed that women did, in fact, read the Torah in certain Orthodox communities. See, for example, Ashkenazi (1953, vol. 1, p. 53); Sperber (2007, pp. 32 and 33, n. 37); Safrai (1997, pp. 399–401); Rosenak (2008, pp. 61–65). These claims are controversial (see, e.g., Shochetman 2005, p. 306), and even if they are true, they refer only to a very small number of communities.

Torah reading—even if the general outline of the argument is accepted—since the WoW are a women-only prayer group. There are simply no men present who might be distracted by their reading of the Torah.

However, in the case of women-only prayer groups, an additional common Orthodox consideration serves as further justification for the prohibition on Women's Torah reading—namely, the requirement of minyan (religious quorum). This Orthodox objection to Women's Torah reading, even in the framework of women-only prayer groups, follows the same logic used to reject women's active participation in public prayers at Orthodox synagogues. Proper conduct for public reading from the Torah requires, just as do public prayers, a minyan. However, a minyan can only be constituted by ten or more Israelite men. Women are simply not counted toward the minyan; ten women are ten individuals, not a minyan.[21]

Despite this, the WoW manner of prayer might have been perceived as legitimate from the Orthodox point of view if the group held Torah readings in a *narrower* format—as, in fact, they requested in their second petition to the court (2410/90).[22] This narrower manner of prayer would accept the following Halakhic restriction: omitting, before the reading of the Torah, the traditional ceremonial blessing *Barechu*. This blessing, in the Halakha, serves as the sanctifying *devarim shebekdusha* whose recitation demands a minyan constituted only by ten or more Israelite men who are a part of the same prayer ritual.[23]

---

21. The Halakhic grounds for this objection to women's public reading of the Torah resembles those discussed at length earlier in the context of the objections to women's praying groups: (a) public readings from the Torah are conducted at fixed times (certain days of the week, holidays, etc.); (b) women are exempt from performing active religious duties at fixed times (*mitzvot asse she-ha-zman gramman*); and (c) those who are exempt from performing a religious duty cannot discharge others of their obligations to perform that duty. By definition, (d) any member of a minyan discharges the other members from various obligations (e.g., the member of the minyan that reads the Torah discharges relevant others from their Torah-reading obligation); therefore, (e) women cannot discharge others from the obligation to read the Torah because they cannot be one of the ten (let alone all of the ten) members of a minyan. In the Orthodox view women are therefore prohibited, even in women-only prayer groups, from reading the Torah (Meiselman, 1978, pp. 136–137; Shochetman, 1997, pp. 165–167; Riskin, 2008, pp. 260–262).

22. It should be noted that this petition does not reflect the heterogeneous, multi-denominational nature of the WoW group; not all members of the group are willing to accept Orthodoxy's restrictions. The Women from Jerusalem, who submitted the first petition of the WoW to the court in 1989 (257/89), demanded the right of women to pray and read Torah exactly as men do (as a minyan, etc.) at the Western Wall (see sect. 2.3). As mentioned in the previous subsection, in spite of such differences, members of the WoW respect each other's varying religious sensitivities and show flexibility in their common worship. However, this flexibility, probably required in order to maintain the WoW as a coherent organization, might not be in line with prevalent Orthodox Halakhic understandings, as explained earlier.

23. For a further, detailed Halakhic examination of this point, which is beyond the contours of this discussion, see Shilo (1999, p. 160).

Women who read from the Torah in this narrower fashion are, therefore, considered only a collection of individuals reading from the Torah and do not form a congregation (*tzibur*) in the technical Halakhic sense. Such individuated readings, in and of themselves, seem acceptable even to the Orthodox, since there is no formal restriction on individual women reading the Torah (Elon, 2005, pp. 133–135).

However, the Orthodoxy objects even to this "narrower" form of Torah reading requested by the WoW and appealed for at the second petition to The Supreme Court (2410/90) alluded to earlier. Justice Elon clearly expressed this objection by claiming that, although reading from the Torah in a reduced and minimal format does not contradict or oppose Jewish law (Halakha) formally, it has never been part of the accepted customs of Judaism. It is a central Halakhic rule that to avoid controversy, one should maintain the established and existing customs rather than adopt innovations (Babylonian Talmud, Pesachim, 50:1–2). Elon asserts that this rule, though general, should be kept with singular stringency at Orthodox synagogues and, of course, the Western Wall since the site functions as the holiest synagogue in the Jewish world.

Just as opposition to the WoW women-only prayer group (at least in its narrower form) was anchored not in formal Halakhic grounds but rather in the claim that it breaches accepted Orthodox custom, so too, the WoW's reading of the Torah is not itself considered counter to the Halakha per se: it is rather perceived to be a breach of accepted Orthodox custom. As we shall see in the next subsection, a similar claim factors into the robust opposition to the WoW's practice of wearing the tallit while praying.

2.1.3. Women Wrapped in the Tallit

We shall now turn to the third and final aspect of the WoW's manner of prayer at the Western Wall that challenges the patriarchy of mainstream Jewish Orthodoxy, namely the wearing of the tallit (prayer shawl). Our discussion of this issue will focus on the Halakhic arguments, both for and against this practice, which were presented before the Supreme Court by various experts in Jewish law during the deliberations regarding the WoW petitions. We have also added references aimed to orient interested readers within the increasingly vast literature devoted to this issue. We begin with the arguments made by those in favor of granting the freedom to wear the tallit at the Western Wall to the WoW, and then we present the arguments of those opposed to granting this freedom. Our conclusion—and this point is so important it needs to be highlighted in advance—is that the intense opposition to the WoW's practice of wearing a tallit cannot be considered Halakhic (as the Halakha suggests various contradicting opinions on this issue) but stems rather from orthodox *custom*. Moreover, the orthodox custom according to which only men pray while wrapped in the tallit, has only been commonly accepted in recent generations.

As mentioned above (2.1.1, 2.1.2), women are exempt from performing religious active duties at fixed times (*mitzvoth asse she-hazman gramman*).[24] As the commandment to wear the tallit or the tzitzit (the small tallit) applies to fixed times (the tallit and tzitzit are obligatorily worn during the day, but do not have to be worn at night), women are exempted from it. Nevertheless, despite the wide-ranging (though not, as will soon become clear, unanimous) agreement to exempt women from the commandment (mitzvah) to wear the tallit, there are disagreements regarding whether women are allowed to wear it if they wish. The varying and, at times, contradictory Halakhic answers to this question are at the heart of the Orthodox and legal debates regarding whether the WoW should be permitted to wear a tallit while praying at the Western Wall.

Those in favor of granting this freedom, including some Orthodox authorities base their support on two arguments presented by Professor Shmuel Shiloh, an expert in Jewish law and an Orthodox rabbi, in his opinion presented to the Supreme Court concerning the WoW (2410/90).[25] First, he notes that there is no sweeping Halakhic prohibition that forbids women from wearing the tallit. To the contrary, there is an enduring and significant Halakhic position that allows for women who so wish to wear the tallit.[26] Several leading orthodox authorities even go so far as to allow for women to say the blessing customarily recited before donning the tallit—namely, "Blessed are you, Lord our God, King of the universe, who has sanctified us with His commandments, and commanded us regarding the commandment of tzitzit." In this, such authorities equate the ritual of women who *wish* to wear the tallit to that of the ritual performed by men who

---

24. The Mishnah in the Tractate Kiddushin (1:7) exempts women from performing active religious duties at fixed times (*mitzvoth asse she-hazman gramman*); the baraita that appears in the Babylonian Talmud's discussion of this Mishnah includes the wearing of the tzitzit in the list of commandments performed at fixed times such as: sukkah, lulav, tefillin, and shofar (BT, Kidushin, 33b–34a).

25. A slightly amended version of the expert opinion prof. Shilo submitted to the Supreme Court (2410/90) was later published as an article in *Techumin*, an annual journal of Jewish law and Modernity (Shilo, 1999; for a discussion of the wearing of the tallit, see esp., pp. 161–163).

26. Maimonides, as all other *rishonim* (leading orthodox authorities who lived, roughly, between the eleventh and fifteenth centuries), rules that women are exempt but that they can wear the tzitzit without reciting the appropriate blessing (MT, Laws of Tzitzit, 3:9). This ruling was accepted by the Sephardic tradition such as with, for example, Joseph Karo and Rabbi Ovadia Yossef. For a discussion with detailed references, see Lubitz (1999); Noam (2013); Elon (2005, pp. 130–133).

are *obligated* to do so.[27] Second, it is a fact that women have worn the tallit and the tzitzit in a variety of manners and circumstances in several historical periods.[28]

We now turn to the arguments in opposition to granting this freedom. Justice Menahem Elon, a major and vocal opponent to granting this permission, argued that the WoW demand to wear the tallit when praying at the Western Wall should be rejected, even though he accepted both of the noted arguments regarding the Halakhic view and the historical data in principle: "In the first and last generations, there were women who wore the tzitzit, and recited the appropriate blessing, upon the opinion of sages,"[29] He insisted, however, that the WoW demand to wear the tallit at the Western Wall should be rejected or declined because "*women did not customarily, at least in the last few generations, wear the tallit or the tzitzit.*"[30] Clearly, Justice Elon does not believe the WoW demand should be rejected on Halakhic grounds (recognizing, as he does, that Halakhic authorities are divided on this matter)[31]; his

---

27. In this context, we can name: Abraham Ben David of Posquieres (Rabad); Rabbi Yizhak Halevi (Rashi's rabbi); Meir b. Baruch of Rothenburg (Maharam); Asher b. Jehyel (Rosh); Gerondi, Nissim b. Reuben (Ran); and Rabbi Moshe Feinstein, among others. For a discussion of these sources, with detailed references, see Noam (2013); Shilo (1999); Shochetman (1997) and Shochetman (1999).

28. According to Noam (2013), who explores the various Halakhic and historic aspects of women wearing the tallit, the position of the *Baraita* (appearing in the BT, Kidushin, 33b–34a)—in which it is determined that women are exempt from the commandment of wearing the tzitzit—reflects the minority position at the time of the Tannaim (i.e., Rabbi Shimon's view). As opposed to this specific position, there are four Tannaic Halakhot which rule that women are obligated to wear the tzitzit. From this, Noam concludes that most women in the Tannaic period did in fact wear the tzitzit. Later, in the Amoraic period, one can mention the example of Rabbi Yehuda—among the greatest Amoraim in the second generation of the Babylonian Talmud—who fastened tzitzit to his wife's apron because he opined that tzitzit was not an active religious duty at a fixed time since it is compulsory both during the day and at night (BT, Menachot, 43a). In fact, the first recorded expression of opposition (discussed above) to women wearing the tzitzit came as late as the fifteenth century. The objection—by Yaakov b. Moshe Levi Moelin (Maharil) [1360—1427], the leader of Ashkenazi Jewry—was raised vis-à-vis, or as a critique of, the women in his surrounding community that *were* wearing the tzitzit. This historical point lends further support for granting the WoW, or any other women who wish to do so, the freedom to wear a tallit at the Western Wall plaza. See also the references in Elon (2005, p. 132, n. 52).

29. Elon (2005, p. 132).

30. Ibid; the emphasis is in the original.

31. Among the orthodox authorities opposed to women wearing the tallit, the following are especially noteworthy: Moses Isserles (Rema); Yaakov b. Moshe Levi Moelin (Maharil); Targum Pseudo-Jonathan; Rabbi Mordecai ben Avraham Yoffe; Rabbi Shaul Yisraeli; Rabbi Yechiel Michel Epstein; Rabbi Yosef Dov Soloveitchik; Yaakov Chaim Sofer. For a detailed discussion with references, see Goldberg (1998, pp. 120–121); Shochetman (1997, 1999); and Elon (2005, pp. 130–133). See, in this context, the comprehensive discussion of Soloveitchik's objection to women's only prayer group in Twersky (1998).

rejection of the demand rests on the fact that it contradicts the Orthodox custom
that has become widely accepted today.

Despite chiefly relying on the widely accepted Orthodox custom, both Justice
Elon's judgment and the expert opinion Professor Shochetman presented to the
Supreme Court, utilize three Halakhic arguments or "oppositions" to women
wearing the tallit. The *first opposition* is the most extreme in Halakhic literature: according to it, women who wear the tallit contravene an explicit Biblical
prohibition: "A woman must not put on man's apparel" (Deuteronomy 22:5).[32]
That is, this view identifies the tallit as specifically "man's apparel."[33] The *second
opposition*, which is more moderate, notes various sages' reservations, arguing
that women wearing the tallit is undesirable because of the apparent "arrogance"
(*yohara*) of this practice. That is, according to this view, women who wear a
tallit are formally within the contours of halakha, but they show disregard for
shared understandings and communal customs.[34] Relying on various Halakhic
sources, Prof. Shochetman argues that "arrogance," in this context, is behavior
that (i) exhibits vulgarity and pride, (ii) shows contempt for others, (iii) separates
oneself from the community, (iv) demonstrates a lack of courtesy or manners,
and (v) changes an accepted custom (Shochetman, 1997, p. 163).

The *third opposition* relies on a letter delivered to the Supreme Court by Rabbi
Tendler, an influential Orthodox authority and the grandson of Rabbi Feinstein
who was among the last of the few Orthodox authorities who allowed women
to bless for and wear the tallit. According to Rabbi Tendler, the permission that
Rabbi Feinstein had given is valid only in cases where the intention of the women
wearing the tallit "is only for the sake of the heavens, without any subversion of
the Torah or the customs of Israel."[35] In other words, Rabbi Feinstein's permission holds only if the tallit is worn in complete compliance with the principled
exemption of women from the commandment of wearing it (as it is an active religious duty at fixed times). Justice Elon, following and adopting Rabbi Tendler's
position, finds that the WoW, however, had "improper motivations" as their

---

32. Unless otherwise noted, all translations of the Hebrew Bible are from the new Jewish
Publication Society translation of the Hebrew Bible (1985).

33. This is Rabbi Mordecai b. Avraham Yoffe's position, which is anchored in the Targum
Pseudo-Jonathan translation of Deuteronomy 22:5. See Shochetman (1997, p. 164) and Elon
(2005, p. 132). As Raday (2007) points out: "This prohibition is reminiscent . . . of the role
which the differentiation between male and female clothing has played in retaining male superiority" (p. 262).

34. This position was adopted by Yaakov b. Moshe Levi Moelin (Maharil), Moses Isserles
(Rema), Rabbi Yechiel Michel Epstein, and others. For sources and critical discussions of their
arguments, see Shochetman (1997, pp. 163–165); Elon (2005, p. 132).

35. Shochetman (1997) adds this letter as one of the appendixes to his article (p. 164).

purpose is "a principled opposition to the very exemption itself as it is hurtful towards women"[36] and, further, to introduce changes to the Halakha. Therefore, this argument concludes that, in the case of the WoW, the permission for women to wear the tallit is void.

However, as previously mentioned, the Halakha is far from being unanimous in its position vis-à-vis women wearing the tallit. Furthermore, and even more specifically, the three Halakhic oppositions presented above are far from being conclusive even from a Halakhic perspective. Indeed, Halakhic counter arguments can be presented against each one of these three oppositions. Against the first opposition—that women should not be allowed to wear the tallit because it is "men's apparel"—one could argue that this is a marginal perspective within Halakhic literature, which as Justice Elon himself mentions, "wasn't accepted by the majority of Halakhic authorities."[37] Against the second opposition—that women wearing the tallit are "arrogant" from a Halakhic perspective—one could simply claim that this opposition is not supported by strong and convincing argumentation: in other Halakhic contexts, as Justice Elon acknowledges in his ruling,[38] the claim that a certain custom is "arrogant" has not necessarily brought about its absolute rejection. An obvious example can be found in another custom related to the wearing of the tzitzit. As Shiloh mentions in his expert opinion for the Supreme Court: "Several of the greatest authorities in Halakha and Kabbalah, such as Isaac Luria and others, have instructed for the tzitzit not to be worn above the other clothing for reasons of arrogance. In spite of this, many observant Jews do wear their tzitzit out."[39] Against the third opposition—that the WoW are driven by improper motivations and wish to change the Halakha—one can point to the WoW's explicit commitment to the Halakha, at least as demonstrated by their second appeal to the Supreme Court (2401/90) (see the discussion in 2.1.1).

---

36. Elon (2005, p. 131).

37. Elon (2005, p. 131). As noted previously, the first opposition is anchored in the *Targum Pseudo-Jonathan* edition of Deuteronomy 22:5. However, as Noam (2013) argues, the *Halakhot* couched in the *Targum Pseudo-Jonathan* are often heretical according to common Orthodox views.

38. Elon (2005, pp. 132–133).

39. Shilo (199, p. 163). Furthermore, a perspective formally external to the Halakhic debate, argues that the term "arrogance" always must be understood within a certain cultural context and its meaning is necessarily derived from social realities and understandings. These realities that give meaning to the term are not internal to Halakha; the Halakha, as any other legal doctrine, needs to "fill" its concepts with certain external meanings. The argument here is that, given changes in women's status in modernity, the WoW behavior should not be viewed as arrogance under any regular meaning of the term (see the discussion of this need to fill legal and moral concepts with meanings that are necessarily external to such systems in Williams, 1985, pp. 140–154).

Given that Halakhic oppositions to women wearing the tallit can be countered with other Halakhic arguments (as acknowledged by Judge Elon himself),[40] it must be concluded that those who oppose the WoW's request base their opposition primarily on the claim that it breaches the commonly accepted customs of Orthodox communities, particularly the customs governing the prayers held at the Western Wall. Justice Elon and Professor Shochetman, therefore, claimed that the rabbi in charge of the Western Wall acted appropriately when he forbade the WoW to pray as they wished at the Western Wall because that kind of prayer contradicts the "custom of the place." This point has strong standing in the Israeli legal system via the "Regulations for the Protection of Holy Places for Jews" (1981), which explicitly prohibit the "holding of a religious ceremony that is not according to the custom of the place, and that offends the sensitivities of the worshipping public towards the place (2(a) (1a))."

In chapter 3, we will provide a lengthy discussion of the contested historical issue of the "custom of the place" at the Western Wall (see 3.2). However, it is already clear, and important to emphasize here, that this issue is not Halakhic; it is historical. Our current discussion, however, is limited to pointing out the recurrence of the argument that the WoW's request should be refused because their manner of prayer is opposed to the accepted prayer customs at the Western Wall. Indeed, this is the central concern of the objection to granting the WoW permission to pray according to their manner: all three aspects of the WoW's practices which we explored above—a women-only prayer group (2.1.1), women's Torah reading (2.1.2), and wearing the tallit (2.1.3)—were condemned as unacceptable by the Orthodox opposition to the WoW's demands primarily because they breach the currently accepted custom.

In conclusion, in spite of the WoW's acceptance of the applicable orthodox Halakhic prohibitions discussed in the last three subsections, the Orthodox opposition to the WoW's manner of prayer at the Western Wall stands. The WoW pray as individuals and not as a minyan (2.1.1), avoid reciting sanctifications (*devarim shebekdusha*) before reading the Torah (2.1.2), and only wear the tallit while adhering to the rulings of Orthodox rabbis (2.1.3); despite this, their practices are deemed to be offensive even though the Halakhic objections do not hold.

Justice Elon, therefore, accurately summarizes the heart of the Orthodox opposition to the WoW's prayer (relying on the opinions of both Chief Rabbis of Israel, Rabbi Mordechai Eliyahu and Rabbi Avraham Shapira) in a statement already mentioned above, but well worth repeating here: "In the prayer plaza at

---

40. Elon (2005, pp. 130–133).

the Western Wall . . . [t]he custom of women prayer has never been carried out . . . [therefore] acquiescing to the appeal of the petitioners [WoW] would involve a clear change of the custom of the place . . . as has been carried out for generations. It is, furthermore, a central Halakhic rule that in order to avoid controversy one should stick to the existing customs (Babylonian Talmud, Pesachim, 50:1–2)."[41] One could argue, and not without merit, that the ongoing twenty-seven year effort to push the WoW out of the Western Wall's plaza in the name of the "custom of the place," has *not* avoided controversy but rather strengthened and intensified it. But perhaps more importantly, Elon's judgment (and the similar opinions of many others who oppose the WoW's requests) relies heavily on the appeal to "the custom of the place" and, therefore, on information regarding historical customs at the Wall. What is clear, without expressing any opinion on the legal and Halakhic expertise of the scholars considered above, is that this particular claim is neither Halakhic nor legal; rather, it is fundamentally a claim about history and historical events that took place at the Wall. In order to verify or falsify this argument, and with it the opposition to the WoW's request to pray according to their manner, a historical discussion is therefore required. We shall conduct this historical survey in chapter 3.

2.2. *Religion and State in Israel: An Overview*

This section succinctly describes religion-state relations in Israel. This topic is wide and multifaceted; our goal here is neither to summarize all of the relevant literature nor to take a stand in the many controversies related to these complex relations. Rather, we seek to provide an adequate and sufficiently detailed survey of this issue to serve as a background to the WoW struggle.

Modern religion–state relations in Israel originated, by and large, in the Ottoman millet system in which religious denominations were recognized by the state and enjoyed exclusive jurisdiction on issues of personal law (the current lack of civil marriages in Israel exemplifies this historical connection; see Barak-Erez, 2009; Liebman & Don Yihia, 1983).[42] However, unlike the Ottoman millet system, Israel does not have an established religion (Neuberger, 1999). Additionally, the Israeli version of the millet system grants denominations, beyond the exclusive

---

41. Elon (2005, p. 153); emphasis is in the original.

42. The millet system is problematic since it "locks" individuals into their religious communities; state toleration exists for communities, not individuals. Members of these communities have no rights of conscience or of association, and every citizen has to be a member of some religious community (Walzer, 1997, p. 17).

jurisdiction over personal law, governmental funding; for example, the state pays the salary of the clergy of various denominations including Jewish and Islamic judges in Halakhic and sharia courts.[43] Now, while the interest of this monograph rests with a religious conflict among Jewish factions, it should be kept in mind that the Millet style religion-state arrangement in Israel applies to its non-Jewish minorities as well (see Karayanni, 2014). Still, we focus on the specific religion-state arrangements that concern the Jewish majority, which consists of close to 75 percent of the population of Israel. This population, in 2016, is roughly divided between 10 percent of ultra-Orthodox Jews, 10 percent of Orthodox Jews, about 40 percent "traditional," and the remaining 40 percent are secular.[44] The body of laws and regulations that provide the basis for the arrangement between religion and state in Israel within the Jewish sector is usually referred to, collectively, as the "status quo compromise" or agreement. This agreement dates back to the period just prior to the ending of the British Mandate. The essence of this agreement is effectively summarized by Barak-Erez:

> [T]the most representative document in this context is the letter that the Jewish Agency—the main Zionist institution at the time (which was controlled by the secular Labor Party)—sent in 1947 to the international organization of Agudat Israel, the hegemonic movement within the ultra-Orthodox Jewish public. This letter, also known as the "status quo document," included commitments to observe certain traditions in the future state. It centered on issues considered important from a religious perspective. It mentioned the recognition of the Jewish Sabbath (Saturday) as the official day of rest; the provision of kosher food in public institutions; the exclusivity of the religious law of marriage and divorce; and a commitment to ensure the autonomy of the ultra-Orthodox educational system. Currently, it is accepted that this document should not be considered as the only source of the status quo regime, but it is certainly a good representative of its spirit. (Barak-Erez, 2009, pp. 2496–2497)

This compromise—which extends to also include the exemption of ultra-Orthodox Yeshiva students from military service, banning both public

---

43. Susser and Cohen (2000); Layish (2006).

44. Such categories are according to self-definition (2011 CBS data). "Traditional" in the Israeli context usually means a person that follows religious requirements to some extent, but is not fully committed to an Orthodox or religious way of life. For many years, this group was under theorized, but in recent years it won much scholarly attention. On the sociology of religion in Israel, see Peres and Ben Rafael (2005); Yadgar (2011).

transportation and the employment of Jews during the Sabbath, and several other concerns—held (albeit imperfectly) well until, roughly, the mid-eighties.[45]

However, starting in the mid-late eighties, several legal, social, and political developments have destabilized the status quo model (Susser and Cohen, 2000). First, in the late eighties, a massive wave of immigrants arrived from the former Soviet Union. Such immigrants arrived from a highly secularized environment and, from an Halakhic point of view, many of them were non-Jews. Many of these immigrants viewed parts of the status-quo agreement as being unjustified and oppressive, especially as it created a situation in which they could not marry in Israel (Cohen and Susser, 2009). *Second*, many native-born Israelis came to view the agreement as unjustified, especially as it limited basic rights such as the freedom to choose to marry and divorce not via the rabbinical courts (Barak-Erez, 2009). *Third*, Israel's legal culture changed, particularly as two new basic laws were enacted: the Basic Law Human Dignity and Liberty and the Basic Law Freedom of Occupation (1992). These laws explicitly pronounced the value of individual rights just as (according to some) a more activist and liberal Supreme Court—which was willing to confront legislation by the Israeli parliament (the Knesset) as well as the status quo—came to office. Such developments made the status-quo agreement increasingly difficult to sustain and to defend (Mautner, 2011).

Fourth, in the early-mid eighties, Israel experienced a massive economic crisis. In response to this crisis, the government decisively changed its economic policies from those that favored a socialist centralized economy to policies of a liberalized, privatized economy. Such changes, accompanied by the rapid adoption of Western consumerist culture, have heavily influenced the Israeli society. While this is not the place to describe such massive changes in economic policy and consumer behavior, they obviously included a certain individualist bent that would view restrictions that religious collectives place on individual choice—such as on civil marriages and the shutting down of businesses and public transportation during the Sabbath—as infuriating coercion (Perez, 2013; Rivlin, 2010).

Fifth, the number of ultra-Orthodox Jews enjoying various exemptions under the status quo agreement (from obligatory army service, to standards applicable to public education, etc.) has risen and so has their reliance on various government-financed welfare programs. Having comprised only a small minority—merely 3 percent of the total population—in the early years of Israel's existence, the ultra-Orthodox constitute about 10 percent of the total population in 2016; exemptions that were tolerable for a small minority seem unsensible and, indeed,

---

45. Some major controversies in religion-state relations took place before this time such as the debate regarding "who is a Jew," as well as the closely connected issue of legitimate conversions to Judaism (Cohen, 2005, pp. 198–217).

unsustainable for much larger numbers. As such exemptions are a part of the status quo agreement, their unsustainability serves to implicate the entire agreement which, consequently, faces growing objections from the secular majority in Israel (Jobani and Perez, 2014a; Perez, 2014).

Sixth, the political balance of power in Israel has changed; during the first three decades of Israel's existence, the labor party had uncontested dominance that allowed it to frame religion-state relations without serious opposition, but since 1977 there has been no hegemonic political party in Israel to establish a framework for religion-state relations through which to address the most divisive, politicized topics facing the Israeli political system. To point to one example, the *Shinui* [lit., "change" in Hebrew] party, in its various incarnations, was formed as an explicitly secularist party with the aim of confronting the status quo agreement. Such a successful party and goal were unimaginable prior to 1977 (Susser and Cohen, 2000; Lerner, 2009).[46]

Lastly, while the dominant Jewish-religious factions in Israel were, historically, Orthodox and ultra-orthodox, other Jewish religious groups—such as the reform and conservative movements, as well as the growing phenomenon of religious feminism—are gradually becoming larger demographics of Israel's population. Such relatively new groups are slow to penetrate to and win recognition from, established judicial and social norms and, thus, face generally inegalitarian treatment from the government. Regardless, these movements present a challenge, both social and legal, to the status quo agreement which, functionally, is only an agreement between an Orthodox minority and a secular majority (Rosenak, 2014; Ross, 2004).

To conclude: the status quo agreement—the organizing arrangement of religion state relations in Israel, at least within the Jewish sector—remains in effect even as it faces fierce criticism and has become unstable. This unbalanced situation can be illustrated with the example of marriage: Jews cannot marry in a civil ceremony in Israel as they are forced to marry via the "Chief Rabbinate," a state organ, which is delegated to Orthodox authorities. However, many Jewish Israelis marry in a civil ceremony outside of Israel, cohabitate without marrying, or marry in religious or semi religious Jewish traditional ceremonies that are unrecognized by the state; each of these approaches help individuals to avoid this heavily unpopular religious-state organ and to express non-religious (or non-Orthodox religious) values (Dovrin, 2006; Ben-Porat, 2013). This example (among many others), points to the somewhat odd and imbalanced situation of the status quo agreement, which, though formally enduring, faces much social hostility.

---

46. The Ratz party was indeed established before that period (toward the 1973 elections), but was much smaller and less influential.

The WoW struggle should be understood against the background of the general divide between secular Jews and ultra-Orthodox regarding the status quo arrangement. However, as a multi-denominational group, the WoW transcend and blur the secular-religious dichotomy in Israeli society by challenging both the secular and ultra-Orthodox assumptions and convictions; the group also functions as bastion of gender egalitarianism, which is usually identified with the secularist "camp" only, though members of the group identify as religiously Orthodox, Reform, Conservative, as well as secular.[47]

This complex character of the WoW is not adequately reflected in the Israeli public's, and Orthodox circles' in particular, image of the group. Generally speaking, both view the WoW as a feminist offshoot of the mainly US-based Jewish Reform movement. Overall, the Reform movement in Israel struggles vis-à-vis its marginalization by the state as well as because of negative public opinion. Nevertheless, the Reform movement is making gradual strides toward achieving legitimacy both formally and socially (Rosenak, 2014; Ross, 2004).

This perceived image of the WoW explains, to some degree, their reliance on judicial means to advance their goals. Regardless of this historical dependency on a legal path, the WoW have gradually found more allies beyond the legal sphere, both from feminist-religious circles among the Jewish Orthodoxy—via organizations such as *Kolech* (Hebrew: "your voice" in a female conjugation)—and among secular feminists who gradually embraced their struggle as a legitimate part of the wider, general feminist agenda. (Shilo, 2006; Shakdiel, 2002). This succinct description of the complex and conflictual religion-state relations in Israel hopefully suffices as the backdrop for a detailed description of the legal aspects of the WoW's struggle, to which we now turn.

2.3. Legal Analysis: An Exploration of Three Major Supreme Court Decisions (1994–2003)

In this section, we trace the long legal odyssey of the WoW in their attempt to win legal permission to pray at the Western Wall according to their manner. The section is organized around the three principled rulings that the Israeli Supreme Court has issued on the matter (which were delivered in 1994, 2000, and 2003).

The importance of these rulings cannot be overestimated: they were delivered by the highest legal entity in Israel and they govern the proper management of the

---

47. There is an important religious feminist movement in Israel, but the description here alludes to social conventions, not to strict sociological reality (see Ross, 2004; Hartman Halbertal, 2002).

holiest Jewish site in the state. These rulings, far beyond their significance to the WoW's struggle, function as legal markings of the contours of legitimate religious conduct in Israel, with all of the social impact that such determinations entail. This follows the importance and the centrality of the Western Wall; as what is accepted as legitimate there, will obviously be accepted elsewhere. No wonder, therefore, that the struggle over prayer arrangements at this site is so heated and difficult to solve. These three Supreme Court rulings employ many theoretical and normative arguments, albeit often articulated in a nascent and inchoate form, that require further critical consideration which will be developed in the following chapters. Examples include the argument that existing arrangements at thick sites should remain unchallenged, specifically because they are couched in long-standing traditions, rooted in the past, that have been transmitted from generation to generation; the argument that offences to religious feelings should set the limits of possible changes in the managements of sacred sites; and the "backlash" argument stating that an expected violent response to revised policies in sacred sites is a sufficient justification for banning such amendments. In this section, however, we merely lay the groundwork for such difficult issues, aiming to provide a clear analysis of the key Supreme Court decisions that created the background to the entire debate surrounding the WoW struggle.

2.3.1. The First Ruling of the Supreme Court

The WoW struggle began in 1988, after a group of women who participated in the first international conference of Jewish feminists, which was held in Jerusalem at the time, was formed. This group, which included a significant number of American-Jewish women, decided to pray, every Rosh Hodesh (the day of the new moon) and during special events, in the women's section (*Ezrat Nashim*) at the Western Wall, wearing prayer shawls traditionally worn by men (*Tallitot*), and reading out loud from the Torah (see 2.1.). Each Rosh Hodesh prayer takes about one hour, thus the WoW request effectively involved very few hours annually. When they first tried to do this, the women encountered violent opposition from other worshippers and were removed from the premises by the police for disturbing public order. In 1989, women from Jerusalem submitted the first WoW petition to the Supreme Court (257/89); in 1990, an additional petition (2410/90) was submitted by women from the United States, whose attempt to pray at the Wall had also been frustrated. Prior to the second petition, but following the initial WoW petition, the minister of religion published an addendum to the 1981 Regulations for the Protection of Holy Places for Jews that prohibited the "holding of a religious ceremony that is not according to the custom of the place, and that offends the sensitivities of the worshipping public toward the place (2(a) (1a))." This amendment allowed the rabbi appointed to the Wall (a position which is formally that of a male-public servant, yet usually held by an ultra-Orthodox person) to forbid the WoW from praying in their manner at the women's section of the Wall.

Justices Elon, Levin, and Shamgar made a joint ruling on the two petitions, after their initial attempts to find a compromise between the two sides proved unsuccessful, in 1994. All three Justices agreed that the WoW were entitled to freedom of religious practice which, in this case, meant they could pray as they wish within their communities and synagogues. However, they disagreed regarding whether this freedom of religious practice should extend to the practice of their manner of prayer at the Western Wall. Elon, the Justice who occupied the seat in the Supreme Court traditionally designated for a scholar in Jewish Law, rejected the WoW petition. In a long and encyclopedic ruling (see 2.1), Elon claimed that though the custom of the WoW did not formally contradict or oppose Jewish law (Halakha), it was not accepted in Orthodox synagogues and thus certainly should not be permitted at the Western Wall since the site functions as the holiest synagogue in the Jewish world. According to Elon, three considerations decisively demonstrate why it should not be allowed: the WoW's prayer practice opposes "the custom of the place" at the Wall, it offends the sensibilities of a majority of worshippers there, and it prevents the other worshipers from fulfilling their own prayer according to Jewish law. Additionally, Elon rejected the WoW's petition because, according to his claim, such consent would lead to violence and turmoil that would endanger the peace and security of the public. This is a clear demonstration of a "backlash" argument; i.e. that an anticipated violent response to a given act, such as a WoW prayer at the Wall, is a sufficient justification for banning this given act (and see chapter 5).

Justice Levin claimed that the WoW had the right to pray according to their manner and rejected Elon's ruling, which was anchored in Jewish law, with a dual consideration. *First*, he insisted that the law for safeguarding holy sites is a distinctly secular law that is not subordinate to religious law even where secular law brings religious law into consideration. *Second*, he noted that the site of the Western Wall has a broad national significance that differs from its religious meaning, thus the fact that it serves as a prayer site does not grant it the status of a "synagogue." Therefore, according to Levin, the court should take into consideration not only the sensitivities of worshippers, but also those of people who visit the site for other purposes in good faith as well. Similarly, the notion of a "custom of the place" should be understood in an open and dynamic sense that reflects the full breadth of beliefs and customs of those who come to worship and visit at the site of the Wall. Levin also rejected the backlash argument, arguing that the anticipated "backlash" is not a legitimate justification for banning religious activities; rather, such a danger points to a duty on the part of the government to ensure freedom of worship. Therefore, Levin ruled that authorities should formulate, within a year, appropriate arrangements that would secure the exercise of the full rights of all worshippers and visitors to the site, including the WoW.

Justice Shamgar (the president of the Supreme Court at the time) recognized the abstract (or "in principle") right of the WoW to pray as they wished at the site, but rejected their petition with the reasoning that the court was not the appropriate place to determine the issue. While indicating that the "doors of the court are always open," he recommended that the government form a committee that would examine possible solutions outside of the courts.

In summary, the Supreme Court rejected the WoW's petitions, according to the majority opinion of Elon and Shamgar (although Shamgar did recognize their abstract right to pray at the Wall and, in that, agreed with Levin), and recommended that a governmental committee be convened to settle the matter.

2.3.2. The Second Ruling of the Supreme Court

Following the Supreme Court's recommendation, the government created three committees that were unable to reach adequate conclusions, or to resolve the dispute over prayer arrangements at the Wall. The first committee, which was comprised of directors of various government Ministries, surveyed four prayer sites near the Wall as potential alternatives: the square at the foot of Robinson's Arch, the area in front of Hulda Gates, the southeast corner of the Wall of the Temple Mount, and the "Small Wall (*Kotel*)" area. After two years of deliberations, and in consideration of police opinion, the committee recommended that the WoW's prayer take place at the southeast corner of the Wall of the Temple Mount, far from the Wall plaza itself.

The second committee was also a Ministerial Committee. After a year of consultations with various security and law enforcement authorities, this committee recommended that the WoW's prayer not be permitted, neither at the Wall nor at any of the four alternative sites suggested by the first committee. Their justification for this recommendation was external security concerns: the sites all pose the danger of causing a conflagration with the Palestinians who look down on these various sites from the Dome of the Rock / Temple Mount; from this vantage, they might consider the recitations of Jewish prayer in these alternative sites to violate the status quo (Raday, 2007).[48]

---

48. This argument exemplifies how important it is to acknowledge the fact that the WoW struggle transcends the local Jewish and Israeli context; it has significant implications for broader international issues like the Israeli-Arab conflict (see section 2.4).

In 1998, a third committee recommended that the WoW's prayer be held at the archaeological site named Robinson's Arch, which is, in fact, a segment of the Western Wall itself. This site is adjacent to the Wall on the south side, though a bridge (the Mugrabi Ascent) that ascends to the Temple Mount, separates it from the main plaza and keeps it out of sight of those praying within the Wall Plaza. It is important to note, however, that Robinson's Arch is a significant archaeological site, which cannot easily be transformed into a prayer site, and has never been a site for traditional Jewish prayer in front of the Wall. Though it is a part of the same Wall, it lacks the deep symbolic meaning attached to the Wall Plaza.

In response to the first committee's suggestions, the WoW again appealed to the Supreme Court (3358/95). In the (second) court ruling, given in 2000, Justices Mazza, Strasberg-Cohen, and Beinisch determined that the right of the petitioners to pray at the Wall as they wished was, in fact, already recognized within the framework of the first ruling (noting the "in principle" consideration of Shamgar and the full support of Levin). Therefore, the recommendations of the different governmental committees—for alternative sites for WoW prayer—effectively opposed the earlier ruling of the Supreme Court even if they originated from that ruling. Further, the Justices rejected all of the sites suggested by the various committees; following a tour of the proposed sites, the Justices concluded that they are either not satisfactory or ill-prepared for prayer services. As a result, the Justices uniformly ruled that the government was to make, within six months, the appropriate arrangements to enable the WoW to pray in their manner at the women section of the Wall Plaza.

2.3.3. The Third Ruling of the Supreme Court

The Supreme Court's second ruling caused public outcry and political turmoil that led the government to request an additional discussion on the matter at the Supreme Court (4128/00).[49] The state claimed that Robinson's Arch, which they defended as a site adequate for the WoW's prayer, provided a fair and feasible solution that responded to the two conditions implicitly set out in the Supreme Court's first ruling. First, since the site of Robinson's Arch is a segment of the Western Wall, this solution maintained the WoW's freedom of access to the Wall. Second, the WoW's prayer at this site would prevent unnecessary offence to and friction with the sensibilities of other worshippers.

The third Supreme Court ruling was delivered in 2003 by an expanded panel of nine Justices. The Justices upheld the right of the WoW to pray as they wished at the Wall Plaza, though they pointed out that this was not an unlimited right

---

49. Regarding the political context, see Shakdiel (2002).

and that any offence to other worshippers should be minimized as much as possible. They ruled that the rights of the WoW and of other worshipers would be best served by establishing an alternative site and thus the government should prepare the site of Robinson's Arch for the WoW's use within a year. If the site was not ready within a year, the WoW would have the right to pray at the Wall Plaza according to their manner. The ruling also noted that, in its current condition, Robinson's Arch also served as an archaeological park under the auspices of the Antiques Authority, and that this authority strongly opposed the preparations necessary to transform the site into a prayer site.[50] Unsurprisingly, this decision did not end the WoW saga. In the next section, we examine some major recent developments of the case.

2.4. Recent Developments

In 2005, the Justice Department issued a statement claiming that the preparations of the Robinson's Arch site were complete, as required by the Supreme Court ruling of 2003 (see previous section), and it was thus the only location at which the WoW would be permitted to pray according to their manner. Though they had accepted the Supreme Court's ruling of 2003, the WoW opposed this claim, asserting that Robinson's Arch was not yet properly prepared. Regardless of this new legal situation, the WoW continued to pray in their manner at the Wall Plaza, as they have done continuously since the establishment of the group in 1988 (albeit with the noted restrictions). Following the 2005 Justice Department statement, WoW members who arrived to the Wall Plaza (to pray), including Anat Hoffman, the chair of the board and founding member, were arrested on the basis of "behaviour in a public place in a way that is liable to disturb the peace," "the violation of a legal ruling," and "a prohibited act in a holy site"; in addition, some of the group members were banned from the Wall for varying periods of time as a result.

Following the arrest of five women from the group in April 2013, however, a dramatic turn has occurred. In a discussion before the Jerusalem Magistrates Court, Justice Larry-Bavly decided to release the detained WoW members without stipulation and rejected the state's request to bar their entry to the Wall for the following three *Rosh Hodesh* prayer services.[51] The state appealed the ruling

---

50. The ruling was made in accordance with the majority opinions of President Barak and Justices Or, Cheshin, Terkal, and Englard and in opposition to Vice President Levin, as well as Justices Mazza, Strassberg-Cohen and Beinisch.

51. [2013] 21352-04-13 State of Israel v. BR Ras and others.

before the Jerusalem District Court, but the appeal was rejected by Justice Sobel of that court.[52] Judge Sobel argued that the third and final ruling of the Supreme Court was worded as a recommendation with stipulations. There is no legal ruling, his decision emphasizes, confirming that the government had fulfilled the appropriate preparations of the Robinson's Arch site as stipulated. Therefore, he insisted that it is not possible to view the Supreme Court's ruling as definitive grounds for assigning criminal liability for the WoW's violation of the 2005 justice Department statement. Further, Judge Sobel argued that the WoW's prayer does not oppose the "custom of the place" according to the broadest interpretation given to that term by the majority ruling in the first Supreme Court decision (see 2.3.1). Finally, Judge Sobel argued, given that the WoW do not employ physical or verbal violence of any kind, they cannot be blamed for endangering the safety of the public or of any person present at the Western Wall Plaza. The legal situation, accordingly, changed and the WoW, as of September 2013, have complete legal backing to pray at the Wall's Plaza according to their custom in all of its three main aspects: (1) praying aloud in a women-only prayer group (*Tfila*); (2) public reading from the Torah; and (3) wearing the ceremonial prayer shawl (tallit) (as discussed in 2.1). Judge Sobel's legal breakthrough, while a considerable step toward granting full legal permission to the WoW to pray according to their manner, did not, however, bring about a situation in which the WoW are free to pray according to their manner at the Wall. Specifically, the WoW are still prevented from reading aloud from a Torah scroll (the second aspect of their manner of prayer).

This de facto situation in which the WoW are allowed to pray aloud in a women-only prayer group, and to wear a prayer shawl, but not to publicly read from the Torah, is explained via a recent regulatory development, as follows. Ultra-Orthodox Rabbi Shmuel Rabinowitz, the Rabbi of the Western Wall and the chairman of the Western Wall Heritage Foundation,[53] relies on a 2010 regulation in order to circumvent Judge Sobel's ruling and to continue to prevent the WoW from praying in their manner at the Wall. The relevant regulation (the "2010 regulation" hereafter),[54] issued by the Western Wall Heritage Foundation

---

52. [2013] 43832-42-33 State of Israel v. BR Ras and others.

53. The Western Wall Heritage Foundation is an Ultra-Orthodox-oriented governmental entity in charge of all activities at the Wall. A standing petition, brought by the Israel Religious Action Center before the Israeli Supreme Court, requests that the Western Wall Heritage Foundation be run by an evenhanded representation of Orthodox, Reform, Conservative, Secular Jews, and also women rather than being dominated by ultra-Orthodox men. See [2013] HCJ 145/13 Israel Religious Action Center v. Western Wall Heritage Foundation.

54. On file with the authors.

(which Rabinowitz chairs) and approved by the Ministry of Justice, forbids all those who wish to pray at the Wall from bringing their own Torah scrolls to the Wall without receiving special, formal permission from the Rabbi of the Western Wall. The 2010 regulation cites the two following justifications for this restriction. First, it will prevent potential disorder that might lead to theft of one of the over 100 Torah scrolls (each one worth between $20,000 and $40,000) which the Western Wall Heritage Foundation provides to worshipers in the men's section of the Wall, (not even one Torah scroll is provided for the women's section).[55] Second, it will prevent the use of Torah scrolls in cases where they would be used, as stated in the 2010 regulation, "in order to hold religious ceremonies that are not according to the custom of the place" (ibid.). Note that, though seemingly general, this formula is, in practice, directed exclusively against the particular prayer manner of the WoW.

Sobel's 2013 ruling clearly stands in contradiction to, and would undermine the second justification of, this 2010 regulation: the inclusive interpretation of the concept "custom of the place," suggested by Sobel, makes the claim that the WoW's manner of prayer opposes the "custom of the place" at the Wall groundless. Nevertheless, relying on the first justification of the above restriction (prevention of theft of Torah scrolls), Rabbi Shmuel Rabinowitz continues to bar the members of the WoW from bringing a Torah scroll into the women's section of the Western Wall.

Parallel to this use of the rather technical 2010 regulation, which might be viewed as problematic and boldly inconsistent with the principles of Judge Sobel's 2013 ruling, Rabbi Shmuel Rabinowitz also prevents the WoW from using one of the Torah scrolls that are available in the men's section. Consequently, the WoW are still prevented (as of August 2016) from fully praying in their manner since they are unable to conduct one of the three main aspects of their manner of prayer (see 2.1).[56]

The WoW, in the meantime, and as a part of their overall goals, also protest against other inegalitarian religious ceremonies taking place at the Wall. For example, in December 2015, during the holiday of Hanukkah, the WoW protested against the exclusion of women from the official, state-sponsored lighting-of-the-candles ceremony at the Wall. The Hanukkah protest of the WoW, which

---

55. This inegalitarian treatment can also be noted from the relative size of the prayer sections allocated for men and women at the main plaza: two-thirds of the plaza are reserved for the men's section, one-third for the women's section (Shakdiel, 2002, pp. 132).

56. In October 2014, they did read from a Torah scroll they had smuggled into the women's section of the Wall (see the detailed description of this historic prayer in the opening of this monograph).

demanded that women be included in the ceremony, also points to the fact that the WoW should be understood not only narrowly, as a group interested in religious equality at the Wall, but also more broadly as a feminist organization aiming to change broader gender inegalitarianism in Israel and the Jewish religion as a whole. The attorney general accepted their formal request, and consequently, the 2015 lighting-of-the-candles ceremony included women for the first time in the history of the Wall. This probably means that the noted ceremony would, from 2015 onward, take place at the upper central plaza of the Wall, about twenty-five meters from the Wall itself and not at the men's section of the central plaza.[57]

In addition to the hindrances posed by the Rabbi of the Western Wall and the Western Wall Heritage Foundation, which he chairs, there are two further attempts to prevent the WoW from praying in their manner at the Wall; the first, disturbances of various kinds coming from ultra-Orthodox women; the second, political power struggles. We shall briefly comment on both.

---

57. Of interest, and in a new development in their long struggle, in March 2016, a few weeks before Passover, the WoW announced their intention to perform for the first time during the holiday a version of the priestly blessing, which they referred to as "Birkat Kohanot" (lit., "Blessings of the Priestesses," as opposed to the traditional "Birkat Kohanim," i.e., "Blessings of the Priests"). This ceremony would have been conducted in parallel to the popular traditional priestly blessing held during Passover at the Western Wall in which tens of thousands of worshippers participate; but instead of men, women, of priestly descent, planned to stand in the women's section of the central prayer plaza wrapped in the tallit, raising their hands and blessing the worshippers. It is important to note that as opposed to other aspects of the WoW prayer practices (discussed at length in the beginning of this chapter; reading the Torah or wearing the tallit, for example), this is not a ceremony (in its women-practiced version) that is common in reformed or conservative Judaism, and it is hard to find support for it in Orthodox Halakha. Moreover, as of yet, the WoW have not asked to integrate the Birkat Kohanot ceremony into their usual prayers (Ettinger, 2016c).

On the twenty-first of April 2016, a few days before Passover, the attorney general, Avichai Mendelblit, held a meeting with representatives of the office of the prime minister, of the Justice Ministry and of the Ministry of Religious Services, as well as the Rabbi of the Western Wall, Shmuel Rabinowitz. The attorney general decided to accept the position of the latter two, according to which the Birkat Kohanot prayer the WoW planned for Passover must be prohibited. The attorney general determined that the ceremony, which has no precedent, contravened the Regulations for Protecting Jewish Holy Places, 1981. These regulations forbid, among other things, prayers that differ from the "custom of the place" (2(a) (1a)). Consequently, during their Passover prayers at the Western Wall on the twenty-fourth of April 2016, the WoW—who were surrounded by a particularly strong police contingent—avoided performing the *Birkat Kohanot* ceremony. Still, they did integrate the ceremony in the first head of the month prayer they held immediately after the holiday (Rosh Hodesh Iyar, April 9, 2016), claiming that the attorney general's interdiction of the ceremony was not sweeping, but rather restricted to Passover only. Following the request of the attorney general, the police did not arrest any of the worshipers in order to avoid further escalating the situation (Ettinger, 2016d). As noted, this is a new development, and it remains to be seen how (and whether) it will be repeated and whether it will influence any attempts to reach a compromise at the Wall.

During 2013, ultra-Orthodox women followed a call issued by ultra-Orthodox leaders and filled the women's section of the plaza in order to disrupt WoW prayer at the Wall (on several occasions, for example on Rosh Hodesh of the Hebrew month of Av—July 2013). This new phenomenon of physical disturbances of WoW prayer at the Wall by ultra-Orthodox women has subsided during 2014–5, but was renewed in August 2016 (Rosh Hodesh of the Hebrew month of Av), when for example, ultra-Orthodox women stood next to the WoW, during prayer, and used whistles in order to disturb WoW prayer (the police failed to intervene). This tactic was complemented by the creation of a Women's group—the "Women *for* the Wall," as distinct from "Women *of* the Wall"—that argues against the WoW manner of prayer and calls for a return to the legal situation that existed prior to Judge Sobel's ruling.[58]

Second, there is growing pressure from political circles to change the legislative and legal situation in ways that are adversarial to the WoW goals.[59] For example, by declaring Robinson's Arch, in its current (2015) incomplete form, as ready to be used for prayer, and consequently aiming to relegate the WoW only to Robinson's Arch site, while banning them from praying at the main plaza.[60] These "behind the scenes" political threats might explain why, despite Judge Sobel's legal breakthrough, the WoW recognized that further steps are required in order to reach a full and stable solution to the conflict over prayer arrangements at the Western Wall; in this context, we turn to the latest attempt at reaching a proper compromise.

Alongside both the ultra Orthodox and the political obstructionism, a renewed attempt to reach a compromise began under the leadership of Natan Sharansky, the head of the Jewish Agency for Israel (which connects Israel and Jewish communities around the world). At the heart of the suggested compromise stands a groundbreaking "third plaza" (or *Ezrat Israel*)[61] plan: the site at the foot of Robinson's Arch would be renovated and designated an egalitarian prayer space for non-Orthodox Jews, and others interested in visiting the Western Wall for various purposes, without the separation of men and women.

---

58. See their website, http://womenforthewall.org/ (accessed February 15, 2015). Lahav points to the historical similarities between the WoW struggle and the suffragists struggle at the end of the nineteenth century and the beginning of the twentieth century, when "groups of women were pitted against each other: one carrying the torch of inclusion, progress and change, the other insisting on the supreme value of tradition and the status quo" (Lahav, 2016, pp. 17–18).

59. The details involve a request by the Rabbi of the Wall from ultra-Orthodox members of parliament to oppose the changes in legislation required for the third plaza plan to move ahead (Ettinger, 2016e; Ettinger and Ravid, 2016).

60. See, for example, Jewish Telegraphic Agency (2013).

61. Literally, "the section of Israel" in Hebrew.

Before turning to the details of this third-plaza plan and to the WoW's response, a brief explanation of the plan's background is required. The third-plaza plan is, obviously, tailored to respond to, not only the WoW's prayers needs, but also to the more general Jewish world beyond Israel's borders; the context in which it should be understood therefore is wider than the WoW struggle. The Israeli government faces significant and growing pressure from liberal Jewish communities, mostly from the United States, to change the status quo at the Wall.[62] In particular, the Reform movement, the largest Jewish movement in North America, leverages its influence with Israeli decision-makers who consider good relations with the Jewish community in the United States to be a crucial asset. The advancement of the third plaza plan should be understood, in this context, as a significant step toward granting a long-sought-for legitimacy to the second largest (after Israel) Jewish community in the world.[63]

According to the suggested plan, this new egalitarian plaza would be open twenty-four hours a day, seven days a week, and have no ultra-Orthodox rabbinic supervision. "The goal"—declares the head of the Jewish Agency for Israel, Natan Sharansky—"is that every Jew on earth can come to the Western Wall and express his identification with the Jewish people in the way he is accustomed to doing so."[64] The planned plaza will be raised at the same height and level as the men's and the women's sections at the central Plaza, and it will be continuous with the Western Wall plaza. The current plaza will remain as it was prior to Sobel's decision and WoW prayer will be banned there.

It is important to note that the suggested location of the third plaza is not altogether new; it is, rather, an expansion of the Robinson's Arch site which is located between the Archeological Park and the Mughrabi Ascent. The third plaza is intentionally planned to be adjacent to the Western Wall on the south side, since a bridge that ascends to the Temple Mount (the noted Mughrabi Ascent) will separate it from the main plaza and keep it out of sight of those praying within the central Wall Plaza.

In October 2013, the WoW presented a list of conditions for the third-plaza plan—pertaining to the section's name, size, budget, status, management, and accessibility—under which they would accept this latest proposal. Collectively,

---

62. See, for example, the protocol of the discussion on the third-plaza plan of the Israeli parliament's committee on women's status (Knesset Protocol, 2013).

63. See Jewish Telegraphic Agency (2014). For a critical evaluation of this involvement, see Aharoni (2014). Note that we do not downplay the growing presence of the reform movement among Israeli Jews, simply noting the political situation.

64. Ettinger (2013).

the conditions mandate that the egalitarian Plaza must have equal funding and status as the central Plaza, and that the authority of the Western Wall Heritage Foundation and the Rabbi of the Wall, which now administer the central Plaza, be restricted to the existing men's and women's sections. A new body, with equal representation for women (including the WoW), would run the third plaza. Moreover, as a multi-denominational women's prayer group, the WoW demand accommodations for those who do not wish to pray as part of a mixed service: the means for women's prayer groups will be available at all times at the new plaza, including a Torah scroll and a temporary partition to surround women's groups during prayer.[65]

Early in 2016 the Israeli government voted to establish this third, egalitarian prayer plaza at the southern part of the Western Wall, adjacent to Robinson's Arch.[66] The details of this new planned plaza, follow, mutatis mutandis, almost all the main aspects suggested by Sharansky, as noted above, but now with the backing and legal authority of a governmental decision. It will be an egalitarian prayer space and will serve non-Orthodox Jews and others interested in visiting the Western Wall for different purposes, without the permanent separation of men and women in place at the central plaza. The authority of the Rabbi of the Wall and the Western Wall Heritage Foundation would not extend to this third, "southern" plaza. Rather, a more representative new council, that would include women and members of reform and conservative Judaism, would be in charge of it. The central plaza will reverse to its legal status in existence prior to Judge Sobel's decision (2013); namely, the WoW's manner of prayer will be banned, and women will be allowed neither to pray while wearing a tallit or tefillin, nor to read from a Torah scroll. At the new egalitarian southern plaza, however, women who *do not* wish to pray as part of a mixed service, will, as mentioned above, have the option and means of doing so; a temporary partition to surround women's groups during prayer will be accessible to them.

However, ultra-Orthodox leaders and Members of Knesset (Israeli Parliament. MK) strongly oppose this new plan,[67] and they skillfully use their strong standing in the coalition as a leverage to delay or cancel it all-together. Note, that even under most convenient circumstances, this plan requires much effort: the new council will have to be established, the new plaza will have to be

---

65. See Jobani and Perez (2014, 495).

66. Governmental decision January 2016 (on file with the authors); the decision followed the recommendations of the advisory team lead by A. Mandeblit on the matter of prayer arrangements at the Wall, convened by prime minister Netanyahu in May 2013, and published early in 2016 (report on file with the authors).

67. See, among many, Rabinovitch (2016); Lau (2016). Lau is the Chief Rabbi of Israel.

built,[68] changes in legislation will have to be introduced. As of August 2016, and given the strength of the ultra Orthodox opposition to the proposed third-plaza plan, none of the mentioned steps was taken.[69]

Adding to the complexity of the matter is a standing petition,[70] submitted in 2016 on behalf of the Center for Women's Justice, asking the Israeli Supreme Court to amend the third plaza plan, as it would ban women's prayer with a Torah scroll at the women's section of the central plaza (this petition was brought on behalf of the splinter group that separated itself from the "women of the wall," called the "original women of the wall"[71]). This ban, the petitioners argue, would violate rights protected by Israeli law. In the state's response (August 2016)[72] it was claimed that, as the planned third (southern plaza) would enable women's prayer with a Torah scroll, the petition ought to be rejected.[73, 74] To conclude: whether

---

68. As of January 2015, the site designated for the third plaza has merely a mid-sized platform that is only accessible via an inconspicuous gate, the platform does not extend to the Wall itself, and the small area between the platform and the Wall is packed with boulders which make the Wall inaccessible for the handicapped and the elderly. A significant amount of work is required in order to make the entrance and the site as a whole into a proper, accessible, and adequate prayer site. The renovations needed at the site are problematic for two reasons. First, such renovations are likely to raise objections from Palestinians and the Arab world as such work may be perceived to be a change in the sensitive status quo in place in the area around the Western Wall. Second, as the site has a significant archaeological value, the Antiques Authority strongly opposed the transformation of the site to a prayer site.

69. The reform movement, in turn, reacted to the ultra-Orthodox tactics in a strongly worded op-ed by Eric H. Yoffie (2016), asking American Jews to support the noted third-plaza plan.

70. A copy of the petition is on file with the authors.

71. Some members of the WoW, including some of the founding members, reject the noted third plaza plan. This segment of the WoW argues that the third plaza does not have equal standing with the Wall's central plaza; that the compromise does not satisfy the long-standing goal of the WoW to pray at the central plaza, and that it is motivated by governmental policies that reflect a fear of ultra-Orthodox violence, an illegitimate consideration. Indeed, this segment has declared that it will ignore the compromise and will continue to pray at the central Plaza, a decision that has created a split within the WoW. See Maltz (2013); Maltz (2014); Jewish Telegraphic Agency (2013). The new splinter group (opposing the third-plaza plan) adopted the name "Original Women of the Wall" for itself; see their Facebook page at, https://www.facebook.com/OriginalWomenoftheWall/

72. On file with the authors.

73. The state's response also had to indicate when the third plaza will be ready for prayer, the noted council established and so on. However, the state's response remains somewhat vague and lacks specific details, and we can carefully conjecture that the reason is political pressures coming from ultra-Orthodox circles.

74. Of interest is that the petition to the High Court of Justice (HCJ) was accompanied with a civil lawsuit directed against the Rabbi of the Wall, and in both, a major claim was that the Rabbi of the Wall is part and parcel of the state, or even a state organ. As such, his actions, are

the third plaza will be established, the noted council convened, and the needed legal changes made, remains to be seen.

2.5. *Conclusion*

The many twists and turns of the recent developments of the WoW struggle—the current struggle to gain permission to read from a Torah scroll, the split within the WoW regarding the third-plaza proposal, and the civil suit put forward against the Rabbi of the Wall—signal that the WoW case is far from being resolved. Moreover, beyond these recent developments, the exploration of the religious, social-political, and legal aspects of the WoW struggle (see sects. 2.1, 2.2, and 2.3, respectively) demonstrate that the current situation demands a solution beyond maintaining the status quo. While this chapter's emphasis on a contextual, details-rich exploration of the case study is essential, in the next three chapters we will shift to a theoretical examination of three models of religion-state relations: the DCV, evenhandedness, and privatization, respectively. Such models aim to organize religion-state relations in a way that would satisfy various different criteria; our exploration of such models will pay special attention to their application to contested-sacred or thick sites in general, and the Western Wall in particular.

---

subject to Israeli laws that pertain to state organs, and their functions in (but not only) public spaces. As such laws have a clear gender nondiscrimination aspect, his actions are a violation of such rules. See chapter 5 for further discussion of this point (both the petition and the civil suit are on file with the authors).

Introduction to Chapters 3 to 5

The following three chapters examine three general, comprehensive models of religion-state relations: the DCV, evenhandedness, and privatization. Each chapter includes a detailed presentation of one model, examines the justifications given for that model, considers some policy implications of the model, and surveys the criticisms raised against the model (and in some cases, point to shortcomings overlooked in the available literature). In each chapter, once we establish a clear outline of a given model, we move to explore its suitability to the contested issue of thick sites, in general, and the Western Wall, in particular.

The three models are "ideal types" in the Weberian sense: they attempt to clearly elucidate and capture what is essential about each model across their various formulations.[75] The models themselves represent three major, prevalent families of religion-state relations that are politically relevant and each is legitimate from a democratic point of view. The three models are also each normative, or "prescriptive," in the sense that they are articulated as a search for an adequate arrangement or "solution" for highly contested thick sites.

The three models do not constitute a comprehensive list of all possible religion-state arrangements. We limited our exploration to models that firmly fit within democratic ideals. As such, the models have to meet certain standards and avoid violating certain principles. Therefore, we accept the view—advanced by Martha Nussbaum (2008), Ronald Dworkin (1977), and Robert Dahl (2006) among others—that citizenship in democratic states, as it grants equal concern and respect to all, places certain constraints on the ways that any democratic government may conduct itself in religious affairs. That is, all three models presuppose and are compatible with certain assumptions and institutional boundaries: basic respect for individual liberty and fundamental rights, a democratically elected government, and respect for minority rights.[76] We omit any discussion of illiberal and undemocratic models (theocracy, oppressive secularism, etc.) and take for granted that the three noted models all explicitly reject blunt discrimination of given religious or national minorities.

---

75. To use Weber's (1904/1949) words: "[C]oncrete individual phenomena ... are arranged into a unified analytical construct (*Gedankenbild*); in its purely fictional nature, it is a methodological utopia [that] cannot be found empirically anywhere in reality" (p. 90).

76. Democracy, to state the obvious, is a contested concept. We prefer an approach that, while not quite minimalist or purely proceduralist (Schumpeter, 1943/2003), is not overly demanding. That is, we seek to define the concept so that it is compatible both with various religion-state arrangements, and with, for example, "negative" and "positive" notions of respect for rights (Gavison, 2003). The literature on the concept of democracy is extensive, for good overviews, see Dahl (2000); Tilly (2007); Christiano (2006).

Beyond agreeing that obvious and blunt discrimination is unacceptable, it will become clear in the following chapters that these three models reach very different conclusions about the proper relations between the state and religions, each model also disagrees about how citizens' entitlements ought to be translated into policies regarding religion generally and thick sites in particular.

In the deliberations to follow, we attempt to provide a balanced and comprehensive examination of each model to assess the advantages and disadvantages of each. Though we argue that the privatization model proves best, we *do not* argue that the only legitimate religion-state model for democratic states is that of privatization. As several legal scholars and political theorists have shown, many perfectly legitimate democracies have an established or endorsed church.[77] Furthermore, arguing that privatization is the only genuinely democratic model would undermine the goal behind the comparison of alternate models, and it would rely on a problematic a priori assumption that *any* deviation from strict separation of religion and state is illegitimate; surely such a view constitutes a conclusion (if it is reached) to be defended, not an axiom to adopt before argumentation even started.

In what follows, we briefly describe each of the models that will be examined more fully in chapters 3, 4, and 5. *First*, the DCV (chapter 3), akin to an endorsed or established church/religion, is a model in which the state favors one dominant religion in various formal and informal ways. Yet, while the state explicitly or implicitly identifies with this religion, it maintains religious toleration broadly. *Second,* in the evenhandedness approach (chapter 4) the state provides resources for religions, but in an equitable and fair manner; while the state itself remains unaffiliated with any specific religion. *Lastly*, the privatization model (chapter 5) leaves religious matters, as much as possible, to the decision of the individual citizen; to accomplish this, the state remains unaffiliated with any given religion and neither supports nor hinders any religion in any material or nonmaterial way.

While the relevance of these models extends well beyond thick sites, the focus of our examination is thick sites, and the Western Wall in particular. While normative thinking regarding religion-state relations is a well-developed field of study, contested sacred sites or "thick sites" demonstrate a surprising dearth of normative analysis; which explains the noted focus. Our conclusion is clear: there are strong reasons to prefer the privatization model, as compared to other models, for the management of disputes over thick sites. We do *not*

---

77. For example, England, Italy, Denmark, and Sweden up to 2000, among others. See Durham (1996); Stepan (2001, pp. 213–253); Fox (2013); Rubinstein and Yakobson (2009).

argue that the two other models are impermissible; however, the considerations of chapter three will show that there are especially strong reasons to object to the DCV.

Finally, note that the conclusion at which we arrive is *not* a "package" argument; one does *not* have to be persuaded that the privatization model is the best model for religion-state relations as a whole in order to be persuaded that it is the best model for thick sites.[78] The specific characteristics of thick sites make the privatization model especially suitable for them, a point that we believe can be persuasively demonstrated even for advocates of other models in general.

---

78. This points to a further issue of how to "fit" a privatized thick site into a nonprivatized religion-state system. We will attempt to provide some answers to this issue in our discussion of the Western Wall in chapter 5; there we will examine what a "privatized solution" would look like for the Wall, even though Israel does not have a privatized model of religion-state relations. However, this is a complex issue that requires a further contextual examination. We view the exploration in chapter 5 as a beginning of a conversation, not its conclusion.

3

The Dominant Culture View and the Women of the Wall

COMPETING SIGNIFICANCES, ELUSIVE TRADITION, AND INEGALITARIANISM

IN THIS CHAPTER, we examine the dominant culture view (DCV) model of religion-state relations and its applicability to thick sites generally and the Western Wall specifically. We are rather critical of this approach because the DCV, as a general model of religion-state relations, faces many challenges that are amplified at thick sites.

This short introduction aims to clarify the basic tenets of the DCV approach; identify the main features of the DCV when concretely embodied by pointing to some real-life examples; establish the basic conditions that must be met for a DCV model to be coherent, meaningful, and relevant to a given country or case; and outline the structure of the chapter.

The DCV adopts, as its point of departure, the claim that there are substantial majorities in some countries that share cultural and religious understandings that, typically, reflect long-standing traditions. These majorities, the DCV argues, can legitimately use governmental actions to advance their religious and cultural traditions, as long as the relevant policies do not violate the core liberties and rights of minority groups (or nonobservant members of these majority groups). In the recent controversy regarding the ban on building minarets in Switzerland, David Miller argued for the adoption of the DCV model, though he did not use this term, as "[a] majority is entitled to ensure that the appearance of public space reflects its own cultural values, so that where those values reflect a Christian heritage, it can insist that Christian buildings and symbols should remain hegemonic" (Miller, 2016, p. 448). An additional, crisp formulation of the DCV position was offered by Judge Bonello of the European Court of Human Rights

(ECHR) in his concurring opinion—in favor of the Italian law that mandates the display of crucifixes in all public-school classrooms—in the *Lautsi* case:[1]

> On a human rights court falls the function of protecting fundamental rights, but never ignoring that customs are not passing whims. They evolve over time, harden over history into cultural cement. They become defining, all-important badges of identity for nations, tribes, religions, individuals.[2]

The DCV, therefore, explicitly condones certain state-sponsored inequalities between adherents of the supported religion (typically the majority) and minority religions. The proponents of the DCV model argue that not all nonegalitarian policies are necessarily illegitimate or discriminatory (Walzer, 1983, p. 313; Miller, 2016; Weiler, 2010, 2011) and suggest several potential justifications, legitimizing such inequalities. Note that, in many DCV cases, religion is intertwined with culture and therefore, as will become clear, defenses of the DCV are often presented as defenses of a national culture of which religion is an important aspect, rather than as defenses of specific religion-state arrangements per se.

What are the main features of the DCV religion-state model when concretely embodied? Because there are many institutional frameworks for DCV style arrangements, and examples of these models in action differ, it is difficult to pinpoint features necessarily shared by all implementations of the DCV model. Although the list is not exhaustive, we do identify the four following features as being typical to embodiments of the DCV:[3] (1) A particular religion receives some form of public support from the state; this support can take various forms: official recognition as the state religion, financial support, symbolic recognition, etc. (2) The religion that receives this public support is well defined and differs significantly enough in creed or practice to be distinct from other religions or other denominations of the same religion. (3) Members of the supported religion enjoy some advantage that is not shared by all citizens, whether it is expressed in financial, symbolic, or other forms. For example, there may be public financial support only for the dominant religion; the weekly cycle and yearly national holidays may be modeled on the calendar of this religious tradition; the symbols of the preeminent religion may be utilized in the national flag, incorporated in state symbols, or

---

1. The *Lautsi* case is discussed in detail in section 3 of the current chapter.

2. Page 38 of the Grand Chamber's decision, Lautsi v. Italy (2011), Application no. 30814/06, ECHR.

3. We rely here, albeit with important modifications, on Whelan (1990).

mandatorily included in the public school system, etc. Note that these advantages make adherence to the supported and (typically) majority religion more attractive, and often less expensive, than adherence to nonsupported religions. (4) The supported religion is seen as an essential part of the state, and there is strong identification of the state with that particular religion.

The DCV model has been embodied in various European countries with officially established churches (England, Greece, Sweden up to 2000, etc.).[4] Additionally, countries without an established religion, but which nevertheless support a given religion in the ways outlined above, can be categorized as belonging to the DCV "group" as well (one can consider Italy and Israel as examples).[5]

In order to defend the relevance of the DCV approach as a model, or its applicability to specific cases, the following conditions will have to be validated or met. First, it must be possible to identify a substantial majority that shares cultural and religious understandings (henceforward, the "shared understandings" condition). Second, it must be possible to identify and follow, within reasonable contours, past traditions and customs that have been transmitted from generation to generation and that express the noted shared understandings (henceforward, the "tradition" condition). These traditions need to be established over a significant timeframe; as Shils points out, "[A]t the minimum, two transmissions over three generations are required for a pattern of belief or action to be considered a tradition." (Shils, 1981, p. 15).[6] Third, it must be clear that no basic rights of the

---

4. It should be noted that the right to self-determination (which has important cultural and religious dimensions similar to those emphasized in the DCV view) is protected in important international human rights conventions. For example, the first article of the landmark UN International Covenant on Civil and Political Rights (1966) states: "All peoples have the right of self-determination. By virtue of that right they freely determine their political status and freely pursue their economic, social and *cultural development*" (italics added). The full original text is available online, see http://www.ohchr.org/en/professionalinterest/pages/ccpr.aspx). For a general discussion of the Covenant, see Cassese (1999). It is unclear what shape the legal protection of this "cultural development" ought to take; we point to this text simply as a legal point of reference.

5. In Italy, state support of Catholicism can be seen, for example, in the requirement that crucifixes be placed in all classrooms of all public schools (Temperman 2012; Perez, 2015); in Israel, such support is notable in the vast system of assistance given to Orthodox and ultra-Orthodox institutions, even though the government has recently started shifting to adopt a more evenhanded approach (see chapter 2, sect. 2.2).

6. Most appeals to the DCV in specific cases are accompanied by claims that both the shared-understandings and the tradition conditions are met. However, there are several exceptions in which countries claim to demonstrate shared understandings without appealing to a shared tradition. This will often be the case following important political occurrences which signal a decisive break from past traditions. The transition from the Ottoman Empire to Atatürk's Turkey, the rise of the socialist Zionist movement from traditional Judaism, and the Bolshevik revolution in Russia serve as three examples showing that, though it is typical, the tradition condition is not mandatory.

individuals who are not members of the majority religion would be violated as a result of adopting a DCV model (henceforward, the "democratic challenge" condition).[7]

In sections 3.1, 3.2, and 3.3 of this chapter, we critically examine each of the three noted conditions that, if met, are supposed to make the DCV applicable and defensible. The centrality of these conditions to the DCV model makes them a suitable focus for our critical review. Indeed, if the first two conditions, that is, "shared understandings" and "tradition," are not met in a particular case, then the major empirical claims articulated by DCV supporters—regarding the preeminence of a dominant religion—will be exposed as vacuous or false. The third condition (the "democratic challenge") constitutes the key justification that DCV adherents offer for condoning the state-sponsored inequality which is an inherent aspect of this model; the successful articulation of such a justification is, therefore, as important as meeting the two prior conditions.

The structure of the chapter is as follows: Section 3.1 examines the first condition that the DCV model must meet—*shared understandings*—and argues that, in the case of the Western Wall, such understandings simply do not exist. Section 3.2 examines the second condition needed for the DCV model to be relevant: *tradition*. In the Women of the Wall case study, the fulfilment of this condition would require the existence of a robust praying tradition in general, the use of a gender divider in particular, and a reliably demonstrated history of this practice. Such traditions, in the case of the Western Wall, are severely contested, if not absent altogether. Section 3.3 explores the democratic challenge to the DCV model and shows that the answers offered by DCV proponents are unpersuasive. The final section of this chapter, section 3.4, asks whether the DCV is a proper model for the management of contested sacred sites; the answer suggested is that the DCV is ill-suited for such sites, and that either evenhanded or privatized solutions (chapters 4 and 5, respectively), better address the complex problems associated with those sensitive locations.

A final comment will complete this introduction: it is important to emphasize that the conditions regarding "shared understandings" and "tradition" are empirical in nature. That is, in order to determine whether they are met, one must examine the empirical—historical and sociological—data of a given case (or cases) rather than theoretical claims. The judgment, at any rate, cannot be made solely on the basis of "armchair philosophy." We therefore turn, in sections 3.1 and 3.2 to the examination of data relevant to our chosen case study: the WoW struggle at the Western Wall. To avoid, or at least reduce, the possibility of

---

7. Since the first two conditions are empirical, they have to be "met by the case"; the third condition, focused on substantive and procedural aspects, is a "condition for the model."

selection bias, these noted conditions are also examined in the appendix with the case study of the Ayodhya dispute. We reach similar conclusions in both cases—namely, that the conditions of "shared understandings" and "tradition" are not met. Indeed, we will argue that more generally speaking, it is extremely unlikely for such conditions to be met in any other similarly contested sacred site.

3.1. Challenging "Shared Understandings": On the Competing Significances of the Western Wall

This section examines the claim that a "shared understandings" model obtains regarding the meaning and significance attributed to and the proper management of the Western Wall by the relevant population of believers. We will consider the differing and, at times, contradictory narratives that various groups attribute to the site. As will be demonstrated, the Orthodox narrative that depicts the Western Wall as a site with a monolithic religious significance is but one among several competing narratives. Thus the "shared understandings" claim can be undermined simply by surveying empirical reality.

We open with an examination of the archaeological narrative that emphasizes the Western Wall's profound historical importance. This narrative supports a demand for the site to be handled according to the accepted archaeological practices of maintenance and care (3.1.1). We will then explore the competing religious narratives of the Western Wall. We will first examine the Orthodox narrative and the sequence of events that lead to its de facto control of the Western Wall plaza (3.1.2). Then we will examine the alternative non-Orthodox narratives that are also attributed to the Western Wall—namely, the conservative and reform narratives that seek to challenge the patriarchal prayer arrangements enacted by the Orthodox and to introduce more egalitarian arrangements. These attempts reflect the fact that non-Orthodox movements share with the Orthodox the insistence on the irreplaceability of the Western Wall and its unique importance in the context of the Jewish tradition (3.1.3). We will end this section with an examination of the Western Wall in the framework of the national narrative and its significance as the location for some of the central rituals of Israel's civil religion, such as the opening ceremony for Israel's official Memorial Day or the swearing in ceremonies of some of the Israel Defense Force's leading brigades (3.1.4).

The tensions between these narratives, which at times flare into open violence, testify to a clear lack of "shared understandings" and, therefore, weaken the case for adopting the DCV model. The sociological reality of conflicting narratives regarding the Wall indicates that one of the model's self-proclaimed central conditions is not met. The notion that the DCV model should be adopted to resolve the religious conflict over prayer arrangements at the Western Wall becomes, therefore, highly unlikely.

3.1.1. The Archaeological Significance of the Western Wall

The Western Wall was erected as part of the grandiose building project initiated by Herod in the first century B.C.E to renovate the second temple. It served as a retaining wall supporting the paved esplanade of the Temple Mount, which Herod had expanded to accommodate the tens of thousands of pilgrims and the sacrificial animals brought to Jerusalem during the three pilgrimage festivals, Passover in particular. According to the latest archeological assessments (published in 2011), while the restoration of the second temple and the construction of structures on the temple mount itself (most likely including some of the retaining walls) were directed by Herod, the Western Wall and Robinson's Arch (a staircase at the southwestern corner of the Temple Mount) were built by his heirs, Herod Agrippa I and Herod Agrippa II (Herod's grandchild and great-grandchild, respectively).[8]

Several archaeological excavations in the area around the Western Wall had taken place in the nineteenth century despite the restrictions that the Ottoman authorities had placed on researchers (Barkai, 2007, pp. 25–26). Comprehensive and thorough archeological research in this area, however, only became possible after the conquest of East Jerusalem during the Six Day War in 1967. Benjamin Mazar (1906–1995), a founding father of Israeli archeology who had served as rector and president of the Hebrew University, stood at the head of the first archaeological delegation that began excavating near the Western Wall in 1968. The controversy sparked by the work of Mazar's archaeological delegation led to the division, still maintained today, of the Western Wall area into a section dedicated to worship (in which excavations are not allowed) and a section reserved for archeological investigation. This controversy proves strikingly revealing regarding the competition between the different meanings attributed to the Wall, and it merits a detailed discussion.

Professor Mazar, whose delegation sought to excavate the area south and southwest of the Western Wall, received permission to do so from the Israeli Antiquities Authority, and his work was undertaken under the auspices of various national institutions, such as the Israeli Academy of Sciences, the Israeli Nature and Parks Authority, and the Jerusalem municipality (in particular, Teddy Kolek, the mayor of Jerusalem at the time). The government did not oppose the excavations but, for the sake of propriety, asked for the permission of the Chief Rabbis of Israel; these rabbis intervened in the name of the Ministry of Religions (as

---

8. Reich and Shukron (2011, pp. 66–73). For a comprehensive depiction of the Temple Mount in the days of the Second Temple that combines historical research, archaeological findings, and information about similar structures in close and contemporaneous cultures, see Bahat and Rubinstein (2011, p. 41).

the Ministry of Religious Services was known at the time) that had acquired the authority over the Western Wall after the Six Day War (Ben-Dov 1982, p. 18–22).

Professor Mazar appealed to the chief rabbis—the Sephardic rabbi Yizhak Nissim and the Ashkenazi rabbi Isser Yehuda Unterman—and asked for their permission to excavate at the Wall. Both categorically rejected the request and insisted that archeological excavations would risk harming the sanctity of the site. In a memorandum sent to the Ministerial Committee for the Holy Places, rabbi Nissim summarized his firm opposition on the basis of the likelihood that "the excavations may go on for many years. In addition, should ancient buildings be found, this will preclude worship. We are in charge of protecting the place from desecration. We must make sure that no deed will in any way impair its sanctity, for praying at the Wall is the main thing, and everything else is incidental" (quoted in Benvenisti, 1976, p. 314). Beyond this official explanation, rabbi Nissim also hinted during his meetings with Professor Mazar that he was concerned that archaeologists would uncover proof that the recognized Western Wall is not actually the historical Western Wall; more generally, he didn't see the point of permitting any activity at this holy site that had the sole purpose of advancing archeological science, which to him was worthless (Ben-Dov, 1982, p. 20). The potential discovery of archaeological "truth,"[9] therefore, threatened the authenticity of the religious narrative recognized by the chief rabbis and the Ministry of Religions.

Professor Mazar rejected the Chief Rabbis' reservations and noted that the excavations were to be undertaken in an area that was not sanctified because no worship had ever taken place at the location chosen for the noted excavations (Bar, 2015, p. 318). The disagreement ended with a compromise that is maintained to this day: the Gate of the Moors, known also as the Mughrabi Gate, and the wooden pedestrian bridge leading to it, effectively divide the Wall into two main parts: (a) the part south of the Mughrabi Gate was expropriated from the control of the Ministry of Religions and was developed as an archeological site administered according to the Israeli law for antiquities, while (b) the traditional place of worship north of the Mughrabi Gate was allocated exclusively to the control of the Ministry of Religions and excavations were banned at this location (Cohen-Hattab, 2010, pp. 31–32).

---

9. The claim—that archaeology reflects the scientific and objective truth—is controversial. Many critics conceive of archaeology in general, and Israeli archaeology in particular, as a tool for disseminating a national narrative that functions as one of the founding blocks of a civil religion. The literature on this debate is vast. See, for example, Feige and Shiloni (2008); Kempinsky (1994); Zerubavel (1995); Silberman (1989); Elon (1971, 1981); Shavit (1997, pp. 51–52); Meskell (1998). Note that this view—that archaeology functions, beyond its scientific role, as part of given national narratives—represents yet another competing meaning attributed to (in our case) the Western Wall. This national narrative, as indicated in section 3.1.4, brings us yet further from any substantial claim to shared understandings regarding the Wall.

Mazar's excavations continued for several years and uncovered a rich variety of findings from various historical periods including the early Muslim, late Byzantine, and Roman periods. Principally, the excavations produced an abundance of remnants of streets and gates from the second temple period on the basis of which an impressive "archeological garden" was established (Bar, 2015, p. 318; Mazar, 1975). In 2013, the Israeli Antiquities Authorities strongly opposed the suggestion to found, in the area of the archaeological garden, a "third plaza" designated for egalitarian prayers (see 2.4 in chapter 2). The Antiquities Authority claimed that the building of such a prayer site would irreversibly harm significant archaeological findings. As Yuval Baruch, a representative of the Antiquities Authority, bluntly argued, "I don't know any intelligent archaeologist who would allow a construction project of that size on the Herodian street. It's inconceivable, just like building such a structure on the Acropolis" (Ettinger, 2013). Dr. Eilat Mazar, the granddaughter of Professor Mazar and a leading archaeologist in her own right, also strongly opposes the "third plaza" plan. "It's not clear to me why they insist on concealing and harming the sole—and impressive—remnant of the fallen stones from the destruction on the Temple Mount during the Second Temple period." Mazar added, "It's the only section of the Western Wall that's still visible above the original street level. If such a (praying) plaza, even a raised one, is constructed there, a great project will be damaged" (Shragai, 2013). The generational change of archaeologists and religious leaders, it seems, did not resolve the conflict between archaeological and religious interest in the area of the Western Wall. Given the inherent differences noted between the narratives, the continuation of such tensions should be expected.

3.1.2. The Orthodox Significance

According to the Orthodox narrative, the Western Wall has been the holiest Jewish site of prayer since the destruction of the Second Temple by the Romans in the first century CE (Charme, 2005, p. 7). The sanctity of the Western Wall is, in this narrative, a consequence of three characteristics that will be examined in the current section: authenticity, continuity, and gender separation.[10]

The first characteristic of the Orthodox narrative is that authenticity is attributed to the Western Wall. This authenticity is anchored in a popular

---

10. There is a wide range of varying and, at times, contradictory Orthodox approaches to rituals at the Western Wall. An aversion to the religious activities at the Wall after its conquest (1967), famously expressed by Yeshayahu Leibowitz (1979, pp. 404–405), is but one example among many of the non-monolithic nature of the Orthodox positions on this issue. In this section, we focus on the central institutional representations of religious orthodoxy, such as the Ministry of Religious Services or the Western Wall Heritage Foundation, which do present a unitary front on this issue.

tradition which perceives the Wall as the last remnant of the Second Temple which was destroyed by Titus and his soldiers in 70 CE (Barkai, 2007, p. 17). In this context, many attribute the famous tenth-century *midrashic* saying—"The Presence of God never leaves the Western Wall" (Exodus Rabba 2:2)[11]—to the Western Wall, despite the fact that this saying originally refers to the western wall of the temple itself, not to the retaining wall that is currently regarded as the Western Wall (Bahat, 2007, p. 33; see also Charme, 2005, p. 8).

A clear example of the orthodox narrative blurring the difference between the Second Temple's western wall and the current Western Wall (the outer retaining wall) can be found on the website of the Western Wall Heritage Foundation, a governmental body with a distinct Orthodox leaning that is in charge of managing the central Wall plaza.[12] This body's website presents the midrashic statement "the Divine Presence will never depart from the Western Wall" as an answer to the question, "Why wasn't the Western Wall destroyed?"[13] This answer is given despite the fact that, elsewhere on the website, the Western Wall is correctly presented as one of the "support walls" around the Temple Mount, rather than a wall of the temple itself.[14]

Because of the authenticity attributed to it (i.e., its mistaken identification with the western wall of the temple rather than with the outer retaining wall of the temple mount), the Western Wall gains a supreme and absolute sanctity in the Orthodox narrative. The sanctity of the Western Wall, as an authentic part of the Second Temple, was maintained in the face of criticism by Zerach Warhaftig, the Minister of Religions who became the authority in charge of the Western Wall plaza after its conquest during the Six Day War. During an interview in 1967, Warhaftig was asked to address the claims that the Ministry of Religions was hiding the fact that the site is not a remnant of the temple from the public, obscuring that it was a retaining wall supporting Herod's expanded esplanade, and concealing the fact that there was nothing holy about the Western Wall in its original context. Minister Warhaftig dismissed these concerns by simply asserting, bluntly, that "no power in the world can take the Western Wall away from

---

11. For a detailed discussion of the traditional belief that God's presence—in Hebrew his *Shekhina*—will never leave the Western Wall, see Peters (1985, pp. 225–227). See also Armstrong (1997, p. 328).

12. Interestingly, even the *Encyclopædia Britannica* wrongly states that the Western Wall is "the only remains of the Second Temple of Jerusalem." See Western Wall. *Encyclopædia Britannica online.* http://www.britannica.com/topic/Western-Wall (accessed February 17, 2016).

13. See the Western Wall's Heritage Foundation's web site at: http://english.thekotel.org/library/article.asp?id=80.

14. Ibid, http://english.thekotel.org/content.asp?id=212.

its holiness" (quoted in Bar, 2015, p. 337). Similarly, in a ceremony held at the Western Wall plaza shortly afterward, Warhaftig insisted that "all of the four walls that surround the temple mount are holy and their holiness stems from the Torah which commands us to protect the temple and all the holiness that is part of it" (quoted in Bar, 2015, p. 342).

The second characteristic that the Orthodox narrative focuses on is the continuous attribution of sanctity to the Western Wall by Jews in the two thousand years that have passed since the destruction of the temple. While this continuity is presented by the Orthodox narrative as undeniable and enduring, historical research indicates that the Jewish tradition only began to view the Western Wall as sanctified in the sixteenth century, and that public prayers at the Wall began only then (Bahat, 2007, p. 33; Barkai, 2007; Charme, 2005, p. 8).[15] On this point, too, the Western Wall Heritage Foundation clearly supports (and assists in creating) the Orthodox narrative. A page on the Foundation's website that presents (what the website refers to as) "facts and figures," simply declares that "[s]ince the destruction of the Temple, the Western Wall has served as an inspiration to the Jewish people."[16]

The third and last characteristic that the Orthodox narrative emphasizes ties the Western Wall's holiness to the gender separation maintained at its plaza. This separation was formally enacted at the Wall as soon as it came under the authority of the Ministry of Religions in 1967. The argument made by the ministry, under the leadership of Warhaftig, was that the gender separation which existed at the temple should also be followed at the Western Wall (Bar, 2015, p. 338). As we saw in chapter 2, this argument was also adopted by various Orthodox authorities, albeit with some modifications, in the Supreme Court deliberations regarding the WoW. Examples include Judge Elon and Professor Shochetman, who served as the state's respondent in the Supreme Court proceedings concerning the WoW's petitions. Shochetman, specifically, ties the gender separation that is customary in Orthodox synagogues to the separation practiced at the temple where, he claims, the sexes were kept separate in order to prevent inappropriate behavior and sinful thoughts. Based on this reasoning, the sexes also should be kept separate at the synagogue, considered a "tiny temple," in order to ensure appropriate conditions for worship (Shochetman, 2005). Adopting Shochetman's logic, Judge Elon claimed that there is a particularly stringent duty to maintain the separation

---

15. The attribution of sanctity followed the changes made to the Wall's surroundings by Suleiman the Magnificent. See section 3.2; Bahat (2007); and Armstrong (1997, p. 327) for a discussion of these changes.

16. See the Western Wall's Heritage Foundation's web site at: http://english.thekotel.org/content.asp?id=28.

of the sexes at the Western Wall as it is considered to be the holiest Orthodox synagogue in the world (Elon, 2005). Such Halakhic considerations are supported
by claims of historical continuity, as exemplified by the arguments of the Women
for the Wall, an organization founded in order to oppose the activity of the WoW
(see chapter 2, sect. 2.4, for discussion). On their official website, they declare—
with a reductive historical account that clearly reflects the Orthodox narrative
while ignoring significant complicating details—that "the traditions of prayer at
the Wall reach back to the days of King Solomon [who founded the first temple
in the tenth century B.C.]."[17, 18]

3.1.3. Non-Orthodox Significance

Non-Orthodox Jewish movements also recognize the Western Wall as the holiest
Jewish prayer site in the world since the destruction of the Second Temple. This
is, in fact, precisely why they consider it important to practice their prayers at the
Wall without gender separation, according to their custom.

Susanne Grossman, a Conservative rabbi, poses significant questions to the
Orthodox narrative in the collection of essays dealing with the status of women
in synagogues that she edited with Rivka Haut, one of the founding members of
the WoW.[19] As shown above, the Orthodox narrative ties the gender separation
practiced in the Orthodox manner of prayer, particularly at the Western Wall,
to the general separation of sexes practiced in the ancient temple. According to
Grossman, however, the practice of gender separation in Orthodox synagogues
stems from one particular ritual—namely, the water-drawing ceremony—which
was held at harvest time, when prayers for rain were performed in the Temple
during the holiday of Sukkot. The Orthodox practice of gender separation
ignores, according to Grossman, the involvement of women in many other rituals performed at the Temple. A careful historical examination of the issue, she
claims, leads to the conclusion that women shared with laymen an almost equal
access to and involvement in the Temple (Grossman, 1993).

The struggle of non-Orthodox movements to pray at the Western Wall without gender separation, as is their practice in general, began as soon as these movements realized that the regulations of worship—set by the Ministry of Religions

---

17. "Our Vision," Women for the Wall website, http://womenforthewall.org/sample-page/
(accessed January 28, 2016).

18. We shall look closely at these historical claims in 3.2; here we merely note them as a part of
listing and examining the different meanings attributed to the Wall.

19. Grossman and Haut (1993).

immediately after the Six Day War in June 1967—made their manner of prayer impossible. In 1968, the Ministry of Religions refused to allow the World Union for Progressive Judaism to open its congress, which was planned for July of that year, with a festive prayer at the Western Wall. The alternative offered was for the ceremony to be held at the upper plaza, about twenty-five meters from the Western Wall. In response, the Union and the League for the Abolishment of Religious Coercion[20] asked prime minister Levi Eshkol to reconsider the matter. In heated debates, both at the Knesset and in various committees, several proposals were made. Some suggested that progressive Jews be allowed to pray at Robinson's Arch, in the area of Professor Mazar's archeological excavation. The minister of tourism, Moshe Kol, supported the Reform movement's request and suggested allocating a permanent section near the Western Wall where they could pray without gender separation. According to Kol, such separation had never been practiced at the Western Wall and would be harmful since it would prevent a significant segment of the Jewish people from praying according to their manner (Cohen-Hattab, 2010, p. 31).

Eventually, the Reform movement's request was refused due to, in part, the claim raised by the Knesset's committee of internal affairs that "we should maintain the custom of prayers at the Western Wall . . . It is preferable to maintain customs and practices as a way to maximize the respect for that which is acceptable and practiced in Jewish tradition."[21] The sense of disappointment among Reform Jews was significant, but threats by ultra-Orthodox factions led them to let go of their demand.[22]

The years that have passed since this initial failure of the Reform movement to gain a foothold at the Western Wall have not solved or healed the controversy about worship practices at the Wall plaza. A notable outburst of open conflict occurred during the *Shavuot* prayers in the summer of 1997. A group of Conservative Jews who tried to perform a non-gender-separated prayer near the entrance to the Wall were violently attacked by dozens of ultra-Orthodox Jews. The resulting commotion was only placated when the police intervened (Sokol & Ilan, 1997). In response to this attack, the Conservative movement organized a massive prayer rally at the Western Wall plaza on the night of *Tisha B'av* (the eleventh of August, 1997), a date traditionally considered symbolic for

20. We thank Noam Hofstadter for providing us with a copy of a letter sent by the League for the Abolishment of Religious Coercion to the prime minister and the head of the interior affairs committee at the Knesset on the twenty-seventh of June, 1968.

21. Quoted by Bar (2015, p. 339), where this polemic argument is examined in detail.

22. Ibid.

the Jewish people's attempt to grapple with gratuitous hatred (*Sinat Hinam*) and inner conflict. However, this event ended when the authorities, in an attempt to avoid a violent clash with ultra-Orthodox factions and a disruption of public order, began the forceful removal of the Conservative worshipers (Hazut, 1997). These events led the government to allot Robinson's Arch, which is situated at the southwest corner of the Wall, for the worship of non-Orthodox groups; to this day these groups perform various rituals and ceremonies at the site, mainly bar- and bat mitzvahs (Cohen-Hattab, 2010, pp. 35–36; see chapter 2 for recent developments regarding this site).

As previously mentioned, intense discussions about establishing a proper "third plaza" with adequate conditions in which non-Orthodox groups could pray without gender separation began in 2013. We have already seen in chapter 2 (2.4) that this third-plaza proposal, according to which the WoW manner of prayer would be permitted but limited to this third plaza alone, lead to a split in the WoW. Some members of the group supported the compromise; others refused to surrender the demand to pray at the central plaza. The controversy, as well as other aspects of the WoW struggle discussed above, indicate that the WoW challenge both the Orthodox and the non-Orthodox regarding adequate prayer practices at the Western Wall; on the one hand, they oppose nonsegregated prayer (and thus do not easily "fit" into the proposed use of the third plaza), and on the other hand, they insist that their manner of prayer be recognized at the central plaza despite the opposition of the Orthodox (and thus they do not easily "fit" there either; see chapter 2 for a detailed discussion of this point).

While Orthodox and non-Orthodox groups agree about attributing preeminent religious significance to the Western Wall, their varying conceptions of religious practice and prayer arrangements preclude any genuine "shared understandings" among the relevant religious groups regarding the site. Moreover, the complexity of the WoW's demand, situated as it is between the Orthodox and the non-Orthodox positions, adds to this fragmentation.

3.1.4. National Significance

Today, the Western Wall is one of the major sites of Israel's civil religion, and many Israelis perceive it as "the culmination of the embodiment of Jewish national resurgence, the pinnacle of the control over Jerusalem and as a symbol that unifies the people" (Kroyanker, 1988, p. 159).[23] With the conquest of the Western Wall in the

---

23. For a comparative study of Israel's major national "shrines"—the Western Wall, Mount Herzl, Ammunition Hill, etc.—see Azaryahu (2002).

Six Day War, its plaza became the stage for some of the central rituals of the civil religion. However, leading up to 1967, the status and significance of the Western Wall had evolved through the various periods of Zionism. One can characterize these developments of the status of the Western Wall in the national narrative as fitting into four periods.[24]

In the *first period*, from the beginning of the first *Aliyah*[25] up until the conquest of the land of Israel/Palestine by the British (1882–1917), the status of the Western Wall was marginal in the Zionist narrative. The beggars and wretchedness which Theodor Herzl saw at and around the Western Wall in 1898 led him to write in his journal that "I resisted feeling a profound elation,"[26] a note that expresses the feeling of many among the pioneers of the New Yishuv (the organized Zionist community in the pre-independence land of Israel/Palestine). Indeed, Jerusalem, in general, and the Western Wall, in particular, did not carry a central significance in the consciousness or activity of the various institutional bodies which, in many respects, shaped the character of the New Yishuv at the time. The Western Wall was attended primarily by members of the Old Yishuv,[27] who used to pray at the Wall and kiss its stones; in the eyes of the New Yishuv, it symbolized destruction and exile. This view was expressed by A. D. Gordon, a philosopher and spiritual mentor to the pioneers of the second Aliyah (1904–1914).[28] The Western Wall was therefore marginal in the world of the second Aliyah pioneers, who scarcely mentioned or visited the site (Aaronson, 1989; Shilo, 1989).

In the *second period*, lasting throughout the British mandate (1917–1948), a clear change occurred in the Western Wall's status. After the British chose Jerusalem as the capital of Palestine/the land of Israel, the importance of the city rose within the Zionist narrative and, with it, the significance of the Western Wall. The Zionist Commission established its headquarters in Jerusalem and the Zionist leadership aspired to make Jerusalem the capital of the future Jewish state. From a symbol of destruction and exile, reflected in the epithet "wailing

---

24. We are here relying, with some slight modifications, on Bar (2015). On the complexity of the relation between Jewish nationalism and the Jewish religion, specifically as reflected in the "civil religion," see Liebman and Don Yihya (1983).

25. *Aliyah* means "immigration" or, literally, "going up [to the Land]."

26. Herzl (1999, p. 54). For a more general examination of Herzl's attitude toward Jerusalem, see Harel (1989).

27. That is, the ultra-Orthodox community that lived in the land of Israel/Palestine prior to the Aliyah and hardly participated in the Zionist revival.

28. Gordon (1982, pp. 166–167). For an examination of Gordon's complex attitude toward the significance of the religious heritage and the secular ethos of the pioneers in the second Aliyah period, see Jobani (2013, 2016c).

wall" common in English and other European languages at the time, the Western Wall gradually became a symbol of national revival and heroism This change was reflected by Itamar Ben-Avi naming it "the Wall of Heroes" (Saposnik, 2009, pp. 181–182).[29]

Conflicts surrounding prayer arrangements at the Western Wall—as a symbol of Jewish secular political power and independence rather than as an exclusively religious site—ignited the 1929 Arab riots which rattled Palestine/the land of Israel (Cohen, 2015). The Western Wall became one of the focal points of the tensions both between the Jews and the Arabs and between the Jews and the British. Thus, in contradiction with the decision of the so called Western Wall Committee that was founded by the League of Nations after the 1929 riots, revisionist Zionist groups used to blow the shofar at the Western Wall (mainly at the end of the Yom Kippur prayers) in order to symbolically assert Jewish sovereignty against the Mandate (Bar, 2015, p. 325). Furthermore, wider and more moderate circles of the New Yishuv, who disagreed with the revisionists' radical positions and actions, also began attributing an increasing centrality to the Western Wall in the national liturgy and daily routine; this tendency, as we shall see, gradually strengthened in the next two periods.

In the *third period*, from the War of Independence to the Six Day War (1948–1967), the physical separation of Israeli citizens from the Western Wall galvanized the yearning for it. As a result, the central importance of the Western Wall in the Zionist narrative increased even more. In a contravention of the armistice agreement signed in 1949, at the end of the War of Independence, the Jordanian authorities refused to allow Jews to visit Jewish places of worship and sacred sites on the eastern side of the city. This included the old city and the Western Wall, and this "inaccessibility of the Wall," as Storper-Perez and Goldberg put it, "became a factor maintaining and even augmenting its appeal in the eyes of many Israeli Jews" (Storper-Perez & Goldberg, 1994, p. 316).

Multiple governmental agencies undertook a variety of initiatives to nurture the growing national bond to the Western Wall, which was perceived as being held captive by a foreign power. For example, the Ministry of Religions organized on Mount Zion, where the conquered parts of the city were visible, a ceremony to commemorate the day on which the old city was conquered by the Jordanians. The Western Wall, however, could not be seen from this site. Along with Mount Zion, there were other vantage points of conquered religious sites, and the effort

---

29. The epithet Wall of Heroes had been coined by Itamar Ben-Avi in 1911. However, it only became commonly used, as Saposnik shows, during the British mandate following the reissue of Ben-Avi's collection of essays about the Western Wall after the 1929 riots. See Saposnik (2009).

demanded by visitors to "reach these out of way siting stations, in order to contemplate the city's strategic and spiritual situation without the possibility of actually seeing the Western Wall, undoubtedly served to heighten its symbolic value" (Storper-Perez & Goldberg, 1994, p. 316).

In 1956, the Ministry of Education determined that it was obligatory that a picture of the Western Wall be hung in every elementary classroom in Israel. It also mandated that explanatory classes be held about the Wall. In 1960, the Governmental Coins and Medals Corporation (which had been founded two years earlier by Ben Gurion) contributed to these efforts by issuing a medal of the Western Wall meant to mark the "eternal bond between Israel and the remnants of the temple" (Bar, 2015, pp. 325–327).

The *fourth period* began with the end of the Six Day War and is ongoing. The year 1967 was a turning point in the history of the Western Wall: the physical, national, and religious features of the site were determined immediately at the end of the war and, mostly, still obtain today. In the next section, we will discuss the prayer arrangements enacted at the Western Wall plaza in this period, here we will focus on the physical and national aspects of the plaza.

Immediately after the conquest of the old city, on the third day of the war, various public figures visited the Western Wall. These initial visitors included the heads of the Ministry of Religions and the Chief Rabbinate who, as mentioned earlier, successfully gained managerial control of the plaza very quickly. The plaza in front of the Western Wall at that time was sixteen meters long and three-and-a-half meters wide (Kroyanker, 1988, p. 159), too narrow to contain the worshipers soon to visit it in unprecedented numbers. According to one estimate, about two million people came to the Western Wall during the first six weeks after the war (Charme, 2005, p. 23). Therefore, under the instructions of various authorities—including the military governor of Jerusalem and the functionaries of the Jerusalem municipality[30]—bulldozers began widening the plaza of the Western Wall by systematically razing 150 houses in the Moroccan quarter. The inhabitants, descendants of Muslim immigrants from North Africa, were evacuated and relocated to available housing in the Muslim quarter (Kroyanker, 1988, p. 159). Bar (2015) writes, "It seems that the original intention was to destroy a limited number of houses and thusly vacate a space by the Western Wall." He notes, however, that "under a mystical-messianic sentiment, the destroyers evacuated hundreds of the inhabitants and destroyed most houses in the area—an

30. Incidentally, many of these authorities refused to take responsibility, in later years, for having ordered the destruction of the Moroccan quarter; see Bar (2015, pp. 328–329).

action that was perceived as obviously necessary by the Israeli public and was performed with barely any protestation" (p. 32).

The significantly wider plaza (60 x 60 meters) that was created through the destruction of the Moroccan quarter completely changed the experience of visiting the site (Cohen, 2009, p. 316; Nitzan-Shiftan, 2011, p. 66). The need to establish a dominant character for this new plaza, as well as regulate the movement of the many visitors (religious, secular, Jewish, and non-Jewish visitors, etc.), fueled the eruption of a controversy among various groups within Israeli society that is ongoing. This controversy, as Cohen-Hattab suggests, serves as a microcosm that reflects the differences of opinions and power struggles in wider Israeli society up to the present day (Cohen-Hattab, 2010).

In the year following the Six Day War, the prayer arrangements at the Wall's central plaza, which are still upheld today, were set. Most importantly, the whole area of the Wall's central plaza, on which the Moroccan quarter used to stand, was placed under the authority of the Ministry of Religions. The expanded plaza was divided into two parts. The first, the part near the Western Wall itself, was set aside to function as an outdoor Orthodox synagogue; in this part of the plaza, the women's section occupies merely a quarter of the space (Bar, 2015, p. 336).[31] The second part of the plaza, to the west of the space reserved for prayer (about twenty-five meters from the Wall itself), was established as a space for various official state ceremonies. The space on the southern side of the Wall, as noted, was allocated for archeological excavations (Cohen-Hattab, 2010).

Although at least some of these arrangements were meant to be temporary, nearly all of them are still in place today. The lack of widely accepted permanent arrangements constitutes a major reason for the continuing polemic in which, throughout the years, many public bodies and institutions have participated; the prime minister's office, the Ministerial Committee for Jerusalem Affairs, the Ministry of the Interior, the Ministry of Religions, the Jerusalem Municipality and the Municipal Engineer, the Company for the Reconstruction and Development of the Jewish Quarter, and so on, have all played a part in this complex debate.[32]

Since 1967, a variety of plans to redesign the Western Wall plaza have been raised and rejected.[33] Apart from the third-plaza plan, which was discussed earlier

---

31. The current (2016) space allocated to men at the plaza is twice as large as the one allocated to women. See Shakdiel (2002, p. 132).

32. As was argued in chapter 1, regarding thick sites as a whole, this inability to reach an agreement is not technical, it is typical to such sites.

33. For a detailed examination of the various plans that have been raised throughout the years, see Kroyanker (1988, pp. 159–167).

(see 2.4), the most famous of these plans has been that proposed by the famed architect Moshe Safdie. At the center of his plan, commissioned by the Company for the Reconstruction and Development of the Jewish Quarter in 1973, was a proposal to conduct archaeological excavations that would expose fourteen more buried courses of stones. This would facilitate the creation of a kind of an amphitheater in front of the Western Wall that would consist of three levels, with the lowest level nearest to the Wall and the highest farthest from it. The level nearest to the Wall—the "holiness plaza"—would be reserved for prayer, and the two further levels would serve secular-national purposes. The purpose of creating three levels was to re-create, for the diverse groups of visitors, the intimacy that had characterized the Western Wall plaza before the Six Day War. Small groups of worshipers would assemble in the lowest plaza nearest to the Wall; larger groups of tourists and other visitors would use the higher levels that, while physically more distant, would offer a good vantage point of the Wall and would still facilitate a sense of nearness to it. The plan went through several transformations as it was the focal point of various political and public polemics. Eventually, as part of the coalition agreement signed in 1977, the demands of the religious parties were accepted and the plan—which the Orthodox claimed would harm the sanctity of the site—was rejected (Kroyanker, 1988, pp. 162–164).

Regardless of such interesting yet eventually unsuccessful plans, the Six Day War significantly changed both the physical reality at the Western Wall and the symbolic significance attributed to it. After its conquest, prayer benches were brought to the Wall immediately, a partition was instituted, and the chief military rabbi festively blew the Shofar. Beyond the traditional religious significance of these actions, they also functioned as iconic representations of the national victory and the recovery of Jewish sovereignty over the site. Additionally, for the more messianic trends within religious Zionism, these actions represent the end of Jewish exile (Troen, 2003, p. 262). The shifting of the aura of holiness and the locus of religious experience from the historic domain of religion to the national domain finds clear expression in the classic photograph by David Rubinger that immortalized the paratroopers at the Western Wall.[34] In that photograph, as Saposnik (2009) puts it:

the soldiers seem to be imbued with a sense of religious awe and merge with the stones of the Western Wall, the holiness of which was diverted from "hyssop and sadness" as in the beginning of the century to the new

---

34. See figure 18 in Saposnik (2015).

holiness of "lead and blood" with the cessation of the battles in June 1967."[35] (p. 188)

After the Six Day War, the plaza gradually turned into one of the central stages for the rituals of the civil religion in Israel. Immediately after the war, various IDF brigades began holding their swearing-in ceremonies at the site. From 1969, the official Memorial Day for fallen soldiers opens at the site with a formal ceremony attended by the president, the chief of staff, and representatives of the families of the fallen. Taken in the aggregate, these steps connect the ancestral Jewish homeland to the modern state of Israel and point to the attribution of a national meaning to the Wall, in addition to its traditional religious meaning (Azaryahu, 2002). Finally, Jerusalem Day, a national holiday commemorating the reunification of the city on the twenty-eighth day of the Hebrew month of Iyyar, was set as an official date for visiting the Western Wall, further pointing to a national, rather than solely religious, meaning attributed to it (Bar, 2015, pp. 333–335). As a further evidence of the national significance of the site, important figures on official visits to Israel are received at the Wall.[36] Distinguished guests—such as Barack Obama and Pope Francis—were brought, as a part of their official visits to Israel, to the Wall and photographed putting notes with their wishes in the stones of the Wall, in the spirit of the popular custom.[37] Prominent Israeli politicians and public figures also regularly visit the Wall to bolster public support through the symbolic connotation of the site as a symbol of unification, security, and national cohesion in the contemporary Israeli national narrative.

To conclude this section, we note that the different meanings attributed to the Wall—including national, religious (both Orthodox and non-Orthodox), and archeological significances—collectively testify to the fact that the condition of a shared understanding, central to the dominant culture view, is not met.[38] We

---

35. For a detailed examination of the changes in the visual representation of the Western Wall, see Saposnik (2015).

36. It should be noted that the Western Wall also functions as a central tourist site; 90 percent of the tourists who come to Jerusalem visit this site (Cohen-Hattab, 2010, p. 29).

37. On this custom, see Bar (2015, p. 330). Today, notes can be "placed" at the Wall from afar, through the website of the Western Wall Heritage Foundation. See http://english.thekotel. org/SendNote.asp?icon=1.

38. In our discussion, we point to the various significant and different narratives attributed to the Wall as a way to reject the shared understandings claim. Beyond noting the various narratives, we did not inquire (if it is even possible to do so) into the proportional weight that each narrative holds for the Israeli public (i.e., the number of each narrative's supporters

move, therefore, to consider the second condition needed for a coherent, meaningful, and relevant DCV model: that of a robust tradition.

3.2. The Elusive Traditions of the Wall: A Subversive Historical Survey of Prayer Practices at the Western Wall

In the previous section, we demonstrated that the Western Wall's current status—both the holiness attributed to it and its centrality to Israel's civil religion—developed through complex and dynamic processes of continuous development, modification, and adjustment. This goes against the tendency of both the religious and the national narratives to present the central meaning of the Western Wall as having been constant through the generations. This section demonstrates that the gender separation practiced at the Western Wall today stems from relatively late modifications to the prayer arrangements that had been maintained at the site for centuries. We will trace the changes made to prayer arrangements generally, and regarding gender separation particularly, through three periods during which the Western Wall was administered under the Ottoman, British, and Israeli sovereignties.

The *first period*, the era of Ottoman rule, extends from the time that Jews began praying at the plaza—originally created by Suleiman the Magnificent in front of the Western Wall as part of the comprehensive reconstructions of Jerusalem that he undertook after the 1564 earthquake—and ends with the conquest of the city by the British in 1917. Though Suleiman issued an official edict

---

and their relative influence). There are several reasons for this. *First and foremost*, the notion of shared understandings is more demanding than the "first past the post" model which does not require a majority vote. The notion of "shared understandings", while not stipulating a specific number, must reflect, at the very least, a majority opinion in order to avoid violating its own underlying principle. The diversity of the significances (and their relative importance and popularity) attributed to the Wall is sufficient to refute claims of shared understandings. *Second*, it is important to note that the Wall is sacred for Jews who are not necessarily Israeli citizens. Israel, through its self-definition as a Jewish state (as well as through laws such as the Law of Return), connected itself strongly with non-citizens Jews; any notion of shared understandings with regard to the Wall should, therefore, include them as well. As a majority of Jews in the United States are either Reform or Conservative, even a "first past the post" system would probably not yield support for the Orthodox model (note that this point would apply to many thick sites). *Third*, examining majorities always raises questions regarding the sources and modes following which such majorities were formed; in the current situation at the Wall, this raises the specter of "sour grapes" and problems associated with preference-revealing under monopolies (see sect. 3.3). *Lastly*, as noted in chapter 2, general religion-state relations in Israel are too highly contested for a clear shared understandings to form; there is no reason to believe that this would be any different in the specific context of the Wall.

(*firman*) permitting Jews to pray at the Western Wall, they were prohibited from installing a gender-divider, or even bringing chairs and benches, as a means of preventing any future claims of ownership of the site (Bahat, 2007; Armstrong, 1997, p. 327).[39] Indeed, from the Muslim perspective, allowing Jews to pray at the Wall was a matter of benevolence, not the recognition of a right.

In this era, Jews perceived the Western Wall plaza as a place of communal gathering where popular folk traditions were acted out; they did not regard the plaza as an outdoor synagogue subject to rabbinical authority and Halakhic laws. Thus, apart from several exceptional cases, no strict gender separation was upheld at the site and no gender-divider was installed. Indeed, based on the various descriptions of the site made during the Ottoman period, the plaza mainly functioned as a place for informal religious devotion. Armstrong (1997), summarizing the period soon after the Jews began using the site, notes that "Jews liked to spend the afternoon there reading the Psalms and kissing the stones . . . They liked to write petitions on slips of paper and insert them between the stones, so that they might remain continually before God" (p. 327).[40] This folkloristic religious activity, like similar rituals described by various visitors during the eighteenth and nineteenth centuries, was conducted without the use of a gender-divider at the site. No concern regarding the natural interaction between men and women at the Wall was recorded during the centuries of Ottoman rule. For example, in the observations made by Gedliah during the opening years of the eighteenth century, women are described as "bitterly weeping" at the Wall on Tisha B'Av—a fast day commemorating the destruction of the Temple—without attracting any particular resistance: neither from the Muslim authorities under whom the site was ruled nor from Jewish men who, given the small size of the plaza at the time and the lack of a gender-divider, certainly would have seen and heard the weeping women (Ben-Dov, 1982, pp. 69–70; Peters, 1985, pp. 528–529; Charme, 2005, pp. 10–11).

As Margalit Shilo demonstrated, the ban on placing a cloth partition to separate the genders facilitated a dominant female presence at the Wall. Shilo notes that "[a]t the Western Wall women were granted a degree of autonomy: it was they who determined the times of assembly, the style of prayer, and the care for the site" (Shilo, 2005, p. 24). In fact, nineteenth-century ultra-Orthodox women even anticipated the WoW when, in 1887, they organized a special "women

---

39. The Western Wall, as Bahat (2007) mentions, was known to Jewish pilgrims before the sixteenth century, yet "none of them mentions praying at the site" (p. 33).

40. For a description of a variety of informal customs that developed at the Western Wall, see Goren (2007, p. 106).

service" at the Wall to celebrate Queen Victoria's jubilee and to express their appreciation of the British monarch (Shilo, 2005, p. 22; Shilo, 2007).

An abundance of postcards, illustrations, photographs, and short films from the late nineteenth and early twentieth centuries that depict the Western Wall all illustrate the lack of a formally organized and constant separation of men and women at the Wall. The two sexes were frequently depicted together, at times only a few feet away from each other. While the genders do, sometimes, appear in separate groups, only rarely can a gender-divider be seen (Charme, 2005, pp.14–15).[41]

Only at the end of the nineteenth and beginning of the twentieth century, did events begin occurring at the Western Wall that involved the exclusion of women at the plaza or use of a gender-divider—such as those honoring visits by important guests or marking other exceptional circumstances. This was the result, mainly, of the rise in power and number of European Ashkenazim in Jerusalem at the time. Ashkenazim tended to be stricter than their Sephardic peers with regard to gender separation. For example, during a prayer held at the Western Wall following a severe drought in 1902, a demand by the Chassidic sects to install a gender-divider at the site was accepted in order to ensure the success of the prayer (Charme, 2005, pp. 15–16). Nevertheless, even when a partition was set up for special events in the late Ottoman period, the formal arrangements at the site were not changed to include a permanent gender partition.

During the *second period*, that of the British Mandate (1917–1948), authorities viewed the repeated attempts by Jews to install a gender partition, as well as chairs and benches, at the Western Wall as preparation for an eventual claim of Jewish political sovereignty over the site. As a consequence, the prayer arrangements at the Wall turned into a contentious topic that concentrated broader friction between Jews and both the Arabs and the British. The British government sought to maintain the religious status-quo upheld at the site during the Ottoman era; the Arabs claimed that setting a partition and bringing chairs and benches to the Western Wall had always been strictly forbidden; the Jews claimed that this interdiction had neither been sweeping nor comprehensively applied as proven by several documented events (Cyrus, 1930; Saposnik, 2015, pp. 1670–1671). The British approach, as exemplified by the 1928 White Paper, was to maintain both the Muslim ownership of the Western Wall and the right of Jews to pray at the site. This approach led British authorities to explicitly forbid the introduction of a divider. Indeed, in the midst of the Yom Kippur prayers that very year, the

---

41. See also this 1918 footage taken at the Western Wall. www.youtube.com/watch?v=8k82Fg-J8VZk (accessed 12 February, 2016).

British forcefully removed a partition that had been raised at the Wall (Storper-Perez & Goldberg, 1994, p. 316; Charme, 2005, pp. 17–18). As mentioned earlier (3.1.4), the tensions surrounding prayer at the Western Wall ignited the 1929 riots. The League of Nations founded, based on British request in the following year, a committee to attempt to regularize the prayer arrangements at the Wall, considering the input of the various concerned parties. The Jewish side claimed that the prayers held at the plaza during the Ottoman period, at least on Shabbat and holidays, were formal public prayers. Therefore, the continuation of these prayers necessitated a divider (which is not obligatory in the context of nonformal, individual prayers such as the recitation of Psalms; Triwaks, 1931).[42] The committee also heard testimonies attesting that the formal prayers requiring a divider have only been held at the site since the end of the nineteenth century, only in specific instances, and not continuously. Muslims testified before the committee that they had never seen a partition, chairs, or benches at the site during regular visits. As Charme claims, the diversity of these various arguments reflect the lack of any permanent and binding arrangement for prayers at the site during the Ottoman era. Eventually, the British reaffirmed the right of Jews to pray at the site but prohibited the establishing of a partition, bringing chairs and benches, and sounding the shofar. These severe restrictions were not accepted by the Jews who occasionally breached them by, for example, demonstratively blowing the shofar at the end of the Yom Kippur fast (see 3.1.4; Goren, 2007, pp. 109–113; Charme, 2005, pp. 18–20).

The *third, and final, period*, beginning with the end of the Six Day War and ongoing, coincides with the establishing of gender separation at the prayer plaza as part of the Orthodox prayer arrangements.[43] Immediately following the war, the Israeli prime minister—Levi Eshkol—sought to transfer responsibility for the Western Wall, as well as for other historical and religious sites within the recently conquered territories, to the Israel Nature and Parks Authority. This organization's focus at the time was the planning of a national garden around Jerusalem's ancient walls. However, vehement opposition by religious parties led to a transfer of the authority over the Western Wall to the Ministry of

---

42. See also International Commission for the Wailing Wall (1931). Various quotes from the Cairo Genizah were brought before the committee in order to demonstrate that Jews already prayed at the Western Wall from the eleventh century onward. According to Bahat (2007), these quotes did not refer to the Western Wall as we know it today, rather they indicated another prayer site to the north of it (p. 33).

43. A detailed examination of the prayer arrangements themselves, as well as of the struggle of non-Orthodox movements to change them, has already been presented (see 3.1.3, as well as the consideration of the debate regarding a third plaza in 1.4).

Religions and a "Rabbi of the Wall," a novel position, was named by the Chief Rabbinate.[44]

The Protection of Holy Places Law (1967)—passed by the Knesset mainly to ensure the safeguarding of Christian and Muslim holy sites conquered during the war, primarily the al-Haram Ash-Sharif and the Church of the Holy Sepulchre—furthered the transfer of authority over the Wall to the Ministry of Religions. In the context of this law, it was decided that holy sites' sanctity would best be protected from desecration by delegating their management to the relevant heads of religion and the Minister of Religions (Bar, 2015, pp. 332–333). Following this new legal principle, which was created to protect non-Jewish holy sites, the Ministry of Religions allocated the management of the Western Wall to the authority of the Chief Rabbinate. They also passed a variety of ordinances pertaining to lawful behavior at the Wall, including prohibitions against: contravening the Shabbat, eating and drinking, organizing assemblies, neglecting to wear a head-cover or skullcap, and inappropriate attire. The most significant and controversial decision of the Ministry of Religions was, however, raising a gender-divider and allocating four times as much space to men as to women (ibid, 336).[45] As we already have dealt with the polemics that arose as a consequence of establishing this partition and the accompanying Orthodox prayer arrangements, we will end this discussion by focusing on the escalation of gender segregation at the Western Wall in recent years. This can be seen in, among other things, the 2008 allocation of a pathway reserved for men without a parallel pathway for women; the occasional enforcement of gender separation in the west of the main prayer plaza ceremonial plaza in 2009; and the geographic distancing of men's and women's toilets in 2010. What started as a controversial step, already contested in 1968, has become an increasingly fortified reality in 2016.

In short, there is little to no evidence supporting the claim that a demonstrable historical tradition of gender separation ever existed at the Western Wall plaza.[46]

---

44. A governmental body that supervises and administers many aspects of Jewish religious life, including: marriage and divorce, burials, conversions, etc. It is, de facto, an ultra-Orthodox body and is unpopular among non-Orthodox Jews and non-observant Jews because they come under its authority if they wish to marry in Israel.

45. As indicated earlier, the current space allocated for men at the plaza is "only" twice as large as that allocated for women.

46. Note that it can be asked whether, *even if* such a tradition existed, it would have any normative value. This question is especially important, since, in many cases, traditions developed in response to decisions and policies enacted by oppressive regimes and, under democratic regimes, would have developed differently (hence the tradition would not have existed had the religion developed freely). We return to this issue in 3.3.2.4; nevertheless, once it is clear that the empirical conditions are not met, this further step is not necessary.

Therefore the "tradition" condition, essential for the applicability of the DCV to the Western Wall, is not met. We can turn, now, to the third condition a legitimate DCV model would have to meet: the democratic challenge.

3.3. *The DCV and Egalitarianism: The Democratic Challenge*

The two previous sections demonstrated the inadequacy of the DCV model for addressing the Western Wall case study because the necessary preconditions of the approach—"shared understandings" and an existing, demonstrable "tradition"—are not met.[47] However, it is worthwhile to ask, if these preconditions could be met, should the DCV be accepted? This section aims to address this principled question.

The main objection that any advocate of the DCV model must answer is the so-called *democratic challenge*: given that modern democratic states represent diverse populations, which hold various religious and ethical views and are divided into different national and cultural groups, a country that chooses to promote one religion with the state apparatus would knowingly and directly create inequality among its population. This inequality requires a justification. In other words, even in cases in which the conditions of shared understandings and tradition *are* met, they are *not* universally shared. Thus, there is still a need to consider the effects that the DCV will have on minorities who do not share the officially recognized "shared understandings" because they find themselves in a state that formally (i.e., monetarily, symbolically, etc.) gives preference to a religion that they do not hold.

The three subdivisions of this section reflect the three main justifications offered by DCV supporters attempting to defend this state-sponsored inequality. Each one of these justifications aims to legitimize such inequality by characterizing it as a permissible inegalitarianism instead of an impermissible discrimination. A first argument is that a given DCV model is required as an instrument for achieving some other goal: maintaining social order, collective cohesiveness, perfectionism in human affairs, support for the welfare state, and so on (3.3.1). Second, proponents argue that the DCV reflects the will of the majority and that its abolition, following a competitive theory of religion-state relations, such as privatization (see chapter 5), will violate the basic democratic value of majoritarianism (3.3.2). Lastly, advocates of this view may insist that there is some intrinsic good in the DCV and in maintaining a given religion-state social order. This

---

47. See the appendix for a survey of the unattainability of these conditions in the Ayodhya conflict as well.

model provides, according to some DCV supporters, a feeling of "being at home" in the public sphere for the members of the supported religion; this "feeling at home" is, according to this argument, important enough to justify state intervention and protection.[48]

Two comments on the DCV model, and the ensuing state-sponsored inequality, are required before we turn to a detailed evaluation of these arguments. *First*, supporters of the DCV do not argue that state support of the majority religion reflects the superiority or the ultimate truth of that religion. Instead, they tend to cite other rationales, such as the importance of shared understandings or instrumental reasons. Accordingly, we shall examine the commonly offered justifications, rather than justifications—relating to a particular faith being truer or superior— that are not championed (to the best of our knowledge) by DCV supporters.

Second, in what follows we will not assume, in an a priori fashion, that *any* deviation from strict neutrality in religion-state relations is, in and of itself, unjust or discriminatory. Such a view begs the question and will fail, in any case, to persuade anyone besides those already committed to liberal neutrality. We will, rather, examine the justifications of the DCV on their own merits; this point should be borne in mind throughout the following deliberations.

3.3.1. The DCV as an Instrumental Good

The first justification for accepting the DCV model despite the inequality it engenders is instrumental in nature; that is, it conceives of the DCV as an instrument, or technique, that is important for achieving some other goal, and is not a good in and of itself. Some typical goals mentioned in this context by DCV supporters are social order, human perfection, collective cohesiveness, and support for the welfare state. The logic here is as follows: in order to achieve some goal, a certain characteristic is required of the body of citizens. If the citizens share some religious or ethical view, they will be more willing to cooperate toward the achievement of some goal, such as maintaining social order or (in a different version) paying high taxes in order to support members of this "extended family" who face financial troubles. If the DCV is abandoned, the achievement of specific social goals will, therefore, be less likely or simply impossible.

---

48. Note that the justifications we will examine were chosen because they are the leading, representative (i.e., frequently repeated, albeit in slightly different versions) attempts to justify the DCV. We make no attempt here to examine all attempts to justify the various versions of the DCV; that would require a book in itself. It should be borne in mind that the term *dominant culture view* is the authors', the justifications to be examined are for models fitting the definition of the DCV offered at the beginning of this chapter; for excellent overviews of this field, see Whelan (1990); Feinberg (1990, pp. 39–80).

Various versions of this position have been promoted by diverse thinkers from different historical periods. Rousseau (1997) offers a classic example; in his well-known discussion of "civil religion" in the *Social Contract*, he notes that "it certainly matters to the state that each citizen have a religion which makes him love his duties . . . which it is up to the sovereign to fix" (p. 150). Durkheim, who viewed religion first and foremost as a social project, asserted that "their [the practices of the religious cult] apparent function is to strengthen the bonds attaching the believer to his god, they at the same time really strengthen the bonds attaching the individual to the society of which he is a member, since the god is only a figurative expression of the society" (quoted in Lukes, 1985, p. 461). Lord P. Devlin (1977), likewise, insisted that

> an established morality is . . . [as] necessary as good government to the welfare of society. Societies disintegrate from within more frequently than they are broken up by external pressures. There is disintegration when no common morality is observed and history shows that the loosening of moral bonds is often the first stage of disintegration, so that society is justified in taking the same steps to preserve its moral code as it does to preserve its government . . . the suppression of vice is as much the law's business as the suppression of subversive activities.[49] (pp. 76–77)

This view of religion as an instrumental good also plays an important part in contemporary (rather dry) analyses of religion as an economic good:

> Tax collection is costly to the government because of resistance by citizens to having their property confiscated. We capture this by assuming that a fraction of each tax dollar collected must be spent on enforcement. This cost will tend to be lower, however, as the government is seen as being more legitimate. As noted, religion can potentially provide this legitimacy, for example by proclaiming that the sovereign is divinely inspired. (Cosgel & Miceli, 2009, p. 405)

Finally, some commentators argue that an established religion is required to advance human perfection. This was argued, for example, by the nineteenth- century British poet and cultural critic Matthew Arnold (1869), in his *Culture and Anarchy*:

---

49. We assume that religion can successfully fulfill the role of "common morality" in Devlin's parlance.

The great works by which, not only in literature, art, and science generally, but in religion itself, the human spirit has manifested its approaches to totality, and a full, harmonious perfection, and by which it stimulates and helps forward the world's general perfection, come, not from Nonconformists, but from men who either belong to [religious] Establishments or have been trained in them. (XIX)

What shall we make of this family of "instrumental" arguments? While there are several ways to examine this family of arguments, our first step is to simply look for evidence that could support such views.

In fact, the argument here is basically empirical: in a country in which the national culture is intertwined with a given religion, the country is permitted to support that religion with the state apparatus in order to achieve some important goal that otherwise would not have been attained or would only have been attained with significantly more effort and cost. Note that the burden of proof rests on those arguing for this instrumental argumentation, as democratic countries adopt a default assumption of equality of treatment by the government toward citizens of different religious and ethical views.[50] Those who argue for a deviation from this default rule, therefore, ought to provide convincing justifications.

Furthermore, establishing any one religion as an official state religion has costs of its own. Beyond the difficulties of establishing, maintaining, funding, and fostering the religion receiving preferred status, there are inherent problems posed by the resulting hegemony: resentment of minorities, corruption of religious organizations, and so on (see chapter 5). The instrumental value of the DCV should therefore be both significant enough and sufficiently certain to obtain that it can offset such costs.

How sound is this instrumental argument? In many cases, the disestablishment (full or partial) of national churches did not lead to the pessimistic predictions that the "instrumental" school of thought suggested, nor did the lifting of restrictions rooted in religious views.[51]

---

50. See the detailed discussion of this point in chapter 5 (5.3). Note the subtle yet important difference between accepting this presumption and arguing that liberal neutrality is the only legitimate model.

51. "As a proposition of fact"—as H. L. A. Hart (1963) dryly noted in his famous debate with Lord Devlin—"it is entitled to no more respect than Emperor Justinian's statement that Homosexuality was the cause of earthquakes" (p. 50). Hart was referring to the ban on homosexual relations supported by Devlin, and the predictions Devlin made regarding the dire results that would follow once such bans are lifted.

Furthermore, the simple empirical fact of religious heterogeneity within large democratic states[52] alone suggests that the "picking and choosing" of one state religion will encourage social divisions and conflicts rather than create social cohesiveness. This empirical reality, when described bluntly, immediately undermines the notion that social stability must explicitly rely on religion in order to ensure "bonds" and avoid "disintegration," as claimed by Durkheim[53] and Devlin, respectively. Once social-religious homogeneity dissipates, picking one religion[54] as the expression of the dominant culture will likely divide rather than unify a population.

Next, the idea that human perfection requires the establishment of religion, as suggested by Arnold, can be undermined both philosophically and pragmatically. *First*, from a philosophical point of view, the concept of human excellence is anchored in a comprehensive and exhaustive system that assumes an absolute point of reference. This point of reference, which Arnold accepts, typically "God" in theology or "Truth" in philosophy, is considered both objectively valid and unconditionally binding for all. However, the critique of religion and ideology that emerged in the second half of the nineteenth century—the period in which Arnold's *Culture and Anarchy* was published—undermined the viability of traditional religions as political justifications and the communal importance of their conceptions of human excellence (Jobani, 2016b).[55]

Second, a pragmatic point of view notes that, beyond the difficulty of measuring Arnold's type of statement, comparing states which enacted disestablishment (the United States, France, Sweden) to states that did not (Greece and the Greek

---

52. Several examples support this point. The Israeli population is divided into Jews (75%), Muslims (roughly 17%), Christians (about 2%), and other groups; each category is divided into further subcategories (Israel's Central Bureau of Statistics data, 2011). In India, the location of our second case study (see the appendix), the population is divided (roughly) into Hindus (80%), Muslims (14%), Christians (2.3%), Sikhs (1.7%), and further religions and groups; however such categories (Hinduism especially) are divided to many further subcategories (Singh, 2015). Other large democratic countries, like the United States and France, have a similar religious heterogeneity; many nondemocratic states also have religiously diverse populations (for support of this empirical assertion, see "Global Religious Diversity," April 4, 2014, retrieved from http://www.pewforum.org/2014/04/04/global-religious-diversity/).

53. Durkheim died in 1917, and the comment above should be read to mean (roughly) an application of parts of his scholarly work to contemporary sociopolitical arrangements.

54. Rather than, for example, constitutional patriotism as suggested by Habermas (1995).

55. Nietzsche, whose declaration of the death of God succinctly expressed the spirit of the time, denied the very existence of an absolute point of reference and, accordingly, undermined all attempts at deriving objectively binding models of human excellence from it. He expressed succinctly his view that directly contradicts Arnold's argument: "I distrust all systematizers and avoid them. The will to a system is a lack of integrity" (Nietzsche 1994, sec. 26, p. 159); in another context, Nietzsche asserts that "the morality of distinction is in its ultimate foundation pleasure in refined cruelty" (Nietzsche, 1997: bk. 1, sec. 30, p. 31).

Orthodoxy, or Bulgaria and Eastern Orthodoxy) does not reveal any obvious and demonstrative advantage in "human perfection." It is far from clear that state apparatuses are the right instruments for achieving human perfection.[56]

The claim—that adopting the DCV maintains and fosters the welfare state—gains no support from empirical data. On the contrary, there is a body of research that suggests a correlation between countries adopting policies that support social *heterogeneity* and increased support for welfare policies (Banting & Kymlicka 2003). The available evidence thus undermines the notion that "an established religion is an indispensable instrument" for the advancement of the welfare state.[57]

To summarize this subsection, there is no reasonable argument or empirically sound evidence that supports the instrumental claim for the DCV.[58] We, therefore, turn to the second justification offered on behalf of the DCV: majoritarianism.

3.3.2. DCV as an Expression of the Wish of the Majority

The second justification for the DCV model equates the dominant culture with the expression of the majority's vote or, more broadly, "will." The basis for adopting the DCV, here, is the idea of majority rule—a basic democratic value.[59] According to this view, replacing the DCV with a competing theory of religion-state relations, such as privatization (see chapter 5), would constitute a blunt violation of majoritarianism.

---

56. This is, of course, a major claim regarding the modern era as a whole. Although it is a contested point, it is defended by many scholarly authorities. See, for example, Strauss (1999); Skinner (2009).

57. A further, related example is the development of trust: according to some scholars, trust among citizens is an important variable for (and indicator of) the functioning of a successful economy. A shared religion, according to this view, would make it easier for such a trust to develop (Miller, 2004). However, when looking at the relevant economic data, we found little or no support for this theory (Alesina, Devleeschauwer, & Easterly, 2002).

58. If further versions of the instrumental argument are advanced, they will have to meet the empirical concerns noted above. Our conclusion is, therefore empirical, rather than philosophical.

59. On the connection between shared understandings and majoritarianism, see Downing and Thigpen (1986); Walzer (1983, p. 313). Note that connecting shared understandings to majoritarianism would create tension between shared understandings and tradition, as the authority of traditions is not based on the idea of expressed consent that is central to majoritarianism. However, in the cases of the Western Wall and the Ayodhya dispute, the basic empirical validation of tradition and shared understandings is falsified, so such further considerations are not required.

The importance of majority rule, or majoritarianism, in democratic theory has been articulated and defended by Robert Dahl (2006):

> If citizens disagree on policies, whose views should prevail? The standard answer in democratic systems is that the decision must follow the will of the majority of citizens, or in representative systems, the majority of their representatives . . . I shall not undertake to justify majority rule except to say that no other rule appears to be consistent with the assumption that all citizens are entitled to be treated as political equals. (pp. 14–15)[60]

Majoritarianism, or the value of majority rule, can certainly be used to ground and to justify the DCV. As J. Weiler, a prominent jurist, suggests in his comments on the *Lautsi* case, theorists can (and perhaps should) shift their point of view from that of a member of a minority, forced to acknowledge her lesser status compared to the majority to which the state "belongs," to that of the many members of a majority asked (or forced) to abolish the symbols of their collective identity from the public sphere. As Weiler (2011) writes:

> But surely Freedom *from* Religion is not absolute, and its vindication has to be so balanced, and the principle collective good against which it should be balanced would, in my view, be the aforementioned collective freedom of a self-understanding, self-definition and determination of the collective self as having some measure of religious reference.[61] (pp. 582)

In the context of the 2009 Swiss referendum that resulted in the prohibition against the building of minarets, David Miller (2016) argued:

> When a people with a distinctive national culture occupy territory over time and transform it to meet their needs, they acquire the right to preserve and enjoy the value they have thereby created . . . In cases where a particular religion has played the dominant role in national life, this will extend to churches, temples, mosques . . . so the value that is created by preserving this heritage is the value of national identity itself. (p. 448)

---

60. We shall not enter further into the discussion of why majoritarianism is appealing beyond the basic idea as introduced by Dahl. Some dispute this view, usually by noting some consequence-derived consideration. See Dworkin (2013, p. 384).

61. It is noteworthy that many European states joined Italy (and, therefore, support the DCV approach) in arguing to the ECHR Grand Chamber that the strict separation of the American model, though legitimate for the United States, is unsuitable for many European states (on the *Lautsi* case, see Temperman, 2012; Perez, 2015).

In the same context of the minarets debate, Moeckli (2011) described the majoritarian based DCV as follows:

> Simply stated, this debate opposes, on the one hand, those who depict the people as the absolute sovereign on whose will, finding its expression in direct democratic processes, no limits can be imposed with, on the other hand, those who argue that in a state based on the rule of law, even the people must comply with certain fundamental rules, including respect for human rights, and that courts can review expressions of the popular will for compliance with these rules. (p. 775)

Note that the majoritarian argument differs from the instrumental view examined earlier. The instrumental view had a derivative, secondary quality, as it presents the DCV as merely an instrument for the achievement of some other goal; the majoritarian argument for the DCV is, conversely, couched in core democratic principles and, as such, carries a central importance in democratic theory, politics, and decision making. We should be careful *not* to assume, a priori, that any deviation from strict equality in religion-state relations immediately signals that majorities by definition have violated the rights of minorities and abused their power. As noted above, such a view begs the important question and, in any case, will not persuade anyone not already committed to liberal neutrality. Furthermore, majorities in democracies are free to reach contested decisions in a wide variety of crucial fields, such as healthcare, social security, national security. Many of these controversial decisions directly influence important human rights. Unless one is willing to severely limit the majoritarian principle in favor of liberal theories of justice (noting that there are many such theories that, at times, are incompatible), one would have to allow some space for majority decision-making (Walzer, 1981; Sen, 2009).[62]

However, the general acceptance of the majoritarian view does not mean that it is adopted without limits; at the very least, some procedural requirements are usually in place. Nevertheless, even if all such requirements are met, it is still unclear whether advancing the DCV model for religion-state relations is a good idea. We shall divide our discussion of this issue between the following four topics: violation of rights (3.3.2.1), Procedural aspects (3.3.2.2), nonreversibility (3.3.2.3), and whether, even if all such somewhat formal criteria are met, the DCV is, simply put, a good idea (3.3.2.4).

---

62. Note that the measure of deviation from the equality standard is an excusing variable; it cannot function as an a priori justification for the deviation itself. This means that the argument made by DCV supporters—that the noted deviation from equality is small—only enters the debate once the deviation itself is justified (Perez, 2015).

3.3.2.1. Violation of Rights

In some cases, adopting the DCV as a model of religion-state relations directly violates the rights of religious minorities or nonbelievers. There is a continuum extending from cases in which the DCV is obviously permissible (say, choosing days of rest that follow the calendar of the majority religion; see Gavison and Perez, 2008) to cases in which the DCV clearly moves beyond what is permissible in a democratic regime (say, the legal situation that existed in the United Kingdom up to 1871, in which the universities of Oxford and Cambridge banned the entry of Catholic students). In between these two extremes, there are many moderate and yet controversial cases, such as the current (2016) Italian law mandating the placement of crucifixes in all public school classrooms (Temperman, 2012) and the decision in India, following the *Shah Bano* case, to limit Muslim women's access to civil remedies in cases of divorce.[63] Now, any judgments about whether such cases exceed the permissible majoritarian grounding of the DCV are bound to be contested. The principled point behind these deliberations should be, however, that majority vote does not provide a carte blanche to advance any religiously motivated law. Majoritarianism is blocked, or reaches its limit, at the point in which minority rights are violated.

3.3.2.2. Procedural Aspects: Duress, Monopoly, and Sour Grapes

In order for the majoritarian argument to be legitimate in the first place, certain procedural requirements regarding the formation of the majority have to be satisfied. Some ways in which majorities are formed are suspect, or improper, as unfair limitations sometimes shape the formation of the majority and the decision it reaches. In such cases, the majoritarian claim should be flatly rejected.[64] This point precedes any substantive debate regarding the DCV, as it is simply a general point guiding any policy grounded in majoritarian arguments. In this section, we identify three categories of such unfair limitations that invalidate a majority opinion and vote.[65]

---

63. See Mohd. Ahmed Khan v. Shah Bano Begum (1985) SCR (3) 844; Spinner Halev (2001).

64. Bernard Williams (2006) elaborated this point and the challenge that it poses:

> What may be called the critical theory principle, that the acceptance of a justification does not count if the acceptance itself is produced by the coercive power which is supposedly being justified, is a sound principle: the difficulty with it, of making good on claims of false consciousness and the like, lies in deciding what counts as having been "produced by" coercive power in the relevant sense. (p. 6)

65. The categories identified here are not exhaustive; they are major examples that deserve our attention. For a more general discussion, see Vermeule (2007).

The first category of an unfair limitation bringing about a given decision is *duress:* if the majority is formed by using threats, bribery, and similar means, it is necessary to reject the claim that (in our context) the dominant culture represents the will of the majority. Any majority formed in such circumstances does not reflect the free choice of the individuals involved.[66]

The other noted categories which might raise procedural issues—*monopoly* and *sour grapes*—are somewhat more complex than the straightforward category of duress. We shall therefore use the case of *Lautsi vs. Italy* as an example, in order to put some flesh on the abstract bones of these two categories of majoritarian procedural problems. This case involves a 2011 decision of the Grand Chamber of the ECHR that concluded that the contested Italian law—requiring the display of crucifixes in each classroom of public schools—does not violate the European Convention on Human Rights.[67, 68]

Let us start with the *monopoly* issue: the mandatory placement of crucifixes in public schools can be viewed as creating a monopoly with legal barriers to entry (and exit), since no public school that does not display the crucifixes is allowed to function. Although private schools are an option, their high tuition costs, as the Grand Chamber decision indicated, requires "disproportionate efforts and acts of sacrifice [from parents]" (2011, chamber decision, para. 55); therefore, they cannot be viewed as a reasonable alternative.[69] If there is only one viable provider of service for the entire citizenry, how can either that service provider or an external observer know the true preferences of those who depend on the service? Unlike companies in the private sector, the *Lautsi* decision could not ignore this question; it appealed to the majoritarian stance as the justification for imposing a monopoly. The idea that the court's decision, accepting the legitimacy of the

---

66. As Walzer points out, in the context of the Jewish Political Tradition, "Rabbis, or some of them, recognize that coerced consent is not morally or legally binding" (Walzer, Lorberbaum, Ackerman, & Zohar, 2003, p. 7).

67. Lautsi vs. Italy (2011), Application no. 30814/06. The discussion here relies on Perez (2015).

68. Our choice of *Lautsi* follows the direct and clear way in which the DCV logic and institutional implications function in this case; but there are other similar cases, see for example, the Canadian case of Mouvement laïque québécois *v.* Saguenay (City), 2015 SCC 16, [2015] 2 S.C.R. 3, in which the Canadian Supreme Court deemed practices, which involved praying, and religious gestures strongly connected to Catholicism, to be impermissible at the municipal council of Saguenay in Quebec. While the final decision was opposed to the decision in *Lautsi*, it is noteworthy that attempts to create DCV style practices in democratic states are certainly present.

69. *Lautsi* passed via several instances. In our context, there were two relevant decisions: the chamber's decision of the ECHR and the Grand Chamber decision. The chamber decision sided with *Lautsi* (against the crucifix law), whereas the final decision of the Grand Chamber sides with Italy's policy. We consider both of these differing decisions of the ECHR.

Italian law, reflects the wishes of the majority in Italy is arguably the crucial and contested point of the case.

If authentic preferences are not reliably revealed through actual choices, then determining preferences will be a particularly problematic challenge. Social scientists, especially economists, are acutely familiar with this problem. Indeed, economist and Nobel laureate James M. Buchanan firmly rejected the idea that a reliable method for discovering such unrevealed preferences exists.[70] To put this point in general terms (looking past the *Lautsi* case), if a given government would like to advance a certain policy—derived from a DCV model—as the "wish of the majority," it will need to provide further evidence to justify that characterization aside from the fact that people follow a legal rule that forces them to be in conformity with the dominant culture.

Sour grapes, or *preference-adaption* problems are an additional potential procedural problem in the context of majoritarian claims. Let us begin with a brief description of the preference-adaption process following Jon Elster's famous exploration of the phenomenon. Elster argues that the satisfaction of wants or preferences should not be considered as a part, or a criterion, of justice. At least, in cases where such preferences are attributable to constraints on the available options and the adaptations made to suit such available options, the satisfaction of wants should not be considered a criterion. If some conditions that give rise to certain adaptations in wants are suspect, the satisfaction of the noted wants should not be a part of a theory of justice (Elster, 1983, pp. 109–140).

Returning to the *Lautsi* case, the mandatory placement of crucifixes directly restricts one option that citizens might have chosen: that of not having crucifixes in classrooms. The custom of placing the symbol in schools is long-standing in Italy (starting in 1860), so it may have given rise to a preference-adaption of both children in public schools and their parents who had studied in a similar environment. A typical adaption of preferences resulting from the elimination of choice—such as not to have crucifixes in classrooms—can take one or both of

---

70. As Buchanan (1959) wrote:

> Economists. . . have generally assumed omniscience in the observer, although the assumption is rarely made explicit. . . , the economist can unambiguously distinguish an increase in welfare independent of individual behavior because he can accurately predict what the individual would, in fact, "choose" if confronted with the alternatives under consideration. This omniscience assumption seems wholly unacceptable. Utility is measurable . . . only to the individual decision-maker. It is a subjectively quantifiable magnitude. While the economist may be able to make certain presumptions about "utility" on the basis of observed facts about behavior, he must remain fundamentally ignorant concerning the actual ranking of alternatives until and unless that ranking is revealed by the overt action of the individual in choosing. (p. 126)

the following forms: *first*, it can diminish the importance of not having crucifixes in classrooms or, *second*, it could detract from the significance of having them in classrooms. Examples of both tactics can be found in both opinions of the courts (i.e., the Chamber and Grand Chamber decisions). Attempts to downplay the significance of having crucifixes in classrooms can be found in the various *Lautsi* decisions in some courts' attempts to argue that the crucifix represents various values aside from its Christian symbolism (see the skeptical discussion of this argument by Evans, 2010–11, p. 356), or in efforts to stress the difference between passive and active religious education. The downplaying of the importance of *not* having crucifixes is evident in (among others) arguments against the adequacy of the separation-between-church-and-state model for the European context (an argument repeated by J. Weiler, 2010, p. 2; see also Langlaude, 2013, pp. 9–11).

Two additional brief comments regarding sour grapes are required. First, the "sour grapes" objection to majority formation is potentially too wide, since it can be applied to many different scenarios. It is therefore advisable to use this objection sparingly, and only in cases (*Lautsi* being one) in which the legal system is clearly and boldly supporting one religious option (especially in the context of public education). Second, the policy lesson to be learned from the sour grapes objection to majority formation generally, and the *Lautsi* case in particular, is that policies should be less restrictive. If there is a concern that individuals wish to maintain a given religion-state model due to a preference-adaptation scenario, the remedy should be to allow for *more* religious (or, indeed, irreligious) options (say, classrooms without the crucifix in Italy, access to and the availability of civil marriages in Israel, etc.).[71]

To conclude: governmental attempts to justify DCV-derived policies in cases in which concerns are raised as to whether majority wishes were formed in suspect ways, merit close examination. Cases in which the legal order permits only one religious option—as in *Lautsi* or the exclusive Orthodox control over prayer arrangements at the Wall's central plaza up to 2013—invite, therefore, close examination of any majoritarian justification for the adoption of a DCV-derived arrangement.

3.3.2.3. *Irreversibility*

In some cases, majority decisions and a version of the DCV model are entrenched in constitutions; or they are otherwise protected by the special majorities or political procedures required to amend them. Such entrenchments can give rise to three problems: unfairness, the countermajoritarian objection, and potential

---

71. For an extended discussion of this point, see Perez (2015); Williams (1985, p. 43).

sour-grapes scenarios. In the face of such problems, it is better, as a general rule, to avoid the institutional entrenchment of DCV arrangements. We shall present an example in order to briefly explain these three problems.

A clear example is the attempt (so far unsuccessful) to get the Israeli parliament to pass the so-called *nationality law*, which is short for "the basic law: Israel as the nation state of the Jewish people." This law assumes a DCV model for religion-state relations and contains several provisions that would entrench the status of the Jewish religion (and culture) in law; amending it would require an absolute majority in the parliament (i.e., 61 of 120 members), despite the fact that an absolute majority is not required for it to be initially enacted.[72]

As mentioned, there are three potential problems with this kind of entrenchment. *First*, regarding fairness. Such an entrenchment would make any attempts to form a new majority and change the noted legal arrangement more difficult; the (current) minority disadvantaged by the DCV will, presumably, regard the law primarily as a tool for maneuvering around important democratic rules. Particularly troublesome, and raising the issue of unfairness, is that some DCV arrangements (as in the case of the nationality law) are protected in a constitutional or semiconstitutional way that makes it rather hard to change or amend them, even for new majorities. The initial legislation that created such a carefully protected status did not require meeting the strict conditions that it imposes. The issue here is not, therefore, that the law is absolutely irreversible; rather it is the *lack of fairness* and symmetry between the creation of the protective mechanism and the effort that would be required for its abolition. This asymmetry signals a violation of the democratic principle of equality of citizens' political rights.[73]

Second, regarding the countermajoritarian objection. Constitutional standing (granted to DCV rules in our context) often means that changes or amendments

---

72. See the full text of the suggested law in the website of Israel's ministry of justice. http://index. justice.gov.il/StateIdentity/ProprsedBasicLaws/Pages/NationalState.aspx (accessed February 2, 2016). [Heb.]. The Swiss minarets ban also fits into this general context, as indicated by D. Miller (2016):

> It looks as though the argument . . . can only justify selective restrictions on building minarets, *and not an outright ban* . . . From the minority's point of view, there is a difference between feeling that you have lost the argument on this occasion, and feeling that a decision has been reached that *forever prevents* you from returning to the table with a similar proposal. Insofar as talk of marginalization or subordination applies, it is surely to the case where a minority is barred by a constitutional rule from advancing its legitimate interests. (p. 453; emphasis added)

73. The notion that such means of self-binding are undemocratic has gained the attention of some scholars; some have vehemently objected to such techniques on democratic grounds (Waldron, 2006). However, J. Elster (1989) has noted in this context that

to such special protected laws would be subject to a judicial review process. Because supreme courts are not elected via regular electoral procedures, the famous danger of the countermajoritarian difficulty always arises.[74] This is not a hypothetical scenario; an example of a judicial decision in favor of "nations" in the abstract can be found in the justification by Judge Bonello—of the ECHR—of the Italian law mandating the display of crucifixes in classrooms in the *Lautsi* case discussed earlier.[75] Such decisions can trigger the countermajoritarian objection, and this is especially troublesome because DCV laws are not part of basic democratic rights or principles that might be eligible for such a protection (Waldron, 2006).

Lastly, regarding 'sour grapes' scenarios. It is important to point out that the symbolic significance of the constitutionally entrenched status of DCV arrangements, as exemplified by the nationality law or the Swiss referendum mentioned earlier, might give rise to sour-grapes scenarios. Such an entrenchment, once given a central position within a country's constitution, will influence how the matter is taught; state education will be invested in promoting and maintaining its importance as part of a self-perpetuating dynamic. This might create special difficulties when attempting to amend such laws. This kind of symbolic granting, therefore, might be as disruptive as the two formal problems of unfairness and countermajoritarianism.

---

the analogy between individual and political self-binding is severely limited. An individual can bind himself to certain actions or at least make deviations from them more costly and hence less likely by having recourse to a legal framework that is external to and independent of himself. But nothing is external to society. With the exception of few special cases, like the abdication of power to the International Monetary Fund, societies cannot deposit their will in structures outside their control: they can always undo their ties should they want to. (p. 196)

Elser is right, of course; nevertheless, this principled ability to undo past arrangements that have won special protection is not subtle enough, and it does not solve the procedural irreversibility difficulty, in at least the three ways noted.

74. As Alexander Bickel (1986) wrote in his classic *The Least Dangerous Branch: The Supreme Court at the Bar of Politics*:

[J]udicial review is a counter-majoritarian force in our system . . . when the Supreme Court declares unconstitutional a legislative act or the action of an elected executive, it thwarts the will of representatives of the actual people of the here and now . . . judicial review is undemocratic. (pp. 16–17)

75. Initially, this point might seem strange—was not the court decision in line with the stance of Italy's government position? Given the monopoly and the 'sour grapes' problems associated with this decision, it is not clear to us what was the position of the majority. Supreme courts reaching decisions about "nations" and "cultures" can raise the countermajoritarian problem, as well as many additional problems (see chapter 5).

3.3.2.4. *Concluding remarks on the DCV*

Let us add the following concluding remarks before turning to examine the application of the DCV to thick sites. Suppose that we meet a person that supports the DCV and, suppose further, that the DCV this person advocates does not fail to meet the aggregated conditions we have discussed here—the conditions of shared understandings and tradition are empirically verifiable, and the formal hurdles are passed (no violations of rights, monopoly, sour grapes, irreversibility, or the other procedural problems noted, etc.)—and that the proposed DCV does *not* aim to fulfill an instrumental role. The particular DCV policy this person recommends, therefore, will be modest, permissible, and, empirically speaking, quite rare. We can still ask upfront, without denying the legitimacy of this particular DCV-style policy, why such a view merits our support. One answer occasionally offered to this question is that the DCV, by mixing religion and national identity, provides the members of the dominant group a feeling of "being at home."[76]

How are we to evaluate this remaining aim that is attributed to the DCV model?

First, our imagined interlocutor should bear in mind that the kind of permissible DCV that she or he supports, which does not violate minority rights and

---

76. A famous, though justly controversial, radical appeal to this wish—to "feel at home" in the public sphere—was offered by Fichte (2009):

> If you ask me how this is to be achieved, then the only comprehensive answer is this: we must become on the spot what we ought to be in any case, Germans. We must not subject our spirit . . . we must formulate sturdy and unshakeable principles to guide us in our thinking and action; life and thought must be of a piece, a single interpenetrating and solid whole . . . and cast off foreign artifice. In a word, we must be German. (p. 154)

A different version of the wish to keep the public sphere in a given state can be found in Lord Devlin's (1965) famous essay *The Enforcement of Morals*:

> [L]aw exists for the protection of society. It does not discharge its function by protecting the individual . . . the law must protect also the institutions, and the community of ideas, political and moral, without which people cannot live together . . . if the reasonable man believes that a practice is immoral . . . and is honest and dispassionate—that no right minded member of his society could think otherwise, then for the purpose of the law it is immoral. (pp. 22–23)

Such sentiments or views are found outside of Europe as well. Consider how a right wing Hindu political party (the Bharatiya Janata Party or the BJP) describes itself in its 1998 public election manifesto:

> The BJP is committed to the concept of "One Nation, One People and One Culture" . . . Our nationalist vision. . . is referred by our timeless cultural heritage. This cultural heritage. . . is a civilizational identity and constitutes the cultural nationalism of India which is the core of Hindutva. (Noorani, 2003b, p. 163)

meets the many of the other conditions noted earlier, will fall quite short of establishing the full legal order necessary for making public spaces feel "home like." Miller's analysis of the 2009 Swiss referendum might throw light on this point. Miller (2016) rightly points out that in Switzerland, a legitimate ban on building minarets—which can only mean "*selective* restrictions on building minarets, and *not* an outright ban" (p. 451)—will fail to guarantee the quality of "feeling at home" that DCV supporters wish to achieve. The necessity of this failure stems from the wish to feel at home in the public sphere itself, as it effectively means a preservation of the public sphere in a "nearly frozen" condition that reflects a certain temporal point. In the Swiss example, it is some point in time prior to the building of minarets. Leaving aside the difficulties of pinpointing such temporal points exactly, no legitimate DCV model can achieve this "freezing," as the deliberations here have made clear. A gap will remain, therefore, between the wishes of the DCV supporter to "feel at home" in the public sphere and the possible achievements of a legitimate DCV model.

Second, the wish to make the public sphere a place where one can feel at home, and using the DCV as an instrument for achieving this goal, faces an additional and wider problem. The public sphere, as described in chapter 1, contains everything that lies between the individual and the state. As such, it contains many things: commercial activities, technical innovations, new architectural styles, the arrival of immigrants, and many more factors. In modernity, these things change rapidly and cause the familiar to become unfamiliar for individual citizens. This is an expected consequence of the basic point of departure for the modernity project, as crisply articulated by Peter Gay (2000): "the conviction that the untried is markedly superior to the familiar, the rare to the ordinary, the experimental to the routine" (p. 2). The changes entailed in such a social project might indeed cause feelings of discomfort or anxiety, since the familiar settings of one's childhood are likely to disappear very quickly. These truths are part and parcel of living in modern society and will remain true regardless of what models of religion-state relations are adopted by the state. To succinctly conclude: the public sphere is a poor place for the individual to fulfill the wish of "feeling at home."[77, 78]

---

77. The idea that a "home" is a secured and unchanging place does not reflect the current social reality that includes, for example, high divorce rates, the changes introduced to the "traditional" family, increased geographic movement for employment, telecommunications, income insecurity, etc. The bases for the analogy drawn between "home" and "national culture" are, therefore, not easily acceptable, if at all.

78. It is indeed possible that the loss of the "feeling at home" can create strong emotional responses. As has been pointed out in the text above, however, the adoption of a legitimate version of the DCV does not necessarily do much to avoid or address this emotional response. With regard to the principled notion that such feelings might provide legitimate reasons

If indeed it is true that the DCV model is an unrealistic way of fulfilling the wish and expectation "to feel at home" in the public sphere in the modern era and that a legitimate DCV model meeting all the requirements noted above is exceedingly rare, *then* the model runs the danger of becoming an empty shell. Lord Thurlow, a nineteenth-century British lord chancellor, desperately attached himself to such an empty position when he asserted: "I'm against you by God, sir, I'm in favor of the Established church; and if you'll get your damn religion established, I'll be in favor of that" (quoted in Feinberg, 1990, p. 65).

3.4. DCV and the Management of Contested Sacred Sites

Having examined the DCV as a general model for religion-state relations, we can now turn to the DCV in the context of sacred sites. The suitability and permissibility of the DCV to such sites should be examined through the three general requirements discussed at length in the three previous sections of this chapter— namely, the empirical conditions of "shared-understandings" and "tradition," as well as the procedural and substantive requirements that must be met in order to address the "democratic challenge." We begin our examination with the two empirical conditions, and then address the requirements connected to the democratic challenge.

---

for a given public policy, both H. L. A. Hart and Ronald Dworkin have argued that strong feelings—such as, in our example, the sadness on seeing the public sphere look different or unfamiliar—are not persuasive arguments. The statement that a person does not like "seeing minarets" or "women praying while wearing *talitot*" or "being in a classroom without a crucifix" expresses a feeling, not an argument. Dworkin (1966) makes this point in the following way: "[W]hen the fever is confirmed, when the intolerance, indignation and disgust are genuine . . . nothing more than passionate public disapproval is necessary . . . when it is clearly met the law may proceed without more" (p. 992). Hart (1977) goes further:

> Surely the legislator should ask whether the general morality is based on ignorance, superstition, or misunderstanding; whether there is a false conception that those who practice what is condemns are in other ways dangerous or hostile to society; and whether the misery to many parties . . . are well understood. It is surely extraordinary that among the things which Sir Patrick says are to be considered before we legislate . . . these appear no where. (p. 87)

Furthermore, and perhaps more broadly, the DCV seems to be strongly connected to conservative views that aim to protect established views and customs; this connection makes this model vulnerable to questions of why this particular aspiration of "feeling at home" should be a part of a theory of justice. Certainly not all customs and past traditions can legitimately continue under evolving modern conditions and norms. The DCV view, succinctly put, encounters the same problems faced by many other conservative views (Strauss, 1999, chap. 6, pt. 2).

As the suitability of any given site for the DCV model rests on the fulfillment of two distinct requirements that are empirical in nature—the existence of shared understandings and an enduring tradition—it is necessary to analyze historical, religious, and sociological realities of a particular site in depth. Such empirical issues cannot be answered by "armchair philosophy"; generalizations, made in an a priori fashion, are simply not relevant here. Only a case-by-case empirical investigation can determine if a given, contested sacred site belongs to the category of thick sites. Not all contested sacred sites fit into the category of a thick site. The contest over meaning and access has to be enduring and substantial in order for a given contested sacred site to qualify as a thick site. This point is important as, once it fits the category of a thick site, a site's inherent contestability means that it cannot meet the shared understandings condition required by the DCV model.[79]

In both cases discussed in this book, the Western Wall and the Ram Janmabhoomi / Babri Masjid, neither of the two empirical conditions required for a "fit" between a given site and a DCV model—shared understandings and a demonstrable tradition—is met. Simon Montefiore (2012) eloquently summarizes this point with regard to the context of Jerusalem as a whole:

In Jerusalem, the truth is often much less important than the myth . . . History is so pungently powerful here, that it is repeatedly distorted; archaeology is itself a historical force and archeologists have at times wielded as much power as soldiers, recruited to appropriate the past for the present . . . Israelis, Palestinians and the evangelical imperialists of the nineteenth century have all been guilty of commandeering the same events and assigning them contradictory meanings and facts" (XXVI).

Likewise, the dual name Ram Janmabhoomi / Babri Masjid itself demonstrates the lack of shared understandings and unified tradition regarding this site. Larson (1995) summarizes this point effectively:

Whether or not the Babri Masjid itself, however, was built from the ruins of an original Hindu temple to Rama and whether or not this particular place in ancient times was considered the birth-place of Rama are matters impossible to determine. Inconclusive 'evidence' can be and has been cited on both sides of the controversy. (pp. 266–267)

---

79. See the definitional terms of "thick sites" in chapter 1 (1.1).

While the case-by-case method precludes making a generalization—such as claiming that contested sacred sites never demonstrate the existence of shared understandings and tradition regarding their management—many, if not all, such sites seem to be prone to the breaking of shared understandings due to their tendencies to raise strong emotional responses from believers. This alone gives reason to suspect the suitability of the DCV to such sites in advance.[80]

We can turn, therefore, to the substantive and procedural conditions that must be met for the DCV model to be a permissible solution for contested sacred sites. It needs to be borne in mind, however, that in many cases, the factual findings indicate that the required empirical conditions were not met and that the rejection of the DCV can be inferred at the "empirical" stage. The following substantive and procedural considerations are not, in such cases, strictly necessary.

Nevertheless, if we wish to examine the permissibility of applying the DCV model to contested sacred sites thoroughly, then we should note that sacred sites reflect and amplify religious tensions more than other sites in the public space. They require special caution when considering varying models of management; anything sensitive and problematic in religion-state relations is even more so at such sites.[81] The reason for this increased sensitivity is that one excusing condition for the DCV is not available in sacred sites: the background condition of plurality. By this, we mean the following: all supporters of the "permissible DCV" that were cited earlier—Weiler (2010, 2011); Miller (2016); and the ECHR *Lautsi* decision (2011, 30814/06)—insist that the DCV (to be legitimate) must coincide with a tolerant and pluralist environment. For example, even if it is mandatory that a crucifix hang on each classroom wall in the public-school system, it does not undermine the freedom of religion in Italy; mosques, synagogues, and the like, still exist. Put differently, as a general rule, the DCV is compatible with an open public sphere in which different religions can geographically coexist without interfering with each other. With sacred sites, however, this coexistence in an open space is much more challenging: one simply cannot build an additional Western Wall or Ram Janmabhoomi / Babri Masjid as one would build another mosque, temple, shrine, church, or synagogue. Any inequality in access, permissible religious activity, representation in councils managing such sites, and so on, would expectedly be seen by believers as blunt discrimination, which would cause significant agitation.

---

80. Sites such as the Temple Mount, the Church of the Holy Sepulchre, and the Cave of the Patriarchs all demonstrate this tendency (Berkovits, 2006; see also Noorani, 2003a, 2003b, 2014, for several examples from India).

81. This point follows the famous Talmudic law of "how much more" (*Kal va-ḥomer*). See Ben Menahem (2008).

The last point is well addressed by Cheryl Birkner Mack, one of the members of the Original Women of the Wall,[82] when the group was refusing to accept the compromise that would delegate the WoW to the third plaza at Robinson's Arch; she insisted that the only place where the group wishes to pray is the women's section at the central Wall plaza: "Nothing has changed. Bigger, better and prettier doesn't increase the Arch's holiness."[83] In any other case, the minor differences between the two locations (both after all, being portions of the same Wall) would probably lead a curious bystander to call her view stubborn or spiteful. This is not the case with a site like the Western Wall. In such sites, anything but complete equality (or something very close to it) is manifestly problematic and creates resentment and instability.

This point hints that the application of the DCV to contested sacred sites—even in the rare cases in which the conditions of shared understandings and tradition are met—will border on the violation of the rights of religious minorities. However, the judgment will depend on the details of the case at hand. What shape does the DCV take in a particular site? This cannot be determined a priori, because it depends on proper description and analysis of the precise arrangements at a given site.

What can be indicated, in a general fashion, is that the increased sensitivity of such sites means that the measure of legitimately acceptable inegalitarianism in other religion-state issues to which the DCV applies (say, budgets, symbolic prominence, etc.) would not be permissible at contested sacred sites. If we consider the details of DCV models, as applied to such sites, we shall see that they must address various complex aspects, such as permissible religious conduct, rights of access, membership in governing bodies over such sites, control over the structure of the site, and so on.[84] An inegalitarian approach toward any of these aspects, such as permissible religious conduct (especially if it takes the shape of a complete ban, but also in cases of less severe, partial prohibitions), amounts to a significant restriction of religious liberties (and therefore fails the "democratic challenge" criterion). For example, we believe that parts of the current (in 2016) arrangements at the Western Wall, such as the granting access to Torah scrolls at the central plaza to men only, are good examples of DCV style

---

82. The group that separated itself from the Women of the Wall and refused to accept the third plaza compromise. See chapter 2.

83. Quoted in M. Chabin, "At 25, Women of the Wall Struggling with Compromise," *Jewish Week*, June 11, 2013, retrieved from http://www.thejewishweek.com/news/israel-news/25-women-wall-struggling-compromise.

84. See chapter 2 above and the appendix for a survey of these aspects with regard to the Western Wall and the Ram Janmabhoomi/Babri Masjid, respectively.

arrangements at a contested sacred site that clearly should be seen as impermissible discrimination.[85]

It is noteworthy (and perhaps obvious) that sites in which shared understandings and tradition exist, and that a proposed DCV arrangement does not constitute impermissible discrimination (and the other substantial and procedural requirements noted earlier, including the failure of instrumental reasons are met), are rare. Perhaps there are cases which meet all of the noted conditions, but it seems implausible that there are many such cases.

Because of this rareness, and given that most DCV-like arrangements are prone to violating the religious liberties of minority members wishing to access contested sacred sites, we conclude that the DCV model should be strongly rejected as a potential solution for such sites; this conclusion is, indeed, more severe than our conclusion regarding the DCV as a general model of religion-state relations. Generally, we argue that it is advisable to look for even-handed or privatized solutions to address competing claims to such sites, as discussed in chapters 4 and 5, respectively. The rejection of the DCV model, it is worth reminding, will not limit the religious liberties of the group supported under the DCV model. Under the DVC model, the liberties of nonsupported groups are not protected. This asymmetry importantly increases in contested sacred sites, and should count as a significant, further argument against the DCV model.

3.5. Conclusion

This chapter examined the dominant culture view model for religion-state relations and found it an unsuitable and highly problematic solution for conflicts regarding contested sacred sites. The DCV model inherently demands that certain empirical conditions be met in order for it to be relevant to a particular location, whether an entire country or a specific site. Whether such empirical conditions—shared understandings and a robust tradition—are met cannot be determined in an a priori fashion. Instead, they require an empirical examination of a given case. We examined whether such conditions are met in the case of the Western Wall in sections 3.1 and 3.2 and reached a negative conclusion. Section 3.3 explored whether the DCV, and its inherent inegalitarianism, could adequately answer the "democratic challenge," that is, whether a sufficient justification can be provided for the deviation from the default democratic assumption

---

85. Note that the question, what would a DCV model at the Western Wall look like? does not arise since the two pre-conditions—shared understandings and tradition—are not met. The example here is a mere illustration.

that citizens holding different religious views will be treated equally. Section 3.3 examined several different answers (instrumental, majoritarian, etc.)—given by advocates of the DCV to the democratic challenge. Our conclusion is that while the model might be permissible, the many conditions that must be met for it to be suitable and permissible ensure that a genuinely appropriate and legitimate DCV model is a rare phenomenon.

With regard to contested sacred sites, our conclusion is that the characteristics of sacred sites—such as their contested histories, their centrality, and the fact that they cannot be replaced by other locations of worship—make the suitability of DCV models to such sites highly implausible. These are highly sensitive locations and the measure of inegaliterianism that (perhaps) might be tolerated with regard to general religion-state relations cannot be tolerated in the context of contested sacred sites. Save rare cases, therefore, it is advisable to approach and manage such sites via evenhanded or privatized models.

4

Evenhandedness, Thick Sites, and the Women of the Wall

PERMISSIBLE BUT INAPPLICABLE?

THIS CHAPTER EXAMINES the second of the three prevalent and influential models of religion-state relations that are considered in this book: *evenhandedness*. The investigation of this model will focus on its applicability to thick sites in general and the Western Wall in particular. The evenhandedness strategy emphasizes the importance of treating all the state's citizens with equal concern and respect, and it endeavors to keep the state strictly unaffiliated with any given denomination. Unlike the privatization approach, however, the evenhandedness model does not adopt a hands-off approach with regard to religion. Rather, this strategy adopts a hands-on approach in which governmental resources are allocated to different religious denominations and groups. The government and the state themselves, as noted, remain unaffiliated with any one denomination and show no preference for any specific religious group.

Joseph Carens (1997) coined the term "evenhandedness" to denote the guiding idea

> that what fairness entails is a sensitive balancing of competing claims for recognition and support in matters of culture and identity. Instead of trying to abstract from particularity, we should embrace it but in a way that is fair to all the different particularities. Now being fair does not mean that every cultural claim and identity will be given equal weight, but rather that each will be given appropriate weight under the circumstances and given a commitment to equal respect for all. History matters, numbers matter, the relative importance of the claim to those who present it matters, and so do many other considerations. (p. 818)

To put Carens's formula in a slightly different way that is more directly applicable to religion-state relations,[1] in an evenhanded approach, the government is expected to provide resources to religious groups, as long as it treats all religions in a similar fair and equitable manner. Note that the evenhanded approach does not insist that all religions receive the exact same quantity of goods; rather, it requires that the allocation of goods follows reasonable, fair, and equitable logic.

The general rationale for adopting the evenhanded approach is the belief that the government should protect citizens' chief interests, as well as their rights, and that citizens' well-being in general should be protected as a part of the role of the welfare state. Governmental resources, according to this view, should therefore be allocated to the state's citizens for use in fulfilling their goals, and the manner of allocation should be equitable and fair. Religious freedom is part and parcel of the interests and well-being of substantial portions of many countries' populations, and so it follows that the state must actively support the capacity of individual citizens to practice their religion.[2]

Two examples will prove illustrative. In Belgium, the government pays the salaries of clergymen of several different denominations (Fox, 2013, pt. 2); in Israel, the state pays the salary of Jewish and Muslim judges in Halakhic and Sharia courts (Cohen & Susser, 2000; Layish, 2006). Other examples include the state's sponsoring of religious education; funding of religious services; maintaining of historic religious sites; granting of tax deductions or exemptions to recognized religions; providing of chaplaincies in hospitals, prisons, and the armed forces; and various other techniques (Fox, 2013; Doe, 2011, chap. 7). As long as such provisions are granted to different religions in an equitable manner, and the state remains unaffiliated with any one religion, religion-state relations should be classified under the evenhanded category.[3]

---

1. Carens (2000) and other scholars, such as Parekh (2000) and Tully (1995), tend to focus on "identity" and "culture" in general. Nevertheless, their theories lend themselves easily to the religious sphere, which is our focus here. In this context, it is noteworthy that those scholars discuss numerous religious examples in their works. Similar formulations of the evenhanded approach were also suggested, in some variation, by Montefiore (1975, p. 6); Bhargava (1998, p. 501); Patten (2014).

2. "Capacity" can be understood in different ways. See below for the difference between result-oriented and procedurally oriented evenhandedness. Here, capacity indicates support beyond mere permissibility—that is, a lack of external impediments (laws)—to use Hobbes' famous formulation (1968, pp. 261–262, chap. 21); the mere absence of prohibitions will not typically satisfy the demands of the evenhanded model.

3. In the US political and constitutional context, religious evenhandedness exists under the title of "nonpreferentialism" (other names used for this system are "general" or "multiple

Note that the evenhanded model does not merely assert that the freedom to practice one's religion is important. Rather, it argues that, in order to satisfy the individual citizen's religious interest, religious freedom (broadly conceived) requires that *the state steps in* and involves itself in the provision of goods and other supportive regulations for religious organizations.[4] With this step, the evenhanded approach goes beyond the privatization model and employs a hands-on rather than hands-off approach. The evenhanded approach, therefore, would have to justify not only the importance of religious freedom per se but also, perhaps mainly, validate this added step of state involvement in the provision of religious goods.[5]

Having clarified the basic tenets of the evenhanded approach, and pointed to some examples of its policy implications, we wish to differentiate two very different kinds of evenhanded approaches that have been developed in the relevant literature. Both share the characteristics identified so far but diverge on the question of whether the evenhanded approach should be *procedural* or *end-result*

---

establishments," and "evenhandedness"). As defined by D. Laycock (1986), "The claim is that the framers of the religion clause intended a specific meaning with respect to the . . . establishment clause: government may not prefer one religion over others, but it may aid all religions evenhandedly" (p. 877); Leonard Levy (1994) offers a similar definition:

> [T]he legislative history of the clause . . . prove an intent to impose upon the national government merely a ban against aiding an exclusive or preferential establishment, which results in their conclusion that government assistance to religion generally, without a hint of discrimination, would not violate the establishment clause. (p. 113)

Both Laycock and Levy strongly reject nonpreferentialism. Levy (1994) summarizes James Madison's famous rejection of nonpreferentialism as follows:

> Madison did not oppose the establishment because it was exclusively a Christian one. He opposed, rather, any government tax for religion because he feared a threat to liberty deriving from an unwarranted exercise of power in a domain forbidden to government. (p. 128).

This fear of threats to liberty, especially in the noted "forbidden domain" of religion, will play an important part in the deliberations of this chapter. See L. Levy (1994) and Curry (1986) for detailed analyses of the entire Madisonian nonpreferentialist debate.

4. As James Madison indicated in his rejection of the nonpreferentialist position in Virginia, this is a questionable argument: "Are religious *establishments* necessary for religion? *no*" (quoted in L. Levy, 1994, pp. 62–63; emphasis added).

5. Note that the evenhanded approach provides support to religions *as such* and should not be confused with approaches that justify the *incidental* allocation of resources to religious activities and institutions as they fulfill some other, nonreligious function (say, charity, education, etc). The leading US Supreme Court decision exemplifying such "incidental" support is *Zelman v. Simmons-Harris* (536 U.S. 639), in which the legitimacy of using state vouchers for religious schools was tested and answered in the affirmative.

oriented. Such different orientations will support very different policies, which the discussion that follows aims to clarify and elaborate.[6]

This chapter is organized around providing a definition of both the end-result and procedural models; examining their justificatory grounding; and identifying their policy implications, blind spots, and weaknesses.[7] Following this multifaceted presentation of each model, we will explore their suitability for application to thick sites generally and the Western Wall in particular. Schematically, this will be divided into explorations of the end-result-orientation of the evenhanded model (4.1), the procedurally oriented evenhanded model (4.2), and the potential applicability of the models to thick sites generally and the Western Wall in particular (4.3).

4.1. End-Result-Oriented Evenhandedness

Having succinctly clarified the broad meaning of evenhandedness, we can turn now to a detailed examination of the end-result-oriented version of the evenhanded model. We open our discussion with a succinct definition of this orientation or version,[8] followed immediately with clarifying comments. We then will turn to consider the justifications of this approach and its policy implications (4.1.1), and conclude by examining the critiques that have been directed toward this approach (4.1.2).

As a preparatory remark, however, it is noteworthy that the conceptual and inherent commitment to results associated with end-result evenhandedness is grounded in the general literature dedicated to equality within current theories of distributive justice. Our usage of the term, and its application to the religious sphere, borrows from such general discussions of equality of consequences or results. Of course, the issue of equality of consequences has attracted significant

---

6. Our interest here is with the different major models of the evenhanded approach, their internal logic and structure, and their political and distributive implications. While we believe that these models are coherent and useful as theoretical tools, and also reflect the dominant trends in the relevant literature, we do not intend to present them as indicative of the entire scope of scholarship on this theory, even within the writings of the scholars whom we identify.

7. In advance, we can note various objections that may be raised against the evenhanded approach. For the purposes of exposition, we divide the objections into two categories: those that focus on the result-oriented evenhanded model, and those that focus on the procedural evenhanded model (and our discussion of these objections is divided accordingly). The division of these objections into these two categories follows the salience and prominence of certain attributes of each evenhanded strategy, but there is some unavoidable overlap, which we shall point to when the need arises.

8. We will use the terms *end-result* and *result* evenhandedness interchangeably.

attention and generated a tremendous amount of literature. We do not aim to summarize all or even some of it;[9] rather, our aim is to simply provide a succinct definition of *result-oriented evenhandedness*, followed by clarifying comments regarding the relevance of this theory for religion-state relations.

Equality of results (or effects), in its application to the religious-identity realm, roughly denotes the following: *the goal of a distributive policy in the religious sphere is that each religious person would be satisfied, as measured by the parameters of his or her given religion, from the noted distribution of religious goods.*

Three brief comments on this definition must be added immediately. *First*, there is an implicit assumption that religion is constitutive of the believer's identity and that the failure to satisfy religious needs amounts to substantial damage to the individual. Thus, any neglect of these needs should be avoided by a schematic allocation of religious goods. This "constitutive view" of religion, in its different variations, provides important grounding for the end-results approach to the evenhanded model, and we examine it in detail. *Second*, "satisfaction" is measured according to the parameters or internal requirements of a given religion, rather than by any external consideration of the "equitable nature" or the "fair manner" of the allocation. This is a corollary of the end-result approach to evenhandedness. *Third*, while the definition points to individual satisfaction, the measurement of such satisfaction will be mediated by the parameters of one's given religious group. This indirect route enables some reasonable policies to be developed out of this view. Obviously, identifying the precise parameters of each religious group involves complex procedural and substantive issues, which we examine here (Jobani & Perez, 2014; Eisenberg, 2009).

The distinctive characteristics of the result-oriented version of the evenhanded model will hopefully become clearer as we point to a specific illustration, to put some flesh on these rather abstract bones. Consider the following example: a given religious education system does not prepare its graduates for the modern labor market, and, consequently, there is a gradual decrease in the number of students within the system. Without the state's increased economic support for the given religious education system, and to its graduates, as a means to offset the negative "exit" dynamics, this group's religious education system

---

9. See Dworkin (2000, chaps. 1 and 2) for a more complete survey of the standard examination of result-oriented equality. See Sen (1992, chap. 6) for a survey of "equality of consequences" in the economic context. Among the many critiques of the "equality-of-results" view, we focus only on those that have direct relevance to the religious sphere. However, one general critique—which notes that the sources of the preferences to be satisfied are problematic—is also crucial to our topic and was therefore examined in detail in chapter 3, in the discussion of sour grapes and the *Lautsi* ECHR case study.

would, simply put, cease to exist. In such scenarios, even though there is no legal or formal oppression of the "dwindling" religion, the result-oriented approach to evenhandedness, properly understood, would demand that the state step in and increase its support of the given religious group. To point to a real life example, *if* the current dynamics in Israel continue—in which a growing number of ultra-Orthodox Jews choose to study in academic colleges and to integrate to the Israeli markets—the number of students in ultra-Orthodox post-high-school religious educational institutions (*Yeshivot*) will diminish to the point of creating a scenario similar to that just outlined (Perez, 2014; Cohen, 2006; and Jobani & Perez, 2014).

This orientation toward results (in this case, protecting a given religious way of life) is exemplified by Avishai Margalit and Moshe Halbertal. They argue that the right to culture justifies assistance to minority cultures that face a danger of "dwindling" or "disappearing" (Margalit and Halbertal, 2004, p. 530); they indicate, specifically, that such assistance is intended as "support for the way of life by the state's institutions so that the culture may flourish" (2004, p. 536). Note that though Margalit and Halbertal use the term "culture," they use ultra Orthodox Jews—a religious group—as one prime example. Their argument is therefore obviously suited to religion-state relations as a whole.

4.1.1. The Result-Oriented Evenhanded Model: Justifications and Policy Implications

In order to provide a fuller picture of the result-oriented approach within the evenhanded model, and to get a clearer view of its policy implications, one should examine its justifications. Obviously, different justifications can support this model; however, for our purposes, one specific justification of this approach can be emphasized—namely, the argument from identity.[10]

Most scholarship on the concept of identity emphasizes the importance of protecting minority groups' rights to culture and religion; this implicitly accepts the empirical reality that no modern state is religiously and culturally homogenous.[11] Views that emphasize identity, therefore, obviously lend support to

---

10. Arguably, "recognition" constitutes another such justification which also has some end result characteristics. See Taylor (1992); Parekh (2000, pp. 259–260); Tully (1995, chap. 1); Perez (2012). We can't enter this further debate here, however, recognition, in its end-result version, would face many of the same kinds of objections noted above. See Orwin (2001).

11. In the discussion that follows, we limit our focus to several scholars who were among the most important working in the "first wave" of the identity-multicultural school of thought; theorizing in this vein certainly continues. See Modood (2013), Eisenberg (2009); Spinner Halev (2000); Pinto (2010, 2016).

evenhanded approaches in which the government commits to the equal support of different identity and religious groups (and as noted above, our focus is on religious groups).[12] For this reason, we examine the arguments of noted identity scholars under the classification of the evenhandedness model.

The substantive core of the identity school of thought's argument is that religion is a constitutive element in many persons' identities. Therefore violations of the integrity of one's religious identity might cause significant harm to one's well-being. Bhiku Parekh (2000), one of the main advocates for multicultural policies in the United Kingdom, exemplifies this argument when he writes:

> [H]uman beings are culturally embedded in the sense that they grow up and live within a culturally structured world, organize their lives and social relations in terms of its system of meaning and significance, and place considerable value on their cultural identity . . . [T]hey are deeply shaped by it, can overcome some but not all of its influences, and necessarily view the world from within a culture. (p. 336)

He further notes that beliefs, cultural norms, and practices

> are constitutive of the individual's sense of identity and even of self-respect and cannot be overcome without a deep sense of *moral loss* . . . it . . . comes closer to a natural inability, [and] society should bear at least most of the cost of accommodating it. (p. 241; emphasis added).[13]

Max Muller (1823–1900), one of the founders of the scholarly field of comparative religion, coined a memorable term that is noteworthy in this context: *mother-religion* (echoing *mother-tongue*), which aptly captures the general view that religion is constitutive of one's persona. According to this view, similar to the way in which one does not choose one's mother, one does not choose one's religion (Muller, 2003, p. 231; see also Masuzawa, 2003, pp. 320–321).

---

12. Identity and religion are somewhat overlapping categories, as can be inferred from reading such scholars as Parekh (2000) and Tully (1995), among others. The many examples that they point to illustrate this overlap. We make no claim, however, that they are identical. We insist merely that there is sufficient similarity to justify applying theorizing about the former to the latter even as our discussion focuses on religious groups.

13. Parekh speaks of identity more generally than we do, but his book *Rethinking Multiculturalism* utilizes many distinctly religious examples, such as the Hijab, Kippah, and Turban (2000, pp. 249–256). See also his discussion of Rushdie, Islam, and free speech in chap. 10 of the book.

A result-oriented evenhanded approach will attract considerable support due to the constitutive function of religion within one's identity: if a given person is unable to continue to practice her religion, she will feel that important interests have been substantially hindered.[14] Here, Muller's concept of *mother-religion* is helpful in suggesting the analogy of religion nurturing and creating one's self understanding; *severance* from this context is analogous, being as painful as being separated from one's mother, which is obviously a setback of an important interest.

As mentioned above, one crucial aspect of the result-oriented evenhanded approach is the assumption that a hands-on approach to religion is required in order to prevent the "moral loss" and "setback of interests" of being severed from one's religion. This would be particularly evident in cases in which a given religious way of life is incompatible with the characteristics of a modern capitalistic society (Kymlicka, 1995, p. 109; Margalit & Halbertal, 2004, pp. 543–547). In such cases, a given religious person's identity and sense of self might be harmed without the aid of state support,[15] as one would find her or his religious community withering away under an indifferent state (i.e., a state that separates religion and state). This concern was illustrated by the example noted earlier of the shrinking number of students in religious schools.

In other cases, the threat to the survival of a group's way of life may come from the state rather than from various social and economic factors.[16] Such cases arise when the state adopts a given (historic or civil) religion and actively encourages a corresponding set of practices, values, and loyalties through the legal system.[17] Such sets of practices and values are, in many cases, in conflict with some religious groups' internal workings. Moreover, modern states typically constitute an expansive bureaucratic apparatus which frequently may collide with the internal workings of given religious groups and, consequently, lead to costly economic and legal challenges for members of such groups.

---

14. For the famous definition of harm employed here, see Feinberg (1984, pp. 31–35).

15. On the interconnectedness between identity, sense of self, and religion, see Taylor (2001, p. 245).

16. See Berger (1990, p. 138); Gill (2008).

17. See Margalit and Halbertal (2004); Perez (2014). Obviously, not all aspects of a state's civil religion find full expression in the legal system. For example, commemoration days of a civil religion can have a very particular nature that makes the experience of religious minorities awkward and uncomfortable. In this sense, the neutrality of the law is indeed "fuzzy." However, we shall focus on clearer cases of explicit state and legal involvement in the religious sphere. For a consideration of fuzzy, inexact, and vague laws, see the clear discussion in Oren Perez (2015, pp. 352–356).

Two examples may be noted to show how common and pervasive this conflict can be. *First,* states usually adopt days of rest that reflect the calendar of the majority religion. On such days, governmental offices, public schools, and many businesses are directed to be closed. Such circumstances are obviously convenient for those who belong to the majority religion, less relevant for non-observant persons, and challenging for individuals belonging to other religions that follow a different weekly cycle. The members of this third group will, therefore, have to negotiate rest days with their respective employers, a difficulty that followers of the majority religion do not share. This might be highly challenging for manual laborers and other workers whose socioeconomic status, and lack of competitive qualifications, might lead them to face complicated choices between loyalty to their religion and (simply put) having a job (Gavison & Perez, 2008; Jones, 1994).

Second, modern states have expansive legal and bureaucratic systems that penetrate more and more of what were previously "free spheres" within a society (Scott, 1999; Epstein, 1990, 1995). As such, cases in which the state apparatus collides with the internal workings of a given religion are becoming more and more frequent. Prevalent examples here would include mandatory service in an army, centralized education standards and curricula, animal slaughtering rules, medical ethics and treatment standards, and the list could be expanded significantly. Such collisions with certain religions are well known and well documented; religious groups typically request exemptions from such rules and regulation (Caney, 2002; Barry, 2001; Greenawalt, 2007).

In *all* of the scenarios noted above, in which a religious practice is threatened by certain social, economic, or political dynamics, the identity approach *requires* a state response that would correct this scenario and enable the continuation of the religious practice, that is, the creation of state policies that are fully sensitive and responsive to claims based on religious identity. The overarching aim of such policies, according to the identity view, should be the protection and maintenance of the full cluster of interwoven elements that constitute a person's identity; first among them, in our case, is religion.

In order to fulfill the goals of the identity school of thought, as just described, several scholars suggest two central and complementary policies. *First,* they strongly favor accommodations of religious requests that necessitate deviations or exemptions from generally applicable laws. As James Tully (1995) puts it, "If a valuable cultural difference is constitutive of the ways a person speaks and acts . . . not to recognise and accommodate it is the injustice of cultural imperialism." (p. 169). "When a culturally derived incapacity," Bhikhu Parekh (2000) claims, "comes closer to a natural inability, society should bear at least most of the cost for accommodating it" (p. 241).

Second, a result-oriented understanding of the evenhandedness approach will strongly support an allocation of resources (of which granting exemptions from generally applicable laws is but one tactic) that serves a particular end-state, that is, that vulnerable or dwindling religious groups would continue to exist so that their members can maintain their identity. As Avishai Margalit and Moshe Halbertal (2004) write:

> The right to culture demands that the state abandon its neutral position and actively assist needy cultures ... a liberal state may not be neutral with respect to the cultures of minorities, especially those in danger of dwindling or even disappearing. The state is obligated to abjure its neutrality ... in order to make it possible for members of minority groups to retain their identity (p. 530; see also Tully, 1995, p. 190; Ann Phillips, 2004; G. A. Cohen, 1999).

4.1.2. The End-Results Evenhanded Model: Critiques

Having summarized the justifications for the end-result evenhanded approach and some of its implications, we turn now to explore four objections to this approach that address: (i) its untenable view of personal identity, (ii) its neglect of religious freedom, (iii) its inability to answer adequately the fundamental "baseline" problem, and (iv) its counterintuitive base argument. We shall take each in turn.

First, the identity argument—which argues for the critical significance of religion in the formation, maintenance and integrity of identity—proves untenable in such rigid terms. While religion is certainly important for personal identity, there is no clear reason to consider it *the* constitutive element of identity. Certainly, many individuals have an almost mechanical relation to their religion in the sense that they follow its rituals and duties out of habitual devotion rather than an active personal need.[18] Furthermore, the fact of conversion demonstrates that individuals can change their religion, become indifferent to it, or even adopt a secular way of life without incurring the "moral loss" or "setback of interests" that identity scholars point to in their arguments. A change in religious affiliation

---

18. Similar claims were often raised in the context of the *Haskalah* (European Jewish Enlightenment). See Sholem Yankev Abramovich (1836–1917), better known by his nom de plume Mendele Mocher Sforim, especially *"In Those Days"* (1910) (available at http://benye-huda.org/mos/bayamim_hahem_I.html [Heb]). In contemporary legal theory, see Laborde (2014, p. 15).

does not necessarily involve a change in one's identity[19]; and even if such a change leads to a significant change in identity, it is not necessarily a damaging change. On the contrary, according to the influential theory which Sandel (1989) labels the "voluntarist" conception of the person, such change often defines the identity of the person more than immediate group membership, "We are not defined by the particular traditions we inhabit or the convictions we espouse; instead, we are independent of our aims and attachments, capable, at least in principle, of standing back to assess and revise them." (p. 598).[20]

Religious change, to restate this point, is not necessarily experienced as damaging to one's identity. Spinoza (1632–1677), for example, indicated no moral loss or setback of interests suffered when he abandoned the Jewish religion and sought salvation (*salus*) beyond the confines of the great historical religions of his time and place (see Yovel, 1992; Jobani, 2008, 2016; Nadler, 2001). There is no doubt that, in some cases, a change of religion can be a case of moral loss that strongly damages one's identity. The forced conversion of Spanish Jews to Christianity in the fifteenth and sixteenth centuries offers such an example. But what created the moral loss, the setback of interests, and the damage to identity in this case is the background events of violence, coercion and duress, not necessarily the fact of change per se. In the cases that interest us here—religious groups dwindling because other religions and ways of life prove more attractive due to aggregated economic and social interests—such problematic background conditions do not arise (Sen, 2007; Jones, 1994; Waldron, 1995).

Second, the argument that religion is central and irreplaceable for an individuals' identity (discussed earlier) inherently treats religion (and, implicitly, religious institutions) as an unchosen attribute of the self, rather than as a matter of individual *freedom*. James Tully provides an illuminative description of this consequence of the "constitutive" religious-identity approach; by presenting religion as an all-encompassing phenomenon, this view suggests that

> people come already constituted in diverse ways by their "identity related" or, in my terms, "cultural" differences' of language, religion and gender. If a valuable cultural difference is constitutive of the ways a person speaks and

---

19. As David Biale (2011) aptly argued, for some luminaries such as Freud and Einstein, the rejection of religiosity and religious rituals "was accompanied by a profound affirmation of Jewish identity" (p. 44).

20. Sandel does not approve of this approach; we are well aware that our "recruitment" of his definition in this context goes against the grain of his argument. Sandel (and others) holds the so-called "communitarian stance," a view which has been met with considerable skepticism. We cannot enter the famous debate between communitarians and liberals here, for a helpful overview see Avineri and de-Shalit (1992); Mulhall and Swift (1996).

acts, then, like custom in ancient constitutionalism, not to recognise and accommodate it is the injustice of cultural imperialism. (1995, p. 169; see also Sandel, 1989, p. 608; Pinto, 2016)

Such a view of religion as an unchosen, central, and irreplaceable aspect of personal identity tends to undermine the significance of religious *freedom* in religion-state relations. Identity theorists describe the relation of a given person to his/her religion almost organically; simply, we are constituted as humans to need our particular religion. In this view, we can't choose to separate ourselves from our *mother-religion*. This seems fundamentally at odds with the ways in which democratic countries and international treaties conceptualize the relations between persons and religion, as well as the ways in which many religious individuals understand their religiosity. The Universal Declaration of Human Rights (UN 1948) serves as an exemplary illustration of the institutional emphasis on religious freedom: "Everyone has the right to freedom of thought, conscience and religion; this right includes freedom to change his religion or belief." (article 18).[21] The second sentence indicates that, instead of a constitutive role for religion in the persona of religious individuals, the focus of the relevant right is primarily the free will of the individual to join or leave a given religion. This context clarifies the importance lying within the counterposition that Abdullahi Ahmed An-Naim (2008) offers, in *Islam and the Secular State*, to the identity argument, "In order to be a Muslim by conviction and free choice, which is the only way one can be a Muslim, I need a secular state. By a secular state I mean one that is neutral regarding religious doctrine." (p. 1). Indeed, if the goal is to respect religious persons' religious affiliation and sense of belonging, it is far from clear that state involvement is required or would be welcomed. Religious minorities in the United States, as an empirical example, accept the idea that the separation model allows religious observance to flourish (Finke & Stark, 2005; chapter 5).

The *third* challenge to the result-oriented evenhanded approach is the baseline problem, that is, the need to establish a specific point in time which should be counted, from an institutional-statist perspective, as the decisive moment of religious existence (in a broader sense) that merits state protection.

---

21. The alleged priority that the identity school grants to the protection of religion over religious freedom or choice should be read against the background of a more general trend revealed in how the various instruments of international law function. As aptly described and analyzed by Lerner (2000), the status that various instruments of international law give to *religious choice*, rather than the protection of *religion per se*, has declined (for a critique of this trend, see Sen, 2007).

A satisfying answer to the baseline problem should include clear and decisive answers to a wide and complex set of questions, such as what should be adopted as the decisive tenets, understandings, and convictions that constitute a religion's state of affairs? what is the religious state of affairs in terms of group size? and what should be designated as sacred sites (number, location, and boundaries)?[22] All such issues are highly controversial and different answers would be suggested to these loaded questions by different members of almost any given religious group, as well as by external observers of such groups. It is, therefore, highly unlikely that there is an answer to the baseline problem that is not arbitrary, and certainly not an uncontroversial one that is available to a state apparatus. The only acceptable institutional response to the baseline problem is to reject arbitrary declarations regarding some imaginary original focal point from which a given religious group ought to be institutionally measured, and to leave such controversies to the conscience of the individual believer.

It is important to note that these intractable problems are not only "philosophical" or "theological," they are also—perhaps mainly—institutional. Once the state adopts a given solution for the baseline problem, it acquires an obligation to continually intervene in religious affairs. Many times (as mentioned above in the "dwindling" scenario), this will take the form of allocating resources in order to maintain or recreate some end state faithful to the arbitrarily adopted baseline. Institutional legitimization of a specific baseline will also necessarily leave some believers outside of the protection of recognized religion altogether. As the evenhanded approach requires the allocation of goods to religious groups, any such institutional decision has important financial, legal, and potentially discriminatory implications that must be borne in mind throughout the current discussion.[23]

The *fourth* challenge that we pose to the end-results evenhanded model is that there is something counterintuitive, perhaps even absurd, in an arrangement that has the state invest more resources as a given religious group loses members. As noted above, identity theorists neglect the role of religious choice in the construction of identity and, as a consequence, the significance of such choice in the perpetuation of religious institutions. The identity justification for the evenhanded

---

22. The baseline problem is especially pertinent to thick sites, given that the geographic-physical status quo in thick sites is typically shaped through the historical accumulation of many injustices and acts of violence. As such, there is no reason to assume that a status quo merits any kind of protection (this point is evident in Ayodhya and Jerusalem, see Friedland & Hecht (1998)). We will return to this point in chapter 5.

23. The discussion in this paragraph owes much to Nozick's famous argumentation regarding the dangers of an expansive state apparatus, and his critique of social end-state policies; as applicable to the religious sphere (Nozick, 1974, pp. 153–155).

model could mean support for a nearly empty shell of a religious institution with very few believers; this counterintuitive result is surely relevant to the evaluation of this approach.

Before turning to the procedural approach to the evenhanded model (4.2), a further nuance is in order. Our discussion, so far, points to the many shortcomings of the identity-grounded and result-oriented evenhanded model. This argument should not be interpreted as a sweeping rejection of all policies of accommodation. Rather, and we shall point to specific cases later on, this argument more naturally serves the conclusion that exemptions and accommodations for religious requests should be justified on other grounds. To point to one chief example, the existence of unfair background rules—stemming, usually, from the state siding with one specific religion among many in a given country—can justify an exemption or accommodation, granted to minority religions.

4.2. *The Procedural Evenhanded Model*

This section examines the second type of approach to evenhandedness: the procedural evenhanded model. We shall divide this discussion into the following aspects: we begin with a description of the procedural evenhanded approach with particular (although not exclusive) attention given to Alan Patten's seminal book *Equal Recognition* (2014)[24]; second, we shall provide some representative examples that will serve as anchors for the theoretical discussion; third, we examine the justifications for this approach (4.2.1); and *lastly*, we point to the weaknesses and blind spots of this approach (4.2.2).

Let us start with a brief description of the procedural evenhanded approach. Similar to the end-result version of the evenhanded model, the procedural version adopts a hands-on approach in which governmental resources of various kinds are allocated to different religious denominations and groups. Likewise, in this approach the government does not show preference to any one religious group and the state remains unaffiliated with any one denomination. However, unlike the end-result version of the evenhanded approach, the procedural version focuses on establishing a fair allocation mechanism rather than on projected consequences. We shall define the procedural evenhanded approach as follows:

The procedural evenhanded model, as we understand it here, involves the allocation of resources to religious groups based on, and only on, criteria of fairness and equitableness toward the individuals whose aggregation constitutes

---

24. Patten prefers to speak of "equal recognition"; the classification of his argumentation under the procedural evenhanded model is ours.

those religious groups. Accordingly, once the threshold of this (assumed) fair
allocation is satisfied, the obligations of the state vis-à-vis religious needs have
ended. What happens to those aggregated groups in the religious realm, from
that point onwards, cannot justify further resource allocations from the state.

This definition requires the following four clarifying remarks. *First and foremost*,
the procedural evenhanded model does *not* depend on any particular end result
in order to be fair and equitable. As Alan Patten (2014) succinctly notes, while
endorsing a version of this model, "justice is not a matter of the outcome" (p. 150).
The fair allocation of resources in the religious realm is aimed to guarantee that
the behavior of each individual believer is the result of her/his choice rather
than the result of some external, typically economic, necessity.[25] Therefore, unlike
in the result-oriented version of the evenhanded approach, *the unequal success of*
religious groups, even to the point of the (occasional) dwindling of some, might be
considered fair in this framework. Inequality as such in the religious sphere is not
deemed a political concern if the state fully ensures the fairness of the background
conditions under which genuine religious preferences and choices of individuals
are made (on the noted "background conditions," see remark three below).

Second, the procedural version of the evenhanded model involves, to return
to the definition above, the allocation of resources according to fair and equitable criteria. This allocation aims to ensure that what brings about the religious
choices of each individual believer is her/his intended will; under a legitimate
evenhanded procedural allocative scheme therefore, the consequences of such
individual choices are legitimate, even if they may lead to the dwindling of religious groups (and the expected agitation and protest that would come from certain believers). The specific consideration and evaluation of variables leading to,
or constituting, this "fair and equitable allocation of resources" must therefore be
both clear and also highly persuasive.

Third, the allocation of resources in the procedural evenhanded approach
aims to enable religious choice and no more or less than this. This marks a point
of clear distinction between the procedural and the end-result approaches to the
evenhanded model. While the end-result version aims to satisfy all, or almost all,
religious claims and requests, the procedural version has no such sweeping aim.
It does aim to enable religious choice and, in order to enable such choice, accepts
the notion that allocation of various resources by the state is required. A. Patten

---

25. The connection between genuine choices, proceduralism, and fair background conditions
is not unique to religious and cultural choice; rather, it is well grounded in preceding developments in the economic realm (especially in the context of the freedom of contract doctrine).
See, generally, Horwitz (1992, pp. 33–65); Fried (2001).

(2014) aptly describes this feature of the procedural evenhanded approach as follows:

> The metric of equality assumed here is broadly "resourcist" rather than "welfarist." By this I mean that equality of recognition depends on facts about the rules that are adopted, the facilities that are made available, the resources that are expended, and so on. It does not depend on the degree to which people who have the relevant conceptions of the good manage to convert these benefits into a successful way of life. It may be that, in a context where comparable facilities, resources, and so forth, are provided to several different cultures, people make choices that leave one of the cultures flourishing and others struggling" (pp. 161–162).

We will demonstrate the applicability of this nuanced yet somewhat abstract formula in the examples below.

Fourth, and lastly, the definition above indicated that the allocation of resources is made to the "*individuals whose aggregation constitute those religious groups.*" This rather cumbersome phrasing reflects an important organizing rationale behind the procedural evenhanded approach: the allocation of resources is aimed at guaranteeing that the religious choices of each individual believer reflect her/his intended will and not external (typically economic) pressures. Therefore, the creation, flourishing, or even the dwindling of religious groups that reflect the aggregation of individual genuine choices, is beyond the boundaries (and, consequently, interests) of this approach (Patten, 2014, pp. 137, 139).[26] The aims of allocations made in the procedural evenhanded model, therefore, are individualistic rather than communal. Nevertheless, the measurement or evaluation of religious needs will be done (typically) according to parameters set by an individuals' given religious affiliation. This is done in order to facilitate consistent and reasonably functioning policy. It should be noted that, in this latter regard, the procedural approach coincides with the end-result approach (see Jobani & Perez 2014; Eisenberg 2009).

Let us turn now to two examples that clarify the policy-related content, and consequences, of the procedural evenhanded approach. For the first example,

---

26. As noted above, one organizing idea of the evenhanded approach, especially in its procedural version, is that the mere retreat of the state is insufficient for enabling genuine and legitimate choices, thus statist allocation of resources is required. This idea relies on, and is strongly connected to, a shift in American legal history from the "freedom of contract" school of thought to a progressive understanding of what constitutes legitimate choices. See Horwitz (1992, pp. 33–63).

take a given state that, beyond its civil court system, also sponsors various religious courts.[27] Let us assume that the state meets the criteria of fairness and equitableness in its support of the different religious courthouses and that it devotes
human and budgetary resources adequately according to such criteria. Let us further assume that fewer and fewer individuals choose to use the services of these
sponsored religious courts and that there are strong grounds to believe that the
shifting preferences of the relevant population—from religious to civil courts—is
the outcome of genuine choices and not some (broadly defined) external necessity. In such cases, the fact that such religious courts are being used by fewer and
fewer people clearly and strongly indicates the noninterest in such services on the
part of the relevant population. This should, therefore, at some point justify the
termination of the support given by the state to such courts. In the framework
of the procedural approach, as Patten (2014) remarks, "there is a cut-off point
determined by an independent standard of fairness beyond which further assistance, accommodation, and recognition for declining cultures is not mandated
by justice" (p. 153).

Note that this example sheds light on several key characteristics of the procedural evenhanded approach. *First*, in order to establish background conditions
adequate for religious choice to be genuine, state involvement is required. Such
involvement is implemented, in our example, through the establishment and
funding of religious courts of all relevant historical religions.[28] *Second*, the allocation of resources in this approach is meant only to enable religious choice. If the
membership of some religious group were to decline even with such support, this
would not raise any pertinent concerns for the proceduralist point of view. *Third*,
once this religious-choice-enabling framework is in place, if individuals choose
not to utilize the available religious services, the state can legitimately interpret
this nonusage as signifying a shifting preference of relevant aggregated individuals. Therefore, rather than call for the state to step in and actively (further) assist
seldom-chosen religious courts (in our example), the proceduralist will call for
the state to suspend funding for such courts given that the relevant individuals
indicate no interest in using them.

For the second example, we will turn to a different kind of "resources" which
religious groups tend to demand: exemptions from generally applicable laws.
Suppose that a state adopts the rest day of the majority religion as its common rest

---

27. As noted above, Israel pays the salaries of Jewish and Muslim judges in institutionalized
Halakhic and Sharia courts (Susser & Cohen, 2000; Layish, 2006).

28. The difficulty of deciding which religions ought to be included in the evenhanded system
is implicit here.

day. On this day, public institutions and most businesses are closed. The choice of this day of rest makes religious observance easier and less costly for members of the majority religion as, unlike members of other religions, their attendance of religious services usually does not conflict with the demands of the weekly work cycle. However, members of minority religions are worse off as their rest days collide with weekly work cycles.

Such examples are familiar from many legal cases that have been extensively discussed in the relevant literature.[29] The privatization model, discussed at length below, unsurprisingly tends to suggest that the state adopt a "hands-off" approach and that members of the minority religion solve the noted conflict via negotiations with their respective employers. The evenhanded approach as a whole, however, will recommend that *some* accommodation be made for minority groups in order to either enable, or reduce the expense of, observing their religious traditions.

Some differentiation between end-result and procedural evenhandedness is possible here as the end-result version would support full (or nearly full) accommodation and the procedural version will recommend a more limited set of policies that would enable genuine religious choice.

The specific parameters of what counts as full accommodation (required by end-result evenhandedness) as opposed to a limited accommodation (required by procedural evenhandedness) are certainly debatable. There is a range of policies that would exemplify each version of evenhandedness. As illustrative examples, the end-result model could suggest that employers be obligated to provide scheduling exemptions based on an employee's religious calendar, or alternatively that such conflicts serve as legitimate justification for collecting unemployment fees (for example, in a small business where an employer simply could not feasibly accommodate deviations from regular weekly cycles). The procedural model might also endorse several different policies. One example would be to create a general policy in which members of recognized (typically historical) religions receive a certain number of exemption-days from regular work-weekly cycles. This exemption-days policy would have different effects on members of different religions as the number of non-regular-days-of-rest varies according to the particular internal workings of their religions. Consequently, some religious minorities will be better off than others under such a procedural policy. This differentiated effect, however, is not a concern for the procedural model as it is not concerned with tailoring rest days exemptions for all religions. As Patten indicated above, the concerns of the procedural view do not extend to how each individual

29. See, for example, Gavison and Perez (2008); Greenawalt (2007); Jones (1994).

believer "converts" this resource to her/his ability to continue to pursue her/his chosen religion. For the proceduralist, only two points matter: that the number of "exemption days" given is fair and equitable, and that the exemption successfully serves to enable genuine religious choice.

Now that we have a better view of the principles, and some implications, of the procedural version of the evenhanded model, we will examine its major justifications.

4.2.1. Justifications for the Procedural Evenhanded Model

Three of the justifications for the procedural evenhanded approach merit consideration here: (i) the special importance of religious choice; (ii) the assumption that state involvement is required in order to provide adequate background conditions that enable genuine religious choice; (iii) the superiority of the procedural version of evenhandedness to the welfarist or end-result version as it rests on the plural grounding of equality, responsibility, and the pragmatic deterrence of free riders.

Let us begin with the *first* justification: namely, the special importance given to religious choice and religious freedom as a whole. On this point, the procedural approach echoes major international treaties such as the 1948 Universal Declaration on Human Rights (article 18) and the European Convention on Human Rights (1953, article 9), as well as major political thinkers such as John Rawls, in recognizing and attributing special importance to freedom of religion (often grounding it in the more general freedom of conscience; see Rawls, 1982, p. 25). This view makes it impermissible for states that accept this principle, for example, to discriminate on religious grounds, to ban religious activities, to ban religious conversion or abandonment, to influence religious faith through government power, and so on.[30] Similar to other such "negative" rights, accepting this point creates constraints on permissible behaviors by the state[31] but does not

---

30. We can't enter here into a full list of the "ingredients" of "religious freedom," and any such list would be contested in any case; for good overviews and discussions of this issue, see McConnell (2000); Durham (2009); Boyle (2007); (Witte 1996); Greenawalt (2007); Nickel (2005); Fox (2016).

31. It is important to note that this negative right is neither trivial nor has it been universally accepted, even among democratic states, historically or in contemporary cases. Multiple examples—India's indifference to (some would say complicity in) the destruction of the Babri Masjid Mosque in 1992, the lack of civil marriages in Israel (since its establishment in 1948), and the Swiss referendum that banned the building of minarets in 2009—all point to the inherent importance of religious freedom as a negative right (on the difference between negative and positive rights, see Gavison (2003)).

sanction, or require, any specific involvement by the state. While the procedural evenhanded approach fully accepts the importance of religious freedom and choice, it moves beyond understanding religious freedom as a "negative" right. This particular attribute of the procedural model serves as its *second* important justification; in order to provide adequate background conditions that enable genuine religious choice, state involvement is required.

As illustrated by the two examples discussed above (religious court systems and days of rest), different techniques and practical steps can be taken in order to achieve this goal: funding of religious courts, paying the salary of religious clergy, instituting exemptions from generally applicable laws, among many other policies and techniques. The argument at the heart of the procedural evenhanded approach is therefore that state involvement is necessary in order to enable genuine religious choices; this assumption is firmly grounded in the history of legal and economic thought, especially in the rejection of the "freedom of contract" school of thought (Horwitz, 1992, pp. 3–65; Fried, 2001).

The argument regarding "state involvement" incorporates several different justifications and, for purposes of clarity, let us briefly examine them. *First*, in order to avoid coercion (economic, religious, or any other), a governmental hands-off policy is insufficient; coercion can arise in the absence of the state or be caused by nongovernmental actors. A typical example in the economic sphere would be a gross imbalance of bargaining power between two transactional parties that leads to an exploitative contract; in our context, an equivalent occurrence arises if and when there is external pressure (social or economic) on vulnerable religious communities that encourages an abandoning of a certain religious activity due to its high cost. *Second*, as there are no realms that are entirely free from state involvement, the issue is not whether the state should or should not intervene in a certain realm. Rather, the issue is how the state is to evaluate, and consequently improve, its involvement in the various realms (religion-state relations included) in which it is already present. Note the tension between these two arguments: the latter would preclude the existence of the former. *Third*, following the two previous points, a given agent would have to command various kinds of resources— sufficient income, adequate education, symmetric information, legal defenses, etc.—in order to enable genuine choices and dispel any suspicion of coercion while making choices, religious ones included.[32]

---

32. Obviously, such a "package" of resources is required in order to defend other interests as well, so it is not only tailored to the freedom to make religious choices. However, we shall avoid here commenting on interests outside of the religious realm and how this "package" protects or provides for them.

These three arguments for "state involvement" all reflect the same fundamental insight, namely that the making of genuine choices requires state involvement. This view, well grounded in the economic-progressive school of thought of the early twentieth century, signals a preference for the positive rather than negative conception of liberty and rights. Specifically, the idea of freedom transforms from a situation of being unconstrained by external, state made impediments to a situation that involves a capacity to act in a certain way.[33]

Many left-liberal thinkers, accepting implicitly or explicitly the "positive view" of freedom and rights, argue that a regular or standard liberal "package" of resources is sufficient for guaranteeing adequate background conditions that enable genuine choices *as a whole* (i.e., regardless of the specific realm of choice); some evenhanded proceduralists claim, against such a view, that a "cultural" or "religious" package of resources is required *in addition* to the regular or standard resources. This point separates many left-liberal thinkers (see Rawls, 1993, pp. 193–197; Barry, 2001, pp. 65, 71; Scheffler, 2007, pp. 110–111) from evenhanded thinkers such as Carens and Patten. The evenhanded model maintains that

> [w]hen the various cultural rights called for by full proceduralism are in place, *alongside* the standard liberal package" as Patten (2014) puts it "then it is more plausible to suggest to minorities who are disappointed with the outcome that they had a fair opportunity to realize their preferred way of life." (p. 156; emphasis added)

The *third* general justification for the procedural version is internal to the evenhanded approach, that is, it serves to demonstrate the superiority of one version (the procedural) of evenhandedness over another version (the end result or welfarist) of evenhandedness. This justification is based on the plural grounding of equality, responsibility, and the pragmatic deterrence of free-riders. We take each in turn.

The argument for the resource-procedural version of evenhandedness that is grounded in considerations of *equality* indicates that religious needs and preferences are varied and differ widely across religions. If the logic of the allocation of religious resources would aim to equally satisfy each believer, citizens belonging to different religions would receive unequal quantities of resources. This would violate a fundamental principle of democratic regimes: that the state is obligated to treat its citizens with equal concern and respect and that it should not discriminate between citizens following their religious affiliations. Allocating a given,

---

33. For this transition, see Miller (1983); Briggs (2006).

equal bundle of resources to each person, and allowing each person to "convert" such resources in order to answer her/his religious needs, would respect the given democratic principle of equal treatment *and* would allow genuine choice in the religious realm.

The second argument supporting the resource version of the procedural even-handed school is grounded in considerations of *responsibility*. The argument here is that, if a person can choose her/his religious belonging, s/he should be responsible for and internalize the gap between the cost of the regular bundle of resources given to all citizens and her/his expensive religious preferences. This argument neatly rests in a common sense understanding of personal responsibility as well as the democratic principle of equal treatment according to which the state should not fund expensive preferences or "tastes" without special justification.[34]

The previous two arguments, regarding equality and responsibility, assume that a given individual can exercise some choice in the religious realm. If this is the case, then these two arguments are potentially powerful. Indeed, both play an important part in the general contemporary theories of distributive justice.[35] However, scholars such as Tully (1995), Parekh (2000), and Margalit and Halbertal (2004)—those who endorse the identity end-result evenhanded approach—reject the relevance of choice in the religious realm. As discussed above, these scholars argue that persons do not choose their religion, but rather that they are born into its bundle of established rituals and comprehensive-lifestyle rules. This was the fundamental insight of Muller's illuminating concept of *mother-religion*.

Furthermore, when we take into account the direct and indirect enforcement mechanisms which religious communities use to monitor their internal work-ings, the immediate relevance of choice and preference in the religious realm begins to appear conceptually and empirically inadequate.

How should we regard such views? The identity school of thought is too rad-ical in its claim that religious identity is not a matter of choice but rather one of ascription. They are correct to emphasize the obvious, but important, point that religious affiliation is not the result of a trivial choice. Clearly, education and socialization from an early age strongly influence one's religious belonging. However, as Catherine Cornille (2003) remarked in noting the phenomenon of multiple religious belongings, "with the gradual dissolution of traditional geo-graphical and spiritual monopolies by particular religions, the religious field has

---

34. See Dworkin (2000, chap. 2).

35. Rakowski (1991) is probably the most ardent advocate of this position.

become wide open and religious belonging increasingly a matter of choice and degree" (p. 43).

Our focus on the important role of choice within the religious realm, as implied by the previous two arguments (regarding equality and responsibility), does not aim at playing down background considerations of education and socialization, nor does it mean that we reduce religious choice to a simple or trivial one. David Gauthier's (1992) adroit words are perfectly applicable to religious choices, "What makes a being autonomous is his capacity to alter given preferences . . . not a capacity to produce preferences with no prior basis" (p. 157). There is a wide continuum—stretching from the radical denial of choice in the religious sphere all together to the view that religious choices are trivial and/or easily reversible— of frameworks for theorizing religious choices.[36] In between the extremes, theories attempt to recognize religious choice as optional without reducing it to a triviality; many international treaties, much sociological literature, and (more recent) economic literature fill in this continuum by providing, describing, and analyzing significant data with regard to religious choice (Finke & Stark, 2005; Gill, 2008). This in-between realm coincides with our preferred approach for analyzing religious choice; we consider, and see examples for such choice both in converting or abandoning religious faith altogether, and as a somewhat more nuanced ability to maneuver within a given religion (Yadgar, 2005; Gal Getz, 2011; the example of the Women of the Wall themselves provides evidence to this ability to maneuver, or choose, within a religious tradition).

It is also important to note, in this context, that there are significant legal and regulatory consequences that follow from the way in which the evenhanded approach is justified and understood; these abstract distinctions directly affect nonbelievers that would have to, for example, fund religious services through their taxes. As such, the two arguments presented—regarding equality and responsibility—have strong general appeal as they limit usage of public funds for religious requests; additionally, when public funds are used to answer these requests, they are used in an egalitarian fashion. The opposing identity justification leads to a more inegalitarian, and expensive—from the point of view of nonbelievers—set of policies toward religious requests (as discussed earlier). This point illustrates, from another perspective, the superiority of the procedural-resource matrix of evenhandedness over the welfarist or end-result version of evenhandedness.

---

36. Z. Bauman (1996) trivializes religious choice, as another example to his general post-modern view, as he writes, "It is now all too easy to choose identity, but no longer possible to hold it" (p. 50).

The third and final argument for adopting the procedural evenhanded view, over the end-result approach, is pragmatic in nature. In the framework of the evenhanded approach (in both versions), governmental resources of various kinds are allocated to different religious denominations and groups without preference. As a relatively new, yet quickly growing body of research on economics and religion has demonstrated, such allocation of resources encourages individuals and organizations to "dress up" their requests for governmental aid in religious "garments." Neither version of evenhandedness discussed here is immune to this human (perhaps too human) tendency to look for, and find, what Walzer (1985) aptly called *material interest in sanctity* (p. 97). The procedural approach, however, is better equipped to cope with this tendency since it rarely coincides fully with—accommodates the entire scope of—religious demands and requests; consequently, it leaves some cost to be covered by the requesting individual. This cost might discourage religious impostors attempting to get a "free ride," and establish the relevant allocating policies in a more prudential manner than the end-result version.[37] This ends our exploration of the justifications for the procedural evenhanded approach, we turn now to examine some of the important counter arguments and critiques that have been brought against this approach.

4.2.2. Critiques of the Procedural Evenhanded Model

The procedural evenhanded approach is an attractive option. It has many merits: it attempts to treat citizens of various denominations with equal concern and respect, it utilizes the scholarly achievements of major proponents of the economic-legal progressive movements in the United States and elsewhere, and it offers a remarkable attempt to ensure that religious choices are genuine rather than coerced. As such, it merits close consideration as, perhaps, the most important rival to the privatization approach. We will show that, while it is certainly permissible in liberal democracies, this model contains three important drawbacks that make it less preferable than the privatization approach: it has an imbalanced view of the connection between an individual and his/her religion (4.2.2.1.); it dedicates insufficient attention to institutional aspects of religions; (4.2.2.2.); and it neglects the empirical reality of thriving religious spheres in countries that do not employ an evenhanded model (4.2.2.3.). Collectively, these reasons raise the doubt as to whether evenhanded policies are required or at all desirable.

---

37. See Gill (2008); Perez (2009); Eisenberg (2009); G. A. Cohen (1999).

4.2.2.1. The individual and her/his religion: an imbalanced *connection*

The first point that merits a critical examination is the connection between an individual and her/his religion. A specific conceptualization of this relation, which we label the *elusive connection*, stands at the heart of the procedural even-handed approach. This point is foundational for each one of the three justifica-tions (equality, responsibility and the so called pragmatic one) offered above; as such, if it proves to be unpersuasive or problematic, then the entire procedural evenhanded approach to religion-state relations—the burdensome apparatus that distributes state funding to religious groups—becomes unnecessary.

Careful attention must be payed to the attempt to understand the exact con-nection that the procedural evenhanded approach draws between an individ-ual and her/his religion. This connection needs to be able to justify the specific nature of the procedural approach; that is, it must be able to justify establishing institutions as a means to creating the background conditions that guarantee genuine religious choices, but it must remain indifferent to the desirability of religious belonging as such.

Any attempt to formulate such a connection accurately and precisely must navigate between two opposite problems: that of rigid views of religious belong-ing on the one hand, and the view that the existing "generic" liberal frameworks are sufficient for protecting religious freedom on the other hand.[38] A rigid identity view would lead to end-result evenhanded policies, while the "generic" framework views—such as those suggested by diverse theorists, extending from left liberals to libertarians, such as Rawls, Barry, Nozick, and Nussbaum—would lead, simply, to the privatization model of religion-state relations.[39]

This in-between character of the procedural-evenhanded approach's under-standing of the connection between an individual and her/his religion lends itself to a substantial *elusive connection* difficulty.

Usually, when a given philosopher or a public policy maker points to the importance of a certain good, and supports allocating resources to meet that interest or need, the aim is that this good will be provided. To point to a simple example, many states recognize the importance of healthcare and, accordingly,

---

38. Note that the point here is the debate regarding what constitutes the adequate defense of religious freedom, not whether religious freedom is important as such.

39. Scholars' views of the background conditions that are required for genuine choices differ in general, and in the religious realm in particular. Nozick (1974) supports a general policy of state non-interference with individual liberty; Rawls (1993), Nussbaum (2008), and Barry (2001) support various left-liberal or egalitarian-liberal theories (leading to the welfare state). However, once those (different) background conditions are satisfied, they all support the pri-vatization model and would object to any (further) allocation of resources to the religious or cultural sphere.

support the allocation of resources to insure that it will be provided to its citizens (i.e., by providing national, cost free health care; subsidizing medical treatments and procedures; encouraging healthy lifestyles; taxing unhealthy products). Usually the aim of state policies in such cases is not only to make a certain good (healthcare, for example) available to people, but to promote or ensure the actual usage or achievement of the given good.[40]

The procedural evenhanded approach is different in that it does not aim to realize a specific state of affairs (i.e., maintaining individual's religious affiliation or the survival of religious groups); it aims only to ensure the background conditions needed to enable genuine choices in the religious realm. However, this model *has no choice but* to point to the special importance of religion as it requires a strong justification for the massive undertaking of establishing relevant institutions (e.g., religious courts), the funding of religious groups, arranging exemptions from laws that conflict with religious traditions, and the overall challenge of guaranteeing the background conditions required for the making of genuine choices in the religious realm.[41] At the same time, this justification must

---

40. Note that the policy implications here are all but trivial: the desirability of a certain end result does not mean that the state will simply obligate citizens to act in a certain way. Concern for liberty and fear of paternalism would prevent such direct action. But the state can support the choice of a certain option by offering subsidies, "choice architecture," etc. (see Thaler & Sunstein, 2009; Perez, 2009—as applied to the religious-cultural sphere).

41. The contested nature of the procedural evenhanded approach is evident through a careful reading of the following justification suggested by Patten (2014):

> When a preference occupies a pivotal role in a person's conception of the good, or when it has a non-negotiable character, or when it is salient to the individual's enjoyment of the recognition and respect of others, then there is reason to think that the individual has a particularly strong interest in being able to fulfill that aspect of her conception of the good. Cultural aspects of a person's conception of the good often possess one or more of these features, and thus persons normally have a weighty interest in being able to fulfill their cultural values. (p. 29)

Note that the terminology used here, to describe the relation between a person and her/his religion, is adopted almost entirely from the identity approach; "pivotal role," "non-negotiable," "salient," and especially "particularly strong interest in being able to fulfill." This terminology, to a considerable extent, emphasizes the significance of religion to one's identity and thus fits the end-result version of evenhandedness more than it does the proceduralist version's focus only on the proper background conditions for genuine religious choices. It should also be noted, briefly, that the procedural evenhanded model is a "starting gate" theory; that is, once the background conditions are properly established, no further allocation of resources is required (to use Dworkin's term and approach). But "starting gate" models assume an initial allocation of resources that is just, and that any subsequent change in ownership is the result of voluntary choices made by individuals. If religion, as Patten seems to indicate, is not a chosen attribute of an individual, then "starting gate" theories are simply not relevant in the manner that Dworkin argued (2000, p. 89).

not be too strong or significant, otherwise the *actual attainment* of the good will be expected to follow (leading back to the end-result evenhanded view).[42]

There is something odd about recognizing the importance of religion and, consequently, arguing that further resources should be allocated in order to ensure genuine religious choices and insisting that the procedural-evenhanded model is completely indifferent to religious affiliation and the survival of religious groups (i.e., the end result). A more straightforward, and also more consistent, view of the matter would be framed as follows: if a particular good is not that important, then the interest corresponding to it (religious freedom, choice, or belonging) ought to be satisfied by "general" or "generic" background conditions. In the case of religious liberty, such background conditions are satisfied through a hands-off approach and, therefore, no further resources ought to be allocated toward this particular good. Alternately, if the particular good is so important that it ought to justify a hands-on approach which will allocate further resources in this realm, then a particular end result will be sought. The procedural evenhanded theory displays an uncomfortable and unbalanced interplay between granting religious affiliation and freedom too little and too much importance in the different stages of its argumentation. Furthermore, this imbalance is rare: most other goods clearly fall under one of the two natural categories identified above [i.e., justifies further resources and the end result *is* important (healthcare); does not justify a special allocation of resources as the end result is not important (playing baseball, for example)]. This rarity, to conclude, this elusive connection, is not a reflection of the special status of religion; it is rather a failure of the procedural evenhandedness theory to be consistent in its different parts, in its treatment of religion.

4.2.2.2. *The Institutional Aspects of Procedural Evenhandedness*

Moving to the second critique, which is focused on the institutional aspects of procedural evenhandedness, we will present two substantial challenges that arise once the procedural evenhanded model faces its potential applicability. When political institutions—courts, state bureaucracy, and so on—adopt the ideas of this approach

---

42. Note that, while other scholarly attempts to provide theories that concern "mere" background conditions while leaving end result open do exist, they differ in that they are general and not tailored to a particular usage; that is, they can be converted or used for many different functions or goals. Rawls' primary goods, or Dworkin's hypothetical auction, have procedural structure (even though both obviously aim to achieve more than merely establishing the background conditions required for genuine choices); however, they are not tailored to a particular realm such as religion or culture. Rather, they aim to ensure the genuine ability to choose between all (or almost all) comprehensive views of the good while requiring no "further" allocation of resources for religion. Therefore, the special further allocation of resources that are not easy to convert to religious groups, according to the procedural evenhanded model we are examining, is what we question, not the procedural aspect per se.

as guidelines for public policy, certain issues will invariably arise. These challenges are not merely practical or technical, in the wide sense of these terms, and we are not arguing that application of the procedural evenhanded model would be complex or difficult. Nor are we arguing that efforts to apply the theory toward public policy would imperfectly transform its ideas. These pervasive difficulties stand in the way of any political theory seeking some form of applicability. We wish to focus on two rather different concrete challenges: (i) any application of the procedural evenhanded approach will conflict with core democratic values that are integral to the procedural evenhanded approach itself; (ii) despite the model's inner logic, its application would "drag" it away from its own formulation to an end-result evenhanded approach. We shall elaborate both points.

The first challenge, which points to the complex and intrusive entanglements that the procedural evenhanded model will create between the government and religions, can be called the *excessive entanglement challenge*. Determining how to allocate resources—in order to ensure the fairness of the background conditions under which religious preferences and choices of individuals are taken—proves to be a complex process. Different religious groups will surely argue that any certain allocation policy affords a given variable too much (or too little) consideration, and that this miscalculation places a burden on their religious choices and limits their freedom. Deciding what is "fair" will require not only a comprehensive collection of data regarding individual religious behavior, but also a distinctive internal understanding of religious tenets and beliefs. The assembling of this information alone is a far from trivial challenge. For example, in the Ayodhya dispute (see the appendix), the commission established in 1992—immediately after the demolition of the Babri-Masjid mosque that lead to the commission's formation—took 17 years (!) to complete the report that it published only in 2009.[43] Furthermore, the adoption of this model could foreseeably fuel complex and extended legal struggles when, in order to be eligible for the allocation of goods, new or unrecognized religions attempt to gain formal recognition from the state.[44]

---

43. The Liberhan Ayodhya Commission Report (2009). Further concrete examples include: the fierce controversy in Israel regarding ultra-Orthodox Jews' request to win an exemption from mandatory military conscription (see Jobani & Perez, 2014; more generally, see Eisenberg, 2009); in the Indian context, the Shah Bano case is infamous (Mohd. Khan v. Shah Bano Begum (1985 SCR (3) 844)), especially the problematic attempt of the Hindu-majority court to examine Islamic religious doctrines (Spinner Halev, 2001; Perez, 2002).

44. A case in point is Scientology in Germany (Zacharias, 2006). See also, more generally, Doe (2011, p. 180). Among other things, deciding who *is* the relevant group that represents a religion often means creating a problematic preference for the conservative members of that group. R. Hardin (2004) aptly articulates this unfortunate situation: "As a variant of liberalism, group liberalism is very odd in that it somehow elevates the relevant group above its members by protecting the group, commonly against its own less than fully committed members" (p. 185).

This need for collecting substantial data, developing nuanced knowledge, and managing subsequent entanglements gives rise to a twofold concern. First, data collection on religious behavior would require governmental prying into private religious choices and personal conduct, actions which conflict with established democratic understanding. Such prying, as Montesquieu (1748/1989) already indicated in his *Spirit of the Laws*, will have negative spillover effects for individual liberty and should be flatly avoided.[45] Second, requiring governmental knowledge of the internal workings of religions would force the government to embark on a mission it is ill equipped to perform, that is, to understand and judge the tenets, beliefs, and creeds of the many religions residing within its borders (furthermore, as will be discussed in 4.3, this knowledge is dynamic, dispersed, and private; collecting it is almost impossible).[46]

Further, collecting such data might harm trust among citizens and fuel suspicion between citizens and their state. Imagine, for example, a member of a minority religion receiving a formal inquiry from the government that asks questions such as, are you a member of this or that congregation? how often do you attend services? and so on. Could a self-respecting citizen fail to be insulted by such an inquiry into the sensitive issue of their religious faith and conduct? Elizabeth Anderson (1999) argued, in her critique of recent theories of distributive justice that overemphasize the notion of responsibility, that to request that citizens display evidence of their personal histories and behavior in order to get aid from the state "is to reduce them to groveling for support." (p. 305). Such prying into the "religious bedroom" of citizens is not an endeavor that should be

---

45. This understanding is couched in Montesquieu's claim that the only true crimes are crimes against private security or public tranquility. There are no crimes against religion since, in such crimes "that wound the divinity, where there is no public action, there is no criminal matter; it is all between the man and god who knows the measure and the time of his vengeance. For if the magistrate, confusing things, even searches out hidden sacrilege, he brings an inquisition to a kind of action where it is not necessary; he destroys the liberty of citizens." (Montesquieu, p. 190, pt. 2, chap. 14). Although the original context is that of criminal law, Montesquieu's argument against prying into private religious matters fits well into the context of religion-state relations as a whole.

46. In some cases, these two issues (intrusion into the privacy of the individual citizen and her liberty as a whole, and the need of the government to reach a detailed understanding of religious creed), become embodied in one particular example, demonstrating the problematic nature of any model involved in such contested practices.

A case in point is the recent heated debate in Israel regarding the questioning of women about their marital status by bath attendants working in the state-funded and operated *mikvot* (ritual baths designed for the Jewish rite of purification). Single women had been blocked from using state-funded *mikvot* in order to signal that the latest "trend" in premarital sex among modern Orthodox singles is not acceptable to the Chief Rabbinate. This amounts to both state prying on private behavior *and* the state siding with contested form of religious interpretation. See Kaplan Sommer (2013); Ghert-Zand (2012).

taken by any democratic state (or even any state that simply values trust between its citizens, and between citizens and the state).

The second institutional challenge to the procedural evenhanded model is that the implications of the approach in practice would "drag" it or "default" it into end-result-oriented policies, and it would do so despite the model's inner logic and explicit principles. This challenge reflects a fundamental *evaluation problem*: how can given policies be evaluated independently of their results? We are skeptical that an evaluative criterion that is independent of an examination of results is available, and as we aim to demonstrate, this evaluation problem reveals a crucial weakness—a blind spot—in the procedural evenhanded approach.

To demonstrate this point, let us return to the example of a country that has established religious courts aside from its civil court system. Let us assume that the state attempts to meet the criteria of fairness and equitableness (however defined) in its support of the different religious courthouses and that it devotes human and budgetary resources accordingly. Let us further assume, again as described earlier, that fewer and fewer individuals choose to use the services of the sponsored religious courts. Here, the procedural evenhanded approach will reach the following conclusion: there are strong grounds for believing that the shifting preferences of the relevant population—from religious courts to civil courts—are the outcome of genuine choices, and not of some (broadly defined) external coercion or pressures of some sort. In such cases, the nonusage of religious courts would clearly and strongly indicate a genuine lack of interest in such services among the relevant population and should therefore justify, at some "cutoff" point, the termination of the state support given to such courts.

Why is this scenario problematic? The principles of the procedural evenhanded model preclude *reading back* from the end result to determine the fairness of the allocation procedure. An absolute aversion to such "reading back" is inherent to the model's principles that maintain that the fair allocation of resources, and only this fair allocation, guarantees that religious choices, such as gradually diminishing use of religious courts, are indeed genuine. Exploring the alternative will clarify why this is an *absolute* aversion: if a decline in the number of persons using such courts provides a reason to allocate more resources to such courts—to ensure background conditions that would enable the shrinking clientele to continue to use them—then a "cut off" point at which the background conditions required for genuine choices are satisfied *will never be reached*. Recurrence of such a scenario would, de facto, commit this model to the end-result of the survival of religious groups, rather than the model's explicit principles. The procedural evenhanded approach, therefore, will have to determine the adequacy of such background conditions independently of results—that is, the number of persons using state-supported religious courts.

However, the attempt to locate a suitable criterion for evaluating the success of a given policy independent of its results is both exceedingly difficult and very unusual. Consider, yet again, the example mentioned above regarding the provision of healthcare. Suppose that a given medical procedure, deemed essential to the population, is offered to the citizens of a state and that various governmental policies seek to ensure that it is used or adopted. To use a concrete example, osteoporosis is a common problem for persons over the age of fifty-five. Suppose a given government that would like to encourage persons above this age to be examined for the disease subsidizes this examination in some way. Suppose, further, that very few people choose to undergo the relevant medical examination. A reasonable policy response, in order to increase the percentage of persons who go through this examination, would be to publicize its importance or to offer some material incentives. The crucial point is that, once the medical procedure is deemed important, at no point is the decision of individual citizens not to use available resources deemed a sufficient reason to cancel these programs altogether. In this medical example, as in many others,[47] the natural way to examine the success of a policy is *to examine its results* and to amend the policies accordingly. The procedural evenhanded approach, however, precludes this exact step.

Several difficulties arise from this *preclusive* characteristic of the procedural evenhanded model. First, if examining results is deemed irrelevant, what criteria can be used to determine that the background conditions are indeed proper? This question is not trivial, and no ready-made answer addresses it: such criteria would require that the government clearly and convincingly define a certain threshold beyond which choices are deemed genuine. But how can such a decision be reached and defended?[48] This point awaits a persuasive answer, and until

---

47. We can point to many similar examples: tax incentives that encourage saving for pensions in order to overcome the tendency to overspend in youth; creating default organ donation rules for driving permit renewal; partially reimbursing the cost of gym membership in order to encourage physical exercise and reduce healthcare costs. In all such examples, if the number of participants is low, it is expected that the rule will be amended in order to be made more effective—that is, there is a "reading back" from results to the formation of the rule or policy (note that at no point does the decision that a result is desirable mean that the government ought to coerce it). See Thaler and Sunstein (2009) for a general discussion and the typology in the realm of religious exemptions offered by Perez (2009, pp. 208–211).

48. We suspect that some attempts to defend a decision regarding this "cut-off" point could draw an analogy between freedom of contract and freedom of religion. There are limits to this analogy, however, and one is particularly important: the progressive critique of the freedom of contract doctrine relied on the harmful effects of that doctrine and amended the defenses that are available to the vulnerable parties in contracts if such bad results continued to appear (Fried, 2001). This reading-back strategy, for reasons explained above, is not open to the procedural evenhanded approach.

one is offered, any formulation of a procedural evenhanded approach will face questions regarding the adequacy of the state in making such complex decisions in the sensitive religious realm.

Second, evaluating the quality and legitimacy of institutions and rules independently of results is unusual. The establishment of rules or institutions almost always addresses a specific need or follows from a specific reason that looks to the achievement of some end. There will be disagreements regarding what, specifically, counts as a success but rarely would the results be ignored entirely.[49]

This point leads to the third difficulty. The evenhanded procedural model underestimates believers' reactions to the dwindling of their religious group. Such believers can be expected to ask the government for additional resources as, they would argue, some variable was not correctly calculated in the creation of the background institutions or rules. This point illustrates, from a different perspective, the claim introduced above: in practice, the implications of the procedural evenhanded approach would "drag" it, default it into end-result-oriented policies and regulations.[50]

4.2.2.3. Is there a Real Need for Evenhandedness in Democratic Societies?

The third and final critique that we shall point to is a simple, almost to the point of being trivial, question: is there a real need for this model in democratic societies? The evenhanded model (in both the procedural and the end-result versions), even under the most prudential and careful political execution, calls for a massive undertaking on the part of the state. It requires identifying relevant groups that are eligible for state support, allocating resources of various kinds (such as the establishment of religious courts and paying the salaries of religious clergy), creating exemptions from generally applicable laws (but with the challenge of doing so all in an equitable way), and this list could easily be expanded. Beyond bureaucratic complexities, there are high institutional, political, and economic costs for such an enterprise, and the hypersensitive religious realm will only amplify

---

49. The explanation for this rare decision to neglect results lies in the imbalanced position that religion has within the procedural evenhanded approach, as noted above in the context of the elusive connection. This *explanation* does not constitute a proper *justification*.

50. Carens' well-known observations regarding Fiji exemplify what might be considered the almost unavoidable tendency of the evenhanded approach to become end-result oriented. His in-depth analysis of the case lead him to conclude that end-result land policies—regarding the absolute ban on selling of land from one ethnic group (Fijians) to non-members of that group (mainly Indo-Fijians)—are both permissible and justified (Carens, 2000, pp. 223, 231). Obviously much gentler policies are available (say, implementing a high sale tax), but the insistence of the members of one group (Fijians) on such end-result policies were decisive for Carens' conclusion to support an absolute legal ban (ibid., 224, 228).

these costs.[51] In order for this model both to be justified and needed, therefore, some real value must be missing in countries that do not employ this model, at least from the perspective of a religious individual. Namely, there must be either a dearth of religious groups, or a weakening of religious observance, and religious persons must be able to claim either circumstance to be the result of lack of state support of religious groups. This lack of state support, the argument might continue, exposes members of (typically) minority religions to troubling, unjust external, economic pressures, forcing them away from their religious observance and belonging.

However, there is very little evidence to support such claims. The United States, rich in religious diversity, is unique among wealthy nations for the high percentage of its citizens who attribute importance to religion.[52] Furthermore, members of religious minorities in the United States are typically strongly supportive of the separation model and see it to be in their interests.[53] France is even richer than the United States in religious diversity.[54] Both states, as is well known, are careful to avoid state support of religion (and see chapter 5).

Such empirical examples support classic analyses of separation models of religion-state relations. Tocqueville, to point to one famous example, reported that religion was stronger in America than in any other country. He famously attributed this strength to the separation of church and state, and he confidently asserted that "during my stay in America, I did not meet a single man, priest or layman, who did not agree about that [explanation]" (Tocqueville 1840/2003, p. 345).[55]

The thriving of religions under the separation model is well explained by the "supply-side" theory of religious markets, which maintains that the lack of governmental involvement in the religious realm encourages more religious groups,

---

51. See Ostrom (2005, chap. 9), both for the problems of establishing such state institutions, and for other, non-statist solutions.

52. See Albright, Kohut, Stokes, McIntosh, Gross, and Speulda (2002); Taylor (2007, p. 2).

53. See, for example, the strong support that American Jews display for the separation of church and state (Mittleman, Licht, & Sarna, 2002); Naim (2008) argues that the Islamic perspective holds a similar view.

54. See Cooperman and Lipka (2014).

55. Two decades before Tocqueville published *Democracy in America*, Madame de Staël (1818/ 2008) wrote,

There is a people who will one day be very great, I mean the Americans . . . What is there more honorable for mankind than this new world which has established itself without the prejudices of the old; this new world where religion is in all its fervor without needing the support of the state to maintain it . . .? (p. 707)

more religious observance, better religious services, and less resentment toward religious institutions (Fox, 2013, pp. 100–102; Stark & Finke, 2000).[56]

To summarize, the simple third challenge that is yet to be answered by an adequate theoretical articulation of the evenhanded approach *is whether it is needed at all*. The thriving of religious groups, religious adherence, and the religious sphere as a whole under regimes that do no support religion at all (the United States and France) is demonstrated by a wide variety of sources, from the reports of classical thinkers such as Tocqueville (1840), Bayle (1686), and Staël (1818), to recent sociological evidence presented by the supply-side theory (see chapter 5). A persuasive answer to this simple query, which needs to be offered by the supporters of the evenhanded model, is yet to be presented.

4.3. *Evenhandedness and Thick Sites*

We are now at a point where we can turn to explore how the evenhanded model would address the various challenges posed by thick sites. Our definition of *thick sites* (chapter 1), such as the Western Wall or Ayodhya's Ramjanmabhumi / Babri Masjid in Uttar Pradesh, is of *sites, typically but not necessarily religious, that are loaded with different and incompatible meanings attributed to them by different agents. From these agents' view, such meanings are highly significant, and consequently these sites are irreplaceable.*

Thick sites pose difficult challenges to evenhanded models, which adopt a hands-on approach in which governmental resources are allocated to different religious denominations and groups without showing preference to any one religious group, while the government and state themselves remain unaffiliated with any one denomination. Perhaps the single most pertinent challenge for the evenhanded approach is the characteristic of *irreplaceability* of such sites owing to their significance for believers' beliefs and identities. Thick sites are not merely the platform on which significant activities are performed (such as religious rituals or ceremonies of a state's civil religion), rather they themselves possess significant meanings—religious, national, and so on—that make them irreplaceable. "The ability of a religious community," as pointed out by Peter Edge (2002), "to designate a place as sacred, particularly as a place of worship, has been seen as one

---

56. We can identify some cases in which a very rigid privatization approach (such as recommended by Barry, 2001; Jones, 1994; and Hardin, 2004) would fall short of the wishes of some religious groups, typically in cases where generally applicable laws collide with religious beliefs and practices. However, there are certainly other legitimate forms of the privatization approach (see chapter 5) and, furthermore, even a privatization model that is more accommodating toward such requests will remain very far from a "full flavor" evenhanded approach.

of the keystones of religious liberty" (p. 161). Michael Lee Ross (2005), in his book examining sacred sites in Canada, asserts that

> sacred sites are crucial to the existence, survival, and well-being of first nations peoples, for their sacred sites distribute their spiritual connection to *particular* portions of the land . . . without their sacred sites . . . (they) would be left with a mere shell of their spiritual relationship with the land . . . what endangers their sacred sites ultimately puts their existence, survival and well-being in jeopardy. Their sacred sites are therefore crucial to their existence, survival and well being. (p. 3; emphasis added)

How, then, would the even-handed model suggest approaching the difficult challenges involved in making worship arrangements and overall managing thick sites? Arguably, the most typical implication of the evenhanded model, as applied to thick sites, would be a policy of *divide and separate*. Such a policy would include the following three features: the state *recognizes* relevant parties and groups; *divides* the thick site; and *separates* the different sublocations via the creation and maintenance of clear and recognized *physical* or *temporal* boundaries within such sites in order to avoid collisions between parties. As will be clear from the following discussion, various empirical arrangements at sacred sites that employ this "triple package" ultimately resemble, or adopt, evenhanded style logic, in the attempt to fairly treat interested parties within the context of such contested sites.[57] Note that, from both empirical and theoretical perspectives, the adoption of the "evenhanded style logic" in order to solve conflicts over sacred sites is not conditioned in any way by the general and principled adoption of an evenhanded approach to the entire realm of religion and state relations.

While seemingly a rather simplistic and crude solution, several states have adopted some version of this divide and separate policy: examining the policies that governments have adopted at the Western Wall, Ayodhya,[58] and other places, such as Samuel's Tomb[59] and the Church of the Holy Sepulchre,[60] shows that this approach has been widely used. Ramjanmabhumi / Babri Masjid was divided into three parts, though that solution was suspended by India's supreme Court; the conflict at the Western Wall, as noted in chapter 2, led to numerous

---

57. Following our contextual approach, we choose to avoid delving into entirely hypothetical implications of the various policies that even-handed models might adopt while confronted with the difficulties distinctive to thick sites.

58. See the appendix.

59. Reiter (2010).

60. R. Cohen (2008). Note that the state of Israel inherited this arrangement from its predecessors, but from our perspective "adopting" and "inheriting" belong to the same category. This point perhaps merits some further discussion that will have to be done elsewhere.

attempts to divide the Wall, including the creation of a third plaza; the site of the Church of the Holy Sepulchre is divided between several Christian denominations; and Samuel's Tomb—"the only place in the world were a functioning synagogue operates underneath an active mosque"—likewise keeps different religious groups separate.[61] Such "separate and divide" arrangements, while not exhausting the policies that the evenhanded model can view as permissible or required, indicate—in all the cases known to us in which the adopted "solution" for thick-sites follows, *mutatis mutandis*, an evenhanded logic (including the Western Wall, Church of the Holy Sepulchre, Ramjanmabhumi / Babri Masjid and Samuel's Tomb)—that the attempted arrangements will ultimately follow an end-result pattern.[62] This, we believe, provides ample and illuminating empirical support for our earlier claim that the end-result pattern is woven, in principle, into the fabric of the evenhanded model.

It should be noted that, far from being a newly formed arrangement, the "divide and separate" approach is a recognized convention in the history of established religion. In the Christian context, for example, one conceptualization of this approach, in which public worship was conducted by adherents of different religious groups at the same location, led to the coining of a neologism: *simultaneum* [shared church].[63] The history of these shared churches goes back to the early sixteenth century, and they can be found in Germany, Switzerland, and Alsace, in France (Kaplan, 2010, pp. 201–203; Brake, 2014, see also Limor, 2007; Kedar, 2001). In these shared churches, there are different strategies for executing the noted "sharing": some divide "time slices" (while sharing the same space), some divide the space, and others employ several other options. Times and places of worship for each community, in such locations, are strictly regulated, using the concepts introduced earlier in the chapter, according to strictly end-result

---

61. Reiter (2010, 158). We approach thick sites from political and historical perspectives, i.e. we are interested in the political and historical solutions suggested to problems posed at such contested locations. In the current discussion, we focus on the solutions that have a clear reference to the evenhanded model. We are well aware of the scholarship arguing that such sites are indivisible due to the social meanings attributed to them from the perspective of the relevant believers. There are, however, two different levels of analysis (that of the political/historical and that of social constructions/meanings) that simply need to be treated differently. For further consideration of the indivisibility claim, see Hassner (2009, chap. 3); for a critique of Hassner's claim regarding the indivisibility of holy sites, see Reiter (2010, pp. 160–161).

62. Berkovits (2000, pp. 229–233); R. Cohen (2008); Coüasnon (1974). See also the appendix. As our focus here is the evenhanded approach and thick sites in the public sphere, we do not delve into the complex issues of ownership relevant to several sacred sites (such as the Church of the Holy Sepulchre) that combine private/communal and public ownership (see chapter 1 for the discussion of the public sphere and chapter 5 for a further discussion of sacred sites and private ownership). See also Bar (2014, pp. 139–140).

63. The German word for a shared church is *Simultankirche*; the origin of this kind of arrangement was the reformation of the sixteenth century.

arrangements. It is perhaps worth noting that the name "shared church" is some-what of a misnomer; the noted arrangements merely duplicate the logic of the divide and separate with regard to the "shared church" structure, rather than indicate any true inter- or intrareligious "sharing."

A policy of divide and separate has some significant advantages: it gives each recognized group access to, and partial control of, the thick site; it enables each group to worship according to its beliefs; it minimizes physical contact between religious groups at the site and therefore reduces the danger of violence[64]; and it is relatively simple and straightforward to apply. No wonder, therefore, it has been adopted (or at least suggested) in contested sites such as the Western Wall, Ramjanmabhumi / Babri Masjid, and the Church of the Holy Sepulchre.

Nevertheless, evenhanded policies suffer from several weaknesses that are typical to end-result policies as a whole, and the case of sacred or thick sites is no exception. The major problem, to put this point in a succinct way, is this solution's *neglect of religious freedom*.[65] The reason that end-result evenhandedness ends up neglecting or violating religious freedom, when applied to thick sites, follows from the *centrally* and *irreplaceability* of these sites for believers. As will be seen momentarily, in general religion-state scenarios, an imperfect application of an evenhanded model means that its allocative system does not extend a given support (financial, legal, etc.) to all religious groups. In thick sites, however, such a failure would usually have the more severe consequence of limiting crucial (and, in some cases, essential) aspects of believers' religious freedom, such as access to or religious practice in such sites. The failure of evenhanded models is, therefore, more troublesome in thick sites than in general religion-state issues. We shall consider this weakness in detail and point to several different examples demonstrating this problem as it has unfolded at the Western Wall.[66]

The ability of the evenhanded model to accomplish its own defined goals in the religious-state realm, that is, to adequately manage religious and identity-based claims, crucially depends on the ability of its regulatory system to "capture" all relevant religious groups. However, as a fact of social and religious life, and in light of various political implications of the model, it appears simply impossible to "capture"

---

64. Donald Forbes (1997), the most ardent critic of the "contact theory," argues that in some cases strict separation is the best way to reduce conflict.

65. See the discussion in 4.1.2.

66. See also the appendix for similar problems that arose at the Ayodhya conflict; this example demonstrates that the failures of the evenhanded model, at least in its application to thick sites, are not case-specific (i.e., not tailored to the Western Wall).

all relevant groups and individual believers within the evenhanded governmental regulatory scheme.

What happens, in practice, is familiar and almost unavoidable: the government picks some "winners" among the competing religious groups in a given state or at particular thick sites, *and* it selects "winners" among the different strands within any given religion (typically the more conservative factions). This means that many other religious groups and individuals, even much of the diversity within the recognized groups, will be excluded from recognition and denied important religious freedoms (or, at the very least, deprived of the full supportive allocations offered by the government to the recognized factions in evenhanded models). In the context of thick sites, such limitations on religious freedoms include some, or all, of the following elements: limited access (complete ban, spatial limitations, temporal limitations, etc.); limitations on manners of worship; limiting permissible conduct; limiting permissible attire (via a strict dress code); and limiting many other aspects of behavior.[67] The end result is a severe violation of religious freedom for the (nonrecognized) person seeking to gain access to and worship at such sites.

Furthermore, the problem of creating a regulatory scheme capable of capturing all relevant groups is not merely a technical challenge of "complex policy planning." Rather it is a practical impossibility due to the inherent characteristics of religious groups and religious choice. As Tocqueville famously argued, the number of associations in a free society tends to grow, change, shift, and split rapidly (Tocqueville, 1840/2003, pp. 595–600). The burden that the evenhanded approach places on governments attempting to execute policies that follow the evenhanded theory—to continually identify relevant groups and then assess and respond to their demands—seems to require unjustifiable optimism regarding the abilities of any government. Such overinvested governments will typically encounter major difficulties when attempting to create evenhanded policies that remain suitable despite the rapid changes within the religious realm.

Hayek's famous critique of centralized economic planning fits well with this aspect of the religious realm and further explains the inability of governments to cope with, and respond to, such rapid changes: the planning of evenhanded policies in the religious realm requires an understanding of information that is dispersed among millions of individuals. Each individual knows, mainly, their own religious preferences and beliefs. Efforts to centrally collect this information

---

67. Eliade (1958) named some such behaviors "gestures of approach," that is, ritual actions that must be taken before entering sacred sites (pp. 370–371). In our context—governmental regulation—such "gestures" are transformed into "gatekeepers" that, de facto, put limits on access to thick sites.

from an entire population are doomed to fail because preferences (including religious ones) constantly change in response to new information and circumstances. A privatized religious realm (see chapter 5) will not face this problem since it avoids governmental mediation of religious beliefs. The evenhanded framework, however, cannot avoid this issue.[68]

Several aspects of the management of the Western Wall exemplify this inherent problem of the evenhandedness model, that is, its neglect of religious freedom. We shall take each example in turn.

The first example points to the ways in which the evenhanded model leads, due to its "picking winners" characteristic, to limitations on religious freedom and practice levied on the non-winning groups. As we saw in the previous chapter (3.1), mixed gendered prayers are not permitted at the Western Wall,[69] a regulation that excludes members of the reform and conservative movements of Judaism from praying according to their manner at the Wall (note that the membership of these two groups constitute a majority of the Jewish people worldwide).[70] The critique here is simple, yet (we believe) powerful: there are too many religious groups, as well as too much internal heterogeneity and diversity within such groups, for any governmental attempt to "capture" all relevant religious groups within a regulatory system to succeed. The unavoidable exclusion of some groups is, as noted, especially dire in the context of thick sites which are irreplaceable and central to the relevant religious groups.[71]

Secondly, the recent split within the membership of the Women of the Wall demonstrates the exact failure of the evenhanded style policy—to include all relevant religious groups, as such groups tend to grow in number and occasionally split—that the noted critical evaluation has led us to expect. As discussed in chapter 2, the Israeli government attempted to adopt an evenhanded styled policy by creating a third plaza where the WoW can pray according to their manner.

---

68. See Hayek (1945). Anderson (2008, p. 247), whom we follow here, eloquently summarizes Hayek's critique of central economic planning.

69. Save for the limited space known as *Ezrat Israel* in its current (early 2016) lamented shape. See chapter 2.

70. One important issue, in this context, is whether nonreligious groups should be included in the evenhanded framework as well; some argue for the extension of any state policies that are supportive of religion to such other religious-like systems of belief (such as secular humanism, pacifism, etc.). This point was raised via Judge Levin's opinion in the first WoW Supreme Court decision, see chapter 2. However, in the present context, it is important to note that even a more inclusive evenhanded system will fail to include all relevant groups. See Eisgruber and Sager (2007); Laborde (2014); Perez (2009).

71. In the appendix we will discuss the deep divisions that exist regarding even the identification of groups to be recognized at Ramjanmabhumi / Babri Masjid.

However, this led to a split within the WoW between those who were willing to accept the third plaza compromise and those who maintained that their core religious beliefs could be respected and guarded only by conducting prayer at the central plaza location. Following the sociological dynamic identified by Tocqueville and Hayek, the religious freedoms of the faction of the Women of the Wall that accepted the third plaza compromise are protected, while the freedoms of the dissenting faction were neglected; not only did the members of this group refuse to be delegated to the third plaza, they were still prohibited from praying according to their manner at the central plaza (according to the noted compromise). This is one more example of the ways in which an evenhanded model limits religious freedom, but there is an important value added by considering the theory in light of this specific case: the sociological dynamic that was identified by Tocqueville and Hayek shows that this failure cannot be prevented or avoided by better "technical" planning solutions.[72]

As a third and final example of the inevitable failure of centralized religious planning at the Western Wall—which the evenhanded approach requires—we can consider the recent case of a Jewish woman, visiting from the U.S, who was denied access to the Wall by security personnel because she was wearing a *kippah* (skull cap).[73] Responding to the event, the Rabbi of the Wall published an apology (as custodians from the Western Wall Heritage Foundation were involved).[74] However, even if the conduct of the security personnel at the Wall was mistaken (and it widely is deemed to be so), such mistakes should be expected. The woman wearing a kippah did not arrive at Rosh Hodesh as a part of the WoW prayer group. This group, at times, includes women wearing a kippah, while most other woman praying at the Wall do not wear a kippah. Thus, this woman did not "fit" neatly into the classifications known to the Wall security personnel and so, following what from the perspective of law and order was seen as a cautious step, she was denied entrance to the Wall. Such cases—of worshippers, who do not

---

72. As another example of the dynamic nature of the religious realm, one can point to recent attempts (August 2015) of the WoW to blow the Shofar during their prayer at Rosh Hodesh (the day of the new moon) of *Elul* within the central plaza. These efforts faced considerable difficulties (which were eventually resolved), as the blowing the Shofar by the WoW was not "covered" in the (then existing) regulations that specified permissible religious conduct for WoW members at the Wall. This event, which was documented and filmed, is available on YouTube, https://www.youtube.com/watch?v=3cFoZYY5P2E&mc_cid=cff543b553&mc_eid=3a27efe83a.

73. T. Pileggi, "Women Barred from the Western Wall," *Times of Israel,* July 6, 2015, retrieved from http://www.timesofisrael.com/woman-barred-from-western-wall-for-wearing-skullcap/.

74. K. Nachshoni, "Kotel rabbi apologizes to woman denied entry for wearing kippah," *YNET,* July 7, 2015, retrieved from http://www.ynetnews.com/articles/0,7340,L-4677153,00.html.

fit neatly into the categories created by the government, facing severe restrictions levied on their religious freedoms at thick sites—should not come as a surprise; they are an inherent problem of the evenhandedness approach. This case exemplifies that the theoretical limitations of the evenhanded model will be manifest as restrictions on the religious freedoms of individuals that do not belong to officially recognized groups. This point is noteworthy since the evenhanded model holds significant bias in favor of certain groups, and thus must be expected to neglect the religious freedoms of individuals unaffiliated with such groups.

4.4. *Conclusion*

Evenhanded theories are, perhaps, the most important alternative to the model of privatization for religion-state relations: they are egalitarian, they aim to be inclusive, and they attempt to guarantee—beyond mere governmental noninterference—the members of various religious groups the capacity to practice their religion.

However, when delving deeper into the logic, justifications, and policy implications of evenhanded models, the difficulties that these models will consistently encounter become clearer. The *identity, result-oriented* version of evenhanded models (see 4.1) requires an untenable view of individual identity and it neglects religious freedom. The second type of evenhanded models, the *procedural version* (see 4.2), successfully avoids some pitfalls of the end-result version, but it suffers from problems such as the "elusive connection" (i.e., the unstable or inconsistent position it grants to the importance of religious belonging), it's rare preclusion of learning from results, and finally it's constant and present likelihood to default into the much less attractive end-result model against its own internal logic.

When applied to thick or sacred sites, evenhanded models face further substantial challenges that stem from two different "sources"; first, the irreplaceability and centrality of such sites, second, the rigid "divide and separate" form these models acquire when applied to such sites. The combined result of these two features would mean that, when evenhanded models are applied to thick sites, the religious practice of nonrecognized groups and unaffiliated individuals will be limited in such sites. This significant weakness of the evenhanded model makes it, arguably, a less attractive solution than the privatization model, which will be the focus of the next chapter.

5

Privatization, Thick Sites, and the Women of the Wall

A SUGGESTED SOLUTION

IN THIS CHAPTER, we examine the third model of religion-state relations explored in this monograph, namely, privatization, and its applicability to thick sites. While no abstract model is perfect in concrete application, the "privatization" model of religion-state relations offers distinct advantages over the two other competing models that we have considered. Such advantages are amplified, rather than diminished, when this model is adequately (i.e., contextually) applied to the sensitive realm of thick sites.

This chapter is structured as follows: it opens with a definition and critical examination of privatization as a comprehensive model for religion-state relations; this includes a succinct exploration of the actual process by which this model could be realized, or at the very least advanced, within a given legal-political reality (section 5.1). We then address two potential misrepresentations or misunderstandings of this model (section 5.2), and analyze several of the major justifications that have been given for adopting this approach (section 5.3). In the extended concluding section, we explore the ramifications of applying the privatization approach to thick sites generally and the Western Wall in particular; we then evaluate the most pressing challenges facing such an application of the privatization model (section 5.4).

5.1. Privatizing Religion: Defining and Illustrating the Model

The privatization model, essentially, keeps the state unaffiliated with any given denomination while employing a strong "hands-off" approach toward religions.

The two main aspects of the privatization approach, as we define it, are the *lack of any state identification* with any specific religion and the *noninterference* of the state in religious conduct, belief, and institutions. As such, the privatization approach reduces governmental entanglement with religion both by strictly limiting the role that religion can play in political institutions and by strictly respecting the autonomy of religious individuals and institutions. The privatization model of religion-state relations aims neither to assist nor to hinder any religious establishment, belief, or practice. Religious beliefs, conducts, and communal belonging, are, therefore, left to the choice of the individual citizen or, through freedom of association, an aggregation of individuals. The government remains indifferent, as it were, to the religious affiliations of its citizens and does not have any religious identity of its own.[1]

The privatization approach means that the state must not only refrain from establishing an official religion, or from intentionally supporting any religious institutions (Patten, 2014: 119–123), but also that it must abnegate state symbols based in religious iconography, reject any religious identification, refrain from using state funds to support denominations, and avoid participation in any form of religious activity. A famous locus classicus for this position can be found in the majority opinion by Justice Black—of the US Supreme Court—in the Everson case:

> Neither a state nor the Federal Government can set up a church. Neither can pass laws which aid one religion, aid all religions or prefer one religion over another. Neither can force nor influence a person to go to or to remain away from church against his will or force him to profess a belief or disbelief in any religion. No person can be punished for entertaining or professing religious beliefs or disbeliefs, for church attendance or non-attendance. No tax in any amount, large or small, can be levied to support any religious activities or institutions, whatever they may be called, or whatever form they may adopt to teach or practice religion. Neither a state nor the Federal Government can, openly or secretly, participate in the affairs of any religious organizations or groups and vice versa. In the words of Jefferson, the clause against establishment of religion by law was intended to erect "a wall of separation between Church and State."[2]

---

1. For various versions of the privatization model, albeit using different terminology, see Nussbaum (2008, pp. 224–232); Rawls (1993, pp., 133–172, 195–201); Laycock (1990); Audi (1989); Barry (2001); Patten (2014, pp. 119–123).

2. Everson v. Board of Education, 330 U.S. 1 (1947), pp. 15–16. Note that the privatization model outlined here is not identical to the current US model of separation (for more on the latter model, see Hamburger, 2004; Taylor, 1998). Some parts of the current American system provide what might be called soft establishment—that is, tax exemptions given to religious

In a similar vein, one can point to the French law that states, in the context of religion-state relations, that "[t]he Republic does not recognize, remunerate, or subsidize any religious denomination" (Robert, 2003, p. 640).

In the framework of the privatization model, a religiously diverse citizenry— including those who don't endorse any religion—will not suffer from legal, material, or even symbolic inequality of treatment based on their religious beliefs or affiliation. Such unequal treatment is likely whenever a state, even one that seeks to maintain formal equality in all areas of rights (political rights, due process, etc.), identifies with one denomination. The privatization model views such an identification as inherently illegitimate.[3]

In order to better understand the privatization model, especially in the context of religion-state relations, it is important to mind the distinction between "public" and "state" domains (Starr, 1989). While a privatized religion-state model prevents religions from recruiting the state for the advancement of their own goals and ideals, these religions are not denied a public presence. Indeed, a wide variety of privately owned entities (religions included) have a conspicuous public appearance apart from state apparatus. Succinctly put, the distinctive feature of privatized religions is not eliminating any public presence or appearance, but rather maintaining their *nonstatist* affiliation (Gavison, 1994).

In the context of the privatization approach, the state creates a system of rules that are applied equally to all with the intention that members of different religions can pursue their beliefs, associate or disassociate with other believers,

---

institutions and legitimacy given to institutionalized prayer, as in the *Marsh* and *Town of Greece* cases (in which the legislature in Nebraska and the municipality at the Town of Greece, New York, were allowed to open their sessions with a prayer; this was permitted, mainly, for the reasons that such practices have been in place for an extended period of time and cannot be considered coercive (see *Town of Greece v. Galloway*, 572 U.S. (2014); *Marsh v. Chambers*, 463 U.S. 783 (1983)). While this is not the place for an extended discussion of the US model, it is important to note that the privatization model is not fully practiced in the United States (McConnell, 1999–2000; Muniz-Fraticelli, 2014; Langvardt, 2014); neither is the US model of separation identical to the French system, which includes some prohibitions that stand in tension with the general thrust of the "noninterference" aspect of the privatization approach (on the French system, see Robert, 2003; Laborde, 2008).

3. One particularly controversial aspect of the privatization approach is the standing that it gives to religious arguments in courts decisions, justification for legislation, and other political and legal usages. John Rawls famously argued that religious arguments should not be used in such spheres unless a parallel liberal argument can be found, or—in rare occasions—when such religious arguments are necessary in order to advance a liberal cause in a certain cultural context (such as the religious arguments of the abolitionists). See Rawls (2001, p. 90; 2001b, p. 584; 1993, pp. 249–251). Rawls' arguments have been met with considerable skepticism, largely focusing on whether liberal arguments are themselves sectarian, and whether disqualifying religious arguments is intolerant (McConnell, 1999). This entire complex debate cannot be further addressed here.

and practice or abandon their religions as they see fit. This "background" system of rules eschews any intent, as mentioned above, of supporting or hindering
any one specific denomination (Patten, 2014, pp. 119–123). Note, however, that
the privatization approach does not attempt to guarantee an equality of effects
that these rules will unavoidably have on different denominations. It is obvious
that many rules—whether safety regulations,[4] mandatory school attendance,[5] or
health regulations[6]—might have different effects on different religious groups
with varying beliefs and traditions. Such "collisions," between the demands of
different religions and generally applicable laws, are becoming more common as
the quantity and complexity of administrative tasks performed by modern states
grows (Epstein, 1990).

Without delving into these complex and controversial issues, we note that in
principle, as long as such laws are general, enjoy reasonable justification, and are
not "tailored" to harm or to benefit specific denominations, they are legitimate
from the viewpoint of the privatization approach. This is the case even if such
laws have different effects on different religions.[7] Of course, while the privatization model does not require that the state attempt to reach equality of effects,
exemptions to general laws can be considered in cases wherein acute difficulties
arise (see, generally, Greenawalt, 2007; Kelly, 2002; Caney, 2002; Perez, 2009;
Gey, 2005; Macedo, 1995).[8]

Having presented privatization as a comprehensive model, or Weberian
"ideal type," we turn to explore the actual process aiming at realizing it either in

---

4. A well-known example of the tension between religious custom and public safety measures
is the *kirpan* (ceremonial sword) which must be worn at all times by observant followers of the
Sikh religion. While ceremonial, many view this sword as a weapon that should be subject to
the same safety rules as any other weapon (Larson, 1995, pp. 234–244; Singh, 2004).

5. In the famous *Yoder* case (Wisconsin v. Yoder, 406 U.S 205 (1972)), the US Supreme Court
decided to grant an exemption, on religious grounds, to the Amish community from generally
applicable laws regarding mandatory attendance at public schools.

6. A famous example of how modern health regulations challenge religious traditions is the
circumcision practiced on male or female infants in some religions. Such practices attract
fierce debate regarding whether exemption from the general rule—which prohibits medically
unnecessary procedures on infants—should be granted on religious and cultural grounds; for
the debate, see Greenawalt (2007); Coleman (2007); Spinner Halev (2000); Shweder (2009);
Shweder (2000).

7. See Barry (2001, chap. 2); Jones (1994); Kurland (1961); the Lockean argument on which
they rely can be found in Locke (2010, pp. 25–26).

8. The willingness to grant exemptions, in certain cases, stands as legitimate so long as such
exemptions do not multiply to the point of a de facto transformation of the privatized model
into a DCV or an evenhanded model. Such exemptions should be considered in cases which
typically involve a general rule which is not impartial; a practice perceived as constitutive or

part or in full. In general, as indicated by Barak-Erez, privatization as a *process* should be understood "as a legal phenomenon [. . .] encompassing any policy that reduces governmental involvement in economic and social life" (Barak-Erez, 2011, p. 140).[9] In the religious realm, this process denotes cases in which a given state had an established or endorsed religion (a version of the DCV model; see chapter 3), but decidedly moves toward a privatized religion-state model. Such a move involves some of the following noteworthy changes: the abolition of an established state-church, the abolition of state funding for religious activities, the abolition of blasphemy laws, and others (Barak-Erez, 2011). From the perspective of the individual believer, there are two important consequences of this process: *first*, any governmental impediments to freedom of religion will be lessened if not abolished; *second*, in cases in which religious services were provided by the state, they will have to be privately purchased or paid for.

A case that demonstrates this process is the abolishment of Lutheran Protestantism's status as Sweden's established church in 2000. In an official publication of the Swedish Ministry of Culture, addressing the "changed relations between the State and the Church of Sweden," the reform was described as follows:

> The decision means that the Church of Sweden has left the public sector and is thus on more of a par with other religious communities [. . .] The reform has given the Church of Sweden full freedom, within the

---

central to the religion requesting the exemption; and additional cardinal considerations such as effects on other interests (safety, nondiscrimination, health considerations, cost to the public, etc.). Lastly, granting an exemption does not necessarily entail that the person or group requesting it should be exempted from dealing with the costs or other associated difficulties the exemption generates (see chapter 4). Balancing the wide variety of considerations that are involved in evaluating such requests—exemptions on religious grounds—is not a trivial task. Ultimately, the issue demands an analysis beyond the bounds of the present inquiry; all that we wish to note here is that the privatization approach does not require the refusal of all such requests.

9. This process can take various forms (Barak-Erez, 2011; Perez, 2013). In the economic sphere, Megginson (2005) suggests the following, narrower definition:

> The political and economic policy of privatization, broadly defined as the deliberate sale by a government of state-owned enterprises (SOEs) or assets to private economic agents, has been one of the most important and visible aspects of this global trend toward greater reliance on markets to allocate resources. (p. 3)

The controversy regarding the success, and efficiency, of the privatization process in the economic sphere lies beyond the boundaries of the current study (see Starr, 1989; Dorfman & Harel, 2013). It is, nevertheless, important to note that there are two different meanings of privatization which are both prominent in the economic context: the change of ownership

framework of the new legislation and existing system of rules, to decide over its own business [. . .] Parishes and church associations no longer enjoy their status as local authorities and their right to levy taxes has been abolished. (Sweden, 2000, "Changed Relations")

Viewing privatization as a process, and not merely as a Weberian "ideal type," is essential for our analysis; not only is it part and parcel of understanding this model, it is also essential in the two case studies chosen for this book (the Western Wall and the Ayodhya dispute). In each case, the solutions attempted so far have not followed the privatization model. Adopting a privatized approach in these cases would, therefore, entail a process leading to a full or partial privatization of the site (see chapter 2; section 5.4; and the appendix).

5.2. Two Potential Misrepresentations of the Privatization Model

This section will clarify two potential misunderstandings of what the privatization of religion is, what it entails, and what its possible outcomes might be. We will look, first, at the conflation of Protestant Christianity with the model of privatization and, second, address the misguided notion that privatization is inherently adversarial to religion.

First, the privatization model is, at times, exclusively associated with a particular and unique set of religious attitudes that are considered typical to, and brought about by Protestant forms of Christianity. According to this criticism, the privatization model is ill-suited to non-Protestant religions with different value systems.[10] Relevant evidence readily demonstrates that this association of Protestantism and privatization is far too simplistic; leading scholars of toleration, such as Zagorin (2003, chap. 5) and Forst (2013, p. 117), have demonstrated that Protestant denominations have historically used the coercive powers of the state in order to advance their religious goals. This phenomenon alone

---

from public to private, and a retreat of the state from a realm that it previously occupied. In the economic realm, the issues of ownership and of the retreat of the state are usually interwoven. Indeed, when the government retreats from a certain economic territory, it allows private individuals and corporations to enter the vacated domain. Markets will replace the government in allocating resources (broadly defined). As will be demonstrated in the discussion below, privatization in the religious sphere, though sharing some aspects with the ways that this concept is used in the economic realm, differs on other grounds. This is especially the case in the context of thick sites (see section 5.4).

10. Casanova (1992, pp. 55–56); Gavison (1994, p. 77); Simon (1982, pp. 9–45).

shows that Protestantism can be directly opposed to the central tenets of the model of privatization. While the rise of Protestantism in early modern Europe, and the religiously diverse states that it created, was obviously connected to the development of new models of religion-state relations—separation included[11]—Protestantism itself was at times strongly associated with given states (Skinner, 1978, vol. 2, pp. 249–254; Labrousse, 1973; Gregory, 2012). Calvin's Geneva and the infamous execution of Michael Servetus in 1553, for example, provide a dramatic demonstration of this point (Friedman, 1978).

Furthermore, Protestantism, especially in its Lutheran version, did not adopt fundamental presuppositions, including the central principle of freedom of conscience, of the privatization model.[12] It should also be noted, as will be demonstrated in section 5.3, that many non-Protestant religious leaders and scholars advocate privatization. In both the legal systems of India (see the appendix) and of Israel (see chapter 2)—two distinctly non-Protestant states—one can identify some elements of the privatization model at work; in the preamble of its constitution, India is defined as a secular state, and many aspects of Israel's legal and political system similarly lean toward privatization (Israel's basic law human dignity and liberty is one notable example).[13]

The idea that the model of privatization in religion-state relations is exclusively rooted in Protestantism, and that the model necessitates a Protestant citizenry and "worldview," is simply incorrect as a matter of historical fact.

A second misunderstanding of the model of privatization is the association of the model with an adversarial approach to religion, or at least with an indifference toward religious belief and practice.[14] As shown in section (5.3), the privatization model is often endorsed by religious scholars and believers specifically as a method of protecting religion from the heavy hand of the state. Indeed, this line of reasoning played an important role in the adoption of this model (or

---

11. In his *Unintended Reformation* (2012), Gregory notes the complexity of Protestantism's role in promoting the separation of religious and civil authorities; he argues that while Catholics, Lutherans, and Reformed Protestants all lost the struggle for supremacy, the conflict itself "fundamentally shaped the subsequent course of Western history in ways *they* could not have foreseen" (Gregory, 2012, p. 160; italics added).

12. Rainer Forst describes how the combination of Luther's antihumanist, antitolerant Protestantism and his fierce aversion to the Catholic Church unintentionally opened the door for religious individualism and freedom of conscience. Luther himself, however, was explicitly averse to both values (Forst, 2013, pp. 117–118).

13. On this basic law, in the context of privatization in Israel, see Hirschl (1998); see also Ben-Porat (2013); Perez (2013); the appendix (regarding India).

14. For a discussion of this association, see Fox (2008, 12–31); Audi and Wolterstorff (1997, esp. pp. 111–113); Williams (2006, p. 93).

something very close to it) in some key legal and political cases, most famously (and influentially) in Virginia in the late eighteenth century.[15]

Furthermore, empirical data indicates that the privatization of institutional religion has beneficial consequences for religious practice. Describing the privatization of religion in Connecticut and Massachusetts in the early nineteenth century, Olds (1994) notes that "[t]he amount of preachers' services consumed surged after privatization in Connecticut and after the partial 1824 privatization in Massachusetts. . . the public church's local monopoly was restraining demand and. . . organized religion gained from the privatization" (p. 282).

More generally, religions thrive under legal orders that share important attributes of the privatization model, as is the case in the United States and France.[16] The association of the privatization model with indifference or opposition toward religion, therefore, does not fit the available data and recognized historical and religious examples; without further evidence, conspicuously lacking at the present, this criticism cannot be accepted.

5.3. Four Justifications of the Privatization Model of Religion-State Relations

A tremendous amount of literature has been dedicated to analyzing and justifying, in various ways, the privatization model of religion-state relations. Our goal, here, is not to cover all of the available justifications for the privatization model; relying on Wittgenstein's paradigm of "family resemblance," our aim is to map out the most important families of justifications given for adopting this model.[17] Succinctly put, we identify four families of justification: *political arguments, equality arguments, liberty arguments*, and *religious arguments*. We adopt here what A. Sen (2009) calls a "plural grounding" (p. 2); that is, we offer several arguments for a certain position without offering a ranking of importance among them.

We begin with the family of political arguments. The first such argument, which concerns the nature of the state, can be called the *state-inadequacy argument*. According to this justification, the government—any government, regardless of its form—is the wrong instrument for conducting theological inquiries, reaching religious decisions, and enforcing any form of religious practice or belief. Consequently, the privatization model proves desirable as it avoids complex entanglements of the government with religion, entanglements which burden the

---

15. See Levy (1994); Curry (1986).

16. See, for the US context, Albright, Kohut, Stokes, McIntosh, Gross, and Speulda, (2002); Taylor (2007, p. 2). For the French context, see Cooperman and Lipka (2014).

17. See Wittgenstein (2009, pp. 36, sect. 66).

government with tasks that it is ill equipped to accomplish (Locke, 1689/2010; Schuck, 2003; Epstein, 1995; Waldron, 1991). Any deviation from the privatization approach, this view argues, will force the state to adopt highly controversial positions, which will implicitly involve selecting the one true faith (if any). This inquiry is best left to clergy, scholars, and the private conscience of individuals, rather than the state bureaucracy.[18]

The second such political argument, which is forward looking, can be called the *social stability argument*. It states that a policy of the privatization of religion reduces hostile competition between different religions that otherwise attempt to recruit the state to promote their values and even to repress other religious groups (Ripple, 1980; Rawls, 1993, pp. 201–206). This argument was eloquently stated by Justice Black of the US Supreme Court, whose opinion is worth quoting at length:

> With the power of government supporting them, at various times and places, Catholics had persecuted Protestants, Protestants had persecuted Catholics, Protestant sects had persecuted other Protestant sects, Catholics of one shade of belief had persecuted Catholics of another shade of belief, and all of these had from time to time persecuted Jews. In efforts to force loyalty to whatever religious group happened to be on top and in league with the government of a particular time and place, men and women had been fined, cast in jail, cruelly tortured, and killed. Among the offenses for which these punishments had been inflicted were such things as speaking disrespectfully of the views of ministers of government-established churches, nonattendance at those churches, expressions of non-belief in their doctrines, and failure to pay taxes and tithes to support them. (*Everson v. Board of Education*, 330 U.S. 1 (1947), p. 9)

These dire consequences—of allowing the recruitment of the state by religions—can be avoided simply by adopting the privatization model. Indeed, under this model, the various religions and denominations would be unable to recruit the state to advance their own particular worldviews (Grim & Finke, 2011). Therefore, the argument goes, the privatization model assists in, and might well be crucial for, the creation of long term social stability.[19]

The second family of justifications for the privatization approach can be labeled the *equality set of arguments*. According to these arguments, citizens of democratic

---

18. In some cases, scholars and decision-makers have attempted to justify an endorsed or an established church not because it represents the one true faith, but because that religion allegedly fulfills a useful social function. We critically explored this argument in chapter 3.

19. John Courtney Murray (1954), the important twentieth-century American Jesuit priest and theologian known for his efforts to reconcile Catholicism with religious pluralism (and who

states rightly expect that their governments will treat them all as equals and safeguard their rights equally. As citizens of Western democracies, and most other contemporary states, tend to hold various different religious beliefs, including none at all, a government that adheres to one given religion would violate its commitment to treat its citizens with equal concern and respect (Rawls, 1993; Dworkin, 1977; Dahl, 2006).[20] Therefore, democratic governments should attempt, as much as possible, to avoid establishing and/or favoring any religion. The endorsement of a religion, as Justice O'Connor of the US Supreme Court argues in her concurring opinion, "sends a message to non-adherents that they are outsiders, not full members of the political community, and an accompanying message to adherents that they are insiders, favored members of the political community" (*Lynch v. Donnelly* 465 US 668, 688 (1984)). A major advantage of the privatization approach, therefore, is that it safeguards the equal status of citizens belonging to different denominations—including those with no religion—by keeping religion and state apart. Furthermore, by respecting the equal status of all citizens through a hands-off approach, the state also respects the rights of citizens to join (or leave) any religious group or association as they see fit (Greenawalt, 1998). This means that the choices which citizens make to associate religiously (if so they choose) are respected since they have no bearing on their status as equal citizens.

A third family of justifications for the privatization approach can be called the *liberty family of arguments*. It is a hallmark of liberalism that states should respect the "presumption of liberty" and that any state interference with individual conduct requires explicit justification. This justification, moreover, should be strong and significant, especially when state intervention will restrict a sphere

---

played a key role, during the Second Vatican Council, in persuading the assembly of Catholic bishops to adopt the council's ground-breaking Declaration on Religious Liberty, *Dignitatis humanae*), argued, regarding the US First Amendment, that

> [f]rom the standpoint both of history and of contemporary social reality the only tenable position is that the first two articles of the First Amendment are not articles of faith but *articles of peace*. Like the rest of the Constitution these provisions are the work of lawyers, not of theologians." (p. 56; italics added)

Note that Murray, a religious person, provided here a nonreligious argument, which appealed to social stability, for his proposed approach to religion-state issues.

20. In Dworkin's (2000) adroit words,

> People of every race, faith and ambition may be born into the same political community, and it is deeply implausible that the characterization of communal life that best fits such a community could be one that assumes that it must choose one faith or set of personal ambitions or ethnic allegiance, or one set of standards of sexual responsibility. . . that characterization not only does not fit the criteria of citizenship; it makes them close to nonsensical. (p. 229)

of considerable importance like the freedom of religion (Gaus, 2000, chap. 4; Hayek, 1978, vol. 2, chap. 9; Hart, 1973).

Citizens in democratic states face a wide variety of state-imposed limitations on their conduct: traffic lights, safety regulations in workplaces, and so on. Most such limitations, however, are not considered particularly controversial or worthy of objection. These limitations become more controversial when they are imposed on core rights that are directly linked to one's well-being, such as (for example) freedom of speech, freedom of movement, etc. In these cases, special justifications are widely deemed to be necessary. The issue of freedom of and from religion is widely considered to be of great significance,[21] and therefore state intervention, or restriction, levied on religious behavior, would have to be justified adequately. Accordingly, unless robust, explicit justifications are provided, the right of freedom of and from religion, just as freedom of speech and other core rights, should not be hindered. The privatization approach, therefore, protects the freedom to practice one's religion; this includes the right to establish, join, or leave religious associations with no fear of unjustified governmental interference. Indeed, this attribute of the privatization model is one of its important advantages over competing models of religion-state relations.[22]

The fourth and final family of justifications for the privatization approach can be called the *religious set of arguments.* Such arguments suggest that adopting the privatization approach is in the interest of religions as such; religious leaders and

---

21. There are many different arguments that emphasize the importance of religious freedom. Some major examples include: (i) the historical argument—that is, that religious freedom are especially important as demonstrated, for example, by the European religious wars that followed the reformation; (ii) the importance of religious freedom for many other key interests, such as the integrity of personal identity; (iii) the role that religion plays in many aspects of human activity and values by answering the "big questions"; (iv) the role of religious freedom in personal autonomy (at times mediated via freedom of conscience), from which the importance of religious freedom is derived.

A different, yet connected, issue is determining the scope of defense from the state and economic forces that religious freedom merits. Here there are two main positions (with a broad continuum between them). The first argues that religious liberties should be accorded an especially strong defense which justifies not only noninterference from the state, but also can justify exemptions from generally applicable laws (to point to one prominent example). The second position argues that the defense accorded to religious liberties should be no different than the defense of any other area in which a person practices or executes her/his liberty. The connection between the justification for, and the scope of religious freedom is not straightforward or linear. This is a fairly developed area of study, see Barry (2001); McConnell (2000); Durham (2009); Boyle (2007); Witte (1996); Greenawalt (2007); Nickel (2005); Fox (2016).

22. McConnell (1999, 2000a) argues for the primary importance of religious freedom, and indicates that he supports the separation of church and state in order to protect this freedom: "My intention here is to defend the idea of religious freedom as our first freedom . . . in defense of religion against the encroachment of the state" (McConnell 1999; 2000a, p. 1244).

scholars whose aim is to protect, defend, or improve religions have developed several such arguments.[23] This "family" of arguments contains two main clusters: the first deals with protecting religions from state interference; the second appeals to the benefits gained by religions who function within the "market situations" that are created by the privatization model.[24] We shall examine each in turn.

Fearing the *corrupting effect* that the state might have on religion, and wishing to protect the purity of religions, several scholars and theorists have favored maintaining a distance between the state and religion in order to preserve religious institutions against political influence.[25] Stanley Hauerwas (2001), a contemporary Christian theologian, argued precisely this: "[W]e shall pollute our Christian faith by making of it a civil religion" (p. 478).

In a similar vein, others noted not only that the state may have a corrupting influence, but also that *the heavy hand of the state* may interfere with religious matters. This is a bitter lesson learned through the many historical instances in which aggressive politicians meddled in the internal workings of religions. In the deliberations held in the American colonies prior to the establishment of the United States, and in the context of the US Constitution and its famous First Amendment, the separation of religion and state was enthusiastically promoted as many contemporaneous religious scholars and leaders argued that separation is desirable from a religious perspective (Levy, 1994; Curry, 1986; Nussbaum, 2008).

---

23. Our use of the term "religious argument" necessitates two brief comments. *First,* we use the term broadly and, therefore, include arguments that refer to religions, as opposed to a "narrow" approach which, as Bernard Williams put it, is limited to arguments that have meaning only within a certain system of thought or belief (1985, pp. 140–152; in his discussion of "thick concepts"). *Second,* it should be emphasized that religious arguments for the privatization model, to be discussed below, do not necessitate that the state attributes importance to religions above and beyond other system of beliefs or conduct; such preference might violate the equality justification for the privatization model noted above (Koppelman, 2013; Gill, 2008). In this context, we note Rawls' general insistence that religious arguments of any kind are to be excluded from certain legal and political institutional contexts. However, even Rawls allows the usage of religious arguments in certain cultural contexts in which they are required for the achievement of liberal goals (alluding, for example, to the abolitionists). See Rawls, 2001a, p. 90; 2001b, p. 584; 1993, pp. 249–251. In our context, a similar logic applies since the privatization approach enables, or protects, important liberal interests as identified above: equality, liberty, and social stability. Furthermore, it might be relevant to note that, historically, such religious arguments were among the most important arguments for the US adoption of the separation model (Nussbaum, 2008, chap. 2).

24. See Berger (1990, p. 138).

25. Smith described this process as follows: "Deprived of the trappings of public office and the coercive power of the state, religion would be privatized, left to the conscience or the inner light of the individual believer" (Smith, 1997, p. 3).

Such religious arguments for privatization can be found across religious boundaries in Christian, Islamic, and Jewish sources.[26] In the Islamic context, for example, An Naim (2010) claims that

> Sharia principles cannot be enacted and enforced by the state as public law and public policy ... if such enactment and enforcement is attempted, the outcome will necessarily be the political will of the state and not the religious law of Islam. The fact that ruling elites sometimes make such claims to legitimize their control of the state in the name of Islam does not mean that such claims are true. (p. 1)

In the Jewish context, Suzanne Last Stone aptly summarizes the view of Hayyim Ozer Grodzinsky, the Ultra-Orthodox rabbinic leader of Lithuania, in the late nineteenth and early twentieth centuries, who "wished to protect the garden of religious Halakha from any state but especially a Jewish state, by separating the two at the outset" (Stone, 2008, pp. 640–641). One can note, additionally, the late Jewish philosopher Yeshayahu Leibowitz (1992), who wrote that "counterfeit religion identifies national interests with the service of God and imputes to the state—which is only an instrument serving human needs—supreme value from a religious standpoint" (pp. 226–227).[27]

Note that we do not claim that such views are dominant within any or all of the religious traditions mentioned. We simply show, here, that arguments for adopting the privatization model for religious motivations can be found within these various religious traditions. This is hardly surprising as state oppression and violence toward individuals and organizations—including religious ones (typically, but not only, toward religious dissenters)— have been common in world history. It is to be expected, therefore, that religious thinkers would seek means by which to restrain state violence and oppression; unsurprisingly, some have attempted to do so by adopting the privatization model.[28]

---

26. See Koppelman (2013); Ravitzky (1998, pp. 49–89); Leibowitz (1992); Stone (2008); An Naim (2010).

27. For an extensive examination of the various models of relations between religion and state within the Jewish tradition, see Walzer (2012); Lorberbaum (2001); Belfer (2004); Ravitzky (1998); Hellinger (2009).

28. Indeed, studies of the history of religious thought reveal an unsurprising similarity between Christian and Jewish sources. See, for example, how J. A. Watt, a prominent scholar of Christian religion-state relations in the Middle Ages, expresses this point:

Another religious argument in favor of the privatization model grounds the immunity of religious groups from state intervention in the existence of a distance, or even a barrier between the state and such groups. The argument is as follows: religious groups that are distanced from the state (i.e., do not receive monetary assistance, legal backing, symbolic recognition, etc.), are able to claim that this "distance" from any statist apparatus means that they are voluntary associations. As such, the fact that individual members are not prevented from exiting such groups (nor were they pressured by the state to join them in the first place) supports these groups' claims to be immune from state intervention, even in cases in which the rules of the "association" are in tension with liberal democratic norms. The status of a "voluntary association" serves, therefore, as an important argument for religious groups' immunity from state intervention, inclusive of the application of nondiscrimination norms that usually apply in statist and public contexts in democratic countries.[29] However, if a religion becomes too closely associated with the state, membership within it can lose its voluntary status; in such a situation, that religion would find itself unable to defend deviations from the usual non-discriminatory norms.[30]

Popes of the early middle ages, concerned to halt imperial intervention in ecclesiastical affairs, had emphasized God's division of the powers and his will that neither power should usurp what was proper to the other's sphere . . . sensitive to the need to conserve libertas ecclesiae. (Watt, 1988, p. 378)

Compare that with the way in which Aviezer Ravitzky (2002), a major scholar of Jewish political thought, argued in the same vein:

Political men will never willingly erect boundaries for themselves or restrict themselves in favor of another authority. For when human beings attain power [...] (it) tends to grow and expand, seeking to burst every constraint [...] such a threat can be anticipated . . . never voluntarily withdrawing in the face of Divine Torah. (p. 88, specifically discussing the thought of the great Jewish thinker, Yitzhak Abrabanel, 1437–1508)

Such views grant support to the notion that the separation of religion and state is intended for the protection of religion from the state (see also Sisk, 1998).

29. While obviously not all justifications for religious freedom adopt this description, it certainly has some important support, see Kukathas (1997); Nickel (2005).

30. This "immunity" argument makes use of contested empirical and normative claims; can religious groups be counted as voluntary associations? What counts as a "real" right to exit? What happens when voluntary membership collides with nondiscrimination claims? What distinctions should be made regarding the strength of immunity granted to different groups? These are weighty questions that cannot be addressed here. The goal of this discussion was simply to outline another religious argument, which has a certain importance in today's legal circles (including the WoW case, as we will note), for distancing state authority from the religious sphere. On the political, moral and legal debate, see Okin (2002); Walzer (1997); Kukathas (1997); Preub (2012); Bagni (1979); Weinstock (2005); Levy (2015).

The "immunity" argument was used, recently, in the context of the WoW case. In late 2015, members of the WoW, via the Center for Women's Justice—an Israeli NGO that deals with issues pertaining to women's equality (broadly conceived) in Israeli society— brought a petition to the Israeli Supreme Court which argued that the legal ban against bringing Torah scrolls to the women's section of the Wall is illegal; they also brought a civil suit against the Rabbi of the Wall that sought compensation for what they claimed to be gender-based discrimination.[31] In both the petition to the Supreme Court and in the civil lawsuit, a central part of the argument was that the Rabbi of the Wall functions as a part of the state. His actions, therefore, must be subject to Israeli laws that pertain to state organs. As such laws clearly forbid discrimination based on gender, the WoW maintained that the rabbi's actions violate the law.

Without judging the merits of the case,[32] the claim can be cited to exemplify the "immunity" argument for privatization: if religions would like to maintain immunity from state intervention and nondiscrimination norms, they should not function so closely with the state as to become, de facto, identical with it and cease being voluntary associations.

The common concern of this first cluster of religious arguments for the privatization of religion—whether addressing "corruption," "aggressive state meddling," or "immunity"—is creating a proper distance between religion and state. That is, the adoption of the privatization model is primarily intended to protect religion from the state in various important ways.

Moving forward, the second cluster of religious arguments for the privatization approach points to the fact that, once they are unable to recruit the state to advance their own agenda, religions must compete for members by demonstrating their virtues and wisdom. Peter Berger (1990) eloquently described the "market situation" of religions created by the privatization model:

> Religious ex-monopolies can no longer take for granted the allegiance of their client populations. Allegiance is voluntary and thus, by definition, less than certain. As a result, the religious tradition, which previously could be authoritatively imposed, now has to be *marketed*. It must be 'sold' to a clientele that is no longer constrained to 'buy.'" (p. 138)

---

31. On file with the authors.

32. It is true that not all connections with the state would make a religious group vulnerable to such lawsuits; we would hesitate to argue that merely receiving funding (as in some even-handed models, see chapter 4) is sufficient to connect a religious group with the state in such a fashion; however, once other factors are added to state funding—for example, the usage of laws and the police to advance a world view that is particular to one religious faction, as is done at the Wall—the connection and affinity between religion and state becomes so substantial as to make the religion vulnerable to such legal interventions.

Believers would, in such a scenario, find a richer variety of denominations, which would be, presumably, more attentive to their needs. Religions will have to adapt in order to attract, and avoid losing, believers. As succinctly argued by Finke and Stark (1988): "to the degree a religious market is unregulated, pluralism will thrive" (p. 42). Simply stated, the second cluster of arguments maintains that a disentanglement of the state from religion would be better for believers, potential believers, *and* the religious institutions themselves in the long run (Bayle, 1686/2005 pp. 199–200; Berger, 1990, chap. 6; Gill, 2007, chap. 2).[33]

This ends our examination of the privatization model of religion-state relations on a general level. We turn now to explore the application of the privatization model to the contested topic of thick sites.

5.4. Privatizing "Thick Sites": Keeping the State at a Proper Distance

The aim of this detailed subsection is to examine the application of the privatization model to thick sites. Our main argument —that the privatization approach is not only the most promising model for religion-state relations as a whole, but also the most adequate governmental response for thick sites—will be demonstrated with reference to the Western Wall and the Women of the Wall case study. As was mentioned in the preface to the chapters dedicated to specific theoretical models (3–5), even scholars who support other models for religion-state relations, in general, might find that the privatization approach is more suitable in the particular case of thick sites than the alternatives.[34] However, given the unique features of thick sites, we do suggest a somewhat nuanced version of the privatization approach, one that we call *context-sensitive privatization*.

This subsection is structured as follows: we begin (section 5.4.1) by exploring the hypothetical application of the privatization model to thick sites in general,

---

33. Nonstatism does not mean that the religious person maintains an attitude of indifference to the public arena or the state; it is simply the understanding that the state is an inappropriate avenue for *religious tikun olam*. Stanley Hauerwas (2001) makes this point insightfully:

> [W]e have a stake in fostering those forms of human association that ensure that the virtues can be sustained. Virtues make it possible to sustain a society committed to working out differences short of violence. What I fear, however, is that in the absence of those associations we will seek to solve the moral anomie of the American people through state action or by a coercive reclaiming of Christian America. (p. 479)

34. Moreover, it is quite possible (even common), for one to be in favor of privatization in the religious sphere and yet opposed to it in the economic sphere. This is Rawls' position, for example, in his *Political Liberalism* (1993); see also Epstein (1990).

and to the Western Wall in particular. We then respond (section 5.4.2) to three potential objections to the application of the privatization approach to thick sites: fear of violence (or the "backlash" problem) (section 5.4.2.1); "baseline" problems (section 5.4.2.2); and, finally, religious incompatibility claims that are often articulated as "offenses to religious feelings" (section 5.4.2.3).

5.4.1. Privatizing Thick Sites

The privatization of thick sites, in simplest terms, means that a government retreats from its heavy presence at, and exclusive management of (usually in association with one particular, dominant religious group), specific thick sites; once such sites are privatized, the state limits itself to providing law and order. However, since thick sites are uniquely irreplaceable and central for various religions, effective application of the privatization model requires special consideration and caution. Succinctly put, the uniqueness of such sites requires a form of privatization that differs from the model of economic privatization that is characterized by (a) transfer of ownership from public to private and (b) the diminution or elimination of governmental control. Indeed, thick sites necessitate a diminution of control *only* and *not* an accompanying transfer of ownership from public to private.[35]

The first step in elaborating this point is to note that thick sites—such as the Western Wall or the Ram Janmabhoomi / Babri Masjid—that are situated on public land[36] are usually heavily regulated (see chapter 2 and the appendix). A privatized model, were it to be applied to such locations, will not usually entail the selling of such land and ownership changing from the state to private hands; rather, it would mean a retreat of the state from the *overregulation* that exists in such contested locations. This goal may not be served if a private owner gains control of the site and might maintain strict regulations once the state retreats. The main goal of privatization, therefore, is not to change ownership of the site. The primary goal is to move the religious decision process that establishes legitimate religious behavior at the site, from the state to the individual.

The theoretical justification for why privatization would entail a diminution of governmental involvement in thick sites, yet not a change of ownership, is as follows. Were thick sites transferred from the state to private ownership, the *irreplaceability* of such sites means that a monopoly over such sites will likely be

---

35. It should be noted that the connection between these two aspects of privatization is anything but simple, as is evident in cases in which the transfer of ownership was accompanied by heavy regulation.

36. See the appendix regarding this point in the context of the Ram Janmabhoomi / Babri Masjid.

created. In economics, a monopoly denotes an enterprise that is the only seller of a good or service, often supported with governmental assistance that legally excludes competition (Stigler, 2008). The usual way to address the problem of monopolies is with competition; as other parties enter the relevant market, consumers can shift from one provider to the next. This choice increases societal welfare. In the sociology of religion, a similar process is described in the context of "religious markets"; the process of governmental retreat results in many religious organizations providing religious services that were formally provided by a single established religion. By allowing consumer choice, this encourages the offering of better service if a religious group wishes to remain in competition for retaining believers (Finke & Stark, 1988). In thick sites, however, this market logic seems inappropriate since the move from public to private ownership does not solve the problematic monopoly situation; there is no market as another Western Wall cannot be produced and no competition can arise.[37] Allowing one person to own a thick site, such as the Western Wall, would thus mean that limitations of access and other modes of behavior could be introduced.[38] Such a situation would bring about the exact opposite of that which the privatization process was set out to achieve in the first place, that is, increasing individual choice at thick sites that are overregulated to the point of limiting religious practice.[39]

If the application of the privatization model to thick sites, such as the Western Wall, does not entail a transfer from public to private ownership, what might privatization of the Western Wall look like? A hypothetical application of this model to the Western Wall would involve, without claiming exhaustiveness, several clear results: the governmental position of the Rabbi of the Wall would be canceled; the Western Wall Heritage Foundation would cease to exist as it currently stands,

37. Lionel Robbins' (1935) classic definition of economics, it is important to remember, was "the science which studies human behaviour as a relationship between ends and scarce means that have *alternative uses*" (p. 15; italics added). Worshippers at sites such as the Western Wall will never agree that there are alternative uses for this location (hence, its irreplaceability); the inadequacy of this particular market logic to thick sites follows from this particular point.

38. A brief comment on the Lockean aspect of the irreplaceability feature is relevant here: Locke, with his "enough and as good" proviso, introduced a well-known limit to the ability to accumulate property. As the irreplaceability feature is, in principle, the exact kind of "thing" that cannot be replicated or further produced, the Lockean proviso would ban exclusive private ownership over it (note, however, that this philosophical point does not settle the practical question of which kind of ownership would best serve believers. On the Lockean proviso, see Locke (1690/1980, p. 19)).

39. We wish, however, to avoid a common mistake of comparing an idealized privatized religion-state model with a worst-case scenario of private ownership in the economic and religious realms. Sufficient empirical research might demonstrate that private ownership provides, on balance, better conservation of, better access to, and less restrictive usage of thick sites than state ownership; the difference between privatization in the economic sphere and the religious sphere might, indeed, prove less distinct than has been assumed.

that is, as a government organ dominated by the Ultra-Orthodox; the specific regulations in both the 1967 and 1981 laws regarding sacred sites, which limit religious practice to avoid "offenses to religious feelings" and to maintain the "custom of the place,"[40] would be revoked; the permanent gender-partition would be removed, though portable dividers would still be permissible (note the difference between outlawing and forcibly installing a divider; privatization, here, means neither forcing nor banning dividers and leaving the matter of their usage as a voluntary choice); and, lastly, the management of the Wall would be taken away from the ministry of religious affairs.[41]

Moreover, the adoption of the privatization model for thick sites would have the further implication of abolishing the term "sacred sites"[42] from all legal discourse and replacing it with a more suitable term such as "thick site." Indeed, the term "sacred" would *not* be ascribed to a site or tradition by the legal system of a state that adopts the privatization model (either in whole or partially). Religious appellations such as "sacred" or "holy," based in particular religious worldviews,[43] are highly disputed. In the Israeli context, for example, the term "holy" appears in the 1967 and 1981 Israeli laws regarding such sites, yet its usage is controversial both across religious affiliations[44] and within the Jewish religion itself.[45] The

---

40. See 2.3.1 for a further consideration of these laws, and the analysis below regarding "offences to religious feelings."

41. It should be noted, in this context, that the department in charge of sacred sites within the ministry of religious affairs was transferred to the ministry of tourism between 2003 and 2013. This was the result of coalition building and political maneuvering in Israel: in 2003, the coalition agreement of two major parties, Likud and Shinui, dissolved the Ministry of Religious Affairs following Shinui's (a radical secularist party) demand. As a consequence, different departments under the authority of this ministry were "moved" to other ministries. The ministry was re-established in 2008, following new coalitional considerations, and the department dealing with sacred sites was returned to it in 2013. While the Ministry of Tourism, obviously, is not the only possible "home" for the management of thick sites, it is relevant that it has functioned as such for a period of ten years.

42. This prohibition would include similar terms, such as "holy," etc.

43. See, in this context, Williams (1985, pp. 140–152).

44. In this context, it is interesting to note that the author of the most comprehensive legal overview of sacred sites in Israel has complained that there is no adequate definition of a sacred site in Israeli law; nor is there a complete list of such sites, which makes the legal defense of them almost impossible. As he writes: "As odd as this lacuna might seem to be, there is no definition of a sacred site in the Israeli law, nor in the British-Mandatory law that preceded the state of Israel!" (Berkovits, 2006, p. 72). The difficulty of defining "sacred"—in a legal context—is noted by other commentators, but we could find none who proposed relocating the definition from the legal-political sphere to the free decision of each individual (Petkoff, 2014). States are simply incapable of correctly identifying and defining "sacredness" across religious divisions. For this reason, in a similar vein, Levi Eshkol wished for the Western Wall to be managed by the Israel Nature and Parks Authority (see chapter 3).

45. See Leibowitz (1982, pp. 134–139); Berkovits (2006, chap. 4).

notion of a "sacred site" should, therefore, be replaced with the much broader concept suggested in this book—that is, "thick site" (other, similar terms could, of course, be suggested); this term effectively captures the vast matrix of national, archaeological, cultural and religious sites that should be given some broad governmental protection. Though no list of thick sites will be perfect or without omission, there is a categorical distinction between a state failing to complete a list based on historical, religious, archaeological, and social worth (similar to the UNESCO world heritage list, for example), and a state that oversteps the limits of its capacities to engage religious concepts and controversies that it is ill equipped to understand or adjudicate.

As a direct result of applying the privatization model to thick sites, such as the Western Wall, religious liberty would be significantly expanded and augmented. Decisions regarding permissible conduct at such sites would be ceded from the state to the worshipping individual. This certainly does not mean that, under a privatized religion-state model, an "anything goes" policy would apply to thick sites. *First,* considerations and prohibitions banning hate speech, incitement, violence, and the like, would function as usual and defend religious people and minorities against potential harms to their interests.[46] *Second,* thick sites, like archaeological sites and museums, certainly carry certain normative expectations with regard to adequate or proper behavior. For example, the Israeli Protection of Jewish Holy Sites (1981) by-law, as noted, contains a list of acts that have nothing to do with religious rituals and that are prohibited in such sites. Some examples include peddling, the presence of animals, allocating publications, making speeches, mendicancy, smoking, and wearing inappropriate attire. While some of these prohibitions may be controversial, the general notion is widely accepted. These are, after all, unique and sensitive sites; there are plenty of other locations in which the activities prohibited by the 1981 by-law can take place and where they are appropriate.

The privatization approach, applied to thick sites, has many merits: it does not restrict the religious liberties of some groups as opposed to others; it does not create inequality between different religious groups and, hence, avoids the social instability that would follow from such inequality; it does not burden the government with complex decisions stemming from state entanglement with religious beliefs; it does not necessitate a repeated assessment and reassessment of various claims raised by different religious groups regarding the proper management of thick sites; it respects the status of all worshipers equally; and finally, the distance created between the state and religions in thick sites serves the interests

---

46. See the legal discussion, in the Israeli context, at Kremnitzer et al. (2003, pp. 94–96).

of religions as discussed above since it discourages the corruption of religious authority and prevents aggressive state meddling in religious affairs.

We are, of course, well aware that the privatization view goes against the position currently adopted by the Israeli government. What the Israeli government has done at the Western Wall is create more regulations and plan more geographical zones in order to facilitate different religious behavior. The pervasive view is that such a complex conflict requires more governmental intervention, not less (see chapter 2; this also applies to the Ayodhya dispute, see the appendix). However, governmental attempts to solve this dispute by creating more regulation— for example, through the proposed third plaza— are, in our view, bound to fail. Against the enthusiasm for more regulation, we approvingly quote James Madison (1785) who noted, in his battle for the separation of religion and state in the State of Virginia:

> Torrents of blood have been spilt in the old world, by vain attempts of the secular arm, to extinguish Religious discord, by proscribing all difference in Religious opinion. Time has at length revealed the true remedy. *Every relaxation of narrow and rigorous policy,* wherever it has been tried, has been found to assuage the disease. (para. 11; italics added)

That is, instead of adding more and more nuanced and complex regulations aimed at achieving the impossible and answering every conceivable struggle between varying religious groups, the best solution is to relax or cancel such regulations.

While the privatization approach indeed has, in our opinion, unrivaled advantages as a model for state-religion relations at thick sites, the fact that such sites are especially contested and prone to raise strong emotions means that an additional sensitivity to context is required. Adopting a context-sensitive approach in thick sites is particularly appropriate, we argue, in cases where applying an overly rigid form of privatization would mean that members of certain denominations would be unable to maintain core practices of their religion; it is, additionally, legitimate given the qualifier that *a context-sensitive approach* will not violate core liberties of the members of other religious groups (nor the core principles of the privatization model itself).

One example, briefly noted above, of how such sensitivity on the part of the government would be appropriate even under the privatization model, is the necessity of allowing a temporary gender-divider at the Wall. This concession is needed so as to avoid (among other considerations) the alienation of Orthodox members of the WoW themselves as they require a divider for their manner of prayer. Here, in order to avoid violating the core principles of the privatization approach, specific conditions are required: the praying party itself (and not the state) would have to provide and place such a divider (during prayers only), and then remove it; the government would not enforce its presence.

5.4.2. Three Potential Objections to the Application of the Privatization Model to Thick Sites

In what follows, we explore and respond to three different challenges raised against the privatization model and its application to thick sites. These are the fear of violence or the "backlash" problem; the "baseline problem"; and the perceived incompatibility of beliefs of the various groups who wish to pray at the site, an issue often raised under a concern to avoid offending religious feelings. While this list does not exhaust all potential challenges, these three objections point to genuine problems that a reasonable observer may raise about the management of a thick site such as the Western Wall or the Babri Masjid / Ram Janmabhoomi. Though these are legitimate concerns, there are convincing answers to each issue.

5.4.2.1. Fear of Violence or the Backlash Problem

The first problem that might arise from an implementation of the privatization model at thick sites is the so called "backlash problem." Believers care deeply about thick sites central to their religion and they often disapprove of the ways in which worshippers from other religions handle themselves at such sites. Thus, deregulating behavioral limits in such places might lead the party that is losing its official support to threaten violence. The members of religious groups that previously enjoyed a dominant position might view deregulation as legalizing sacrilegious or heretical activities at a highly sensitive religious site; they might, therefore, act violently toward other worshippers, the police, and so on. The backlash claim, succinctly put, holds that the threat of violence could, and perhaps should, justify the maintenance of a given inegalitarian order at a thick site that is biased in favor of a faction that may otherwise resort to violence.[47] In other words, it argues that an anticipated violent response to a given act is a sufficient justification for banning this given act (Spinner Halev, 2001).

In order to properly evaluate the backlash argument, one should distinguish the *empirical* and *philosophical* claims it relies on; that is, separate the empirical claim that deregulating behavior in thick sites might be followed by violence

---

47. It should be noted that the backlash argument is not only a hypothetical challenge to the privatization approach raised in theoretical discussions, but one that was actually raised in the context of both the WoW's struggle and the Ayodhya dispute. See chapter 2 and the appendix, respectively.

from the philosophical claim that an anticipated violent response to a given act provides sufficient justification for banning this otherwise legitimate act. We shall analyze both claims.

From an *empirical* perspective, one needs to keep in mind that threats, by their nature, are not about what has (empirically) happened or is happening; they are about what might happen in the (yet unknown and speculative) future. A case in point is the reality at the Western Wall since 2013, when Judge Sobel's decision allowed the Women of the Wall almost complete freedom to pray according to their manner at the site. As noted at length in chapter 2, several governmental committees and judges, prior to Sobel's decision, raised concerns of violent responses by the Ultra-Orthodox and cited this concern as a reason to legally ban the WoW from prayer at the Wall. That is, they clearly adopted "backlash" logic. However, the few instances of violence at the Wall targeting the members of the Women of the Wall have, at no point, reached the levels that alarmists predicted. Warnings, or predictions, regarding violent responses at the Wall should therefore be considered refuted, and speculative reasoning presented as empirical justification should be viewed suspiciously. Assessments of the potential for future violence have to be empirically validated in a case by case fashion; in some instances (as in the WoW case) such assessments have already been refuted. To give this point a clear formulation: if someone would like to limit religious freedom due to the fear of a violent reaction should that limit be lifted, then concrete, specific, and convincing empirical evidence must be provided as justification for such action. A general concern about "backlash" made abstractly is surely insufficient.

Furthermore, religious extremism intensifies when the state adopts one particular religion, not when it retreats from the religious arena. This general point, following observations made by Adam Smith, provides another principled reason to doubt the empirical claims of a backlash argument in cases of a state retreat from thick sites. The fear that religious radicalism will follow from a retreat of the state, Smith argues, follows a backward logic.[48] Once religious organizations and individuals assume that the state can be used to advance one particular religious position, many problems and conflicts will arise. Thus, the fears that the

---

48. This criticism includes, most famously, David Hume (1858), who argued

> that in reality the most decent and advantageous composition which [the civil magistrate] can make with the spiritual guides is to bribe their indolence, by assigning stated salaries to their profession, and rendering it superfluous for them to be further active than merely to prevent their flock from straying in quest of new pastures. (vol. 3, p. 129).

privatization of religion would lead to violence, assume a situation in which such a "recruitment" option exists. As Smith (1979) notes:

> But if Politicks had never called in the aid of religion . . . had . . . never adopted the tenets of one sect more than those of another . . . it would probably have dealt equally and impartially with all the different sects, and have allowed every man to choose his own priest and his own religion as he thought proper. There would in this case, no doubt, have been a great multitude of religious sects . . . The teachers of each sect, seeing themselves surrounded on all sides with more adversaries than friends, would be obliged to learn that candour and *moderation* which is so seldom to be found among the teachers of those great sects whose tenets being supported by the civil magistrate, are held in veneration by almost all . . . This plan of ecclesiastical government, or more properly of *no* ecclesiastical government . . . would probably by this time have been productive of the most philosophical good temper and *moderation* with regard to every sort of religious principle. (Smith, 1979, pp. 792–793; italics added)

In short, the backlash argument inherently lacks the empirical evidence that it presupposes, and we could reasonably expect the reverse causation.

Let us turn now to the second component of the backlash argument: the philosophical, or principled, claim that violence anticipated as a response to a given legitimate act provides sufficient justification for banning it. This claim, even if empirical evidence supported the correlation that it draws, should be dismissed. In fact, it violates a basic principle—almost a trivial assumption—of democratic states, namely that threats and violence should not be rewarded with political or legal legitimacy. As Rawls (1999) succinctly noted, "each according to his threat advantage is not a conception of justice" (p. 116). Therefore, if a religious faction loses a previously enjoyed privileged position, and responds with threats of violence against a new and egalitarian arrangement, the state is not justified in retreating from the new egalitarian, privatized arrangement.[49]

However, in some rare cases—typically in such cases in which complex conflicts pose the likelihood of all-around and potentially uncontrolled violence— there might be a place, albeit qualified and carefully constructed, for backlash considerations to play a part in determining temporary transitional arrangements for thick sites. Although even in such cases, there is a range of policies that can be adopted, and there is no reason to grant backlash considerations a carte blanche

---

49. For a comprehensive inquiry into Rawls' category of "threat advantage," see Barry (1989).

to determine the arrangements in a given thick site. Nevertheless, such transitional arrangements may deviate from the privatization approach without discounting the model in general, and without rendering it illiberal.[50]

5.4.2.2. *Baseline Problems*

Thick sites tend to have long and remarkably disputed histories, a characteristic that gives rise to conflicting claims of ownership and, as the practical ramification of ownership, proper management of such sites. Such disputes put not only the existing *physical/geographical* contours of thick sites into question, but also the assumption that such sites actually reside on state land, that is, that they are located in the public sphere. As the privatization approach is suitable and applicable only to state or public holdings, such historical claims of ownership can significantly limit the applicability of the privatization approach to thick sites residing on uncontested state land. To point to two examples: in the Ayodhya dispute, the Islamic Wakf claims that the entire area is Muslim property and that any action other than giving it back to the Wakf is simple thievery (see the appendix); in the Western Wall context, some maintain that the fact that the plaza, or a significant portion of it, was built on a razed Arab neighborhood means that it belongs to that community (Ben-Dov, Naor, & Aner, 1983).

Indeed, how should a scholar assess the wide variety of historical claims and counterclaims regarding wrongs committed by different religious groups against each other, wrongs which often affected fundamental issues of legal ownership, the physical condition, and the boundaries of a given thick site? Moreover, such claims and counterclaims, especially in thick sites, often go back hundreds of years. How should an interested observer approach such opposing claims coming from many different groups with various legitimate concerns?

The problem of establishing the "baseline" is a familiar one that is usually associated with the "boundary problem" in political theory—the question of how to divide parts of the earth between groups of people as part of an effort to justify (or criticize) current borders.[51] Robert Dahl (1989) describes this

---

50. A full discussion of the requirements that would have to be met for such arrangements to be legitimate cannot be presented here, but we can identify at least three "families" of relevant considerations: *first*, empirical verification of the likelihood of potentially uncontrolled violence erupting; *second*, the use of various instruments, developed in the literature of proportionality, that can limit the scope of such arrangements so as to avoid, among other concerns, exaggerated limitations on religious liberty (see Barak, 2012); and *third*, in order to avoid what Margalit famously labeled a "rotten compromise," concessions should not be made to aggressive parties that are likely to ask for more concessions, nor should concessions be made by only one side in a conflict (see Margalit, 2009; see also the appendix for further discussion of this point).

51. On this debate, see Michael Walzer (1983, chap. 2); Margaret Moore (2015); Chaim Gans (2003); and Ferdinand Teson (2015), to name a few prominent examples.

debate over territorial units as follows: "[T]he criteria of the democratic process presupposes the rightfulness of the unit itself. If the unit is not proper or rightful ... then it cannot be made rightful simply by democratic procedures" (p. 207). When translated to the specific issue of thick or sacred sites, the baseline problem exposes that any model of religion-state relations (privatization included) would have to assume, or accept, that some *unit* indeed constitutes the contested sacred or thick site and that the considerations of a privatized system apply to that unit. Such considerations are, as Dahl noted, external to any model of religion state relations, privatization included.

Though the baseline problem, as applied to thick sites, poses a challenge, it is not as formidable as it seems initially. The two following considerations make this evident: the lack of clear and well documented "status quo ante" at thick sites *and* the lack of a just focal point of reference. *First,* one needs to keep in mind the so called "mirage of the status quo ante." In some trivial cases, suggesting a given status quo ante, may not constitute a significant problem. If, say, John steals Jane's laptop from her table at the coffee shop, runs away with it, and is stopped by a passing police officer immediately, then we know that the status quo ante is Jane sitting at her table in the coffee shop with the laptop on her table. With thick sites, however, we enter a world of difficulties that is familiar from debates regarding past wrongs and intergenerational justice. We don't have a clear image, or a counterfactual, of the status quo ante: at many thick sites, the disputes go back so many years, if not centuries, that the mutual stories of offenses, violence, and oppression quickly move from the historical to the "narrative" and the "mythical," that is, the type and reliability of available information deteriorates quickly.[52]

Second, conflicts pertaining to thick sites typically lack a just focal or original point of reference. This is a consequence of such sites' long, complex, and often violent histories. This point was famously made by Hume (1748) while discussing the origins of all states, but the comments are highly relevant to thick sites as well: "Almost all the governments which exist at present, or of which there remains any record in story, have been founded originally, either on usurpation or conquest, or both, without any presence of a fair consent or voluntary subjection of the people." To put this point in a straightforward way for cases at thick sites: even if a clear and well-documented status quo ante would present itself, as unlikely as this might be, the circumstances surrounding the contours, shape, and ownership of thick sites are themselves the result of past wrongs; as argued by Hume, and it is not clear why any such status quo ante based on past injustice should have any normative importance.

---

52. See Waldron (1992); Perez (2012); Cohen (2015); Weinrib (2012).

These two considerations lead us to conclude that, if indeed epistemological and normative grounds that follow from the typical histories of thick sites preclude the return to a status quo ante, any changes to the current status quo should rest on nonreligious grounds—improving access, creating shelter from the elements, and so on—and nothing else. The reason is that, once a return to a status quo ante is understood to be unattainable, the only reasons to change the current status quo in a religiously significant way will involve choosing a preferred religion. Such a choice is precluded by the privatization approach. Stated simply, while the privatization model can't fix past wrongs, it can be impartial and fair at present. Perhaps this *present egalitarianism* is the best available answer to the troubled events of the past.

5.4.2.3. *Problems of Religious Incompatibility*

One of the most notable characteristics of thick sites—that the various meanings attributed to such sites are not only different, they are incompatible with each other (see chapter 1)—is reflected in individuals' deep concern regarding the behavior of persons from differing religions or denominations at such sites. If, as the privatization model prescribes, the state were to retreat from a given legal order at a given thick site, then persons holding incompatible religious beliefs could be directly exposed to each other's religious practices. These practices, in some cases, may be perceived to be not merely disturbing but to actually interfere with other groups properly practicing their religion. Such incompatibility can take two different forms: either a physical incompatibility or an incompatibility related to beliefs (sometimes presented via the language of offenses to religious feelings). Each deserves consideration.

Let us begin with cases of physical incompatibility. In some cases, the usage of a thick site by members of one religion would physically prevent the usage of this site by the members of another religion. Once the state retreats from a given arena, other forces will attempt to occupy it. For example, at the Western Wall, there was an attempt by Ultra-Orthodox leaders to have Ultra-Orthodox women fill the women's section of the Western Wall Plaza, on the day of the new moon, in order to prevent the WoW from entering the location (see chapter 2). If the privatization model remains solely within the contours of providing law and order and little else, the result would be a de facto ability of the majority religious group to prevent the minority religious group from practicing at this thick site. In such cases, therefore, there is no avoiding state involvement. However, the involvement should be procedural rather than substantive, that is, it should not endorse one religion. It should, rather, be largely technical, akin to traffic lights or a regulation regarding parking permits, as the state ensures that religious observance leaves sufficient space for all interested parties in an orderly fashion.

The state does not, furthermore, determine who those interested parties might be but rather verifies that all such parties, whether various groups or interested individuals, will be able to worship at the site. Once this largely technical requirement is satisfied, state obligations end. An illustration of such a minimal, almost technical management, is that of famous museums, whose gentle yet decisive management of visitors wishing to see famous pictures, such as Rembrandt's the *Night Watch* in the Rijksmuseum in Amsterdam or Botticelli's the *Birth of Venus* at the Uffizi Gallery in Florence. If, among the many people who wish to see those famous pictures, a particular group speaks too loudly or delays excessively in front of these famous paintings during busy hours, or in any way prevents other people from seeing them, museum stewards certainly should (and will) require such visitors to adjust their behavior.[53]

Before turning to an analysis of the category of belief-oriented incompatibility, and the ways that the privatization model ought to approach it, a brief example will clarify what this category denotes. In the first Israeli Supreme Court ruling regarding the Women of the Wall, Judge Elon insisted:

> An undisputed fact is that the vast majority of those praying at the Western Wall each and every day believe. . . that the changes requested [by the WoW] in the petitions before us would, if granted, defile the prayer plaza of the Western Wall. . . and according to Halachic law, such men and women would be prevented from praying at the Western Wall.[54]

Similar arguments were raised in the Ayodhya dispute as part of the conflict between Muslims and Hindus over the management of the Babri Masjid / Ram Janmabhoomi; indeed, the incompatibility of beliefs at this site is poignantly reflected in the controversy surrounding the placement and worship of deities, which is obligatory for Hindus but banned by Islam.[55]

For such problems of belief based incompatibility, the general and principled answer provided by the privatization model would be governmental noninterference. The state acceptance and enforcement of *one* view in such cases would

---

53. Beyond its commonsensical soundness, this idea of "technical management" reflects the famous Lockean proviso (developed in the context of property rights, but easily applied to thick sites) that others are left "enough and as good" time and space at the sacred site. On the Lockean Proviso, see Locke (1690/1980, p. 19).

54. Para. 61 of his judgment, HCJ 257/89.

55. See Pokharel and Beckett (2012, p. 4) for a description of this exact point in their detailed description of the events that transpired at the Babri Masjid / Ram Janmabhoomi (see the appendix for elaboration).

amount to a de facto establishment of a state religion; thus a concession on this point would directly contradict the major tenets of the privatization approach. What each person thinks or believes, regarding the religious belief or behavior of another person, falls outside of the borders of a state apparatus that follows the privatization approach (see section 5.1).

Such belief based incompatibilities, as noted above, are at times presented in the language of offenses to religious feelings.[56] A further, more specific analysis of how the privatization model addresses this category is required as this particular way of discussing incompatibility gained particular prominence in the WoW case. A government that, in its regulation of thick sites, explicitly attempts to avoid "offenses to religious feelings" must assume that, in cases in which certain behaviors by group A are deemed to offend the religious feelings of group B, the legal system is justified in limiting or banning such acts by group A. The current relevant by-law in Israel, to point to one pertinent example, prohibits any religious ceremony that "offends the sensitivities of the worshipping public"; this bylaw was used in the WoW case to limit certain religious practices of the WoW (see chapter 2).[57]

Therefore, the question arises whether the privatization model can accommodate a law that bans acts that are likely to bring about offenses to religious feelings as legitimately applicable to thick sites?[58] It must be noted that offenses

---

56. For a comparative-legal discussion of offences to religious feelings and blasphemy laws, see Doe (2011, pp. 140–156).

57. The main law that bans offences to religious feelings in sacred sites is the Protection of Holy Places (1967) by-law, the main aspects of which are as follows:

> The Holy Places shall be protected from desecration and any other violation and from anything likely to violate the freedom of access of the members of the different religions to the places sacred to them or their feelings with regard to those places. (1) Whoever desecrates or otherwise violates a Holy Place shall be liable to imprisonment for a term of seven years. (2) Whosoever does anything likely to violate the freedom of access of the members of the different religions to the places sacred to them or their feelings with regard to those places shall be liable to imprisonment for a term of five years.

To this 1967 law, the Protection of Jewish Holy Sites By-Law (1981) was added; the relevant lines from this law are "within such sacred sites . . . (1.a) it is forbidden to perform a religious ritual opposed to the custom of the place, and which offends the sensitivities (or feelings) of the worshipping public." The Western Wall is just one of the noted holy sites addressed by this by-law. For a full list and discussion, see Berkovits (2006, chap. 4); the full text of the laws can be found at: https://www.nevo.co.il/law_html/Law01/P224K1_001.htm (the 1967 law), and https://www.nevo.co.il/law_html/Law01/P224K1_002.htm (the 1981 law).

58. The notion that there are identifiable local customs, both historically verified and uncontested (or nearly uncontested), plays an important role in the discourse regarding offences to religious feelings in thick sites. The question, "offenses against what?" is answered by "local customs"; these customs are often what augments the otherwise bare notion that members

to religious feelings constitute a rather opaque category. For example, hate speech—defined as deliberately demeaning and/or insulting speech aimed at a vulnerable minority, which aims to stir, or create hate against this minority—covers rather distinct ground (even though its boundaries aren't always perfectly clear) and can thus be legally banned.[59] The category of offenses to religious feelings, in comparison, covers a far more extensive and less carefully defined ground; prohibitions against such offenses could potentially limit speech, behaviors, and religious rituals that are not demeaning or humiliating. Additionally, this category does not necessarily protect a specific, vulnerable minority. The sweeping grounds that "offenses to religious feelings" cover already provide a reason to be skeptical regarding legally prohibiting such actions. Consequently, the privatization strategy will usually oppose legislation directed against "offending religious feelings."[60] Four main considerations shape this stance.

First, the privatization approach seeks a retreat from religious affairs and, ipso facto, would be reluctant to adjudicate claims relating to "offending" religious feelings as they lead to state entanglements with religious sensitivities. Indeed, in order to enable any balanced consideration and judgment of such cases, the state would need, at the very least, to obtain sufficient knowledge of the core beliefs of a given religion in order to determine the legitimacy of the claimed "offenses."[61] Such entanglement with a religion is precisely one of the major problems that the privatization model seeks to address in the first place.[62] Furthermore, such a

---

of a particular religion are offended by a given behavior (see chapter 2). A rough formulation of this point would be as follows: an offense to some believers stems (typically) from a scenario in which a long-established custom, central to the belief system of their religion, is disrupted by some people, and this disruption offends the feelings of said believers. As was shown in chapters 2 and 3, however, historical claims such as those about "established customs" are almost always disputed. This is especially true in thick sites, so we are left with the "bare" problem of "offenses."

59. Waldron (2012); see also the skeptical view of Weinstin (1999) regarding the regulation even of such hate speech.

60. While we believe that the offense argument is problematic as a whole, we focus exclusively on thick sites here. There are some cases in which the offense category might be legitimate, such as cases where the "cost" to the nonbeliever is very small and the interest of the believer is cardinal. One such case is, in Israel, the issue of closing the roads during the Jewish Sabbath prayers in some Ultra-Orthodox neighborhoods. The debate regarding legitimate offenses arguments, however, is beyond the current discussion. See Statman (2000); Pinto (2010); Statman and Sapir (2014); Israel Supreme Court decision (HCJ) 5016/96 Horev vs. Minister of Transportation (1997).

61. See (HCJ) 5016/96 Horev vs. Minister of Transportation (1997) for such a balancing test; the decision is available in English via the Cardozo law school, http://versa.cardozo.yu.edu/opinions/horev-v-minister-transportation.

62. As Australian scholar H. Pringle (2011) writes:

governmental approach will fuel, most likely, ever more impassioned attempts of believers to prove that they are "truly offended" or that they are "more offended" by another's behavior than vice versa.

Second, it is quite likely that different religions will be offended for different, and occasionally opposing, reasons. In some cases, all relevant possible behaviors may offend some party. For example, while some Ultra-Orthodox are offended by the WoW prayer practice, some members of the WoW are offended by the gender segregation of the Ultra Orthodox prayer practice in the first place (Chesler & Haut 2002, p. 3). In such cases, whatever action the state takes, *some party will be offended.*[63] We should also add, though it is perhaps an obvious point, that externally imposed limits on religious practice that are meant to avoid offending some other party will surely offend the party whose religious freedom is thus restricted. Governmental regulation aimed to avoid religious offense can therefore be rejected by a reductio ad absurdum of the logic behind such arguments.

Third, the offense category applies far beyond the relatively clear "hate speech" category. Such religious offenses are likely to be caused by the banal behaviors of law-abiding citizens, whether nonobservant persons or members of (typically) minority denominations; such "offenses" could very well be an incidental byproduct of minority religious rituals or various nonoutstanding behaviors. Thus, the offence category must ultimately demand that the state regulate normal behavior if it is going to avoid offending members of a given religion. This is a far-reaching conclusion that the liberal privatization approach dismisses from the start. As Joel Feinberg argues, regarding extremely susceptible persons,

[I]t is not the role of law in a modern secular state to adjudicate as to the truth or falsity of (religious) ideas. Such a role would involve the state's taking on. . . "state sponsorship of religion" by defining the boundaries of religiously permissible expression. . . adjudication of disputes under such laws will inevitably involve making judgments as to theological truth and falsity. (p. 325)

Furthermore, the report "Prisoners of Belief," by the US Commission on International Religious Freedom (2014) demonstrates that the use of blasphemy laws is in many cases directly political and often abused to serve ends that have nothing to do with religion.

63. The attempts by the Israeli government to regulate behavior at the Cave of the Patriarchs serve as another good example of the reductio ad absurdum of this type of objection (leaving issues of sovereignty aside); the Jewish and Arab worshippers each had different, and at times opposing, expectations regarding what constitutes a religiously required, permissible, or forbidden behavior; these disagreements led to a complex and, at times, conflicting set of unstable instructions regarding, for example, drinking wine (banned from the perspective of Muslims, required for certain Jewish rituals) and for funeral rituals (Guinn, 2006, pp. 62–63, while not without merits, the current situation which adopts a version of the "divide and separate" solution does not assuage the reductio ad absurdum objection).

the more fragile our sensitive sufferer's psyche, the less protection he can expect from the criminal law ... If a mere sneeze causes a glass window to break, we should blame the weakness or brittleness of the glass and not the sneeze.[64]

Instead of seeking state protection, the offended person may: explain her/his view to the person with which s/he disagrees, write an op-ed or a book, upload a video explaining her/his view to YouTube—the various methods individuals have at their disposals in a democratic state to express their opinions; this offended person may not turn to the state however asking to ban a given behavior.

Fourth, regulating thick sites to avoid "offense to religious feeling" proves not only problematic for the government in charge of the site, but also for the very religious believers it is meant to shield. The same reasons that were indicated above—religious reasons for adopting the privatization model—are relevant here. To point to two central ones: (a) such legislation brings about a meddling of the state in religious affairs and religious doctrines. Indeed, the state would have to decide which religious doctrines merit defense; this means government agents not only must learn substantial information about a given religion, but also that they must make decisions they are ill-equipped to make about the veracity and importance of many religious doctrines. (b) Such legislation can always backfire: if a given religious group loses its prominence (Marshall & Shea, 2011). A religious person might therefore hesitate to suggest that a state should attempt to defend her/him from offenses to their religious feelings since the harm to religious interests may be much more severe than the noted "offenses" themselves.[65]

Our discussion, of religious incompatibility and offenses to religious feelings, suggests that the privatization approach to debates regarding appropriate behavior at thick sites favors relocating such debates from the legal arena to societal and normative ones.[66] Beyond dealing with obvious obstructions—or technical

---

64. Feinberg (1985, p. 34).

65. Even members of the dominant religious group should be weary of a situation in which the relative legal-religious prominence of religious groups depends on civil authority. As Madison (1785) argued:

Who does not see that the same authority which can establish Christianity, in exclusion of all other Religions, may establish with the same ease any particular sect of Christians, in exclusion of all other Sects? that the same authority which can force a citizen to contribute three pence only of his property for the support of any one establishment, may force him to conform to any other establishment in all cases whatsoever? (para. 3).

66. See, generally, Whitman (2000); Kremnitzer, Goldman and Tamir (2003); Levy (2010).

rules as, for example, in the Museum scenario—the state should not attempt to ban, limit, regulate, or encourage various behaviors at thick sites. Indeed, public debates and norms are certainly not less significant than governmental decisions or court rulings in establishing widely accepted behaviors. It is, therefore, possible (although not certain) that the retreat of the state will eventually lead to a voluntary arrangement between worshippers of various kinds. In fact, there is significant empirical data regarding "order without law," and similar important concepts, which examine voluntary arrangements that replace governmental regulations; this data demonstrates the impressive success of such voluntary arrangements. The lessons of such arrangements can be applied to thick sites.[67]

5.5. *Conclusion*

The privatization model of religion-state relations is the last comprehensive model examined in this book. This model is characterized, fundamentally, by the creation of a proper distance between the sphere of religion and the state; this distance is maintained by rejecting any state identification with a religion, refraining from supporting or hindering religion in any way, and maintaining a strict hands-off approach to religion. Matters of religious belief, practice, and membership in a given religious group are left to the free decision of individual believers. Put into practice as a process, privatization generally means a retreat of the state from some religious realm that it previously occupied: disestablishing a state religion, discontinuing the funding of religious services, etc. The core principle of privatization— whether in an "ideal," complete model or a partial process of diminution of state involvement in religious affairs—is that decisions regarding matters in the religious sphere lie with the individual, not the state.

This model has many clear advantages over the others that we have considered: it protects religious liberty; it guarantees that the state treats citizens that hold different religious views (or none at all) with equal concern and respect;

---

67. See Ellickson (1994); Ostrom (1990, 2005). The sociological literature on religion-state relations sometimes argues that religious incompatibility is not unchangeable, permanent, and rigid (Barkan, 2015). In our context, this means that once the state retreats, a noted incompatibility might be diminished or even disappear; religious people adapt to the presence of other religions, and a fascinating corpus of historical and sociological literature recounts various ways in which sacred spaces come to be shared in practice (Kedar, 2001; Limor, 2007; Reiter, 2010; Bigelow, 2010). However, we do not wish to claim that such a change is, empirically speaking, expected, nor that it is required for the privatization model to be applicable to thick sites. The reason is internal to the privatization approach: how individual believers *view* other religious beliefs and practices is beyond the contours of state actions, and while the noted sociological view regarding the adaptability of religious views is interesting, it is not required (nor is it sought) by the privatization model.

it unburdens the state from functions it is ill equipped to handle or manage; it avoids state entanglement with contested religious affairs and disputes; and lastly, but very importantly, it protects religious groups and institutions from being corrupted by being tied to the heavy and, at times, aggressive hand of the state.

The application of the privatization model to thick sites that have been under state management means that the government retreats from its typical heavy presence at, and exclusive management of, these sites (management that usually was conducted in association with one particular, dominant religious group). Instead, the state limits itself to providing law and order while guaranteeing, when required, that no group holds a de facto monopoly over such sites; that is, the state adopts a role akin to that of a traffic officer or museum steward. The application of the privatization approach to thick sites, when done in the context-sensitive manner discussed here, affords three particularly significant advantages to other approaches: it protects the religious liberties of all relevant religious groups and individuals equally; it does not entangle the state in bitter religious conflicts at these highly sensitive locations; and, lastly, it serves the interests of religions themselves by avoiding any religion-state collusion, in which one religious faction uses state powers to limit religious practices of other groups.

Concluding Remarks

EARLY IN 2016, the Israeli government voted in favor of establishing a third, egalitarian prayer plaza adjacent to Robinson's Arch at the southern part of the Western Wall. As outlined in chapter 2, this new plaza is intended to be an egalitarian prayer space that will serve non-Orthodox Jews and others interested in visiting the Western Wall for various purposes; this new plaza will not enforce the separation of men and women, in place at the central plaza. Neither the Rabbi of the Wall nor the Western Wall Heritage Foundation would have any authority over this third "southern" plaza. Rather, a more broadly representative new council, one that would include women and members of Reform and Conservative Judaism, would be in charge of managing this site. The legal status of the central plaza will revert to what it was prior to Judge Sobel's decision (2013)—namely, the Women of the Wall's manner of prayer will be banned: women will be allowed neither to pray while wearing a tallit or tefillin nor to read from a Torah scroll. However, there will be no such enforced unified-custom at the new egalitarian southern plaza. Women who *do not* wish to pray as part of a mixed service will have the option and means of doing so; a temporary partition to surround women's groups during prayer will be accessible to them.

This is a detailed and complex plan that attempts to be sensitive to, and to satisfy, many different groups and perspectives. Its significance lies in the following: *first*, it obviously expands the prayer plaza at the Western Wall in order to create the new prayer space; *second*, it provides formal recognition to Reform and Conservative Jews at the Western Wall which, given the centrality of the site, means a significant improvement in their status within Israel as a whole; *finally* and perhaps most importantly, it provides for women a place at the Wall to pray in ways which were previously illegal, and it makes them full members of the governmental entity in charge of one of the holiest sites in the Jewish tradition. This, as our considerations above have shown, is not a small matter and it has far-reaching consequences for the status of women in Israel beyond the religious realm. Even if this decision ultimately fails to be realized—and the obstacles are indeed formidable—the fact that it came about is in and of itself important;

substantial thought and effort went into developing this plan, and much political capital was spent for it to pass a governmental vote.[1]

As sensitive as this plan might be, and as complex as its considerations are, even at this preliminary phase it has been met with highly mixed responses. Among these responses, three are particularly notable for the present study: while the Women of the Wall endorsed the third-plaza plan; their splinter group—the *Original* Women of the Wall—opposed it, as did the ultra-Orthodox. The official responses of these groups are worth quoting at some length. The Women of the Wall, through their website, declared:

> The approval of the Mendelblit Plan [the new southern plaza] is the first step to women's full equality and empowerment at the Western Wall, the holiest site for Jews and a public space in Israel [...] For Women of the Wall, representing religious women from across the Jewish denominational spectrum, the creation of a third section of the Kotel sets a strong precedent in women's status in Israel: women as administrators of a holy site, women as leaders, women as influential force not to be ignored or silenced.[2]

An opposing view—offered by Shulamit S. Magnus, one of the leaders of the *Original* Women of the Wall splinter group—defies such a compromise:

> [No] deal which says, either adopt *haredi* prayer practice in order to stay at the Kotel, or go to Robinson's, a site of prayer practices contrary to your religious commitments, and a place with no resonance or meaning for any of us;- is one we will accept. We are about Jewish women's prayer, at the Kotel. Neither aspect is negotiable. Nor is our solidarity as Jewish women [...] No back of the bus for us [...] Coercion is wrong in religion, and it is wrong in public policy. It is wrong, above all, at the Kotel, which should be a place of inclusiveness for all the Jewish people, a place of mutual respect and accommodation [...] Let us keep our eyes on the prize. The real one [...] no substitutes.[3]

---

1. It should be noted that the third-plaza plan belongs to a "family" of plans that attempt to resolve conflicts by redesigning the Western Wall plaza, chief among them Safdie's plan (1973). That plan, like the current third-plaza plan, includes some important aspects of the even-handed approach. As discussed in chapter 3, Safdie's plan was rejected in 1977 due to political maneuvering (Kroyanker, 1988, 159–167; see also Bar, 2015, 329–331).

2. Available on their website, see http://womenofthewall.org.il/2016/02/revolution-for-women-and-jewish-pluralism-in-israel/

3. Available on-line at http://www.jpost.com/Opinion/Deal-or-no-deal-We-shall-not-be-moved- 443135

Aryeh Mahlouf Deri, an ultra Orthodox leader and (as of early 2016) the minister of interior affairs, voted against the southern plaza plan at the official vote. According to Deri, who voiced the wide, fierce ultra Orthodox opposition to the plan,

[T]he state of Israel operates according to Judaism as traditionally understood. This entire problem of Reform and Conservative Judaism has not existed in the state of Israel so far, and I have no intention to allow it to happen now. No compromise on the matter is acceptable.[4]

These three reactions suggest that the governmental vote has not resolved the fundamental issue.

Despite the thought and effort behind the creation of this complex compromise, the diverse reactions—including two out of the three main parties bluntly rejecting it with strong language of "back of the bus," "coercion," "no compromise"[5]—demonstrate that this largely evenhanded solution is problematic. Even if the third southern plaza is built, and even if the noted council is established, the struggle over the management of the Western Wall and the proper prayer arrangements will be far from over.

THIS ENTIRE RESEARCH project was motivated by a desire to understand why, exactly, the conflict over prayer arrangements at the Western Wall, and similar conflicts at contested sacred sites located in the public sphere, prove so intractable. This specific concern lead us to the conceptualization of "thick sites" in order to specify and clarify the precise nature of the problem. Specifically, by carefully attending to the details of the Women of the Wall conflict and the Ayodhya dispute, we used an inductive process to develop the novel concept of a *thick site* as a category that attempts to elucidate the unifying characteristics of an entire class of disputed sacred sites.

---

4. http://news.walla.co.il/item/2930318 [Heb.]. In the same vein, the Rabbi of the Wall, Shmuel Rabinovitch, wrote to ultra-Orthodox MKs (Rabinovitch, 2016), labeling the new compromise as "blasphemous," a "grave danger," and a "darkness covering the land." See also Ettinger (2016a) for the overall Ultra Orthodox rejection of the plan.

5. Note that these quoted statements do not exhaust the entire spectrum of opposition to the plan; our survey does not consider, for example, the strong opposition of the Archaeological Council of Israel, which argues that the southern plaza would seriously harm the important archeological garden at Robinson's Arch (Ettinger, 2016b).

With the term *thick site*, as we have said, we denote a site typically but not necessarily religious, which is loaded with different and incompatible meanings that are attributed to it by different agents. From these agents' view, such meanings are highly significant and, consequently, these sites are irreplaceable. The following characteristics of thick sites, in the aggregate, create the tense social dynamic that at times deteriorates into severe violence (typically directed against minority groups): there are various and different meanings attributed to such sites; such sites are significant, indeed, irreplaceable from the perspective of the believers; and, finally, at least some beliefs of one group are incompatible with the beliefs of other groups.

This understanding of the characteristics underlying the conflicts over thick sites, reached through an inductive process, allowed us to suggest an answer to the question: *what is the best way for states to manage thick sites?* The answer is counterintuitive but simple: governmental agencies should not attempt to manage thick sites or should manage them as little as possible. This means, in practice, adopting the privatization model of religion-state relations for thick sites. States should, therefore, retreat from any current management of thick sites, aside from providing law and order and filling a few other narrowly defined technical roles. Typical state-enforced measures of legal "management" that would be abolished, were the privatization model applied to thick sites, include: dividing such sites into geographical areas that each belong to a specific religious group; appointing, and remunerating, religious clergy in charge of the sites; banning the religious practices of (typically) minority religious groups to prevent "offenses to religious feelings" or departures from "local customs"; and several other examples that have been pointed to here. Returning to the central case study of this monograph, adopting the privatization model at the Western Wall would necessitate several important changes to the current legal situation, including: abolishing the position of the Rabbi of the Wall; canceling any bans on religious behaviors that are based on claims that such behaviors "offend the sensitivities of the worshiping public" and are "contrary to the custom of the place"; dismantling the Western Wall Heritage Foundation; and removing the permanent gender-divider (temporary, portable dividers would be allowed, see chapter 5). All matters of religious decision-making at the site, to succinctly summarize the goal of privatization, would lie with the individual rather than with the state (see the detailed discussion in chapter 5).

Two main considerations led us to the conclusion that *not* managing thick sites— that is, applying the model of privatization to them—is the best available option for states facing conflicts at such contested sites. The first consideration is that governments are ill-equipped to manage such sites and, when they do attempt to manage them, they often cause substantial harm. The second is that keeping the state at a proper distance from thick sites, as the privatization model suggests, yields tangible benefits. We shall briefly discuss both. *First*, states are ill-equipped for the task of managing thick sites, even though many of them attempt to do just that, as the contradictory demands made by different religious groups—all wishing to uphold their beliefs and practices in the same physical space—present the state with extraordinarily difficult challenges. Facing the social conflict that thick sites tend to create and magnify, governments that search for the "right" way to manage such sites can only resort to creating increasingly comprehensive, detailed regulatory schemes meant to address these incompatible religious practices and demands. Such regulatory schemes, however, will inherently be imperfect and, whether intentionally or not, often be marred by the exclusion of many religious interests. Such imperfections and exclusions add fuel to the already heated disputes between religious groups at thick sites. Given that thick sites are irreplaceable, the likely failure of such regulatory attempts will have spectacular costs in terms of social stability, religious freedom, financial resources, and so on. Typically, each concerned group will claim to receive unfair treatment at such sites; any groups that were completely excluded from such arrangements will understandably be furious; mistrust between opposing groups will be augmented; and the temptation to appeal to the government to improve the standing of one's religious group will only increase.[6]

Second, applying the privatization model to thick sites yields a variety of important benefits for religious individuals, groups and the citizenry as a whole. To name just a few: the protection of the religious liberties of concerned religious groups and individuals (and those that wish to visit such sites for nonreligious reasons); the egalitarianism of the model; the social stability that it promotes and maintains; and, finally, it protects religions from the corruption (or worse) often associated with state authority and power.

We wish to conclude with a brief anecdote regarding an event that transpired in Jerusalem recently, as told to the authors. A woman, wearing a tallit, walked on the sidewalk of a street in the neighborhood of Rehavia, which is outside of the

---

6. The possibility of recruiting the state to give support to one religious group creates an especially harmful dynamic, in which the "option" of recruiting state assistance proves to be a temptation that is hard to resist. Further, each group prefers a situation in which the state enforces its particular preferences, and each fears a situation in which another group wins the recruitment "game." All groups understand this dynamic, and therefore (willingly or unwillingly) will feel compelled to join the "race" to recruit the state. The result will be, typically, a suboptimal level of religious freedom. To elaborate: one group will win the recruitment game, with detrimental results for other groups. With the privatized approach, in which the state cannot be recruited, the level of religious freedom for all will be better protected. This "collective action" scenario that is encouraged or even created by state involvement usually leads to the corrupt entanglement of the state with religion. This harmful dynamic will cease to exist once privatization is adopted as the guiding model for religion-state relations as applied to thick sites.

old city. An ultra-Orthodox man that was standing next to a nearby kiosk looked at the woman and examined her for a few seconds. While he, unsurprisingly, did not seem to like her wearing a tallit, the specific comment he yelled at her to show his displeasure was noteworthy: "Where do you think you are, at the Western Wall?" If a woman is wearing a tallit, it seems that she naturally belongs, even for an ultra-Orthodox man, at the Western Wall.

Thick Sites, "Gag Solutions," and the Ayodhya Dispute

The Babri Masjid/Ram Janmabhoomi site, located in the ancient city of Ayodhya (Uttar Pradesh, India), is the focus of a prolonged, violent, and bitter conflict. This particularly contested thick site is held as sacred by various Hindu and Muslim groups (both Sunni and Shia). In this appendix, we examine the Ayodhya conflict in order to widen our perspective regarding disputed thick sites beyond the Women of the Wall case study and to minimize, as much as we can, selection bias. The appendix is divided into three parts: *first*, a brief explanation of the methodological rationale for exploring an additional case study, and of the reasons for choosing the Ayodhya dispute; *second*, a succinct description of the history of this highly complex and violent dispute; *lastly*, a theoretical reexamination, using the contextual method, of the three religion-state models that were explored in chapters 3 to 5 (DCV, evenhandedness, privatization). More specifically, this re-examination will show that in our subject matter of thick sites, even though we remain convinced that privatization usually constitutes the best option, sensitivity to context might force us to shift to other models (at times as second-best solutions for limited periods). In this last section, the added value of considering a second case study is revealed in two specific ways; the dispute over Ayodhya gives rise to a legitimate fear of significant violence that necessitates considerations not raised by the Women of the Wall case study, and the de facto solution adopted by the Indian government lies outside the contours of the three noted models that we have covered and should be examined as a heretofore unconsidered alternative. Specifically, the government has severely restricted access and worship by enacting a gag solution. We reject the gag solution and advocate, in its place, an evenhanded solution—dividing the site—which we will justify and explain at the end of the appendix.

A.1. A Brief Methodological Explanation

The Women of the Wall's struggle over the official prayer arrangements at the Western Wall demonstrates important characteristics of religion-state relations in cases of disputes over the management of sacred sites. Nevertheless, we worried that the particulars of the dispute might constrain or misdirect our thinking. So we asked ourselves: What (if any) common aspects of disputes over the management of sacred sites are missing at the Western Wall? What solutions were adopted in other cases, and how do they differ from the ones adopted or suggested in the Western Wall case study? How successful are these alternative solutions? These questions led us to consider whether an additional case study might influence our analysis of the three models that we have explored at length. Such concerns lead us to add a second case study to this monograph and to use it specifically to better understand the general category of disputes over sacred sites. The decision to focus on the Ayodhya dispute for our second case study is based on several considerations,[1] some of which emphasize the differences between the two conflicts and others which point to their similarities.[2] *First*, as an obvious difference, the Ayodhya dispute has nothing to do with either Israel or the Jewish religion. The geographic, cultural, and religious distance between the two conflicts facilitates, therefore, a broader view of the general category of struggles over sacred sites. *Second*, and more specifically, the WoW's struggle is an intrareligious dispute, while the Ayodhya dispute is interreligious. This is an important difference that likely contributes to the severity of the Ayodhya conflict, since the cultural familiarity between opponents is minimal, and this unfamiliarity fuels increasingly severe incompatibility of the relevant parties' religious practices.[3] *Third*, the gender aspect, while central to the WoW case study, is virtually absent from the Ayodhya dispute. We were careful to choose a case in which gender is not a central variable in order to avoid making our study underrepresentative of the wider range covered by the general category of disputes over sacred sites.[4] *Fourth*, the Ayodhya dispute emphatically shows that the conflict is not only religious: it is part

---

1. Several valuable, newly edited volumes examine sacred sites from political and legal perspectives; we leave the task of including these sites, along with the WoW and the Ayodhya conflicts, in a systematic analysis to future research (on these studies of sacred sites, see Ferrari & Benzo, 2014; Barkan & Barkey, 2015; Breger, Reiter, & Hammer, 2010).

2. Aside from the methodological literature outlining the contextual approach of political theory, and the political science case-study method (both pointed to in chapter 1), we also have relied on scholarship regarding the adequate comparison of case studies, see Lieberson (1991); Lijphart (1971); Pierson and Skocpol (2002); Seawright and Gerring (2008).

3. Note that, by making this specific point, we do not thereby subscribe to Huntington's (2011) clash of civilizations theory; indeed, his thesis was challenged and discredited on empirical grounds by studies arguing that conflicts internal to a culture are actually more severe than those between cultures (Henderson, 2005).

4. For example, Mount Athos, a holy mountain and peninsula in Northern Greece, is a contested thick site wherein gender plays a central part in the dispute. It is both an autonomous

of a broader political and regional conflict.[5] *Fifth*, the level of hostility and violence at Ayodhya was much higher and more severe than what was experienced by the WoW at the Western Wall. The level of exclusion that some Hindu groups imposed on Muslims at Ayodhya—culminating in the destruction of the Babri-Masjid mosque in 1992—goes far beyond what the WoW experienced at the Wall. *Lastly*, the de facto solution adopted at Ayodhya, a severe restriction of access and religious practice, referred to as a "gag solution," was never even considered for the Wall.[6]

Despite these important differences, there are several important similarities. First, the conflict at Ayodhya is, after all, a conflict over the management and ownership of a sacred or thick site. As such, regardless of the interreligious nature of the Ayodhya dispute, the questions that must be addressed are very similar to those raised in the WoW conflict—that is, who owns the site? What religious practices should, or should not, be allowed? What solutions have been offered for this site? Were they successful? Second, a rapidly growing body of literature in political science, and adjacent fields, draws comparisons between India and Israel in general, and Jerusalem's sacred sites and the Ayodhya dispute in particular. We therefore contribute to and build on an existing body of literature that identifies these states as similar enough to allow for useful comparisons.[7] Among the several significant similarities between India and Israel are the similar dates of independence, the fact that the independence of both was gained from the British Empire, and the ongoing relevance of the geographical and political partitions established at the time of their independence, among others. Lastly, an interesting similarity arose in the legal and political deliberations concerning the suggested solutions for the two sites. In both the Ayodhya and the WoW cases, it was suggested that the space at the site be divided between the different religious groups (or subgroups). This proposed shared solution, highly disputed at both sites, makes the comparison especially intriguing.

---

polity that does not allow any entrance of women into its borders, and a World Heritage Site. The ban against women stands even though it violates important EU laws regarding gender equality (Papadopoulou, 2014). As noted above, selecting this as a second case would artificially narrow the pool of cases to the point of being unrepresentative of the full category of disputes over sacred sites.

5. This "broader" scope is also represented in the WoW case, as demonstrated by the support that American Jewry give to the WoW. However, the "broader" scope of the conflict, as will be clear from the discussion above, is much more dominant in the Ayodhya dispute; the difference in degree justifies classifying this as a "difference" of the two cases (Noorani, 2014). The most comprehensive, updated attempt to analyze the complex relations between American Jews and the state of Israel is Rynhold (2015).

6. While there were attempts to restrict or ban WoW prayer at the Wall, such solutions were never applicable to members of the WoW as individuals wishing to pray; in any case, such solutions were defeated in the legal sphere and with the eventual third-plaza solution (see chapter 2).

7. Harel (2010); Perez (2002); Kumaraswamy (2013); Walzer (2015); Friedland and Hecht's (1998) research specifically compares the conflicts over the Temple Mount in Jerusalem to the Ayodhya dispute.

A.2. The Ayodhya Dispute: The Details of the Case

On the sixth of December 1992, a crowd of more than two hundred thousand Hindu volunteers, known as *Kar Sevaks*, destroyed the Babri Masjid. The Babri Masjid was a mosque built, in 1528, at Ayodhya during the reign of Babur, the first Mughal emperor of India (Rajamony, 2007, pp. 121–122). This demolition was the culmination of a long dispute between Hindus and Muslims regarding ownership of and rights to worship at the site. We shall begin our description of this case by briefly looking at the significance of the site for Hindus (section A.2.1) and Muslims (section A.2.2) respectively, and then succinctly present some central historical and legal dimensions of the dispute and describe the current management (as of 2015) of the site (section A.2.3). Even the following brief historical survey of the case, which unavoidably touches on the mythical, is heavily disputed.[8] While acknowledging that neutrality here is virtually impossible, we have attempted to navigate the sensitive area between history and myth that forms the background of many bitter arguments at such contested locations.[9]

A.2.1. The Hindu Narrative

The Hindu epic *Ramayana* identifies Ayodhya, located in the Faizabad district of the Northern Indian state of Uttar Pradesh, as the birthplace of the god Ram, an avatar of Vishnu (Mehta, 2015, p. 2). The *Ramayana* and the *Mahabharatha* are the two great expressions of the epic period in classical Hinduism (500 B.C.–A.D.500) during which the structure and mores of Hindu society were developed and temple-centric forms of worship arose. Among the many deities worshiped, the gods Vishnu and Shiva gained preeminence in the epic period; in Northern India, the benevolent Vishnu was believed to have descended into the world in ten incarnations, or avatars, in order to restore righteousness (Rajamony, 2007, p. 94). Among these ten avatars, Krishna and Rama gained the most widespread devotion. Rama, the seventh avatar of Vishnu, is said to have saved the world from the power of demons and then righteously ruled Ayodhya; he maintained an order of purity during a long, prosperous, and happy reign (Rajamony, 2007, p. 111).

The events of Ram's rule occurred, according to the *Ramayana*, during the mythical age of *Treta-Yuga*, thousands of years before our present age, the *Kali-Yuga*. According to Hindu traditions, the city of Ayodhya disappeared at the end of the Treta-Yuga period and was rediscovered in the present age by King Vikramaditya—the legendary first century B.C.E. Emperor of Ujjain—through meditation. Though archaeological

---

8. Noorani (2003a) collected an impressive number of original documents regarding the Babri Masjid/Ram Janmabhoomi conflict. See, for example, his survey of the raging controversy regarding archeological findings, in which every discovery and reported finding is bitterly disputed (pp. 18–172).

9. See the detailed discussion in chapters 2 and 3 regarding the Western Wall.

and historical evidence are inconclusive and controversial, traditional Hindu accounts maintain that King Vikramaditya constructed a large temple on the birth site of Ram. The *Sangh Parivar*, a term used to refer to various Hindu militant organizations, claim that Vikramaditya's temple was destroyed in order to facilitate the construction of the Babri Masjid in 1528; these groups insist, therefore, that their ownership claims to the site predate Muslim claims (Majid, 2015, p. 560).

The cult of Rama became particularly popular in Northern India during the eighteenth century and has continued to be predominant, especially in the state of Uttar Pradesh (Rajamony, 2007, p. 94). Large numbers of *Ramanandhis* settled in Ayodhya and established the city's importance as a major pilgrimage center. By 1991, more than six thousand Hindu temples had been built in the city and its economy heavily relied on pilgrims (Rajamony, 2007, pp. 111–112).

A.2.2. The Muslim Narrative

Muslims, too, trace their connection to Ayodhya to mythical events in the distant past. In fact, they claim that their attachment to the site dates to the pre-Islamic period: they identify Ayodhya as the burial place of both Seth, one of the sons of Adam and Eve, and of the biblical figure of Noah. The origins of these traditions are unknown, though their authenticity was already disputed in the sixteenth century by the famed Muslim Scholar Abul Fazl. Despite these long-standing doubts, both tombs still attract many Islamic pilgrims (Rajamony, 2007, p. 112).

The first Muslim invasion of Ayodhya took place, most probably, in the eleventh century. The region became part of the Mughal Empire when Babur, the first Mughal Emperor, defeated the ruler of Ayodhya; under Babur's rule, the Babri Masjid was built in 1528 (Mehta, 2015b, p. 398). An inscription in the mosque itself claimed that one of the nobles of Babur's court, Mir Baqi, erected the masjid (Rajamony, 2007, p. 114).

Ayodhya remained under Muslim rule until the British period, which began when the British army took control in 1856 (Ratnagar, 2004, p. 239). It is widely considered to be a holy city for Muslims and is, at times, referred to as a "khurd Mecca" or "small Mecca"; not only are the tombs of Seth and Noah allegedly located there, the tombs of many Muslim holy persons and saints are in the city. There are more than fifty *Dargahs*—shrines built over the graves of, mainly, Sufi saints—in Ayodhya, approximately one hundred mosques, and more than a hundred Muslim graveyards (Rajamony, 2007, pp. 112–113).

A.2.3. The Historical and Legal Dispute

As mentioned above, according to radical Hindu organizations known as the Sangh Parivar,[10] Babur destroyed an ancient temple dedicated to Ram in order to build the Babri

---

10. Including the Vishwa Hindu Parishad (VHP), the Rashtriya Swayamsevak Sangh (RSS), etc.

Masjid. Ram Sharan Sharma, the eminent twentieth-century Indian historian, endorsed the Muslim view that no such temple had existed on the site; yet his view is disputed (Rajamony, 2007, p. 113) and has not in any way assuaged the claims of Hindu nationalists (Bacchetta, 2000, pp. 256–257). Sangh Parivar groups tend to think of Muslims as alien invaders who never genuinely assimilated with Indian culture and, most specifically, as demolishers of sanctified Hindu temples (Freigang, 2015, p. 26); against such a polemical characterization, they insist on Hindu ownership of the site (Rajamony, 2007, p. 106). This claim gained some support, in 2003, when the archeological survey of India (ASI) reported that their excavation of the site had uncovered evidence of a large tenth-century structure, similar to a Hindu temple, that would have preexisted the Babri Masjid. The report, however, was controversial.[11]

The first historically recorded religious dispute near the Babri Masjid involved Muslims seizing a nearby Hindu temple and repurposing it as a mosque during the early years of the British rule. Shah Gulam Hussein led a party of his followers to oust Hindus from the Hanumangarghi temple where, he claimed, there had been a mosque earlier. They were overpowered and Hindus killed many of the Muslims involved; if not for the intervention of the British forces, the communal clashes would likely have been more severe (Rajamony, 2007, p. 116; Panikkar, 1993). In 1857, a Mahant—a Hindu priest—constructed a raised platform in the Babri Masjid compound on which he placed idols of Hindu gods for worship. Local Muslims objected and petitioned the local magistrate. This dispute was soon after resolved, when both parties agreed to raise a wall between the mosque and the platform (Ratnagar, 2004, p. 240). In 1885, a Hindu Mahant filed the first legal suit by Hindus concerning the Babri Masjid. In the suit, he demanded the legal title to the land and permission to construct a roof over the noted platform. The claim was dismissed, as were two subsequent appeals, and there seem to have been no further legal disputes for more than forty years (Ratnagar, 2004, p. 240).

In 1934, a riot broke out near Babri Masjid, in a village near Ayodhya, because of the slaughter of a cow on the eve of the important Muslim festival of Bakr-id. While the riot was not related to the central issue of claims about Ram's birthplace, the Babri Masjid did come under attack. Another pre-independence dispute over the site occurred, not between Muslims and Hindus, but rather between Shia and Sunni Muslims (Bacchetta, 2000, pp. 254–265). Consequently, in March 1946, a civil judge ruled the site was to be owned and managed by the Sunni Central Board of Waqf (Rajamony, 2007, p. 117; Noorani, 1993).[12]

In 1949, soon after India gained its independence, several Hindus—the majority community in Ayodhya—placed the idols of Rama and other figures inside the mosque (Rajamony, 2007, p. 117). To state the obvious, this was done without asking permission from the relevant Muslim clergy at the Mosque. In response, the courts did

---

11. See "Ayodhya: High Court Relies on ASI's 2003 Report," *Economic Times*, October 1, 2010.

12. With regard to the Shia/Sunni controversy, see the original documentation provided by Noorani (2003, esp., pp. 190–198, 296–300).

not order the removal of the idols, nor did they restore the property to the Muslim community; rather, through an interim injunction, they locked the Babri Masjid and denied entry to both Muslims and Hindus (Ratnagar, 2004, p. 240). The dispute gained renewed political attention when, in 1983, D. D. Khanna, a former minister in the congress government of Uttar Pradesh, wrote to Indira Gandhi, then the Indian prime minister, to demand the restoration of the destroyed temple at Ayodhya (as well as other sites).

At this time, the Vishwa Hindu Parishad (VHP), an Indian right-wing Hindu nationalist organization, sought to organize popular Hindu support in favor of (re) building the Ram temple. This led to the formation of an organization whose sole purpose was liberating the Ram Jamastan site, Ram's birthplace, from Muslim control (Bacchetta, 2000, p. 267). Hindu nationalist forces gave a deadline to the government, demanding that the locks of the mosque be removed by March 6, 1986, after which they would forcibly break the locks and seize the site. Eventually, a direct court order led to the locks of the Babri Masjid being opened for Hindus, in March 1986; Muslims were still not allowed to enter the site (Majid, 2015, p. 560).

Following the establishment of the Muslim Babri Masjid Action Committee (BMAC), the dispute escalated and its impact spread beyond the borders of Uttar Pradesh. In 1987, a rally was organized in Delhi in order to protest the unlocking of the Babri Masjid to Hindus only and demanding that the right to pray at the site be restored to Muslims. The VHP, too, expanded their campaign beyond Uttar Pradesh to reach large parts of India. The results of the 1989 parliamentary elections meant that the Janathan Dal Party formed the government with outside support of the Bharathyia Janatha Party [BJP]; (Majid, 2015, p. 560); this coalition moved the Ram Janmabhoomi issue to the national political stage.

The Ram Janmabhoomi issue was a significant concern for L. K. Advani, an important Indian politician and a senior leader of the BJP, who launched a *rath yatra*—a campaign based on the Hindu tradition of chariots transporting deities—to promote the notion of building a Ram temple in place of the Babri Masjid. There were sporadic disturbances of public order along the chariot's route (Noorani, 2003b, pp. 171–172) and, at the end of 1990, parliamentary calls were made to stop the *yatra*; Advani was arrested in Bihar, which led to a clash between BJP supporters and police forces in Ayodhya (Van Der Veer, 1992, p. 102). In their attempt to clear the Babri Masjid area, police resorted to the use of force with fatal results for several Kar Sevaks and the injury of many others. The ashes of the volunteers who had been killed in the clashes were sent to different parts of the country by the Sangh Parivar, which created further tensions that included riots and violence. The BJP withdrew its support from the government, which led to the coalition's fall and the holding of new elections. In the June 1991 elections for the Lok Sabha (the lower house of India's bicameral Parliament), the Indian National Congress party emerged as the single largest party in the Parliament and formed the governing coalition under Narashima Rao. Meanwhile, in the elections for the Uttar Pradesh assembly, the BJP gained the majority and formed the governing coalition for the region (Rajamony, 2007, p. 121).

Emboldened by the BJP majority in the Uttar Pradesh assembly, the Sangh Parivar declared that the rebuilding of the Ram temple would begin on the sixth of December, 1992. On the first day of December, Kar Sevaks from many parts of India started arriving in Ayodhya; by the sixth of December, more than two hundred thousand Kar Sevaks were present in the city. At eleven o'clock that morning, people gathered near the disputed area to listen to speeches; shortly after, some of the Kar Sevaks breached the security cordon and entered the disputed area itself. They began throwing stones at the mosque, as well as the police who were guarding it. The police quickly fled the scene and other security forces of the Uttar Pradesh state failed to intervene. Members of the Kar Sevaks crowd climbed the mosque with ropes and dismantled the domes with iron rods. At around 12:45, the idols, collection boxes, and portraits of Ram were carried from the building. Soon after, the domes collapsed and the mosque was reduced to rubble. Meanwhile, Muslims in Ayodhya were attacked and many of their houses were set ablaze (Noorani, 2003b, pp. 1–85; Rajamony, 2007, p. 122). The demolition of the Babri Masjid led to the resignation of the Uttar Pradesh state government and, under article 356 of the Indian constitution, the imposition of presidential rule in response to the failure of the state government.

In the hours following the demolition of the Masjid, a makeshift temple was constructed and idols of Ram were installed in it. On the morning of the eighth of December, paramilitary forces assumed control of the site and no Kar Sevaks were allowed to stay inside the temple. Yet, upon receiving the permission of the High Court of Allahabad, worship at this make-shift temple resumed (Mehta, 2015a, p. 4).

In the days following the demolition of the mosque, a judicial commission was set up under a High Court judge, Justice Liberhan, to conduct an inquiry into the events at Ayodhya (though its report was not published until 2009, see below). In 1994, the Indian Supreme Court unanimously declined to give its opinion, in response to a presidential request, regarding whether a Hindu temple existed prior to the construction of the Babri Masjid (Rajamony, 2007, p. 123). In the 1996 general parliamentary elections, the BJP emerged as the single largest party; the party's success was largely due to its role in the Babri Masjid / Ram temple dispute. The BJP leader, Vajpayee, became the prime minister (Ratnagar, 2004, p. 241), though this government fell after only thirteen days. In the subsequent elections, the BJP campaigned with the promise to work towards building a Ram temple at the site of the demolished Babri Masjid. The party gained more seats than they had won in the previous elections, though they were unable to gain a majority. Again Vajpayee became prime minister and, again, he did not last long. Another general election was held in 1999. Having campaigned heavily on the Ram temple issue, Vajpayee became prime minister for the third time. Though he was finally able to complete his five-year term in full, he did so without building the temple. In the 2004 elections, the BJP lost to the Congress party which, with Manmohan Singh at its head and the outside support of left-wing parties, pushed a more secular platform.

As these events unfolded in the political sphere, the general civil unrest and violence surrounding the Ayodhya dispute continued. In February 2002, for example, several

Ram devotees returning by train from Ayodhya, were burned alive when one of the train compartments was torched. This led to massive riots in the state of Gujarat, governed by the BJP, where within three days more than two thousand people—mainly from the minority Muslim community—were killed and hundreds of rapes were reported.

The above mentioned Liberhan commission, though set up ten days after the demolition of the Babri Masjid, only finished and submitted its report on the thirtieth of June 2009, almost seventeen years after it began its inquiry. The report puts most of the responsibility for the demolition of the mosque on the political parties and the Hindu organizations involved: "The blame or the credit for the entire temple construction movement at Ayodhya must necessarily be attributed to the Sangh Parivar" (Liberhan Ayodhya Commission, p. 939). It also stated that "Immediately after entering into office, the government of Uttar Pradesh headed by Kalyan Singh embarked on the pogrom leading up to the events of December 6th 1992" (ibid., p. 951). Muslim leadership, too, is blamed for providing "the rabid Hindu ideologues sufficient cause to instill fear into the common citizen of India" (ibid., p. 946). In its recommendations, the commission notes that

> while it may be useful and indeed desirable to import certain aspects of ethics and morality into the political arena, the use of religion, caste or regionalism is a regressive and dangerous trend, capable of alienating people and dividing them into small sections [. . .] The events of December 6th 1992 and the many subsequent events have already shown to the nation the danger and the disruptive potential of allowing the intermixing of religion and politics. (ibid., p. 963)

While initially not made public, the commission's inquiry is now fully available on the website of the India Ministry of Home affairs.[13]

On the thirtieth of September 2010, the Allahabad High court pronounced its verdict on four land title suits related to the Ayodhya dispute. It decreed that the disputed site was to be divided into three parts: a third of the site would be dedicated to Ram Lalla (the infant Lord Rama), as represented by the Hindu Maha Sabha (a nationalist Hindu group and party), for the eventual construction of the Ram temple; a third of the site would be placed under the management of the Islamic Sunni Waqf board; and the remaining third of the site would be managed by the Hindu religious denomination Nirmohi Akhara.[14] However, in May 2011, the Supreme Court of India—having heard the appeals of Hindu and Muslim parties[15]—stayed the high court order that split the

---

13. See online at: http://mha.nic.in/LAC (accessed February, 2016).

14. The court's decision is available online at: http://elegalix.allahabadhighcourt.in/elegalix/DisplayAyodhyaBenchLandingPage.do; see also Mehta (2015a, p. 3).

15. Each of the claimants demands the area to itself, as indicated above (Noorani, 2014, pp. 379–396).

disputed site. Their de facto suspension of this plan noted that "this is very strange and surprising. Nobody has prayed for partition of the area. The Allahabad High Court has given a new relief which was not sought by anybody" (Patnaik & Mudiam, 2014, p. 384). The case, as of late 2015, therefore still awaits a decision by the Indian Supreme Court and no clear solution is in sight. In the meantime, no religious activity of any kind is permitted, save for Hindu religious rituals at the small Ram Lalla makeshift temple made in the aftermath of the mosque's destruction; the building of new or additional houses of religious prayer or worship was strictly banned (Venkatesan, 2015). The court seems to be in no particular hurry to deliver its decision, as reported in the Indian media: "The top court pointed out that the records in the case were in several languages—Arabic, Persian, Sanskrit, Hindi, Urdu and Punjabi—and would have to be translated into English before appeals could be taken up. "The record is massive and the documents in the case are of varied kinds . . . It may be a long road to final adjudication. But you must proceed in a methodical manner," a bench headed by Justice T. S. Thakur (the current, as of January 2016, Chief Justice of India) said" (Sinha, 2015). Thus, the site has been effectively shut down once again.

The ban on almost all religious activity at Babri Masjid / Ram Janmabhoomi is accompanied by the rather unwelcoming heavy security presence, security checks, and lack of adequate facilities—including drinkable water and even toilets[16]—all of which reflect and complement the legal ban on religious activity. In the aggregate, this policy arguably creates (see the next section) a de facto policy of deterring all would be worshippers from using the site. Certainly, if no one uses the site, any and all collisions at the place can be prevented (Pokharel and Beckett, 2012, pp. 55–56). The heavy security and the neglect of essential facilities seem to be intentional policies aimed at decreasing the number of visitors and, consequently, decreasing the likelihood of a recurrence of the events of 1992.

A.3. *Gag Solutions and the Ayodhya Dispute: Returning to the Models*

What major lessons are to be learned from the complex case of the Ayodhya dispute, and how do these lessons assist us in achieving a better understanding of state responses to disputes over thick sites in general?

Following the contextual method (introduced in chapter 1), we will analyze both the characteristics of the Ayodhya conflict and the various solutions adopted there

---

16. The lack of facilities was described by one reporter as follows: "[P]ilgrims, who are devotees of Lord Rama, are deprived of even basic facilities like drinking water and toilets and face difficulty due to inadequate arrangements made by both the Centre and UP government," *Times of India*, August 15, 2015, retrieved from http://timesofindia.indiatimes.com/india/ SC-allows-repairing-offacilities-at-makeshift-Ram-Lalla-Temple-in-Ayodhya/articleshow/ 48420064.cms). In late 2015, the Indian Supreme Court allowed minor repairs at the place (inclusive of the makeshift temple). These repairs were immediately contested by Muslim leaders, who regarded them as further support of a status quo that they view as discriminatory and that must be opposed, as described in Sinha (2015): "Hours after Monday's decision, AIMIM chief and Hyderabad MP Asaduddin Owaisi urged the All India Muslim Personal Law Board (AIMPLB) to appeal against the Supreme Court order."

while moving between the details of the case and of the relevant theories (DCV, even-handedness, and privatization) in order to sharpen our understanding of both. The Ayodhya case, therefore, is not merely an illustrative example for further exploring the *application* of the principles already noted above, but an opportunity to *add* valuable insights to the models themselves.

This section is divided to three parts: we begin with an analysis of the de facto solution implemented at Ayodhya—that is, a severe restriction of worship and access— and place it within the relevant literature on "gag solutions" (section A.3.1); we then evaluate the instrument of "gag solutions" as compared to the DCV, evenhandedness, and privatization models for religion-state relations (section A.3.2); and, lastly, we reconsider the particulars of the Ayodhya case and reach the conclusion that the gag solution ought to be rejected in favor of an evenhanded model (section A.3).

A.3.1. Ayodhya: Restricting Access and Worship, "Gag Solutions," and Thick Sites

A survey of the Ayodhya dispute provided us with an additional and important instrument that states can use for handling conflicts over thick sites: the severe restriction of access and of religious practice (including bans on building new houses of worship). Such restriction of access and worship belongs to a family of policy solutions often referred to as "gag rules" or "gag solutions" (Holmes, 1997).[17] In order to properly evaluate the policy chosen at Ayodhya, a succinct examination of the "gag" approach is required. Simply stated, the term "gag rule" or "gag solution" indicates a situation in which one is prevented from saying something or acting in a specific way, either legally or through social norms, in order to avoid severely offending feelings or interests as well as in order to avoid creating social instability.[18]

In the literature exploring such "gag" solutions, their merits are described as follows: "sealing one's lips [. . .] because open airing would mortally offend prominent

---

17. Note that some aspects of the restrictions in place at Ayodhya are formal and some are informal. The ban on building new temples is formal (i.e., enacted by a court decision), while withholding basic services (toilets) for pilgrims is informal (Venkatesan, 2015). As such, the analysis of the overall policy as "gagging" is an interpretive decision of the authors and differs from any official declaration of the government.

18. The term "gag rule" or "gag solution" is typically used to denote things that one is prevented from saying, either legally or through the norms of conversation. However, the term has also been used to describe the preclusion of prosecution after a certain temporal point, the avoidance of topics all together—such as slavery in the United States—during certain periods, or religion in some institutional contexts. The justifications for such rules or norms vary and depend on context: politeness, maintaining adequate procedures in a court of law, protecting the separation of religion and state, maintaining social stability, and the list can be expanded (Holmes, 1997; see also chapter 5.) The term indicates an obvious agreement with Rawls' (1993) version of political liberalism; it was met with some objections, typically by those who argue that such rules are restrictive either vis-à-vis liberalism (Isaac, Filner, & Bivin, 1999) or vis-à-vis religion (McConnell, 1999). In any case, the diverse and wide usage of such restrictions certainly imply

individuals or sub groups and permanently injure the cooperative spirit." (Holmes, 1997, p. 19); Holmes continues:

> No issue is more frequently classified as "worthy of avoiding" than religion [. . .] Religious disputes [. . .] cannot always be resolved politically [. . .] the "wall" between church and state does not merely shelter the private sphere from unwanted incursions; it also unburdens the public sphere of irresolvable problems" (p. 23).

The "unburdening" justification given in support of a gag rule nicely explains the "gagging of access and worship" in the Ayodhya dispute; it serves the government in its attempt to avoid making a substantial religious decision in this case. While this unburdening of the government is also a feature of the privatization approach, there the policy enacted is the exact opposite. Indeed, by opening up a thick site to all worshippers, as recommended by the privatization model, the government is similarly relieved of the need to make substantial religious decisions. Examining the gag solution, however, immediately reveals two highly problematic issues. *First*, the "gagging of access and worship" solution is in tension with basic democratic principles. The severe restriction of access and worship, especially when levied on a thick site, amounts to a severe limitation of religious freedom that is protected in many international treaties and constitutions[19] (including that of India).[20] As such, even if such a ban were applied equally to all concerned parties (which is not the case in the Ayodhya dispute), it will be deeply problematic. *Second*, gagging solutions tend to be self-defeating, pragmatically speaking;[21] that is, in the context of thick sites, they tend to intensify conflicts rather than assuage them, at least over time. Denying access and worship likely creates resentment which, eventually, will increase the perceived importance of the site for the relevant believers and increase their desire to worship at the "gagged" site. Thick sites, it is well worth remembering, are irreplaceable from the believers' perspectives and there are no alternatives to them (see chapter 1).[22]

---

that the term "gag rule" can be used to describe an attitude towards acts rather than speech only; thus, in our analysis we adopt the terms "gag solution" or even "gagging access."

19. See, for a full discussion, Ferrari (2014); Barry (2001); McConnell (2000); Durham (2009); Boyle (2007); Witte (1996); Greenawalt (2007); Nickel (2005); Fox (2016).

20. See articles 25–28 of the Indian constitution; the preamble defines India as a secular state, and article 25 indicates (among other things) that "all persons are equally entitled to freedom of conscience and the right freely to profess, practice and propagate religion."

21. By "self-defeating" we denote, following Parfit's famous definition, cases in which a given school of thought believes that what needs to be done under certain conditions is X, yet X will cause their own aims to be worse achieved (Parfit, 1979, p. 533).

22. When Jordanian authorities refused to allow Jews access to the Western Wall (1948–1967), they only intensified its religious significance. "The inaccessibility of the Wall," as Storper-Perez and Goldberg (1994, p. 316) put it, "became a factor maintaining and even augmenting its appeal in the eyes of many Israeli Jews." For a detailed discussion of this point, see chapter 3.

A.3.2. "Gagging" Solutions: Evaluating the Instrument vis-à-vis the Models of DCV, Evenhandedness, and Privatization

How should we evaluate the instrument of "gagging"—uncovered by the Ayodhya case-study—as an alternative to the three models of DCV, evenhandedness, and privatization? These three models aim to regulate religion-state relations without violating democratic principles and religious freedoms; as explained in the preface to chapters 3–5, models that violate such criteria are simply outside the boundaries of our study. The gagging solution does not meet this standard because, by definition, it consists of a severe restriction of religious freedom. It, therefore, cannot be approached as another, fourth model of regulating religion-state relations. "Gagging" also does not have the complex wealth of institutional use and theoretical justification that the three models demonstrate. As such, we should approach it as an instrument, not as a comprehensive model. Despite its somewhat illiberal nature, the gagging technique can be adopted as a particular, usually temporary, solution when the three legitimate models are rendered inapplicable by extreme circumstances.

Adopting this problematic instrument can be justified if it prevents significant harm to basic human interests, such as major violent collisions between religious factions like Hindus and Muslims. As such, the "gagging" solution is a potential second-order option.[23] Its adoption, even when justified, needs to meet the criteria of proportionality that was pointed out in chapter 5 with regard to the notion of "backlash": is it the least restrictive means available? Is there a logical connection between the policy adopted and the desired goal? Furthermore, the policy must be evaluated periodically as its usefulness is time sensitive; it may indeed remain in effect even though it is no longer needed (Barak, 2012).[24]

A.3.3. The Particulars of Ayodhya: Gagging or Evenhandedness?

Having explored the details of the Ayodhya dispute, and considered the status of the gagging instrument relative to the three more comprehensive models, we can evaluate the solution that has currently been adopted for the Ayodhya dispute. We conclude that the problematic "gagging" instrument is not the best available solution and that an evenhanded solution should be adopted as a preferable alternative. As a preliminary

---

23. This "second-order" characterization points to two issues: first, while not inherently desirable, it is (arguably) the best that can be achieved at some given point in time; second, it precludes a decision of a more substantial type (i.e., more permanent decisions with regard to the site). On second-order solutions, see Sen (2009, pp. 15–18); on second-order decisions, see Sunstein and Ullmann-Margalit (1999).

24. There is also the perennial question of who should be authorized to make such liberty-limiting decisions in the first place. See, on political judgment generally, Ruderman (1997); Wolin (1990, pp. 100–119). For the Aristotelian notion of practical wisdom (*phronesis*), see Aristotle (2000, pp. 103–118); see also chapter 1 for our discussion of the contextual method and its justifications.

comment, it should be noted that the gagging instrument currently applied in Ayodhya is incomplete and discriminatory. It is discriminatory as worshipping at the makeshift Hindu Ram Lalla temple is permissible, while all other religious activities—first and foremost those of Muslims—are not allowed. This arrangement is clearly discriminatory. Such discrimination is especially intolerable given that it was directly shaped by the violent demolition of the Babri-Masjid in 1992; the victims of that attack, initially denied their freedom to worship at the Mosque through a violent act, continue to be denied access to their sacred site. If an adopted "gag" solution is to be permissible, *it must be applied equally*; that is, it must restrict access and worship to all parties equally. A discriminatory application of a gagging order, like the one "on the ground" at present, likely will also fail to promote stability. If anything, such a discriminatory measure will increase suspicious attitudes, hostility, and violence between Muslims and Hindus. Furthermore, the discriminatory character of the "gagging" response does not absolve the government from "picking and choosing" a particular religion to support among many, as it does favor one specific group. Therefore, one major advantage of the "gag" approach—unburdening the government from the need to make substantial religious decisions—does not apply. Assuming that the gag solution was universally and equally applied to all relevant religious groups that wish to worship and pray at the site, how would this solution compare to those indicated by the DCV, evenhandedness, or privatization models? We argue that the gagging solution is worse than what is prescribed by these models and that it ought to be rejected, even if applied in an equitable fashion, in favor of less restrictive means of preventing violence. The evenhanded solution that was suggested by the Allahabad High Court (see section A.2) constitutes the most preferable option. Less restrictive, this evenhanded solution preserves a measure of religious liberty without destabilizing the situation on the ground. We grant that the fear of violence is a serious and legitimate concern which, given the particularities of the case at hand, makes this evenhanded model preferable to the privatized model that we have advanced above. Let us elaborate. It is necessary to critically consider why the evenhanded approach was rejected by the Indian Supreme Court. Thus we consider the arguments of Justice Lodha, one of the judges of India's Supreme Court, who was a member of the panel that stayed (and de facto canceled) the evenhanded solution that would have divided the site into three parts:

> The High Court's judgment[25] is something strange. A new dimension has been given by the High Court as the decree of partition was not sought by the parties. It was not prayed for by anyone. It has to be stayed. It's a strange order. How can a decree for partition be passed *when none of the parties had prayed for it?* It's strange. Such kind of decrees cannot be allowed to be in operation. It is a difficult situation now. The position is that the High Court verdict has created a litany of litigation. (quoted in Venkatesan 2015; italics added)

---

25. That is, the judgment of the Allahabad High Court, the high court of the state of Uttar Pradesh.

Justice Lodha argues that the tripartite solution should be rejected specifically because no party requested such a solution, and numerous parties have petitioned against it. However, since ownership, management, and rights of usage and access at thick sites such as the Babri Masjid / Ram Janmabhoomi are heavily disputed, "non-contestability" clearly sets the bar for acceptable solutions too high. It is unrealistic to expect that any solution would be tailored perfectly to the wishes of even one party in the dispute, let alone several of them. The more modest criteria of maintaining a reasonable level of stability and of religious freedom for interested parties offer a more feasible target.

We wish to suggest, therefore, that the Allahabad High Court's decision to split the site into three sections—a third to the Hindu Maha Sabha (a nationalist Hindu group and party) for the eventual construction of the Ram Lalla (infant Lord Rama) temple, a third to the Islamic Sunni Waqf board, and the remaining third to the Hindu religious denomination Nirmohi Akhara—is the best solution as things stand at present. This solution is admittedly far from perfect. As the detailed analysis of evenhanded theories in chapter 4 has led us to expect, it is not fully inclusive (Shia Muslims, for example, for whom the site is also sacred, are not recognized in this solution)[26]; it demands that the government become directly involved in religious affairs; it is rigid ("end state," in the language used in chapter 4); and it would force the government to continually assess and reassess new developments in the religious sphere. It is also highly likely that such evenhandedness would involve the banning of some legitimate religious behaviors at the site. Furthermore, each of the involved parties are unsatisfied with this solution, each one wishes to gain exclusive management of the whole area.[27] These considerations had lead us, in chapter 4, to reject the evenhanded model as means of addressing thick sites and to favor the privatization model (examined in detail in chapter 5). However, in the Ayodhya dispute, the fear of violence, which was the driving force behind the Indian government's semi-formal adoption of the gag solution, has forced us to reconsider this conclusion. As was noted in our methodological discussion of the differences and similarities between the WoW case and the Ayodhya dispute, one of the important differences between the two cases was the magnitude of the violence taking place in Ayodhya, and the fact that the larger context—regional, national, and international— means that the conflict can spread quite extensively. The WoW case does not lie within such a sweeping adversarial context.

Even though we recognize the imperfections and disadvantages of an evenhanded model in general, we argue that for the Ayodhya dispute, the Allahabad High Court's

26. It has been suggested that, in the Indian context, the nature of such categories (religion as a whole, communities recognized versus those that are not recognized or participants in this particular dispute) were heavily influenced by theories and distinctions introduced by the British Empire. An analysis of this claim points well beyond the contours of the current research. See Srikantan (2012).

27. The Wakf, for example, argues that any shared allocation is illegitimate since it is the sole party with a legitimate ownership claim (Noorani, 2014, pp. 379–396).

decision to divide the site into three parts in an evenhanded fashion constitutes the best available solution. There are two major advantages of an evenhanded solution for the Babri Masjid / Ram Janmabhoomi case. *First*, the solution to divide the site into three maintains some level of religious freedom and egalitarianism, even if only for the members of the three "chosen" groups, that the gag solution does not replicate. *Second*, this evenhanded solution avoids the dangers of day to day "collisions" between worshippers belonging to different religions at this thick site (at least, if the different three areas of the site are properly constructed). That is, while pilgrims and worshippers from different sects will encounter each other elsewhere, a properly enacted tripartite arrangement could guarantee that they would not encounter each other within the thick site, a focal point where such encounters might ignite hostilities[28] (see the "divide and separate" technique discussed in chapter 4).

Our conclusion is, therefore, that the evenhanded solution of "divide and separate" presents a less restrictive means of maintaining reasonable levels of security than is otherwise available. It is superior to the gag solution which, even in its "pure form," inherently leads to far more severe violations of religious freedom for most or all of the concerned parties. We should also note that, once the divide and separate arrangement is established and each group gets some of what it desires,[29] the fact that several religions or denominations worship at the site will become a routine practice; eventually, a process of privatization might be considered, given its general advantages over evenhandedness that were outlined in chapter 5.

A.4. Concluding Remarks

What can be learned from the analysis of the Ayodhya case? The Ayodhya dispute adds several important dimensions to our discussion of the preferred religion-state arrangement at the Western Wall and, more broadly, to our attempt to better understand the proper management of thick sites in general: *first*, the heightened levels of violence in the Ayodhya case, and its context of wider overall conflict, is a significant difference from the WoW case that makes an alternate solution necessary; *second*, the Ayodhya case introduced a new and significant instrument to the "tool kit" for managing thick

---

28. As Voltaire (1733) famously wrote:

> Take a view of the Royal Exchange in London, a place more venerable than many courts of justice, where the representatives of all nations meet for the benefit of mankind. There the Jew, the Mahometan, and the Christian transact together, as though they all professed the same religion, and give the name of infidel to none but bankrupts" (p. 44).

29. In such contested sites, if one party receives all that it desires, it is likely that the end result, the compromise, is "rotten" in that it deprives other parties of important rights and freedoms; such a solution is likely to, eventually, lead to more violence. See Margalit (2009); and chapter 5.

sites: a gag solution—that is, severely restricting access to, and worship at, thick-sites; *third*, the details of the Ayodhya case reinforced one of the major claims—that thick sites do not have a demonstrably unified tradition and shared understandings, two features required for a coherent and applicable DCV model—presented in our critical evaluation of that model (chapter 3); *finally*, given the particulars of the Ayodhya case, we were forced to reconsider our conclusion from chapters 3 to 5 that the privatization model is indeed preferable to the competing models of DCV and evenhandedness. Such previously unconsidered (at least in the aggregate) particulars include the heightened levels of violence that extend well beyond the site and the relative fairness of the evenhanded compromise suggested by the Allahabad High Court. Indeed, this compromise was not endorsed by any of the parties and, therefore, could not be "rotten"; further, it would maintain a level of religious freedom that was otherwise difficult to imagine. All of these variables, combined, led us to shift our support from the privatization model to the evenhanded approach in this case, at the very least as a "second order" solution. The Ayodhya dispute, therefore, added valuable insights to our research regarding thick sites. Such insights, gained from this additional case study, point once again to the advantages of the contextual approach; it is highly unlikely that such richness would have been provided by any kind of abstract "armchair philosophy."

References

Aaronson, Ran. (1989). Jerusalem in the eyes of members of the First Alyiah. In Hagit Levski (Ed.), *Jerusalem in Zionist vision and realization* (pp. 47–66). Jerusalem: Zalman Shazar Center for Jewish History. [Heb].

Abramovich, Sholem Yankev. (1910). "*In Those Days*". [Heb]. Retrieved from http://benyehuda.org/mos/bayamim_hahem_I.html.

Abudarham, David Ben-Yosef. (1927). *Sefer Abudarham*. Deva, Romania: Weinstein and Friedmann.

Adler, Rachel. (2001). Innovation and authority: A feminist reading of the "women's minyan" responsum. In Walter Jacob & Moshe Zemer (Eds.), *Gender issues in Jewish law* (pp. 3–32). New York: Berghahn.

Aharoni, Leah. (2014). Stop the division at the Western Wall. *Jerusalem Post*, October 14. Retrieved from http://www.jpost.com/Opinion/Stop-the-Division-at-the-Western-Wall-378846, accessed February 17, 2016.

Albright, Madeleine K., Kohut, Andrew, Stokes, Bruce, McIntosh, Mary, Gross, Elizabeth M., & Speulda, Nicole. (2002). Among Wealthy Nations: U.S. stands alone in its embrace of religion. (Pew Research Center Essay). Retrieved from http://www.pewglobal.org/2002/12/19/among-wealthy-nations.

Alesina, Alberto, Devleeschauwer, Arnaud, Easterly, William, Kurlat, Sergio, & Wacziarg Romain. (2002). Fractionalization. (NBER Working Paper Series, no. 9411). Cambridge, MA: National Bureau of Economic Research.

Alexander, Elizabeth Shanks. (2013). *Gender and timebound commandments in Judaism*. Cambridge: Cambridge University Press.

An Naim, Abdullahi A., (2010). *Islam and the secular state*. Cambridge, MA: Harvard University Press.

Anatoli, Jacob b. Abba Mari. (1886). *Malmad ha-Talmidim*. Lyck: M'kize Nirdamim. [Heb].

Anderson, Elizabeth. (1999). What is the point of equality? *Ethics, 109*(2), 287–337.

Anderson, Elizabeth. (2008). How should egalitarians cope with market risks? *Theoretical Inquiries in Law*, *9*, 239–270.

Anderson, Elizabeth. (2010). *The imperative of integration*. Princeton, NJ: Princeton University Press.

Aristotle. (2000). *The Nicomachean Ethics*. (R. Crisp, Trans.). Cambridge: Cambridge University Press.

Armstrong, Karen. (1997). *Jerusalem: One city, three faiths*. New York: Ballantine Books.

Arnold, Matthew. (1869). *Culture and anarchy*. (Project Guttenberg e-text). Retrieved from http://www.gutenberg.org/cache/epub/4212/pg4212.html.

Ashkenazi, Shlomo. (1953). *The woman in the perspective of Judaism*. (3 vols.). Tel Aviv: Jezreel.

Audi, Robert. (1989). The separation of church and state and the obligations of citizenship. *Philosophy and Public Affairs*, *18*(3), 259–296.

Audi, Robert. (2011). *Democratic authority and the separation of church and state*. Oxford: Oxford University Press.

Audi, Robert, & Wolterstorff, Nicholas. (1997). *Religion in the public square*. Lanham, MD: Rowman and Littlefield.

Avineri, Shlomo, & de-Shalit, Avner (Eds.). (1992). *Communitarianism and individualism*. Oxford: Oxford University Press.

Azaryahu, Maoz. (2002). (Re)locating redemption. Jerusalem: The Wall, two mountains, a hill and the narrative construction of the Third Temple. *Journal of Modern Jewish Studies*, *1*(1), 22–35.

Baader, Benjamin M. (2012). Jewish difference and the feminine spirit of Judaism. In Baader, Benjamin M., Gillerman, Sharon, & Lerner, Paul. (Eds.), *Jewish masculinities: German Jews, gender, and history* (pp. 50–71). Bloomington: Indiana University Press.

Bacchetta, P. (2000). Sacred space in conflict in India: The Babri Masjid affair. *Growth and Change*, *31*(2), 255–284.

Bagni, B. N. (1979). Discrimination in the name of the Lord: A critical evaluation of discrimination by religious organizations. *Columbia Law Review*, *79*(8), 1514–1549.

Bahat, Dan. (2007). On the sanctification of the Western Wall. *Ariel: Journal for Knowledge of the Land of Israel*, *180*(July), 33–54. [Heb].

Bahat, Dan, & Rubinstein, Chaim T. (2011). *The Carta Jerusalem Atlas*. Jerusalem: Israel Map and Publishing Company. [Heb.]

Bakker, H. (1991). Ayodhyā: A Hindu Jerusalem; an investigation of "Holy War" as a religious idea in the light of communal unrest in India. *Numen*, *38*(1), 80–109.

Banting, Keith, & Kymlicka, Will. (2003). Do multiculturalism policies erode the welfare state? (Working Paper 33. School of Policy Studies). Kingston: Queen's University.

Bar, Doron. (2007). *Sanctifying the land: The Jewish holy places in the State of Israel*. Jerusalem: Yad Izhak Ben-Zvi Publications. [Heb].

Bar, Doron. (2014). The debate over the designation of holy places and historical sites in the State of Israel, 1928–1967. *Cathedra, 154*, 137–162. [Heb].

Bar, Doron. (2015). The struggle over the Western Wall, 1967–1973. In Yehoshua Ben-Arieh, Aviva Halamish, Ora Limor, Rehav Rubin, &Ronny Reich (Eds.), *Study of Jerusalem through the ages* (pp. 318–346). Jerusalem, Yad Ben-Zvi Pulications.

Barak, Aharon. (2012). *Proportionality.* Cambridge: Cambridge University Press.

Barak-Erez, Daphne. (2008). *Outlawed pigs: Law, religion, and culture in Israel.* Madison: University of Wisconsin Press.

Barak-Erez, Daphne. (2009). Law and religion under the status quo model: Between past compromises and constant change. *Cardozo Law Review, 30*, 2495–2508.

Barak-Erez, Daphne. (2011). The private prison controversy and the privatization continuum. *Law and Ethics of Human Rights, 5*(1), 138–157.

Barkai, Gabriel. (2007). The Western Wall. *Ariel: Journal for Knowledge of the Land of Israel, 180*(July), 17–27. [Heb].

Barkan, Elazar, & Barkey, Karen. (2015). Introduction. In E. Barken & K. Barkey (Eds.), *Choreographies of Shared Sacred Sites* (pp. 1–32). New York: Columbia University Press.

Barkay, Gabriel, & Schiller, Eli (Eds.). (2007). *The Western Wall.* Special issue of *Ariel: Journal for Knowledge of the Land of Israel, 181*, 17–27. [Heb].

Barry, Brian. (1989). *Theories of justice.* Berkeley: University of California Press.

Barry, Brian. (2001). *Culture and equality.* London: Polity.

Bauman, Zygmunt. (1996). Morality in the age of contingency. In P. Heelas, S. Lash, & Paul Morris (Eds.), *Detraditionalization* (pp. 49–59). Oxford: Blackwell.

Bayle, Pierre. (2005). *A philosophical commentary on these words of the gospel.* Indianapolis, IN: Liberty Fund. (Original work published in 1686).

Belfer, Ella. (2005). *A split identity: The conflict between the sacred and the secular in the Jewish world.* Ramat Gan, Israel: Bar-Ilan University Press. [Heb].

Bellah, Robert N. (1964). Religious evolution. *American Sociological Review, 29*(June): 258–374.

Ben-Dov, Meir. (1982). *In the shadow of the temple: The discovery of ancient Jerusalem.* Jerusalem: Keter.

Ben-Dov, Meir, Naor, Mordechai, & Aner, Zeev. (1983). *The Western Wall.* (Raphael Posner, Trans.). New York: Adama Books.

Ben-Menahem, Hanina. (2008). Is Talmudic law a religious legal system? A provisional analysis. *Journal of Law and Religion 24*, 379–401.

Ben-Porat, G. (2013). *Between state and synagogue: The secularization of contemporary Israel.* Cambridge: Cambridge University Press.

Benvenisti, Meron. (1976). *Jerusalem: The torn city.* Minneapolis: University of Minnesota Press.

Benzo Andrea. (2014). Towards a definition of sacred places: Introductory remarks. In S. Ferrari & A. Benzo (Eds.), *Between cultural diversity and common heritage legal and religious perspectives on the sacred places of the Mediterranean* (pp. 17–24). London: Ashgate.

Berger, Peter L. (1974). Some second thoughts on substantive versus functional definitions of religion. *Journal for the Scientific Study of Religion 13*(2), 125–133.

Berger, Peter L. (1990). *The sacred canopy: Elements of a sociological theory of religion.* New York: Anchor Books.

Berkovits, Shmuel. (2000). *The battle for the holy places: The struggle over Jerusalem and the holy sites in Israel, Judea, Samaria and the Gaza District.* Or Yehuda, Israel: Hed Arzi. [Heb].

Berkovits, Shmuel. (2006). *How dreadful is this place! Holiness, politics and justice in Jerusalem and the holy places in Israel.* Jerusalem: Carta. [Heb].

Bhargava, Rajeev. (1998). What is secularism for? In Rajeev Bhargave (Ed.), *Secularism and its critics* (pp. 486–542). Oxford: Oxford University Press.

Biale, David. (2011). *Not in the heavens: The tradition of Jewish secular thought.* Princeton, NJ: Princeton University Press.

Bible. Old Testament English. Jewish Publication Society. (1985). *Tanakh: A New Translation of the Holy Scriptures according to the Traditional Hebrew Text.* Jewish Publication Society.

Bickel, Alexander M. (1986). *The least dangerous branch: The Supreme Court at the bar of politics.* (2nd ed.) New Haven, CT: Yale University Press. (Original work published in 1962).

Bigelow, Anna. (2010). *Sharing the sacred: Practicing pluralism in Muslim North India.* Oxford: Oxford University Press.

Boyle, Kevin. (2007). Freedom of religion in international law. In Javaid Rehman & Susan C. Breau (Eds.), *Religion, Human Rights and International Law*, (pp. 23–51). Leiden: Martinus Nijhoff Publishers.

Brake, Wayne T. (2014). The contentious politics of religious diversity. In Chris Tilly & Michael Hanagan (Eds.), *Contention and trust in cities and states* (pp. 229–248). New York: Springer.

Breger, Marshall J., Reiter, Yitzhak, & Hammer, Leonard (Eds.). (2010). *Holy places in the Israeli-Palestinian conflict.* London: Routledge.

Briggs, Asa. (2006). The welfare state in historical perspective. In Christopher Pierson, Francis G. Castles, & Ingela K. Naumann (Eds.), *The welfare state reader* (pp. 16–30). London: Polity.

Brown, Iris. (2008). The big Pesika dilemma: Between individual distress and the needs of a system. *Akdamot 21*, 203–214. [Heb].

Buchanan, J. (1959). Positive economics, welfare economics, and political economy. *Journal of Law and Economics 2*, 124–138.

Caney, Simon. (2002). Equal treatment, exceptions and cultural diversity. In Paul Kelly, (Ed.), *Multiculturalism reconsidered* (pp. 81–101). Cambridge: Polity

Carens, Joseph H. (1997a). Liberalism and culture. *Constellations, 4*(1), 35–47.

Carens, Joseph H. (1997b). Two conceptions of fairness: A response to Veit Bader. *Political Theory*, *25*(6), 814–820.

Carens, Joseph H. (2000). *Culture, citizenship, and community*. Oxford: Oxford University Press.

Carens, Joseph H. (2004). A contextual approach to political theory. *Ethical Theory and Moral Practice*, *7*(2), 117–132.

Carens, Joseph H. (2013). *The ethics of immigration*. Oxford: Oxford University Press.

Carpenter, Kristen A. (2004–5). Property rights approach to sacred sites cases. *UCLA Law Review*, *52*, 1061–1148.

Casanova, Jose. (1992) Private and public religions. *Social Research*, *59*(1), 17–57.

Cassese, Antonio. (1999). *Self-determination of people: A legal appraisal*. Cambridge: Cambridge University Press.

Charme, Stuart L. (2005). The political transformation of gender traditions at the Western Wall in Jerusalem. *Journal of Feminist Studies in Religion*, *21*(1), 5–34.

Chesler, Phyllis, & Haut, Rivka (Eds.). (2002). *Women of the Wall: Claiming Sacred Ground at Judaism's Holy Site*. Woodstock, VT: Jewish Lights Publishing.

Christiano, Tom. (2006). Democracy. In *The Stanford Encyclopedia of Philosophy*. (Spring 2015 edition). Edward N Zalta (Ed.). Retrieved from http://plato.stanford.edu/archives/spr2015/entries/democracy, accessed April 21, 2016.

Cohen, Ailene Nusbacher. (1999). Efforts at change in a traditional denomination: The case of Orthodox women's prayer groups. *Nashim*, *2*, 95–112.

Cohen, Andrew I. (2015). Corrective vs. distributive justice: The case of apologies. *Ethical Theory and Moral Practice*. Published online, December 11. Retrieved from http://link.springer.com/article/10.1007/s10677-015-9674-5, accessed April 21, 2016.

Cohen, Asher, & Susser, Brenard. (2000). *Israel and the politics of Jewish identity*. Baltimore: Johns Hopkins University Press.

Cohen, Asher, & Susser, Brenard. (2009). Jews and others: Non-Jewish Jews in Israel. *Israel Affairs*, *15*(1), 52–65.

Cohen, Bezalel. (2006). Economic hardship and gainful employment in Haredi society in Israel: An insider's perspective. Jerusalem: Floersheimer Institute.

Cohen, Gerald A. (1999). Expensive tastes and multiculturalism. In Rajeev Bhargava, Amiya Kumar Bagchi, & R. Susdarshan (Eds.), *Multiculturalism, liberalism, and democracy* (pp. 80–100). Oxford: Oxford University Press.

Cohen, Gerald A. (2012). Rescuing conservatism. In *Finding oneself in the other* (pp. 143–174). Princeton, NJ: Princeton University Press.

Cohen, Haim. (2006). *Being Jewish*. Tel Aviv: Kinneret-Dvir. [Heb].

Cohen, Hillel. (2015). *Year zero of the Arab-Israeli conflict 1929*. Boston: Brandeis University Press.

Cohen, M. (2009). The Western Wall (Wailing Wall) Plaza. In Doron Bar & Eyal Meiron (Eds.), *Planning and conserving Jerusalem: The challenge of an ancient city*, (pp. 316–323). Jerusalem: Yad Izhak Ben-Zvi.

Cohen-Hattab, Kobi. (2010). Holiness, nationality and tourism: Conception of the Western Wall Plaza in Jerusalem after the Six-Day War (1967). *Horizons in geography*, *75*, special Issue: *Tourism*. [Heb].

Cohen, Raymond. (2008). *Saving the Holy Sepulchre: How rival Christians came together to rescue their holiest shrine*. Oxford: Oxford University Press.

Coleman, Doriane L. The Seattle compromise: Multicultural sensitivity and Americanization. *Duke Law Journal*, *47*(4), 717–783.

Collier, David, & Mahoney, James. Insights and pitfalls: Selection bias in qualitative research. *World Politics*, *49*(1), 56–91.

Collins, Richard B. (2003), Sacred sites and religious freedom on government land. *Journal of Constitutional Law*, *5*(2), 241–270.

Cooperman, Alan, & Lipka, Michael. (2014). U.S. doesn't rank high in religious diversity. Pew Research Center Essay. Retrieved from http://www.pewresearch.org/fact-tank/2014/04/04/u-s-doesnt-rank-high-in-religious-diversity, accessed April 21, 2016.

Cornille, Catherine. (2003). Double religious belonging: Aspects and questions. *Buddhist-Christian Studies*, *23*(1): 43–49.

Cosgel, Metin, & Miceli, Thomas J. (2009). State and religion. *Journal of Comparative Economics*, *37*(3), 402–416.

Coüasnon, Charles. (1974). *The Church of the Holy Sepulchre in Jerusalem*. London: Oxford University Press.

Curry, Thomas, J. (1986). *The first freedoms*. Oxford: Oxford University Press.

Cyrus, Adler. (1930). *Memorandum on the Western Wall: Prepared for the Special Commission of the League of Nations on behalf of the Jewish Agency for Palestine*, Philadelphia. [Heb].

Dahl, Robert. (1989). *Democracy and its critics*. New Haven, CT: Yale University Press.

Dahl, Robert. (2000). *On democracy*. New Haven, CT: Yale University Press.

Dahl, Robert. (2006). *On political equality*. New Haven, CT: Yale University Press.

Day, Abby. (2005). Doing theodicy: An empirical study of a women's prayer group. *Journal of Contemporary Religion*, *20*(3), 343–356.

Denzin, Norman K. (1989). *Interpretive interactionism*. Newbury Park, CA: Sage.

Devlin, Patrick. (1965). *The enforcement of morals*. Oxford: Oxford University Press.

Devlin, Patrick. (1977), Morals and the criminal law. In Ronald Dworkin (Ed.), *The Philosophy of law* (pp. 66–82). Oxford: Oxford University Press.

Doe, Norman. (2011). *Law and religion in Europe*. Oxford: Oxford University Press.

Dorfman, Avihai, & Harel, Alon. (2013). The case against privatization. *Philosophy and Public Affairs*, *41*(1): 67–102.

Dorfman, Avihay. (2008). Freedom of religion. *Canadian Journal of Law and Jurisprudence*, *21*(2), 1–23.

Dovrin, Nurit. (2006). Marriages of Israelis abroad and the part of the immigrants from the Soviet Union in the phenomenon. *Megamot*, *44*(3), 477–506. [Heb].

Downing, Lyle A., & Thigpen, Robert B. Thigpen. (1986). Beyond shared understandings. *Political Theory*, *14*(3), 451–472.

Dunleavy, Patrick. (1993). The state. In Robert E.Goodin, Philip Pettit, & Thomas W. Pogge (Eds.), *A companion to contemporary political philosophy* (pp. 793–803). Oxford: Blackwell.

Durham, W. Cole, Jr. (1996). Perspectives on religious liberty: A comparative framework. In John D. Van der Vyver & John Witte Jr., *Religious human rights in global perspective: Legal perspectives* (pp. 1–44). Boston: Martinus Njhoff.

Durham, W. Cole Jr. (2009). The doctrine of religious freedom. In Scott W. Cameron, Galen L. Fletcher, & Jane H. Wise (Eds.). *Life and Law* (Vol. 2, pp. 65–82. Provo, Utah: Brigham Young University.

Dworkin, Ronald. (1966). Lord Devlin and the enforcement of morals. *Yale Law Journal, 75*(6), 986–1005.

Dworkin, Ronald. (1977). Liberalism. In Stuart Hampshire (Ed), *Private and public morality* (pp. 113–143). Cambridge: Cambridge University Press.

Dworkin, Ronald. (1977b). *Taking rights seriously*. Cambridge, MA: Harvard University Press.

Dworkin, Ronald. (2000). *Sovereign virtue*. Cambridge, MA: Harvard University Press.

Dworkin, Ronald. (2001). Liberalism. In *A matter of principle* (pp. 181–214). Oxford: Oxford University Press.

Dworkin, Ronald. (2006). The right to ridicule. *New York Review of Books*, March 23.

Dworkin, Ronald. (2013). *Justice for hedgehogs*. Cambridge, MA: Harvard University Press.

Eaton, Richard M. (2000). Temple desecration in pre-modern India. *Frontline, 17*(25/26), December 22, 2000, and January 5, 2000.

*Economic Times. (*2010). Ayodhya: High Court relies on ASI's 2003 Report. October 1.

Edge, Peter W. (2002). The construction of sacred places in English law. *Journal of Environmental Law, 14*(2), 161–183.

Eisenberg, Avigail. (2009). *Reasons of identity*. Oxford: Oxford University Press.

Eisenstadt, Leora F. (2007). Privileged but equal: A comparison of US and Israeli notions of sex equality in employment law. *Vanderbilt Journal of Transnational Law, 40*(2), 357–416.

Eisgruber, Christopher L., & Sager, Lawrence G.. *Religious freedom and the Constitution*. Cambridge, MA: Harvard University Press.

Eliade, Mircea. (1958). *Patterns in comparative religion*. London: Sheed and Ward.

Ellickson, Robert C. (1994). *Order without law: How neighbors settle disputes*. Cambridge, MA: Harvard University Press.

Elon, Amos. (1971). *The Israelis: Founders and sons*. London: Weidenfeld and Nicolson.

Elon, Menachem. (2005). *The status of women: Law and judgment, tradition and transition, the values of a Jewish and democratic state*. Tel Aviv: Kibutz HaMeuchad. [Heb].

Elster, Jon. (1983). *Sour Grapes: Studies in the subversion of rationality*. Cambridge: Cambridge University Press.

Elster, Jon. (1989). *Solomonic Judgments*. Cambridge: Cambridge University Press.

Epstein, Richard. (1990). Religious liberty in the welfare state. *William and Mary Law Review, 31*(2), art. 11.

Epstein, Richard. (1995). *Simple rules for a complex world.* Cambridge, MA: Harvard University Press.

Ettinger, Yair. (2013). Sharansky sees egalitarian section at Western Wall within two years. *Haaretz.com*, May 7. Retrieved from http://www.haaretz.com/israel-news/sharansky-sees-egalitarian-section-at-western-wall-within-two-years.premium-1.519761, accessed January 31, 2016. [Heb].

Ettinger, Yair. (2016a). The Archeological Council to PM Netanyahu: the Western Wall compromise will create a substantial harm to Robinson's Arch. *Haaretz.com*, April 4, 2016. Retrieved from http://www.haaretz.co.il/news/education/.premium-1.2903978, accessed April 4, 2016. [Heb].

Ettinger, Yair. (2016b). The Government approved: Egalitarian section at Western Wall. *Haaretz.com*, January 31. http://www.haaretz.co.il/news/politi/1.2835301, accessed April 21, 2016. [Heb].

Etinger Yair. (2016c). The Women of the Wall introduce a religious innovation: Birkat Kohanot. *Haaretz.com*, March 23. Retrieved from http://www.haaretz.co.il/news/education/.premium-1.2889829, accessed May 16, 2016. [Heb].

Etinger Yair. (2016d). Women of the Wall hold priestly blessing ceremony at Kotel, Despite AG prohibition. *Haaretz.com*, May 9. Retrieved from http://www.haaretz.com/jewish/news/.premium-1.718650, accessed May 16, 2016.

Etinger, Yair. (2016e). The Rabbi of the Wall distances from Mendelblit's plan. *Haaretz.com*, March 14, 2016. Retrieved from http://www.haaretz.co.il/news/politi/1.2882769 [Heb], accessed May 16, 2016.

Ettinger, Y., & Ravid, B. (2016). PM Netanyaho admits difficulties in implementing the Western Wall compromise. *Haaretz.com*, March 23, 2016. Retrieved from http://www.haaretz.co.il/news/politi/1.2895668, accessed April 21, 2016. [Heb].

Evans, Malcolm D. (2010–11). From cartoons to crucifixes. *Journal of Law and Religion*, *26*(1): 345–370.

Federalist Papers. Library of Congress online. Retrieved from https://www.loc.gov/rr/program/bib/ourdocs/federalist.html, accessed December 20, 2016.

Feige, Michael, &Shilony, Zvi. (2008). *Archeology, religion and nationalism in Israel.* Sde-Boker: Ben-Gurion Research Institute. [Heb].

Feinberg, Joel. (1984). *Harm to others.* Oxford: Oxford University Press.

Feinberg, Joel. (1985). *Offense to others.* Oxford: Oxford University Press.

Feinberg, Joel. (1990). *Harmless wrongdoing.* Oxford: Oxford University Press.

Ferber, Alona. (2014). Women of Wall slip Torah scroll into Western Wall bat mitzvah. *Jewish Daily Forward*, October 24, http://forward.com/articles/207879/women-of-wall-slip-torah-scroll-into-western-wall, accessed April 21, 2016.

Ferrari, Silvio. (2014). Introduction: The legal protection of the sacred places of the Mediterranean. In Ferrari Silvio & Andrea Benzo (Eds.), *Between cultural diversity and common heritage legal and religious perspectives on the sacred places of the Mediterranean* (pp. 1–16). London: Ashgate.

Ferrari, Silvio, & Benzo, Andrea. (Eds.). (2014). *Between cultural diversity and common heritage legal and religious perspectives on the sacred places of the Mediterranean.* London: Ashgate.

Fichte, Johenn G. (2009). *Fichte: Addresses to the German nation* (ed.) G. Moore. Cambridge: Cambridge University Press.

Finke, Roger, & Rodney Stark. (1988). Religious economies and sacred canopies. *American Sociological Review, 53*(1), 41–49.

Finke, Roger, & Rodney Stark. (2000). *Acts of Faith.* Berkeley: University of California Press.

Finke, Roger, & Rodney Stark. (2005). *The churching of America.* New Brunswick, NJ: Rutgers University Press.

Forbes, Donald. (1997). *Ethnic conflict: Commerce, culture, and the contact hypothesis.* New Haven, CT: Yale University Press.

Forst, Rainer. (2013). *Toleration in conflict.* Cambridge: Cambridge University Press.

Fox, Jonathan. (2008). *A world survey of religion and the state.* Cambridge: Cambridge University Press.

Fox, Jonathan. (2013). *An introduction to religion and politics.* New York: Routledge.

Fox, Jonathan. (2016). *The unfree exercise of religion.* Cambridge: Cambridge University Press.

Frazer, Nancy. (1990). Rethinking the public sphere: A contribution to the critique of actually existing democracy. *Social Text, 25,* 56–80.

Freigang, Lisa. (2015). Identity and violence: Sectarian conflict in post-independence Indian literature. In Marlene Bainczyk-Crescentini, Kathleen Ess, Michael Pleyer, & Monika Pleyer (Eds.) *Identities: Interdisciplinary Perspectives* (pp. 25–37). Heidelberg: Heidelberg Univeritat.

Fried, Barbara H. (2001). *The progressive assault on laissez faire.* Cambridge, MA: Harvard University Press.

Friedland, Roger, & Hecht, Richard. (1998). The bodies of nations: A comparative study of religious violence in Jerusalem and Ayodhya. *History of Religions, 38*(2), 101–149.

Friedland Ben Arza, Sara. (2003). Prayer without men's assistance. *Nekoda 267,* 36–93. [Heb].

Friedman, Jerome. (1978). *Michael Servetus: a case study in total heresy.* Geneva: Droz.

Frimer, Aryeh A., & Frimer, Dov I. (1998). Women's prayer services: Theory and practice. *Tradition, 32,* (2), 5–118.

Gal Getz, Poriya. (2011). *Leaving religion behind: A journey into the world of ex-Orthodox Jews.* Tel Aviv: Am-Oved. [Heb].

Galston, Willian A. (2010). Realism in political theory. *European Journal of Political Theory, 9,* no. 4, 385–411.

Gans, Chaim. (2003). *The limits of nationalism.* Cambridge: Cambridge University Press.

Garrick, David. (1998). *Shaped cedars and cedar shaping: A guidebook to identifying, documenting, appreciating and learning from culturally modified trees.* Vancouver: Western Canada Wilderness Committee.

Gaus, Gerald. (2000). *Political concepts and political theories.* Boulder, CO: Westview.

Gauthier, David. (1992). The liberal individual. In Shlomo Avineri & Avner de-Shalit (Eds.), *Communitarianism and individualism* (pp. 151–164). Oxford: Oxford University Press.

Gavison, Ruth. (1992). Feminism and the private-public distinction. *Stanford Law Review, 45*(1), 1–45.

Gavison Ruth. (1994). Religion and state: Separation and privatization. *Law and Governance, 2,* 55–96. [Heb].

Gavison, Ruth. (2003). On the relationships between civil and political rights, and social and economic rights. In Jean-Marc Coicaud, Michael W. Doyle, & Anne-Marie Gardner (Eds.), *The globalization of human rights* (pp. 23–56). Tokyo: UN University Press.

Gavison, Ruth, & Perez, Nahshon. (2008). Days of rest in multicultural societies: public, private, separate? In Peter Cane, Carolyn Evans, & Zoe Robinson (Eds.), *Law and religion in theoretical and historical context* (pp. 186–213). Cambridge: Cambridge University Press.

Gay, Peter. (2000). *Modernism: The lure of heresy.* New York: W. W. Norton.

Geertz, Clifford. (1966). Religion as a cultural system. In Michael Banton (Ed.), *Anthropological approaches to the study of religion* (pp. 1–46). New York: Praeger.

Geertz, Clifford. (1973). *Interpretation of cultures.* New York: Basic Books.

Geertz, Clifford. (2000). Anti anti-relativism. In *Available light: Anthropological reflections on philosophical topics* (pp. 42–67). Princeton, NJ: Princeton University Press.

Gerring, John. (2004). What is a case study and what is it good for? *American Political Science Review, 98*(2), 341–354.

Gey, Steven G. (2005–6). Free will, religious liberty, and a partial defense of the French approach to religious expression in public schools. *Houston Law Review, 42*(1), 1–80.

Ghert-Zand, Renee. (2012). Single ladies want mikveh access. *Forward,* January 18. Retrieved from http://forward.com/sisterhood/149642/single-ladies-want-mikveh-access/, accessed May 5, 2016.

Gill, Anthony. (2008). *The political origins of religious liberty.* Cambridge: Cambridge University Press.

Goldberg, Zalman Nehemiah. (1998). Women's public prayer (a response). *Techumin, 18,* 120–222. [Heb].

Gomm, Roger, Hammersley, Martyn, & Foster, Peter (Eds.). (2009). *Case-study method* London: Sage.

Gordon, Aharon David. (1982). Man and nature. In Eliezer Schweid (Ed.), *The Writings of A. D. Gordon* (pp. 49–174). Jerusalem: Zionist Library. [Heb].

Goren, Dotan. (2007). The struggle between Jews and Arabs over the Western Wall. *Ariel: Journal for Knowledge of the Land of Israel 180,* July, 105–113. [Heb].

Greenawalt, Kent. (2007). Moral and religious convictions as categories for special treatment: The exemption strategy. *William and Mary Law Review, 48*(5), 1605–1642.

Greenawalt, Kent. (1998). Freedom of association and religious association. In Amy Gutmann (Ed.), *Freedom of association* (pp. 109–144). Princeton, NJ: Princeton University Press.

Gregory, Brad. (2012). *The unintended reformation.* Cambridge, MA: Harvard University Press.

Grim, Brian J., & Finke, Roger. (2011). *The price of freedom denied.* Cambridge: Cambridge University Press.

Grossman, Susan. (1993). Women and the Jerusalem Temple. In Susan Grossman & Rivka Haut (Eds.), *Daughters of the king: Women and the synagogue* (pp. 15–37). Philadelphia: Jewish Publication Society.

Grossman, Susan, & Haut, Rivka (Eds.). (1993). *Daughters of the king: Women and the synagogue.* Philadelphia: Jewish Publication Society.

Guinn, David. (2006). *Protecting Jerusalem's holy sites.* Cambridge: Cambridge University Press.

Habermas, Jurgen. (1993). *The structural transformation of the public sphere.* (T. Burger, Trans.). Cambridge, MA: MIT Press.

Habermas, Jürgen. (1995). Citizenship and national identity: Some reflections on the future of Europe. In Ronald Beiner (Ed.), *Theorizing citizenship* (pp. 255–282). Albany: State University of New York Press.

Hamburger, Philip. (2004). *Separation of church and state.* Cambridge, MA: Harvard University Press.

Hardin, Russell. (2004). Subnational groups and globalization. In Keith Dowding, Robert Goodin, & Carole Pateman (Eds.), *Justice and democracy* (pp. 179–194). Cambridge: Cambridge University Press.

Harel, Chaya. (1989). Herzl's attitude to Jerusalem. In Hagit Levski (Ed.), *Jerusalem in Zionist vision and realization* (pp. 75–90). Jerusalem: Zalman Shazar Center for Jewish History. [Heb].

Harel Shalev, Ayelet. (2010). *The challenge of sustaining democracy in deeply divided societies: Citizenship, rights, and ethnic conflicts in India and Israel.* New York: Lexington.

Hart, H. L. A. (1963). *Law, liberty and morality.* Stanford, CA: Stanford University Press.

Hart, H. L. A. (1973). Rawls on liberty and its priority. *University of Chicago Law Review, 40*(3), 534–555.

Hart, H. L. A. (1977). Immorality and treason. In Ronald M. Dworkin (Ed.)., *The philosophy of law* (pp. 83–88). Oxford: Oxford University Press.

Hartman-Halbertal, Tova. (2002). *Appropriately subversive: Modern mothers in traditional religions.* Cambridge, MA: Harvard University Press.

Hassner, Ron. (2009). *War on sacred sites.* Ithaca, NY: Cornell University Press.

Hauerwas, Stanley. (2001). A Christian critique of Christian America. In John Berkman, & Michael Cartwright (Eds.), *The Hauerwas Reader* (pp. 459–480). Durham, NC: Duke University Press.

Hauptman, Judith. (1993). Women's voluntary performance of mitzvoth from which they are exempt. *Proceedings of the World Congress of Jewish Studies* Devision C, 1, pp. 161–168.

Haut, Rivka. (1992). Women's prayer groups and the Orthodox synagogue. In Susan Grossman & Rivka Haut (Eds.), *Daughters of the king, women and the synagogue: A survey of history, Halakha, and contemporary realities* (pp. 135–157). Philadelphia: The Jewish Publication Society.

Haut, Rivka. (2003). Orthodox women's spirituality. In Phyllis Chesler & Rivka Haut (Eds.), *Women of the Wall: Claiming sacred ground at Judaism's holy site* (pp. 263–287) Woodstock: Jewish Lights Publishing.

Hayek, Friedrich A. (1945). The use of knowledge in society. *American Economic Review, 35*(4), 519–530.

Hayek, Friedrich A. (1978). *Law, legislation, and liberty.* New York: Routledge.

Hazut, Rami. (1997). Fight in the Kotel. *Yedioth Aharonoth,* August 12, p. 3. [Heb].

Hellinger, Moshe. (2009). Religious ideology that attempts to ease the conflict between religion and state: An analysis of the teachings of two leading religious-Zionist rabbis in the State of Israel. *Journal of Church and State, 51*(1), 52–77.

Henderson, Errol A. (2005). Not letting evidence get in the way of assumptions: Testing the clash of civilizations thesis with more recent data. *International Politics, 42,* 458–469.

Herzl, Theodor. (1999). Letter written October 31, 1898. In *Die Judensache* [The Jewish cause]. (Vol. 2) *Diaries 1895-1904* (p. 54). Jerusalem: Bialik Institution and the Central Zionist Archives. [Heb].

Hirsche, Samson R. (1962). *The Pentateuch translated and explained.* (Vol. 3) *Leviticus* (pt. II). (Issac Levy, Trans.). London: L. Honig and Sons.

Hirschl, Ran. (1998). Israel's 'Constitutional Revolution': The legal interpretation of entrenched civil liberties in an emerging neo-liberal economic order. *American Journal of Comparative Law, 46*(3), 427–452.

Hobbes, Thomas. (1968). *Leviathan* (Edited and with an introduction by C. B. Macpherson). London: Penguin.

Holmes, Oliver Wendell, Jr. (1992). Lochner vs. New York, Dissent, reprinted in Richard A. Posner (Ed.), *The Essential Holmes* (pp. 305–307). Chicago: University of Chicago Press. (Original article published in 1905).

Holmes, Stephen. (1997). Gag rules, or the politics of omission. In Jon Elster, & Rune Slagstad (Eds.) *Constitutionalism and Democracy* (pp. 19–58). Cambridge: Cambridge University Press.

Horwitz, Morton J. (1992). *The transformation of American law, 1870-1960.* Oxford: Oxford University Press.

Hume, David. (1748). Of the original contract. Constitution Society website. Retrieved from http://www.constitution.org/dh/origcont.htm, accessed April 24, 2016.

Hume, David. (1858). *The history of England*. (Vol. 3). Boston: Phillips Sampson and Company.

Huntington, Samuel. (2011). *The clash of civilizations and the remaking of world order*. New York: Simon and Schuster.

International Commission for the Wailing Wall. (1931). Report of the commission appointed by His Majesty's government in the United Kingdom of Great Britain and Northern Ireland, with the approval of the Council of the League of Nations, to determine the rights and claims of Muslims and Jews in connection with the Western or Wailing wall at Jerusalem, December, 1930. London: H.M.S.O.

Irshai, Ronit. (2013). Dignity, honor, and equality in contemporary Halachic thinking: The case of Torah reading by women in Israeli modern orthodoxy. *Modern Judaism, 33*(3), 332–356.

Issacs, Alick. (2006). Kavod Ha-Tsibbur: A feminist approach. *Nashim, 12*, 261–288.

Isaac, Jeffrey C., Filner, Matthew F., & Bivin, Jason C. (1999). American democracy and the New Christian Right: A critique of apolitical liberalism. In Ian Shapiro & Casiano-Hacker Gordon (Eds.). *Democracy's edges* (pp. 222–264). Cambridge: Cambridge University Press.

Jefferson, Thomas. (1984) Notes on the constitution of Virginia. In Merrill D. Peterson (Ed.), *Thomas Jefferson: Writings* (pp. 123–326). New York: Library of America. (Original work published in 1785).

Jewish Telegraphic Agency. (2013). Women of Wall Founders Reject Leader's Compromise on Prayer at Western Wall. *Forward*. October 14. Retrieved from http://forward.com/articles/185571/women-of-wall-fouders-reject-leaders-compromise-on/#ixzz3RtoQZCPu, accessed April 25, 2016.

Jewish Telegraphic Agency. (2014). Netanyahu to Reform Jews: Western Wall belongs to all. *Times of Israel*, December 16. Retrieved from http://www.timesofisrael.com/netanyahu-to-reform-jews-western-wall-belongs-to-all/, accessed April 25, 2016.

Jobani, Yuval. (2008). Ethical or political religion? On the contradiction between two models of amended religion in Spinoza's "Theological Political Treatise." *Hebraic Political Studies, 3*(4), 396–415.

Jobani, Yuval. (2013). The true teacher: Jewish secularism in the philosophy of A.D. Gordon. In Jan Wolenski, Yaron Senderowicz, & Józef Bremer (Eds.), *Jewish and Polish Philosophy* (pp. 198–216). Krakow: Austeria Publishing House.

Jobani, Yuval. (2016). *The role of contradictions in Spinoza's Philosophy: The God-intoxicated heretic*. New York: Routledge.

Jobani, Yuval. (2016b). The secular university and its critics. *Studies in Philosophy and Education, 35*(4), 333–351.

Jobani, Yuval. (2016c). The lure of heresy: A philosophical typology of Hebrew secularism in the first half of the twentieth-century. *Journal of Jewish Thought and Philosophy, 24*(1), 95–121.

Jobani, Yuval, & Perez, Nahshon. (2014). Women of the Wall: A normative analysis of the place of religion in the public sphere. *Oxford Journal of Law and Religion*, 3(3), 484–505.

Jobani, Yuval, & Perez, Nahshon. (2014a). Toloration and illiberal groups in context: Israel's ultra-orthodox 'society of learners'. *Journal of Political Ideologies*, 19(1), 78–98.

Jones, Peter. (1994). Bearing the consequence of belief. *Journal of Political Philosophy* 2(1), 24–43.

Kaplan-Sommer, Allison. (2013), Don't ask, don't tell: The new Mikveh policy. *Haaretz. com*, May 10, 2013. Retrieved from http://www.haaretz.com/blogs/routine-emergencies/don-t-ask-don-t-tell-the-new-mikveh-policy.premium-1.523291, accessed May 5, 2016.

Kaplan, Benjamin. (2010). *Divided by faith*. Cambridge, MA: Harvard University Press.

Karayanni, Michael M. (2014). The multicultural nature of the religious accommodations for the Palestinian-Arab minority in Israel: A curse or a blessing? In René Provost (Ed.), *Mapping the legal boundaries of belonging: Religion and multiculturalism from Israel to Canada* (pp. 225–251) Oxford: Oxford University Press.

Kashner, Rita. (2014). The bat mitzvah girl who made Kotel history. Forward.com. *The Sisterhood* (blog), October 28. Retrieved from http://blogs.forward.com/sisterhood-blog/208090/the-bat-mitzvah-girl-who-made-kotel-history, accessed April 24, 2016.

Kedar, Benjamin Z. (2001). Convergences of Oriental Christian, Muslim, and Frankish worshippers: The case of Saydanya and the Knights Templar. In Zsolt Hunyadi & József Laszlovszky (Eds.), *The Crusades and the military orders: Expanding the frontiers of Medieval Latin Christianity* (pp. 89–100). Budapest: Central European University.

Kelly, Paul (Ed.). (2002). *Multiculturalism reconsidered*. Cambridge: Polity.

Kempinski, Aharon. (1994). The influence of archaeology on Israeli culture and society. In Gabriel Barkai & Eli Schiller (Eds.), *Landscape of Israel: Azarias Alon Jubilee Volume, Ariel: Journal for Knowledge of the Land of Israel, 100–101* (pp. 179–190). Jerusalem: Ariel, [Heb].

Kershner, Isabel. (2014). With guile and tiny Torah, women hold a bat mitzvah at the Western Wall. *New York Times*, October 24. Retrieved from http://www.nytimes. com/2014/10/25/world/middleeast/women-hold-western-wall-bat-mitzvah-in-jerusalem.html?_r=0, accessed April 24, 2016.

Koppelman, Andrew. (2013). *Defending American Religious Neutrality*. Cambridge, MA: Harvard University Press.

Kremnitzer, Mordechai, Shahar, Goldman and Eran Tamir (Eds.). (2003). *Religious feelings, freedom of expression and the criminal law*. Jerusalem: Israel Democracy Institute [Heb].

Kroyanker, David. (1988). *The struggle over the city structure and its appearance*. Tel Aviv: Zmora-Bitan and the Jerusalem Institute for Israel Studies.

Kukathas, Chandran. (1997). Cultural toleration. In Ian Shapiro & Will Kymlicka (Eds.). *Nomos XXXIX: Ethnicity and Group Rights* (pp. 69–104). New York: New York University Press.

Kumaraswamy, P. R. (2013). The maturation of Indo-Israeli ties. *Middle East Quarterly*, 39–48.

Kurland, Philip, B. (1961). Of church and state and the Supreme Court. *University of Chicago Law Review*, *29*, 1–97.

Kymlicka, Will. (1995). *Multicultural citizenship*. Oxford: Oxford University Press.

Laborde, Cecile. (2008). *Critical republicanism: The Hijab controversy*. Oxford: Oxford University Press.

Laborde, Cecile. (2014). Equal liberty, nonestablishment, and religious freedom. *Legal Theory*, *20*(1), 52–77.

Labrousse, Elisabeth. (1973). Religious toleration. In Phillip P. Weiner (Ed.). *Dictionary of the History of Ideas* (Vol. 4, pp. 112–121). New York: Charles Scribner's Sons.

Lahav, Pnina. (forthcoming). The woes of WoW: The Women of the Wall as a religious social movement and as metaphor. In John Berthrong (Ed.), *Religion, conflict and peace making: Seeking wisdom in interdisciplinary dialogue*.

Lahav, Pnina. (2015). The Women of the Wall: A metaphor for national and religious identity. *Israel Studies Review*, *30*(2), 50–70.

Langlaude, Sylvie. (2013). Lautsi v Italy: Coercion and lack of neutrality in the classroom?, *Annuaire Droit et Religions*, *6*, 601–617.

Langvardt, Kyle. (2014). The lawless rule of the norm in the government religious speech cases. *Washington and Lee Journal of Civil Rights and Social Justice*, *20*, 405–455.

Larson, James G. (1995). *India's agony over religion*. Albany: State University of New York Press.

Lassman, Peter. (2000). The rule of man over man: Politics, power and legitimation. In Stephen Turner (Ed.) *The Cambridge companion to Weber* (pp. 83–98). Cambridge: Cambridge University Press.

Lau, David. (2016). There will be no compromise at the Western Wall. Facebook post by Rabbi David Lau (Chief Rabbi of the State of Israel), June 29, 2016. Retrieved from https://www.facebook.com/rabbidlau/posts/1087460121320569?comment_id=1087463357986912&comment_tracking=%7B%22tn%22%3A%22R%22%7D, accessed, August 18, 2016.

Laycock, Douglas. (1986). "Nonpreferential" aid to religion: A false claim about original intent. *William and Mary Law* Review, *27*, 875–923.

Laycock, Douglas. (1990). Formal, substantive and disaggregated neutrality toward religion. *DePaul University Law Review*, *39*(3), 993–1018.

Layish, Aharon. (2006). Adaptation of a jurists' law to modern times in an alien environment: The case of the Shariʿa in Israel. *Die Welt des Islams*, n.s., *46*(2), 168–225.

Lecce, Steven. (2008). *Against perfectionism: Defending liberal neutrality*. Toronto: University of Toronto Press.

Leibowitz, Yeshayahu. (1979). *Judaism, the Jewish People and the State of Israel*. Tel Aviv: Schocken [Heb].

Leibowitz, Yeshayahu. (1975). *Yahadut, Am Yehudi u-Medinat Yisrael* [Judaism, the Jewish people, and the State of Israel]. Tel Aviv: Schocken. [Heb].

Leibowitz, Yeshayahu. (1982). *Belief, history, and values*. Jerusalem: Hebrew University Student Union Press [Heb].

Leibowitz, Yeshayahu. (1992). *Judaism, human values, and the Jewish state*. E. Goldman (Ed.) and (E. Goldman, Yoram Navon, & Zvi Jacobson, Trans.). Cambridge, MA: Harvard University Press.

Lerner, Hanna. (2009). Entrenching the status-quo: Religion and state in Israel's constitutional proposals. *Constellations 16*(3), 445–461.

Lerner, Natan. (2000). International Norms on Freedom of Religion and belief. *Brigham Young University Law Review, 3*, 905–932.

Levy, Jacob. (2007). Contextualism, constitutionalism and *modus vivendi* approaches. In Anthony S. Laden & David Owen (Eds.), *Multiculturalism and political theory* (pp. 173–197). Cambridge: Cambridge, University Press.

Levy, Jacob. (2010). Multicultural manners. In Michel Seymour (Ed.), *The plural states of recognition* (pp. 61–77). New York: Palgrave.

Levy, Jacob. (2015). *Rationalism, Pluralism, and Freedom*. Oxford: Oxford University Press.

Levy, Leonard. (1994). *The establishment clause: Religion and the First Amendment*. Chapel Hill: University of North Carolina Press.

Lieberson, Stanley. (1991). Small N's and big conclusions: An examination of the reasoning in comparative studies based on a small number of cases. *Social Forces, 70*, 307–320.

Liebman, Charles, & Don-Yihya, Eliezer. (1983). *Civil religion in Israel*. Berkeley: University of California Press.

Lijphart, Arend. (1971). Comparative politics and the comparative method. *American Political Science Review, 65*(3), 682–693.

Limor, Ora. (2007). Sharing sacred space: Holy places in Jerusalem between Christianity, Judaism and Islam. In Iris Shagrir, Ronnie Ellenblum, & Jonathan Riley-Smith (Eds.). *Laudem Hierosolymitani: Studies in crusades and medieval culture in honour of Benjamin Z. Kedar* (pp. 219–231). Aldershot, UK: Ashgate.

Locke, John. 2010. A letter concerning toleration. In *Locke on toleration*, Richard Vernon (Ed.). Cambridge: Cambridge University Press. (Original work published in 1689).

Locke, John. (1980). *Second treatise of government*. C. B. Macpherson (Ed.). (Hackett Classics). Indianopolis, IN: Hackett. (Original work published in 1690).

Loew, Judah b. Bezalel [Maharal]. (1972). Drush al ha-Torah. In *Sifrei Maharal: Be'er ha-Golah*. Jerusalem: no publisher name. [Heb].

Lorberbaum, Menachem. (2002). *Politics and the limits of law: Secularizing the political in medieval Jewish thought*. Stanford, CA: Stanford University Press.

Lorberbaum, Menachem. (2007). Making space for Leviathan: On Hobbes' political theory. *Hebraic Political Studies, 2*(1), 78–100.

Lubitz, Rivka. (1999). Regarding women's prayer (a response). *Techumin*, *17*, 165–167. [Heb].

Lukes, Steven. (1985). *Emile Durkheim, his life and work: A historical and critical study*. Stanford, CA: Stanford University Press.

Macedo, Stephen. (1995). Liberal civic education and religious fundamentalism: The case of God v. John Rawls? *Ethics*, *105*(3), 468–497.

Madison, James. (1785). Memorial and remonstrance against religious assessments. *The Founders' Constitution*. (Vol. 5) Amendment I (Religion), document 43. Retrieved from http://press-pubs.uchicago.edu/founders/documents/amendI_religions43.html, accessed April 24, 2016.

Majid, Abdul. (2015). The Babri Mosque and Hindu extremists movements. *Journal of Political Studies*, *22*(2), 559–577.

Maltz, Judy. (2013). Women of the Wall divided as dissenters refuse to budge from women's section. *Haaretz.com*, October 30. Retrieved from http:// www.haaretz.com/jewish-world/jewish-world-news/.premium-1.555238, accessed April 24, 2016.

Maltz, Judy. (2014). Orthodox feminist group breaks ranks with Women of the Wall: joins other dissenters in opposing move to new mixed prayer section. *Haaretz.com*, February 4. Retrieved from http://www.haaretz.com/news/national/.premium-1.572443, accessed April 24, 2016.

Margalit, Avishai. (2009). *On compromise and rotten compromises*. Princeton, NJ: Princeton University Press.

Margalit, Avishai, & Raz, Joseph. (1990). National self-determination. *Journal of Philosophy*, *87*(9), 439–461.

Margalit, Avishai, & Halbertal, Moshe. (2004). Liberalism and the right to culture. *Social Research*, *71*(3), 529–548.

Margolin, Ron. (2011). *The inner religion: The phenomenology of inner religious life and its manifestation in Jewish source*. Ramat Gan, Israel: Bar-Ilan University Press. [Heb].

Marshall, Paul, & Nina Shea. (2011). *Silenced*. Oxford: Oxford University Press.

Masuzawa, Tomoko. (2003). Our master's voice: F. Max Müller after a hundred years of solitude. *Method and Theory in the Study of Religion*, *15*(4), 305–328.

Mautner, Menachem. (2011). *Law and the culture of Israel*. Oxford: Oxford University Press.

Mazar, Bengamin. (1975). *The mountain of the Lord*. New York: Doubleday.

McConnell, Michael W. (1990). The origins and historical understanding of free exercise of religion. *Harvard Law Review* *103*(7), 1409–1517.

McConnell, Michael W. (1999). Five reasons to reject the claim that religious arguments should be excluded from democratic deliberation. *Utah Law Review 3*, 639–658.

McConnell, Michael W. (2000a). The problem of singling out religion. *DePaul Law Review*, *50*(1), 1–48.

McConnell, Michael W. (2000b). Why is religious liberty the first freedom? *Cardozo Law Review*, *21*(4), 1243–1265.

Megginson, William. (2005). *The financial economics of privatization*. Oxford: Oxford University Press.

Mehta, Deepak. (2015). Naming the deity, naming the city: Rama and Ayodhya. *South Asia Multidisciplinary Academic Journal 12*, 1–16.

Mehta, Deepak. (2015b). The Ayodhya dispute: The absent mosque, state of emergency, the jural deity. *Journal of Material Culture, 20*(4), 397–414.

Meiselman, Moshe. (1978). *Jewish women in Jewish law*. New-York: KTAV Publishing and Yeshiva University Press.

Meskell, Lynn M. (Ed.). (1998). *Archaeology under fire: Nationalism, politics, and heritage in the Eastern Mediterranean and Middle East*. London: Routledge.

Mill, J. S. (1997). On Liberty. In Alan Ryan (Ed.), *Mill, texts and commentaries*. New York: Norton.

Miller, David. (1983). Constraints on freedom. *Ethics, 94*(1): 66–86.

Miller, David. (2004). Social justice in multicultural societies. In Philippe Van Parijs (Ed.), *Cultural diversity versus economic solidarity* (pp. 13–33). Bruxelles: De Boeck.

Miller, David. (2016). Majorities and minarets: Religious freedom and public space. *British Journal of Political Science, 46*(2), 437–456.

Mittleman, Alan, Licht, Robert, & Sarna, Jonathan D. (2002). (Eds.) *Jews and the American public square: Debating religion and republic*. Lanham, MD: Rowman and Littlefield.

Modood, Tariq. (1998). Anti-essentialism, multiculturalism, and the "recognition" of religious groups. *Journal of Political Philosophy, 6*(4), 378–399.

Modood, Tariq. (2013). *Multiculturalism*. London: Polity.

Moeckli, Daniel. (2011). Of minarets and foreign criminals: Swiss direct democracy and human rights. *Human Rights Law Review, 11*(4), 774–794.

Mommsen, Wolfgang J. (1989). Max Weber on bureaucracy and bureaucratization: threat to liberty and instrument of creative action. In Wolfgang Mommsen (Ed.), *The political and social theory of Max Weber: Collected essays* (pp. 109–120). Chicago: Chicago University Press.

Montefiore, Allen. (1975). *Neutrality and impartiality*. Cambridge: Cambridge University Press.

Montefiore, Simon S. (2012). *Jerusalem: The biography*. London: Phoenix.

Montesquieu, Charles Louise de Secondat. (1989). *The spirit of the laws*. Cohler, Anne M., Miller Basia C., & Stone, Harold S. (Eds.). Cambridge: Cambridge University Press.

Moore, Margaret. (2015). *A political theory of territory*. Oxford: Oxford University Press.

Mulhall, Stephen, & Swift, Adam. (1996). *Liberals and communitarians*. Oxford: Blackwell.

Müller, Max. (2003). *The essential Max Müller: On language, mythology, and religion*. Jon R. Stone (Ed.). New York: Palgrave MacMillan.

Muñiz-Fraticelli, Víctor M. (2014). The distinctiveness of religious liberty. In Rene Provost (Ed.), *Mapping the legal boundaries of belonging: Religion and multiculturalism from Israel to Canada* (pp. 99–118). Oxford: Oxford University Press.

Murray, John Courtney. (1954). Civil unity and religious integrity (pp. 45–78). Woodstock Theological Library at Georgetown University website. Retrieved fromhttp://www.library.georgetown.edu/woodstock/murray/whtt_c2_1954d, accessed April 24, 2016.

Nachshoni, Kobi. (2015). Kotel rabbi apologizes to woman denied entry for wearing kippah. *YNET*, July 7. Retreived from http://www.ynetnews.com/articles/ 0,7340,L-4677153,00.html, accessed April 25, 2016.

Nadler, Steven. (2001). *Spinoza's heresy: Immortality and the Jewish mind.* Oxford: Oxford University Press.

NDTV. (2010). Ayodhya verdict: Allahabad High Court says divide land in 3 ways, October 1. Retrieved from http://www.ndtv.com/india-news/ayodhya-verdict-allahabad-high-court-says-divide-land-in-3-ways-433808, accessed April 25, 2016.

Neuberger, Benyamin. (1999). Religion and state in Europe and Israel. *Israel Affairs, 6*(2), 65–84.

Nickel, James. (2005). Who needs freedom of religion. *University of Colorado Law Review, 76*, 941–964.

Nietzsche, Friedrich. (1994). *The anti-Christ, ecce homo, twilight of the idols and other writings.* (J. Norman, Trans.). Cambridge: Cambridge University Press.

Nietzsche, Friedrich. (1997). *Daybreak: Thoughts on the prejudices of morality.* (R. J. Hollingdale, Trans.). Cambridge: Cambridge University Press.

Nitzan-Shiftan, Alona. (2011). Stones with a human heart: On monuments, modernism and preservation at the Western Wall. *Theory and Critic, 38–39*, 65–100. [Heb].

Noam, Vered. (2013). None may object. *Makor Rishon*, July 26. [Heb].

Noorani, Abdul G. (1993). Legal aspects to the issue. In Sarvepalli Gopal (Ed.), *Anatomy of a confrontation: Ayodhya and the rise of communal politics in India* (pp. 58–98). London: Zed Books.

Noorani, Abdul G. (Ed.). (2003a). *The Babri Masjid question 1528-2003.* (Vol. 1). New Delhi: Tolika.

Noorani, Abdul G. (2003b). *The Babri Masjid Question 1528-2003.* (Vol. 2). New Delhi: Tolika.

Noorani, Abdul G. (2014). *Destruction of the Babri Masjid: A National Dishonour.* New Delhi: Tolika.

North, Douglass. (1990). *Institutions, institutional change and economic performance.* Cambridge: Cambridge University Press.

Nozick, Robert. (1974). *Anarchy state and utopia.* New York: Basic Books.

Nussbaum, Martha. (2000). *Women and human development.* Cambridge: Cambridge University Press.

Nussbaum, Martha. (2008). *Liberty of conscience.* New York: Basic Books.

Okin, Susan. (2002). "Mistresses of their own destiny": Group rights, gender, and realistic rights of exit. *Ethics, 112*(2), 205–230.

Olds, Kelly. (1994). Privatizing the church: Disestablishment in Connecticut and Massachusetts. *Journal of Political Economy*, *102*(2), 277–297.

Oren, B. Michael. (2015). *Ally: My journey across the American-Israeli divide.* New York: Random House.

Orwin, Clifford. (2000), Charles Taylor's pedagogy of recognition. In R. Beiner & W. Norman (Eds.), *Canadian political philosophy* (pp. 232–249). Ontario: Oxford Uuniversity Press.

Ostrom, Elinor. (1990). *Governing the commons.* Cambridge: Cambridge University Press.

Ostrom, Elinor. (2005). *Understanding institutional diversity.* Princeton, NJ: Princeton University Press.

Otto, Rudolf. (1958). *The idea of the holy.* (John W. Harvey, Trans., 2nd rev. ed). Oxford: Oxford University Press. (Original work published in 1917).

Panikkar, Kavalam N. (1993). A historical overview. In Sarvepalli Gopal (Ed.), *Anatomy of a confrontation: Ayodhya and the rise of communal politics in India* (pp. 22–37). London: Zed Books.

Papadopoulou, Lina Triantafyllia. (2014). Law and religion in Greece. *Brill's Encyclopedia of Law and Religion online.* Retrieved from http://www.brill.com/products/online-resources/encyclopedia-law-and-religion-online, accessed April 24, 2016.

Parekh, Bhikhu. (1990). The Rushdie affair: Research agenda for political philosophy. *Political* Studies, *38*(4), 695–709.

Parekh, Bhikhu. (2000). *Rethinking multiculturalism: Cultural diversity and political theory.* New York: Palgrave.

Parfit, Derek. (1979). Is common-sense morality self defeating? *Journal of Philosophy*, *76*(10), 533–545.

Patnaik, Arun K., & Mudiam, Prithvi Ram. (2014). Indian secularism, dialogue and the Ayodhya dispute. *Religion, State and Society*, *42*(4), 374–388.

Patten, Alan. (2014). *Equal recognition: The moral foundations of minority rights.* Princeton, NJ: Princeton University Press.

Peres, Yochanan, & Yaar, Ephraim. (1998). *Between agreement and discord.* Jerusalem: Israel Democracy Institute. [Heb].

Perez, Nahshon. (2002). Should multiculturalists oppress the oppressed? On religion, culture and the individual and cultural rights of un-liberal communities. *Critical Review of International Social and Political Philosophy*, *5*(3), 51–79.

Perez, Nahshon. (2009). Cultural requests and cost internalization: A left liberal proposal. *Social Theory and Practice*, *35*(2), 201–228.

Perez, Nahshon. (2012). *Freedom from past injustices.* Edinburgh: Edinburgh University Press.

Perez, Nahshon. (2013). The privatization of Jewishness in Israel (or: on economic post-Zionism). *Israel Affairs* *19*(2), 273–289.

Perez, Nahshon. (2014). The limits of liberal toleration: The case of the Ultra-Orthodox in Israel. *Journal of Church and State*, *56*(2), 223–247.

Perez, Nahshon. (2015). Lautsi v. Italy: Questioning the majoritarian premise. *Politics and Religion*, *8*(3), 565–587.

Perez, Oren. (2015). Fuzzy law: A theory of quasi-legal systems. *Canadian Journal of Law and Jurisprudence*, *28*(2), 343–370.

Peters, Francis E. (1985). *Jerusalem: The holy city in the eyes of chroniclers, visitors, pilgrims, and prophets from the days of Abraham to the beginnings of modern times*. Princeton, NJ: Princeton University Press.

Petkoff, Peter. (2014). The legal protection of sacred places. In Silvio Ferrari & Andrea Benzo (Eds.), *Between cultural diversity and common heritage: legal and religious perspectives on the sacred places of the Mediterranean* (pp. 57–74). London, Ashgate.

Phillips, Anne. (2004). Defending equality of outcome. *Journal of Political Philosophy* *12*(1), 1–19.

Pierson Paul, & Skocpol Theda. (2002). Historical Institutionalism in Contemporary Political Science. In Ira Katznelson & Helen V. Milner (Eds.), *Political Science: State of the Discipline* (pp. 693–721). New York: W. W. Norton.

Pileggi, Tamar. (2015). Women barred from the Western Wall. *Times of Israel*, July 6. Retrieved from http://www.timesofisrael.com/woman-barred-from-western-wall-for-wearing-skullcap, accessed April 25, 2016.

Pin, Andrea. (2014). (European) stars or (American) stripes: Are the European Court of Human Rights' neutrality and the Supreme Court's wall of separation one and the same? *St. John's Law Review*, *85*(2), 627–664.

Pinto, Meital. (2010). What are offences to feelings really about? *Oxford Journal of Legal Studies*, *4*, 695–723.

Pinto, Meital. (2016). The absence of the right to culture of minorities within minorities in Israel: A tale of a cultural dissent case. *Laws*, *4*(3), 579–601.

Plato. (1968). *The Republic*. (A. Bloom, Tran.). New York: Basic Books.

Pokharel, Krishna, & Beckett, Paul. (2012). *Ayodhya: The battle for India's soul*. A *Wall Street Journal* special report. Retrieved from http://blogs.wsj.com/indiarealtime/2012/12/10/ayodhya-the-battle-for-indias-soul-the-complete-story, accessed April 24, 2016.

Ponterotto, Joseph G. (2006). Brief note on the origins, evolution, and meaning of the qualitative research concept "thick description." *Qualitative Report*, *11*(3), 538–549.

Porat-Rouash, Hadas. (2008). The respectful minyan: Kevod Ha-Tzibur versus Kevod Ha-Briyot. *Deot*, *38*, 25–29. [Heb].

Posner, Richard. (2011). *Economic analysis of law*. (8th ed.) New York: Wolters Kluwer.

Preub, Ulrich K. (2012). Associative rights. In Michel Rosenfeld & András Sajó (Eds.), *Oxford handbook of comparative constitutional law* (pp. 949–966). Oxford: Oxford University Press.

Pringle, Helen. (2011). Regulating offence to the godly. *University of New South Wales Law Journal*, *34*(1): 316–332.

Ray, S. A. (1988), Property rights and the free exercise clause. *Hastings Constitutional Law Quarterly*, *16*, 483–511.

Puterkovsky, Malka. (2014). *Walking on her path: Life challenges from a Halachic and moral perspective*. Tel Aviv: Yediot Aharonot. [Heb].

Rabinovitch, Shmuel. (2016). Letter to the leaders of the ultra orthodox parties in the *knesset* entitled "Legislation Aiming to Protect the Status Quo at the Western Wall." March 14, on file with the authors.

Raday, Francis. (1995). Religion, multiculturalism and equality: The Israeli case. *Israel Yearbook on Human Rights, 25*, 193–241.

Raday, Francis. (2007). Claiming equal religious personhood: Women of the Wall's constitutional saga case. In Winfried Brugger & Michael Karayanni (Eds.), *Religion in the public sphere: A comparative analysis of German, Israeli, American and international law* (pp. 255–298). Berlin: Springer.

Rajamony, Christu. (2007). Sacred sites and international law: A case study of the Ayodhya dispute (Doctoral dissertation). Oxford: Oxford Brookes University.

Rakowski, Eric. (1991). *Equal justice*. Oxford: Oxford University Press.

Ratnagar, Shereen. (2004). Archaeology at the heart of a political confrontation: The case of Ayodhya. *Current Anthropology, 45*(2), 239–259.

Ravitzky, Aviezer. (1998). *Religion and state in Jewish thought*. Jerusalem: Israel Democracy Institute [Heb].

Ravitzky, Aviezer. (2002). *Religion and state in Jewish philosophy*. Jerusalem: Israel Democracy Institute.

Rawls, John. (1999). *A theory of justice*. (Rev. ed.). Cambridge, MA: Harvard University Press. (Original work published in 1971).

Rawls, John. (1982). The basic liberties and their priority. In Sterling M. McMurrin (Ed.) *The Tanner lectures on human values*, vol. 3 (pp. 3–87). Salt Lake City: University of Utah Press

Rawls, John. (1993). *Political liberalism*. New York: Columbia University Press.

Rawls, John. (2001a). *Justice as fairness: A restatement*. Cambridge, MA: Harvard University Press.

Rawls, John. (2001b). The idea of public reason revisited. In Samuel R. Freeman (Ed.), *Collected papers* (pp. 573–615). Cambridge: Harvard University Press.

Raz, Joseph. (1986). *The morality of freedom*. Oxford: Clarendon Press.

Reich, Ronny, & Shukron, Eli. (2011). Excavations in Jerusalem beneath the paved street and in the sewage channel next to Robinson's Arch. *Qadmoniot: A Journal for the Antiquities of Eretz-Israel and Bible Lands, 142*, 66–73. [Heb].

Reiter, Yitzhak. (2010). Contest or cohabitation in shared holy places? The Cave of the Patriarchs and Samuel's Tomb. In Marshall Berger, Yitzhak Reiter, & Leonard Hammer (Eds.), *Holy places in the Israeli-Palestinian Conflict* (pp. 158–177). London: Routledge.

Reiter, Yitzhak. (2016). Feminists in the temple of orthodoxy: The struggle of the Women of the Wall to change the status quo. *Shofar: An Interdisciplinary Journal of Jewish Studies, 34*(2), 79–107.

Richardson, H. S. (2002). *Democratic Autonomy: Public Reasoning about the Ends of Policy*. Oxford: Oxford University Press.

Ripple, Kenneth F. (1980). The entanglement test of the religion clauses: A ten-year assessment. *UCLA Law Review*, *27*, 1195–1239.

Riskin, Shlomo. (2008). Women's Aliyah to the Torah. *Techumin*, *28*, 258–270. [Heb].

Rivlin, P. (2010). *The Israeli Economy from the foundation of the state through the 21st century*. Cambridge: Cambridge University Press.

Robbins, Lionel. (1935). *An essay on the nature and significance of economic science*. London: Macmillan.

Robert, Jacques. (2003). Religious liberty and French secularism. *Brigham Young University Law Review*, *2*, 637–660.

Robinstein, Amnon, & Yakobson, Alexander. (2008). *Israel and the family of nations*. New York: Routledge.

Rogowski, Ronald. (1995). The role of theory and anomaly in social-scientific inference. *American Political Science Review*, *89*(2), 467–470.

Rosenak, Avinoam. (2008). Kevod Ha-Tzibur as a protective concept: A look at the Pesika of Rav yosef Mashash. *Akdamot*, *20*, 55–70.

Rosenak, Avinoam. (2014). *Reform Judaism: Thought, culture and sociology*. Jerusalem and Tel-Aviv: Van Leer Jerusalem Institute and Hakibbutz Hameuchad.

Rosen-Zvi, Ishay. (2012). *The Mishnaic Sotah ritual: Temple, gender and Midrash*. Leiden: Brill.

Ross, Lee Michael. (2005). *First Nations sacred sites in Canada's courts*. Vancouver: UBC Press.

Ross, Tamar. (2004). *Expanding the palace of Torah: Orthodoxy and feminism*. Waltham, MA: Brandeis University Press.

Rothbard, Murray N. (2003) *The ethics of liberty*. New York: New York University Press.

Rothstein, Gidon. (2005). Women's Aliyyot in contemporary synagogues. *Tradition*, *39*(2), 36–58.

Rousseau, Jean Jacques. (1997). *Rousseau: The social contract and other later political writings*. (V. Gourevitch, Trans. and Ed.). Cambridge: Cambridge University Press.

Ruderman, Richard S. (1997). Aristotle and the recovery of political judgment. *American Political Science Review*, *91*(2), 409–420.

Rumpf, Christian. (1995). Holy places. In Rudolf Bernhardt (Ed.), *Encyclopedia of Public International Law*, *2*, 863–866. Amsterdam: Elsevier.

Ryle, Gilbert. (1971). *Collected papers*. (Vol. 2). *Collected essays, 1929-1968*. London: Hutchinson.

Rynhold, Jonathan. (2015). *The Arab-Israeli conflict in American Political Culture*. Cambridge: Cambridge University Press.

Safrai, Shmuel, & Chana. (1997). All are invited to read. *Tarbiz 66*(3), 395–401. [Heb].

Sandel, Michael J. (1989). Religious liberty: Freedom of conscience or freedom of choice, *Utah Law Review* (3), 597–615.

Sapir, Gideon, & Statman, Daniel. (2014). *Religion and state in Israel*. Tel Aviv: Yediot Aharonot. [Heb].

Sapir, Gideon, & Statman, Daniel. (2015). The protection of holy places. (Unpublished manuscript, on file with the authors).

Saposnik, Arieh. (2009). Zionist sacredness in the making of the "New Jew." *Yisra'el: A Journal for the Study of Zionism and the State of Israel, 16*, 165–194. [Heb].

Saposnik, Arieh. (2015). Wailing walls and iron walls: The Western Wall as sacred symbol in Zionist national iconography. *American Historical Review 120*, no. 5, 1653–1681.

Sassoon, Isaac. (2011). *The Status of women in Jewish tradition*. Cambridge: Cambridge University Press.

Scarboro, Allen, Campbell, Nancy, & Stave, Shirley A. (1994). *Living witchcraft: A contemporary American coven*. Westport, CT: Praeger.

Scheffler, Samuel. (2007). Immigration and the significance of culture. *Philosophy and Public Affairs, 35*(2), 93–125.

Schelling, Thomas C. (1984). *Choice and consequence*. Cambridge, MA: Harvard University Press.

Schuck, Peter. (2003). *Diversity in America*. Cambridge, MA: Harvard University Press.

Schumpeter, Joseph A. (2003). *Capitalism, socialism and democracy*. London: Routledge. (Original work published in 1943).

Scott, James C. (1999). *Seeing like a state: How certain schemes to improve the human condition have failed*. New Haven, CT: Yale University Press.

Seawright, Jason, & Gerring, John. (2008). Case selection techniques in case study research. *Political Research Quarterly, 61*(2), 294–308.

Sen, Amartya. (1992). *Inequality re-examined*. Oxford: Oxford University Press.

Sen, Amartya. (2007). *Identity and violence: The illusion of destiny*. New York: Norton.

Sen, Amartya. (2009). *The idea of justice*. Cambridge, MA: Harvard University Press.

Seneca. (1986). *Trojan women*. (F. Ahl, Trans.) Ithaca, NY: Cornell University Press.

Shakdiel, Leah. (2002). Women of the Wall: Radical feminism as an opportunity for a New Discourse. *Journal of Israeli History, 21*(1–2), 126–163.

Shapiro, Mendel. (2001). Qeriat Ha-Torah by women: A Halakhic analysis, *Edah Journal, 1*(2), 1–52.

Shavit, Yaacov. (1997). Archaeology, political culture, and culture in Israel. In Neil Asher Silberman & David B. Small (Eds.), *The archaeology of Israel: constructing the past, interpreting the present* (pp. 48–61). Sheffield: Sheffield Academic Press.

Shilo, Margalit. (1989). From Jaffa to Jerusalem: the attitude of the Zionist Organization to Jerusalem during the Second Aliyah. In Hagit Levski (Ed.), *Jerusalem in Zionist vision and realization* (pp. 91–106). Jerusalem: Zalman Shazar Center for Jewish History. [Heb].

Shilo, Margalit. (2005). *Princess or prisoner? Jewish women in Jerusalem, 1840–1914*. Waltham, MA: Brandeis University Press.

Shilo, Margalit. (2006). A religious orthodox women's revolution: The case of Kolech (1998–2005). *Israel Studies Forum, 21*(1): 81–95.

Shilo, Margalit. (2007). Women by the Wall. *Ariel: Journal for Knowledge of the Land of Israel*, *180*, 55–59. [Heb].

Shilo, Shmuel. (1999). Women's communal prayer in the Kotel Square. *Techumin*, *17*, 160–164. [Heb].

Shils, Edward. (1981). *Tradition*. Chicago: University of Chicago Press.

Shklar, Judith. (1984). *Ordinary vices*. Cambridge, MA: Harvard University Press.

Shklar, Judith. (1998). The liberalism of fear. In Stanley Hoffmann (Ed.), *Political thought and political thinkers* (pp. 4–20). Chicago: University of Chicago Press.

Shochetmen, Eliav. (1997). Women's Minyamim at the Kotel. *Techumin*, *15*, 161–184. [Heb].

Shochetman, Eliav. (1999). More regarding the question of women's Minyanim (a response to a response). *Techumin*, *17*, 168–174. [Heb].

Shochetman, Eliav. (2005). Women's Aliyah to the Torah. *Sinai*, *135–136*, 271–349. [Heb].

Shragai, Nadav. (2013). Whose wall is it anyway? *Israel Hayom*, April 19. Retrieved from http://www.israelhayom.com/site/newsletter_article.php?id=8729, accessed January 31, 2016.

Shweder, Richard A. (2000). What about female genital mutilation? And why understanding culture matters in the first place. *Daedalus*, *129*(4), 209–232.

Shweder, Richard A. (2009). Shouting at the Hebrews: Imperial liberalism v. liberal pluralism and the practice of male circumcision. *Law, Culture and the Humanities*, *5*(2), 247–265.

Shweder, Richard A. (2010). Geertz's challenge: Is it possible to be a robust cultural pluralist and a dedicated political liberal at the same time? In Austin Sarat (Ed.), *Law without nations* (pp. 185–231). Stanford, CA: Stanford University Press.

Swedberg, Richard (2005). *The Max Weber dictionary: key words and central concepts*. Stanford, CA: Stanford University Press.

Silberman, Neil Asher. (1989). *Between past and present: Archaeology, ideology and nationalism in the modern Middle East*. New York: Holt.

Singh, R. S. V. (2015). Muslim population growth. *The Hindu*, August 25, updated August 27. Retrieved from http://www.thehindu.com/news/national/census-2011-data-on-population-by-religious-communities/article7579161.ece, accessed April 25, 2016.

Singh, Swaran P. (1998). Caring for Sikh patients wearing a *kirpan* (traditional small sword): Cultural sensitivity and safety issues. *Psychiatric Bulletin*, *28*(3), 93–95.

Sinha, Bhadra. (2015). Ayodhya case files will need decade to read: Supreme Court. *Hindustan Times*. Updated August 11. Retrieved from http://www.hindustantimes.com/india/ayodhya-case-files-will-need-decade-to-read-supreme-court/story-WyrhrWlgkYJYA5kkfLP4WL.html, accessed April 25, 2016.

Sisk, Gregory. (1998). Stating the obvious: Protecting religion for religion's sake. *Drake Law Review*, *47*(1), 45–166.

Skinner, Quentin. (1969). Meaning and understanding in the history of ideas. *History and Theory*, *8*(1), 3–53.

Skinner, Quentin. (1978). *The foundations of modern political thought*. (Vol. 2) *The age of reformation*. Cambridge, MA: Cambridge University Press.

Skinner, Question. (2009). A genealogy of the modern state. (British Academy Lecture). *Proceedings of the British Academy*, *162*, 325–370.

Smart, Ninian. (1996). *Dimensions of the sacred: An anatomy of the world's beliefs*. Berkeley: University of California Press.

Smith, Adam. (1979). *An inquiry into the nature and causes of the wealth of nations*. R. H. Campbell & A. S. Skinner (Eds,). Oxford: Clarendon Press.

Smith, Steven B. (1997). *Spinoza, liberalism, and the question of Jewish identity*. New Haven, CT: Yale University Press.

Sokol, Sami, & Ilan, Shachar. (1997). Ultra-Orthodox attacked Conservatives, Palestinians and police-officers in Jerusalem. *Haaretz*, June 12. [Heb].

Sperber, Daniel. (2002). Congregational dignity and human dignity: Women and public Torah reading. *Edah Journal 3*(2), 1–13.

Sperber, Daniel. (2007). *The path of Halacha: Women reading the Torah; a case of Pesika policy*. Jerusalem: Rubin Mass.

Spinner Halev, Jeff. (2000). *Surviving diversity*. Baltimore: Johns Hopkins University Press.

Spinner-Halev, Jeff. (2001). Feminism, multiculturalism, oppression, and the state. *Ethics*, *112*(1): 84–113.

Spinner Halev, Jeff, & Eisenberg, Avigail (Eds.). (2005). *Minorities within minorities*. Cambridge: Cambridge University Press.

Spinoza, Benedict de. (2007). *Theological-political treatise*. (Michael Silverthorne & Jonathan Israel, Trans.). Cambridge: Cambridge University Press.

Srikantan, Geetanjali. (2012). The difficulties of religious pluralism in India. Asia Research Institute, National University of Singapore, research paper, no. 187.

Staël, Germaine de. (2008). *Considerations on the principal events of the French Revolution*. Aurelian Craiutu (Ed.). Indianapolis, IN: Liberty Fund. (Original work published in 1818).

Starr, Paul. (1989). The meaning of privatization. *Yale Law and Policy Review*, *6*, 6–41.

Statman, Daniel. (2000). Hurting religious feelings. *Democratic Culture*, *3*, 199–214.

Stepan, Alfred. (1978). *The State and society: Peru in comparative perspective*. Princeton NJ: Princeton University Press.

Stepan, Alferd. (2001). *Arguing comparative politics*. Oxford: Oxford University Press.

Stepan, Alfred. (2011). Multiple secularisms of modern democratic and non-democratic regimes. In Craig Calhoun, Mark Juergensmeyer, & Jonathan VanAntwerpen (Eds.), *Rethinking secularism* (pp. 114–144). New York: Oxford University Press.

Stigler, George, J. (2008). Monopoly. *The Concise Encyclopedia of Economics*. David R. Henderson (Ed.). Liberty Fund. (Library of Economics and Liberty). http://www.econlib.org/library/Enc/Monopoly.html, accessed September 16, 2015.

Stone, Suzanne Last. (2008). Religion and state: Models of separation from within Jewish law. *ICON*, *6*(3–4), 631–661.

Storper-Perez, Danielle, & Goldberg, Harvey E. (1994). The Kotel: Toward an ethnographic portrait. *Religion, 24*(4), 309–332.

Strauss, Leo. (1999). *Natural rights and history.* Chicago: Chicago University Press.

Sunstein, Cass. (2014). *Simpler: The future of government.* New York: Simon and Schuster.

Sunstein, Cass, & Ullmann-Margalit, Edna. (1999). Second Order Decisions. (University of Chicago Public Law and Legal Theory Working Paper, no. 1).

Susser, Bernard, & Cohen, Asher. (2000). *Israel and the politics of Jewish identity: The secular-religious impasse.* Baltimore: Johns Hopkins University Press.

Taylor, Charles. (1992). The politics of recognition. In Amy Gutmann (Ed.), *Multiculturalism and the politics of recognition* (pp. 25–73). Princeton, NJ: Princeton University Press.

Taylor, Charles. (1998). Modes of secularism. In Rajeev Bhargave (Ed.), *Secularism and its critics* (pp. 31–54). Oxford: Oxford University Press.

Taylor, Charles. (2001). *Sources of the self: The making of the modern identity.* Cambridge, MA: Harvard University Press.

Taylor, Charles. (2007). *A secular age.* Cambridge, MA: Harvard University Press.

Temperman, Jeroen (Ed.). (2012). *The Lautsi papers: Multidisciplinary reflections on religious symbols in the public school classroom.* Leiden: Brill.

Teson, Ferdinand. (2015). The mystery of territory. *Social Philosophy and Policy, 32*(1): 25–50.

Thaler, Richard, & Sunstein, Cass. (2009). *Nudge.* London: Penguin.

Thompson, Dennis. (1984). Political theory and political judgment. *PS 17*(2), 193–197.

Tilly, Charles. (1985). War making and state making as organized crime. In Peter B. Evans, Dietrich Rueschemeyer, & Theda Skocpol (Eds.), *Bringing the state back in* (pp. 169–191). Cambridge: Cambridge University Press.

Tilly, Charles. (2007). *Democracy.* Cambridge: Cambridge University Press.

Tocqueville, Alexis de. (2003). *Democracy in America.* (G. E. Bevan, Trans). New York: Penguin. (Original work published in 1840).

Triwaks, Isaac Abraham (Ed.). (1931). *The sentence of the Wall: The account of the International Committee for the Western Wall.* Tel Aviv: Tel Aviv. [Heb].

Troen, Ilan. (2003). *Imagining Zion: Dreams, Designs and Realities in a Century of Jewish Settlement.* New Haven, CT: Yale University Press.

Tully, James. (1995). *Strange Multiplicity: Constitutionalism in an Age of Diversity.* Cambridge: Cambridge University Press.

Twersky, Mayer. (1998). Halakhic values and Halakhic decisions: Rav Soloveitchik's pesak regarding women's prayer groups. *Tradition 32*(3), 5–18.

Van Alstyne, William. (1984). Trends in the Supreme Court: Mr. Jefferson's crumbling wall; a comment on Lynch vs. Donnelly. *Duke Law Journal 33*(4), 770–787.

Van der Veer, Peter. (1992). Ayodhya and Somnath: Eternal Shrines, Contested Histories. *Social Research 59*(1): 85–109.

Venkatesan, J. (2015). Supreme Court stays Allahabad High Court verdict on Ayodhya. *The Hindu,* March 31. Retrieved from http://www.thehindu.com/news/national/

supreme-court-stays-allahabad-high-court-verdict-on-ayodhya/article2003448.
ece, accessed April 25, 2016.

Vermeule, Adrian. (2007). *Mechanisms of democracy*. Oxford: Oxford University Press.

Villaroman, Noel. (2015). *Treading on sacred grounds*. Boston: Brill.

Voltaire. (1733). *Letters on the English*. (Internet modern history sourcebook). Fordham University website. Retrieved from https://legacy.fordham.edu/halsall/mod/1778voltaire-lettres.asp, accessed December 21, 2016.

Waldron, Jeremy. (1991). Locke: Toleration and the rationality of persecution. In John Horton & Susan Mendus (Eds.), *John Locke: A letter concerning toleration in focus* (pp. 98–124). London: Routledge.

Waldron, Jeremy. (1992). Superseding historic injustice. *Ethics, 103*(1), 4–28.

Waldron, Jeremy. (1995). Minority cultures and the cosmopolitan alternative. In Will Kymlicka (Ed.), *The rights of minority cultures* (pp. 93–112). Oxford: Oxford University Press.

Waldron, Jeremy. (2006). The core of the case against judicial review. *Yale Law Journal, 115*, 1346–1406.

Waldron, Jeremy. (2012). *The harm in hate speech*. Cambridge, MA: Harvard University Press.

Walzer, Michael. (1981). Philosophy and democracy. *Political Theory, 9*(3), 379–399.

Walzer, Michael. (1983). *Spheres of justice*. New York: Basic Books.

Walzer, Michael. (1984). Liberalism and the art of separation. *Political Theory, 12*(3), 315–330.

Walzer, Michael. (1985). *Exodus and revolution*. New York: Basic Books.

Walzer, Michael. (1994). *Thick and thin*. Notre Dame, IN: University of Notre Dame Press.

Walzer, Michael. (1997). *On toleration*. New Haven, CT: Yale University Press.

Walzer, Michael. (2012). *In God's shadow: Politics in the Hebrew Bible*. New Haven, CT: Yale University Press.

Walzer, Michael. (2015). *The paradox of liberation*. New Haven, CT: Yale University Press.

Walzer, Michael, Menachem Lorberbaum, Ari Ackerman, & Noam J. Zohar (Eds.). (2003). *The Jewish Political Tradition*. (Vol. 2) *Membership*. New Haven, CT: Yale University Press.

Watt, John A. (1988). Spiritual and temporal powers. In Jean H. Burns (Ed.), *The Cambridge history of medieval political thought* (pp. 367–423). Cambridge: Cambridge University Press.

Weber, Max. (1946). Politics as a vocation. In Hans H. Gerth & Charles R. Mills (Eds. and Trans.), *From Max Weber* (pp. 77–128). New York: Oxford University Press.

Weber, Max. (1949). Objectivity in social science and social policy. In Edward A. Shils & Henry A. Finch (Eds. and Trans.), *The methodology of the social sciences*, Glencoe, IL: Free Press.

Weber, Max. (1978). *Economy and Society: An outline of interpretive sociology*. Berkeley: University of California Press.

Weber, Max. (2011). The Meaning of ethical neutrality in sociology and economics. In Edward A. Shils (Ed.), *Methodology of social sciences*. (New ed.). New Brunswick, NJ: Transaction Publishers. This is a reprint of the 1949 edition published by the Free Press, Glencoe, IL. Weber's essay originally published in 1917.

Weiler, Joseph. (2010). Lautsi: Crucifix in the classroom redux. *European Journal of International Law, 21*(1), 1–6.

Weiler, Joseph. (2011). State and nation: Church, mosque and synagogue; on religious freedom and religious symbols in public places. In Mary Ann Glandon & Hans F. Zacher (Eds.), *Universal rights in a world of diversity: The case of religious freedom* (pp. 578–588). Vatican City: The Pontifical Academy of Social Sciences.

Weinrib, Ernest J. (2012). *Corrective justice*. Oxford: Oxford University Press.

Weinstein, James. (1999). *Hate speech, pornography, and radical attacks on free speech doctrine*. Boulder, CO: Westview.

Weinstock, Daniel. (2005). Beyond exit rights: Reframing the debate. In Jeff Spinner-Halev & Avigail Eisenberg (Eds.), *Minorities within minorities* (pp. 227–248). Cambridge: Cambridge University Press.

Weiss, Avraham. (2001). *Women at prayer: A Halakhic analysis of women's prayer groups*. Hoboken, NJ: KTAV Publishing House.

Weiss-Goldman, Ruhama. (1999). I want to put tefillin on you. In David Yoel Ariel, Maya Leibovich, & Yoram Mazor, et al. (Eds.), *Blessed be he who made me a woman? Women in Judaism from the Bible until modern times* (pp. 105–120). Tel Aviv: Yedioth Acharonoth. [Heb].

Whelan, Frederick G. (1990). Church establishments, liberty and competition in religion. *Polity, 23*(2), 155–185.

Whitman, James. (2000). Enforcing civility and respect: Three societies. *Yale Law Journal 109*(6), 1279–1398.

Williams, Bernard. (1985). *Ethics and the limits of philosophy*. Cambridge, MA: Harvard University Press.

Williams, Bernard. (2005). *In the beginning was the deed*. Princeton, NJ: Princeton University Press.

Williams, Bernard. (2006). *Philosophy as a humanistic discipline*. Princeton, NJ: Princeton University Press.

Winslow, Anastasia P. (1996). Sacred standards: Honoring the establishment clause in protecting Native American sacred sites. *Arizona Law Review, 38*, 1291–1343.

Witte, John, Jr. (1996). Essential rights and liberties of religion in the American Constitutional Experiment. *Notre Dame Law Review 71*, 371–445.

Wittgenstein, Ludwig. (2009). *Philosophical investigations*. (Rev. 4th ed.). (G. E. M Anscombe, P. M. S. Hacker, & Joachim Schulte, Trans.). West Sussex: Wiley-Blackwell.

Wolin, Sheldon S. (1990). *The presence of the past*. Baltimore: Johns Hopkins University Press.

Wygoda, Michael. (2010). The three kinds of holy places in Jewish Law: The case of Nachmanides' Cave in Jerusalem as a third kind. In Marshall Berger, Yitzhak

Reiter, & Leonard Hammer (Eds.), *Holy places in the Israeli-Palestinian conflict: Confrontation and co-existence* (pp. 92–103). London: Routledge.

Yadgar, Yaacov. (2005). *Masortim in Israel: Modernity without secularization.* Jerusalem: The Shalom Hartman Institute. [Heb].

Yoffie, Eric, H. (2016). Arrest and civil disobedience: What U.S. Jews need to do to support religious freedom in Israel. *Haaretz.com.* Retrieved from http://www.haaretz.com/opinion/.premium-1.713031?date=1459968971610, accessed April 6, 2016.

Yovel, Yermiyahu. (1992). *Spinoza and other heretics: The Marrano of Reason.* Princeton, NJ: Princeton University Press.

Zacharias, Diana. (2006). Protective declarations against Scientology as unjustified detriments to freedom of religion: A comment on the decision of the German Federal Administrative Court of 15 December 2005. *German Law Journal, 7,* no. 10, 833–842.

Zagorin, Perez. (2003). *How the idea of religious toleration came to the West.* Princeton, NJ: Princeton University Press.

Zerubavel, Yael. (1995). *Recovered roots: Collective memory and the making of Israeli national tradition.* Chicago: University of Chicago Press.

CANADIAN SUPREME COURT DECISIONS

Mouvement laïque québécois v. Saguenay (City), 2015 SCC 16, [2015] 2 S.C.R. 3

Tsilhqot'in Nation v. British Columbia, [2014] 2 SCR 257

US SUPREME COURT

Everson v. Board of Education, 330 U.S. 1 (1947)

Wisconsin v. Yoder, 406 U.S. 205 (1972)

Frontiero v. Richardson, 411 U.S. 677 (1973)

Marsh v. Chambers, 463 U.S. 783 (1983)

Lynch v. Donnelly, 465 U.S. 668 (1984)

Lyng v. Northwest Indian Cemetery Protective Association, 485 U.S. 439 (1988)

Zelman v. Simmons-Harris, 536 U.S. (2002), 639

Town of Greece v. Galloway, 572 U.S. (2014)

EUROPEAN COURT OF HUMAN RIGHTS

Lautsi v. Italy (2011), Application no. 30814/06

ISRAELI COURT RULINGS, PETITIONS, STATE RESPONSES

[2013] 21352-04-13 State of Israel v. BR Ras and others

[2013] HCJ 145/13 Israel Religious Action Center v. Western Wall Heritage Foundation

HCJ 257/89 and 2410/90 Hoffman v. Ministry of Religious Affairs
HCJ 3359/95 Hoffman v. Director-General of the Prime Minister's Office
[1997] (HCJ) 5016/96 Horev v. Minister of Transportation
CWJ petition to the HCJ
State response to CWJ petition, 8.2016.

WEBSITES

The official website of the Women of the Wall. http://womenofthewall.org.il/
The official website of the Western Wall Heritage Foundation. http://www.thekotel.
    org/content.asp?Id=361
The official website of 'Women for the Wall': http://womenforthewall.org/

KNESSET PROTOCOLS AND GOVERNMENTAL DECISIONS (ISRAEL)

Governmental decision (January 2016) regarding prayer arrangements at the Western
    Wall (on file with the authors).
Knesset Protocol. (2013), Committee on Women's Status, 19th Knesset, First Session
    (April 30), Prayer Arrangements at the Western Wall. Retrieved from http://www.
    knesset.gov.il/protocols/data/rtf/maamad/2013-05-07.rtf, accessed April 25, 2016.
    [Heb].

INDIAN COURT RULLINGS

Mohd. Ahmed Khan v. Shah Bano Begum. (1985) SCR (3) 844.
The Allahabad High Court, Decision of Hon'ble Special Full Bench hearing
    Ayodhya Matters. Retrieved from http://elegalix.allahabadhighcourt.in/elegalix/
    DisplayAyodhyaBenchLandingPage.do, accessed April 25, 2016.

OFFICIAL PUBLICATIONS AND REPORTS

Changed Relations Between the State and the Church of Sweden. Fact sheet, offi-
    cial publication. Sweden, Ministry of Culture (2000). Retrieved from http://
    www.sst.a.se/download/18.4c1b31c91325af4dad3800015546/1377188428760/
    Fact+sheet+about+state-church+relations.pdf, accessed April 25, 2016.
Israel's Central Bureau of Statistics, (2011), ethnicity and religiosity report, (Heb.), on
    file with the authors.
Prisoners of Belief. the U.S. Commission on International Religious Freedom (2014).
    Retrieved from http://www.uscirf.gov/reports-briefs/policy-briefs-and-focuses/
    policy-brief-prisoners-belief-individuals-jailed-under, accessed April 25, 2016.
The Liberhan Ayodhya Commission Report (India), 2009. Retrieved from http://
    mha.nic.in/LAC, accessed April 25, 2016 (on file with the authors).

INTERNATIONAL TREATISES

1948 Universal Declaration on Human Rights (article 18).
1953 European Convention on Human Rights (article 9).

REPORTS

Global Religious Diversity. Pew Research Center. Religion and Public Life report, April 4, 2014. Retrieved from http://www.pewforum.org/2014/04/04/global-religious-diversity/.
Report of the advisory team lead by A. Mandeblit to the matter of prayer arrangements at the Wall, convened by PM Netanyahu in May 2013, and published early in 2016; (on file with the authors).

Index

Note: Page numbers followed by n and another number refer to a numbered footnote

Abrabanel, Yitzhak, 155–156n28
Abudarham, David Ben-Yosef, 15, 21, 23–24, 23n9–10
Agudat Israel, 36
Al-Haram Ash-Sharif, 79
Aliyah (immigration) periods, 69, 69n25, 69n27
allocation of resources
  eligibility for, 9
  evenhandedness and, xxi, 104n5, 111, 115–118, 125–128, 131
American Jewry, support for Women of the Wall, xvii, 185n5
Anatoli, Jacob ben Abba Mari, 24n13
Aner, Zeev, 2n1
archaeological significance, of the Western Wall, 61–63, 67
Archeological Park, 49
archeological survey of India (ASI), 188
Armstrong, Karen, 76
Arnold, Matthew, 82–83, 84
Ashkenazi Jewish tradition, 31n28
avatars, in Hindu epics, 186–187
Ayodhya dispute, 183–199. See also Ram Janmabhoomi / Babri Masjid (RJBM)

Allahabad High Court
  pronouncement, 191, 192
belief-oriented incompatibility, 170–171
DCV model and, 183, 193, 195–196, 199, 913
details of the case, 186–192
evenhandendness and, 183, 193, 195–199
gag solutions, 192–196, 193–194n18
Hindu narrative, 185, 186–187
historical and legal dispute, 170, 187–192
interreligious nature of, 184
Kar Sevaks and, 186, 189–190
methodological explanation, 184–185
Muslim narrative, 167, 187
privatization model and, 163, 193, 194, 195, 196, 197
shared understandings and, 85n59
Supreme Court of India and, 191–192
WoW conflict comparison, 184–185

Babri Masjid. See Ram Janmabhoomi / Babri Masjid (RJBM)
Babri Masjid Action Committee (BMAC), 189

Babur (Mughal emperor), 186–188

Babylonian Talmud, 29, 30n24, 31n28, 35

Barak-Erez, Daphne, 36, 147

Barkay, Gabriel, 2n1

Barry, Brian, 126, 126n39

Baruch, Meir b., 31n27

Baruch, Yuval, 63

Basic Law (Israel)
    Freedom of Occupation, 37
    Human Dignity and Liberty, 37, 149

Bauman, Z., 124n36

Beinisch, Dorit, 43

Belgium, evenhandedness example, 103

Bellah, Robert N., 8n12

Ben-Avi, Itamar, 70

Ben-Dov, Meir, 2n1

Berger, Peter, 157

Bharatiya Janata Party (BJP), 94n76, 189–191

Bhargava, Rajeev, 103n1

Biale, David, 112

Bickel, Alexander, 93n74

Birkat Kohanot ("Blessings of the Priestesses") ceremony, 47n57

Black, Hugo, 144

Bonello, Judge, 56–57, 93

The Book of Abudarham (Abudarham), 23

Brennan, William J., 22

British Mandate (1917–1948), 36, 69, 70n29, 77–78

Buchanan, J., 90n70

Calvin, John, 149

Canadian Supreme Court, 89n68

Carens, Joseph
    on evenhandedness, 102–103, 103n1
    "identity" and "culture" focus, 103n1
    observations on Fiji, 133n50
    on research methodology, 14–15

Center for Women's Justice, 51

Chesler, Phyllis, xix

Chief Rabbis of Israel, 26, 34, 61. *See also* Eliyahu, Mordechai; Shapira, Avraham

Christian shared churches *(simultaneum)*, 137–138

Church of the Holy Sepulchre, 79, 136, 137, 138

church/religion-state separation model
    American Jews support for, 134n53
    Forbes on, 138n64
    in France, 144–145n2
    Gregory on, 149n11
    Jefferson on, 144
    Madison on, 163
    McConnell on, 153n22
    privatization and, 54, 144n2
    Protestantism and, 149, 149n11
    "supply-side" theory of religious markets and, 134–135
    Tocqueville on, 134
    in the U.S., xviii, xxi, 113, 134, 144, 154, 154n23, 163
    Watt on, 155–156n28

"civil religion" (Rousseau), 10

clash of civilization theory (Huntington), 184n3

Cohen-Hattab, Kobi, 72

Company for the Reconstruction and Development of the Jewish Quarter, 72, 73

compromise efforts
    by Israeli Supreme Court, 41
    by Sharansky, 48
    third plaza plan, xx, 48n49, 49, 51, 63, 72, 178

congregation *(tzibur)*, 25, 27n19, 29

Conservative Judaism, xvii, 24, 39, 45n53, 67–68, 74–75n38, 177, 179

"constitutional patriotism" (Habermas), 10

Cornille, Catherine, 123

countermajoritarianism, 91–93, 93n75
Culture and Anarchy (Arnold), 82–83, 84
Curry, Thomas J., 103–104n3

Dahl, Robert, 86, 167–168
David, Abraham Ben, 31n27
DCV model, of religion-state relations.
    See dominant culture view (DCV)
    model, of religion-state relations
Declaration of Religious Liberty (Second
    Vatican Council), 151–152n19
Deri, Aryeh Mahlouf, 179
devarim shebekdusha
    (sanctifications), 25, 34
Devlin, Lord P., 82, 83n51, 84, 94n76
Dome of the Rock / Temple Mount, 42,
    43. *See also* Temple Mount
    (al-Haram Ash-Sharif)
dominant culture view (DCV) model,
    of religion-state relations, xx,
    56–101. *See also* majority rule
    (majoritarianism), DCV model and
    Ayodhya dispute and, 183, 193, 195,
    196, 199
    Bonello on, 56–57
    countermajoritarian objection, 92–93
    defense of relevance of, 58–59
    democratic challenge and, 80–96
    egalitarianism and, 80–96
    embodiment of, in Europe, 58
    evaluation of aims of, 94–96
    as expression of the wish of the
        majority, 85–93
    fairness issues, 92
    as an instrumental good, 81–85
    issues of emotional response to,
        95–96n78
    main features, 57–58
    management of contested sacred sites
        and, 96–100
    Miller's argument for, 56

nationality (basic) law and, 92, 92n72, 93
    shared understandings and, 59, 60–75,
        80–81, 94, 96–100
    state-sponsored inequalities
        condoned by, 57
    violation of rights and, 88
Durkheim, Emile, 82, 84
Dworkin, Ronald, 95–96n78,
    128n42, 152n20

Eaton, Richard M., 4n7
Edge, Peter, 135–136
egalitarianism
    DCV model and, 80–96
    evenhandedness and, 198
    gender egalitarianism, xvii, 18, 39, 47
    privatization model and, 169, 181
Eliade, Mircea, 139n67
Eliyahu, Mordechai, 34–35
Elon, Judge Menachem
    on Abudarham, 23n10
    on opposition to WoW's prayer, 15–16,
        26, 34–35
    ruling on Supreme Court petition, 7,
        41–42, 65–66
    on Western Wall prayer plaza, 26
    on women wearing the tallit, 32–33
Elster, Jon, 90, 92–93n73
end-result-oriented model of
        evenhandedness, 105–115
    allocation of resources and, 111
    attraction of support by, 109
    baseline problem objection, 113–114
    characteristics, 106–107
    counterintuitiveness objection, 114–115
    critiques of, 111–115
    full accommodation requirement of, 119
    Halberta/Margalit on, 107
    identity and, 107–115, 142
    justifications/policy implications,
        107–111

end-result-oriented model of
     evenhandedness (*Cont.*)
  Muller and, 108–109
  Parekh and, 108, 110
  state *vs.* religious conflicts, 109–110
  support for allocation of resources, 111
  Tully and, 108n12, 110
The Enforcement of Morals
     (Devlin), 94n76
Equal Recognition (Patten), 115
Eshkol, Levi, 78
European Court of Human Rights
     (ECHR), 56–57, 86n6, 89, 91
evenhandedness model, of religion-state
     relations, 102–142. *See also* end-result-
     oriented model of evenhandedness;
     procedural model of evenhandedness
  allocation of resources and, xxi, 104n5,
     111, 115–118, 125–128, 131
  Ayodhya dispute and, 183, 193, 195–199
  Carens on, 102–103, 103n1
  divide and separate policy, 136–138,
     142, 173n63, 198
  end-result-orientation, 105–115
  examples of / rationale for
     adopting, 103
  identity approach to, 102–103, 107–115
  need for in democratic societies, 133–135
  objections to, 105n7
  "picking winners" characteristic, 140
  procedural orientation, 115–135
  regulatory scheme challenges,
     139–140, 163
  religious freedom and, 104, 111, 113,
     120–121, 126, 128, 138–139
  thick sites and, 135–142
  third-plaza plan and, 140–141
  U.S. "nonpreferentialism" comparison,
     103–104n3
  U.S. religious evenhandedness,
     103–104n3
  weaknesses of, 138

Everson v. Board of Education (1947;
     U.S.), 144, 144–145n2
Ezrat Nashim. See women's section
     (*Ezrat Nashim*), Western Wall

"family resemblance" paradigm
     (Wittgenstein), 150
Feinberg, Joel, 173–174
Feinstein, Moshe, 31n27, 32
Fichte, Johenn G., 94n76
First Amendment (U.S. Constitution), 154
Forbes, Donald, 138n64
Forst, Rainer, 16n28, 148, 149n12
France, religion-state relations in, 145
Francis (Pope), 74
Frazer, Nancy, 12

Gate of the Moors (Mughrabi Gate), 62
Gauthier, David, 124
Gay, Peter, 95
Geertz, Clifford
  on contested sites, 2–3, 3–4n3
  on religion, 8
  on thick description, 2–3
  on webs of significance, 3n4
gender egalitarianism, xvii, 18, 39, 47
gender hierarchy, in Judaism, 21n6
gender inegalitarianism, 47
gender separation
  Elon on, 65–66
  Grossman on, 66
  Ministry of Religions on, 65, 66–67
  non-Orthodox view on, 66–68
  Orthodox narrative on, 65–66
  Ottoman era rule and, 75–77
  Schochetman on, 65
  Six Day War era and, 78–79
Gordon, A. D., 69
Governmental Coins and Medals
     Corporation, 71
Grand Chamber, European Court of
     Human Rights (ECHR), 86n6, 89, 91

Gregory, Brad S., 149n11

Grodzinsky, Hayyim Ozer, 155

Grossman, Susanne, 66

Gurion, Ben, 71

Habermas, Jurgen, 10, 11–13

Halakhic considerations

  on gender separation, 66

  perspectives on WoW's manner
    of prayer, 19–35, 20n2

  on Soviet immigrants, 37

  on Western Wall's historical
    significance, 66

  on women's exclusion from
    minyan, 21, 25, 28

  on women's exemption from
    performing active religious duties at
    fixed times, 21–22, 23, 24, 28n21, 30

  on women's wearing of the tallit, 29–35

  Women Tefilah Groups
    legitimacy and, 7

Halbertal, Moshe, 107, 109n17, 123

Halev, Yizhak, 31n27

Hanukah protest (2015), 46–47

al-Haram Ash-Sharif (Temple Mount),
  42, 49, 61, 63–65, 98n80, 185n7

Hart, H. L. A., 83n51, 95–96n78

Hartman-Halbertal, Tova, 25

Haskalah (European Jewish
  Enlightenment), 111n18

Hauerwas, Stanley, 154

Haut, Rivka, xix, 7, 25, 66

Herod Agrippa I, 61

Herod Agrippa II, 61

Herzl, Theodor, 69

High Court of Justice (HCJ), 51–52n74

Hindu Maha Sabha (nationalist
  group), 197

Hindu narrative, of Ayodhya dispute,
  186–187

Hirsch, Samson Raphael, 15, 21–22,
  22n7, 24

Hobbes, Thomas, 7, 11, 103n2

Hoffman, Anat, 44

Hofstadter, Noam, 67n20

Hume, David, 165n48, 168

Huntington, Samuel, 184n3

Hussein, Shah Gulam, 188

identity

  Bauman on, 124n36

  Carens'/Parekh's/Tully's focus
    on, 103n1

  end-results evenhandedness and,
    107–115, 142

  procedural evenhandedness and,
    123–124, 126, 127n41

  religion's overlap with, 108n12

  religious-identity realm, 106

identity-multicultural school of
  thought, 107n11

India. *See also* Ayodhya dispute;
  Ram Janmabhoomi / Babri
  Masjid (RJBM)

  archeological survey (ASI), 188

  Bharatiya Janata Party, 94n76,
    189–191

  Hindu Maha Sabha, 197

  privatization model in, 149

  Ram Lalla temple, 197

  Vishwa Hindu Parishad, 187n10, 189

Indian National Congress party, 189

inegalitarianism, in Israel, 47

International Commission for the
  Wailing Wall (1931), 78n42

International Covenant on Civil and
  Political Rights (UN), 58n4

irreplaceability of thick sites, 4, 135,
  160nn37–38

irreversibility, DCV model and, 91–92,
  92–93n73, 94

Islamic argument for the privatization
  model, 155

Islamic Sunni Waqf board, 197

Israel
Aliyah (immigration) periods, 69, 69n25, 69n27
Basic Law: Freedom of Occupation, 37
Basic Law: Human Dignity and Liberty, 37, 149
Belgium comparison, 103
Knesset (parliament), 37, 50, 67, 67n20, 79
nationality (basic) law, 92, 92n72, 93
religion-state arrangements in, 35–39
religious divisions data, 84n52
religious feminist movement in, 39n47
sacred sites under conflict in, 4n7
Soviet emigrations to, 37
status quo compromise, 36–38
Western Wall administration by, 78–80
Israeli Academy of Sciences, xii, 61
Israeli Antiquities Authorities, 63
Israeli Justice Department, 44
Israeli Nature and Parks Authority, 61, 78, 161n44
Israeli Supreme Court, 7, 15
Israeli Action Center petition, 45n53
1994 ruling, 40–42
2000 ruling, 42–43
2003 ruling, 43–44
on women wearing the tallit, 33
WoW petitions, 7, 23n10, 25, 28–29, 28n22, 35, 40–43
Israel/Palestine, 69
Israel Religious Action Center, 45n53

Janathan Dal Party, 189
Jefferson, Thomas, 144
Jehyel, Asher b., 31n27
Jerusalem Day (holiday), 74
Jerusalem District Court, xv, 19, 45
Jerusalem Magistrates Court, 44
Jerusalem Municipality, 72
Jewish Agency for Israel, 36, 48, 49
Jewish Orthodoxy. *See* Orthodox Judaism

Jewish Political Tradition, 89n66
Jewish Reform movement (U.S.), 39, 49, 67

Kabbalah, 33
Karo, Joseph, 30n26
Kar Sevaks, 186, 189–190
kippah (skull cap), 108n13, 141
kirpan (ceremonial sword), 146n4
Kol, Moshe, 67
Kolek, Teddy, 61

Labor Party (Israel), 36, 38
Larry-Bavly, Sharon, 44
Larson, James G., 97
Lautsi vs. Italy (2011)
ECHR's ruling on, 56–57
majoritarian procedural problems and, 89–91, 93, 98, 106n9
Weiler's comments on, 86
Laycock, D., 103–104n3
League for the Abolition of Religious Coercion, 67
League of Nations, 78
The Least Dangerous Branch: The Supreme Court at the Bar of Politics (Bickel), 93n74
Leibowitz, Yeshayahu, 63n10, 155
Leviathan (Hobbes), 11
Levin, Shlomo, 41–43
Levy, Jacob, 17
Levy, Leonard, 103–104n3
Liberhan Ayodhya Commission Report (2009), 129n43, 191
Likud Party, 161n41
Loew, Judah b. Bezalel, 22
Lorberbaum, Menachem xii, 11n19, 89n86, 155n27
Luria, Isaac, 33
Luther, Martin, 149n12
Lutheran Protestantism, 147, 149
Lutt, Sasha, xv–xvi
Lynch v. Donnelly (1984; U.S.), 152

Mack, Cheryl Birkner, 99
Madison, James, 104n4
Magnus, Shulamit S., 178
Mahabharatha (Hindu epic), 186
Maharal of Prague, 22, 22n8
majority rule (majoritarianism), DCV
    model and, 80–81, 85–93. *See also*
    countermajoritarianism
  duress issues, 89
  irreversibility and, 91–92, 92–93n73, 94
  Lautsi vs. Italy and, 89–91, 93,
      98, 106n9
  monopoly issues, 89–90, 93n75, 94
  sour grapes problems, 74–75n38, 89,
      90–93, 94, 106n9
  violation of rights and, 88
Malmud he-Talmidim (Anatoli), 24n13
Margalit, Avishai, 107, 109n17, 123
Mazar, Benjamin, 61–63, 67
Mazar, Eilat, 63
Mazza, Eliyahu, 43
McConnell, Michael W., 153n22
Members of Knesset (Israeli parliament),
    37, 50, 67, 67n20, 79
Mendelblit, Avichai, 47n57, 50n66
Mendelblit Plan, 178
methodology used for study, 14–18
mikvot (ritual baths) debate, 130n46
Miller, David, 86, 95, 98
millet system
  in Israel, 35–36
  in the Ottoman Empire, 35
Ministerial Committee for Jerusalem, 72
Ministry of Religions, 61–62, 64, 65, 67,
    70, 71, 72, 79
minyan (religious quorum)
  exclusion of women from, 21, 24,
      28, 28n21
  Haut on, 25
  requirements of, 28
  WoW's demand for participation in,
      25, 28n22

Mishnah, Tractate Kiddushin, 30n24
Moeckli, Daniel, 87
Moelin, Yaakov b. Moshe Levi, 31n28
monopoly issues, majority rule and,
    89–90, 93n75, 94
Montefiore, Simon, 97, 103n1
Montesquieu, Charles Louise de
    Secondat, 130
mother-religion concept (Muller),
    108–109, 113, 123
Mount Athos (Greece), 184–185n4
Mughrabi Ascent, 49
Mughrabi Gate (Gate of the Moors), 62
Muller, Max, 108–109, 113, 123. *See also*
    mother-religion concept
Murray, John Courtney, 151–152n19
Muslim narrative, of Ayodhya
    dispute, 187
mutatis mutandis, 11n19, 50, 137

Naor, Mordechai, 2n1
Nashim Sh'ananot, 22n8
nationality (basic) law, 92, 92n72, 93
national significance, of the Western
    Wall, 68–75
New Yishuv (Zionist
    community), 69–70
Nietzsche, Friedrich, 84n55
Nissim, Rabbi Yizhak, 62
Noam, 31n28
"noble lies" (Plato), 10
non-Orthodox Jewish movements, 38,
    48, 50, 66–68, 74
nonpreferentialism, 103–104nn3–4
Noorani, Abdul G., 186n8
Nozick, Robert, 126, 126n39
Nussbaum, Martha, 126, 126n39

Obama, Barack, 74
O'Connor, Sandra Day, 152
Olam Haba, 22
Old Yishuv, 69

Original Women of the Wall
  Mack's leadership of, 99
  Magnus's leadership of, 178
  opposition to third-plaza plan, 51n71,
    99, 178
  split with Women of the Wall, 51n71
Orthodox Judaism, 24, 39, 45n53, 74–
    75n38. *See also* ultra-Orthodox Jews
  on classification of WoW, 20–21n4
  gender separation in synagogues, 66
  objections to women praying in
    public, xx, 20–26
  objections to women wearing
    tallit, 29–35
  portrayal of women in, 23
  Western Wall's significance for, 63–66
  WoW's disagreement with, 6, 14
Ottoman Empire
  millet system, 35
  transition in Turkey, 58n6
  Western Wall administration,
    61, 75–78

Palestinian Territories, 4n7
Parekh, Bhikhu, 103n1, 108, 108n13, 109,
    110, 123
Parfit, Derek, 194n21
Patten, Alan, 103n1, 115, 116, 118,
    119–120, 127n41
Plato, 10
political obstructionism, 48
prayer leaders (*Hazzanit*), 26
privatization model (of religion-state
    relations), 143–176. *See also*
    privatization of thick sites
  advantages of, 175–176
  aims/description of, 143–144
  applicability to thick sites, 143,
    158–172, 174–176, 179–181
  Ayodhya dispute and, 163, 193, 194,
    195, 196, 197
  "background" system of rules in,
    145–146

context-sensitive approach, xxii, 158,
    163, 176
corrupting influence of the state, 154
endorsement by religious believers,
    scholars, 149–150
equality arguments, 151–152
exemptions, 146–147n8
in France, 150
"hands off" approach toward
    religions, 143–148
immunity argument, 156–157, 156n30
in India, 149
Islamic argument for, 155
Jewish argument for, 155
justifications of, of religion-state
    relations, 150–158
liberty family of arguments, 152–153
"market situation" of religions
    created by, 157
misrepresentations of, 148–150
Protestantism and, 147, 148–149
Rawls on, 145n3
of religion, in Connecticut and
    Massachusetts, 150
religious exclusivity of, 148–149
religious set of arguments, 153–156
social stability argument, 151
state-inadequacy argument, 150–151
in Sweden, 147–148
privatization of thick sites, 158–176
  advantages of, 175–176, 180–181
  Ayodhya dispute and, 163
  backlash problem objection,
    164–167, 164n47
  baseline problems, 167–169
  consumer choice benefits, 160
  context-sensitive approach, xxii, 158,
    163, 176
  description, 159–164
  emotional impact of, 163
  impact on government, 159–160
  implications of adoption of, 161–162
  merits of, 162–163

objections to, 164–175
religious extremism and, 165–166
religious incompatibility problems,
169–175
procedural model of evenhandedness,
115–135
allocation of resources in, 115–118,
125–128
critiques of, 125–135
definition, 115–117
elusive connection concept and,
126–127
evaluation problem, 131–132
examples, 117–120
excessive entanglement challenge, 129
identity and, 123–124, 126, 127n41
institutional aspects of, 128–133
justifications for, 120–125
partial accommodation requirement
of, 119
Patten on, 127n41
preclusive characteristic, 132–133
religion's importance in, 127–128
religious freedom justification, 120–121
Protection of Holy Places Law (1967),
79, 171n57
Protestantism, 147, 148–149
public sphere
conflicts over thick sites in, 6n11, 7
effects of religion in, 8, 10
feminist scholars on, 12n22
Habermas's definition, 11–13
as an "in-between" sphere, 12
the state and, 12n21
"thin" view of, 13–14

Rabinowitz, Rabbi Shmuel (Rabbi of
the Western Wall). *See also* ultra-
Orthodox Jews; Western Wall
Heritage Foundation
accusation of WoW's deception, xvi
civil lawsuit against, 51–52n74
Mendelblit's meeting with, 47n57

on third-plaza plan, 50
"2010 regulation" of, 45–47
WoW's demand for meeting with, xv
Raday, Francis, xii, 20n1, 24n12, 32n33, 42
Ramayana (Hindu epic), 186
Ram Janmabhoomi / Babri Masjid
(RJBM), 129
Ayodhya dispute and, 183–199
belief-oriented incompatibility
dispute, 170–171
DCV model and, 97, 98
divide and separate policy, 138
division into parts, 136
documents related to, 186n8
historical background, 187–192
mutatis mutandis and, 137
objections to management of, 164, 170
shared understandings and, 97
violent Hindu-Muslim encounters at,
5, 16
Ram Lalla (infant Lord Rama)
temple, 197
Rashtriya Swayamsevak Sangh (RSS),
187n10
Ravitzky, Aviezer, 155–156n28
Rawls, John, 126, 126n39, 128n42, 145n3,
154n23, 166
Reform Judaism, xvii, 24, 39, 45n53,
74–75n38, 177, 179
Regulations for the Protection of
Holy Places for Jews (1981), 34,
40–41, 47n57
religion
custom *vs.* public safety measures, 146n4
as an economic good, 82
Geertz's functional definition, 8
human perfection and, 82–83, 85
identity's overlap with, 108
as an instrumental good, 82
Miller on, 86
privatization of, 143–148
social-religious homogeneity, 84
Weiler on, 86

religion-state relations, 35–39. *See also*
        dominant culture view (DCV)
        model, of religion-state relations
    changing political balance, 38
    DCV model, 56–101
    denomination data, 36, 38
    evenhandedness model, 102–142
    privatization model, 143–176
    sociological literature on, 175n67
    status quo compromise, 36–38
    "who is a Jew" controversy, 37n45
"religious argument," 154n23
religious evenhandedness, 103–104n3
religious-feminist challenges of WoW
        (Halakhic analysis), 19–35
    women-only prayer group, 20–26, 45
    women's Torah reading, 26–29
    women wrapped in the tallit, 29–34
religious feminist movement, 39n47
religious freedom
    arguments on the importance of,
        153nn21–22
    evenhandedness and, 104, 111, 113,
        120–122, 126, 128, 138
    global interests in, 103
    Western Wall limitations, 140
    WoW's goal of, xvii, xxi
religious incompatibility issues at thick
        sites, 169–175
result-oriented model of evenhandedness.
        See end-result-oriented model of
        evenhandedness
Rethinking Multiculturalism
        (Parekh), 108n13
Robbins, Lionel, 160n37
Robinson's Arch, 42–45, 48–50, 61,
        67–68, 99, 177
Ross, Michael Lee, 136
Rousseau, Jean Jacques, 10, 82
Rubinger, David, 73
Ryle, Gilbert, 2–3n3

Sabbath laws, status quo compromise
        and, 36–37
sacred sites. *See also* thick sites; *specific
        sacred sites*
    baseline problem and, 168
    causes of conflicts at, 7
    conflicts over, xvi, 5, 6, 7, 18, 179
    contested sites, and DCV
        model, 96–100
    DCV and, 96–101
    Eliade on, 139n67
    evenhandedness and, 136, 137n62, 142
    Geertz and, 3
    Jordanian restrictions on Jews
        visiting, 70
    laws (1967, 1981) regarding, 161–162
    legalistic definitions of, 2n2, 161n44
    Lockean proviso and, 170n53
    management issues, xvii, 13, 16n28, 40,
        96–101, 161n41, 184
    privatization model and, 161
    Protection of Holy Places law
        and, 171n57
    Ross on, 136
    shared understandings and, 96–100
Safdie, Moshe, 73
Samuel's Tomb, 136, 137
sanctifications *(devarim
        shebekdusha),* 25, 34
Sandel, Michael J., 112
Sangh Parivar (Hindu militant
        organizations), 187–190
Saposnik, Arieh, 73–74
Sassoon, Isaac, 23n9–10
Schiller, Eli, 2n1
Scientology, 129n43
Second Temple, 61, 63–64, 66
Second Vatican Council, 151–152n19
self-determination rights, 58n4
Seneca, 10n18
Sephardic Jewish tradition, 30n26

Servetus, Michael, 149

Shah Bano case, 129n43

Shamgar, Justice Meir, 41–43

Shapira, Avraham, 34–35.

Sharansky, Natan, 48, 49, 50

shared churches *(simultaneum)*, 137–138

shared understandings
    Ayodhya dispute and, 85n59
    DCV model and, 59, 60–75, 80–81,
        94, 96–100
    Ram Janmabhoomi / Babri Masjid
        and, 97
    sacred sites and, 96–100
    Western Wall and, 59, 60–75

Sharia courts, 36, 103, 118n27

Sharia principles, 155

Sharma, Ram Sharan, 188

Shilo, Margalit, 76

Shiloh, 33, 33n39

Shils, Edward, 58

Shinui Party, 161n41

Shochetman, Eliav, 26n16, 27n18, 31n27,
    32, 34, 65

Shofar, WoW's efforts at blowing, 141n72

Shweder, Richard A., xii, 146n6

simultaneum (shared churches), 137–138

Singh, Kalyan, 191

Six Day War (1967), 64, 66–73

Smart, Ninian, 8n13

Smith, Adam, 166

Smith, Steven B., 154n25

Sobel, Judge Moshe, 45–46, 48–50,
    165, 177

Social Contract (Rousseau), 82

sour grapes (preference-adaption)
    problems, DCV model and,
    74–75n38, 89, 90–93, 94, 106n9

Spinoza, Benedict de, 11, 112

Spirit of the Laws (Montesquieu), 130

the state. *See also* religion-state relations
    definitions of, 9–10

heavy handed, corrupting effect on
    religion, 154

public sphere and, 12n21

state-religion conflicts, 109–110

Weberian definition of, 9–11,
    10n17, 11n19

status quo compromise, 36–38

Stone, Suzanne Last, 155

Strasberg-Cohen, Tova, 43

Suleiman the Magnificent (Ottoman
    ruler), 75–76

Sweden, privatization model in, 147–148

Switzerland, ban on building minarets, 95

tallit (prayer shawl), wearing of, by
    WoW, 29–35

Talmudic law: "how much more" *(Kal
    va-homer)*, 98n81

Temple Mount (al-Haram Ash-Sharif),
    42, 49, 61, 63–65, 98n80, 185n7

Tendler, Rabbi, 32–33

Theological-Political Treatise (Spinoza), 11

thick sites. *See also* Ayodhya dispute;
    Mount Athos; privatization of thick
    sites; Ram Janmabhoomi / Babri
    Masjid; Samuel's Tomb; Temple
    Mount; Western Wall
    Christian shared churches, 137–138
    definitions/characteristics of, 1–7,
        135, 180
    divide and separate policy, 136–138,
        142, 173n63, 198
    Edge on, 135–136
    evenhandedness and, 135–142
    gag solutions and, 192–194, 197–199
    Hume's comment on, 168
    incompatibility of meanings
        attributed to, 3–4
    irreplaceability of, 4, 135, 160n37
    meanings attributed to, 2–3, 3–4
    privatization of, 158–176

thick sites (*Cont.*)
  Protection of Holy Places Law and,
    79, 171n57
  significance of meanings
    attributed to, 4
"Thinking and Reflecting" (Ryle), 2–3n3
"The Thinking of Thoughts: What Is 'le
    Penseur Doing?'" (Ryle), 2–3n3
third-plaza plan
  Antiquities Authorities and, 63
  Center for Women's Justice and, 51
  description, 49, 178n1
  divide and separate policy, 137
  evenhandedness and, 140–141
  gender separation consideration, 68
  initial implausability of, xxiii
  Mazar, Eilat, opposition to, 63
  Members of Knesset opposition, 50–51
  Original WoW opposition to, 51n71,
    99, 178
  reform movement and, 51n69
  required renovations, 51n68
  Sharansky's suggestion for, 48, 49, 50
  the state's opinion of, 51, 51n73
  ultra-Orthodox opposition, 48n49,
    50–51, 178
  WoW's acceptance of, 178, 179
  WoW's conditions for, 49–51
  WoW split caused by, 52, 68
Thurlow, Lord, 96
Tocqueville, Alexis de, 139
Toleration in Conflict (Forst), 16n28
Torah
  barring of WoW from bringing to
    Western Wall, xv–xvi
  Halakha's objections to women's
    public reading of, 28n21
  reading by women, 26–29
  smuggling of, into women's section of
    the Wall, 46n56

Treta-Yuga, 186–187
Tully, James, 103n1, 108n12, 110,
    112–113, 123
"2010 regulation," 45–46
tzitzit (small tallit), 30–31, 30n26, 31n28,
    33. *See also* tallit (prayer shawl),
    wearing of, by WoW

ultra-Orthodox Jews (Judaism). *See also*
    Rabinowitz, Rabbi Shmuel
  disagreements with WoW, 6, 14, 39, 41
  1887, special "women service," 76–77
  Reform Jews conflict with, 67
  request for military service
    exemption, 129n43
  road-related Sabbath
    restriction, 172n60
  running of Western Wall Heritage
    Foundation, 45n53
  state support given to, 58n5
  status quo compromise and, 36–38
  supervision of aspects of religious
    life, 79n44
  tallit wearing by women
    opposition, 182
  third-plaza plan opposition, 48n59,
    50–51, 178, 179n4
  violence/fears of violence by, 51n71,
    67–68, 165
  Western Wall Heritage Foundation
    domination, 45n53, 160–161
  women's disruption of WoW, 47, 48, 169
  WoW's demand to meet with, xv
Unintended Reformation
    (Gregory), 149n11
UN International Covenant on Civil and
    Political Rights, 58n4
United Kingdom, xvi, 88, 108
UN Universal Declaration of Human
    Rights, 113

U.S. Constitution, 154
U.S. Supreme Court
  Everson v. Board of Education,
    144, 144n2
  Lynch v. Donnelly, 152
  Wisconsin v. Yoder, 146n5

Vajpayee (BJP leader), 190
Vishwa Hindu Parishad (VHP),
  187n10, 189

Walzer, Michael, 2–3n3, 3n9, 23n11,
  89n66, 125
Warhaftig, Zerach, 64–65
Weber, Max, 9–10, 11n19, 16n32
Weiler, J., 86, 98
Western Wall. *See also* third-plaza plan
  archaeological significance of,
    61–63, 67
  British administration of, 77–78
  cast study methodology, 14–18
  competing significances of, 60–75
  Conservative movement prayer
    rally, 67–68
  divide and separate policy, 138
  failure of centralized planning at, 141
  first-fourth Aliyah periods and, 69–71
  gender separation established at, 78–79
  irreplaceability of, 160
  Israeli administration of, 78–80, 163
  Jewish-Arab tensions at, 70
  Jordanian authorities ban of Jews
    at, 194n22
  Ministry of Religions and,
    61–62, 64–65
  objections to management of, 164–165,
    167, 169–170
  ongoing rejection of design
    plans, 72–73
  Ottoman administration of, 61, 75–78
  partition removal, by British, 77–78
  prayer arrangement conflicts at, 70
  prayer practices and, 75–80
  privatization's impact on, 162
  religious freedom limitations at, 140
  Saposnik on, 73–74
  shared understandings and, 59, 60–75,
    74–75n38
  significance, for non-Orthodox,
    66–68, 74
  significance, for Orthodox, 63–66
  significance, national, 68–75
  site regulation controversies, 71–72
  Six Day War and, 68–69, 71, 72, 73, 74
  southern plaza plan, 179
  as a thick site, 1–7
  ultra-Orthodox women's special
    service at, 76–77
  as "Wall of Heroes," 70
  women's section *(Ezrat Nashim),*
    xv–xvi, 40–41, 46, 47n57, 48–51,
    72, 99, 157, 168
  WoW's challenges in liberation of, 19–35
Western Wall Heritage Foundation, xv,
  45–47, 45n53, 50, 63–65, 74n37, 141,
  160–161, 177, 180
White Paper (1928), 77
Williams, Bernard, 154n23
Wisconsin v. Yoder (1972; U.S.), 146n5
Wittgenstein, Ludwig, 150
Women *for* the Wall, 48, 66, 179
*Women of the Wall: Claiming Sacred
  Ground at Judaism's Holy Site* (eds.
  Chesler and Haut), xix
women-only prayer group *(Tfila),* 20–26,
  28, 28n21, 29, 34, 45
  Abudarham's objections to, 23
  growing Halakhic legitimacy of, 7
  Halakhic perspectives, 20n2
  Hirsch's objections to, 21–22

women-only prayer group (*Cont.*)
    Maharal of Prague's objections to, 22
    physical attacks against, 7
    reasons for Orthodoxy's objections
        to, 20–21
    WoW's united challenge of exclusion
        from, 24–26
women's section (*Ezrat Nashim*),
    Western Wall, xv–xvi, 40–41, 46,
        47n57, 48–51, 72, 99, 157, 168
Women Tefilah Group, 7

World Heritage Sites, 184–185n4
World Union for Progressive
    Judaism, 67

Yossef, Ovadia, 30n26

Zagorin, Perez, 148
Zelman v. Simmons-Harris (U.S.
    Supreme Court), 104n4
Zionist Commission, 69
Zionist movement, 36, 69, 73

Printed in the USA/Agawam, MA
August 1, 2017